SOUTH FLORIDA STUDIES IN THE HISTORY OF JUDAISM

Edited by
Jacob Neusner
William Scott Green, James Strange
Darrell J. Fasching, Sara Mandell

Number 68
SOURCES OF THE TRANSFORMATION
OF JUDAISM
From Philosophy to Religion
in the Classics of Judaism

by
Jacob Neusner

SOURCES OF THE TRANSFORMATION
OF JUDAISM
From Philosophy to Religion
in the Classics of Judaism

A Reader

SOURCES OF THE TRANSFORMATION OF JUDAISM

From Philosophy to Religion
in the Classics of Judaism

A Reader

by
Jacob Neusner

Scholars Press
Atlanta, Georgia

SOURCES OF THE TRANSFORMATION OF JUDAISM

From Philosophy to Religion
in the Classics of Judaism

©1992
University of South Florida

Publication of this book was made possible by a grant from the Tisch Family Foundation, New York City. The University of South Florida acknowledges with thanks this important support for its scholarly projects.

Library of Congress Cataloging in Publication Data
Neusner, Jacob, 1932-
    Sources of the transformation of Judaism: from philosophy to religion in the classics of Judaism: a reader/ by Jacob Neusner.
        p. cm. — (South Florida studies in the history of Judaism; no. 68)
    Includes bibliographical references and index.
    ISBN 1-55540-813-3 (alk. paper)
    1. Rabbinical literature—History and criticism.   2. Judaism--History—Talmudic period, 10-425.   I. Title. II. Series
BM496.5.N48223   1993
296.1'206—dc20   92-42836
                                                         CIP

Printed in the United States of America
on acid-free paper

Table of Contents

Preface ix

Part One
HISTORICAL CONSIDERATIONS

1. From Mishnaic Philosophy to Talmudic Religion: The Transformation of Judaism Between ca. 200 and 400. A Summary 3

Part Two
JUDAIC CLASSICS OF THE AGE OF CONSTANTINE

2. The Talmud of the Land of Israel in Literary Context 29
3. Leviticus Rabbah and the Hebrew Scriptures 69
4. From Exegesis to Syllogism. How Leviticus Rabbah Makes Intelligible Statements: Listmaking and Classifying Facts 105
5. Genesis Rabbah and the History of Israel 121

Part Three
PRINCIPLES OF JUDAISM IN THE AGE OF CONSTANTINE

6. When Did Judaism Become a Messianic Religion? 161
7. What, Exactly, Do We Mean by "An Event" in Judaism? History in the Formation of Judaism 173

Part Four
TORAH, ISRAEL, AND GOD

8. The Transformation of the Torah 195
9. The Redefinition of "Israel": Judaism and Its Social Metaphors 211
10. God: Principle, Presence, Person, and Personality in the Formation of Judaism 253

Index 293

Preface

Between 200 and 400 Judaism changed from a philosophy to a religion. In this book I explain the meaning of that simple sentence. That is the thesis of my *The Transformation of Judaism. From Philosophy to Religion* (Champaign, 1992: University of Illinois Press). Here I treat subjects insufficiently presented there, yet required for a full understanding of the argument of that work. The problem I address concerns the transformation, by continuator documents, of a Judaic system of the social order, one that was fully set forth in its initial document and both carried forward and vastly recast by continuator documents. That problem therefore directs attention to systemic description, analysis, and interpretation of documentary evidence, for by comparing one set of writings with another I compare one system of a religion to another system within that same religion.

This book forms a supplement to *Transformation*. The necessity for such a supplement came to mind when I taught a course at the University of South Florida on "the formation of Judaism," and found that reading in my principal work leading to this one, *The Economics of the Mishnah* (Chicago, 1989: The University of Chicago Press), *Rabbinic Political Theory: Religion and Politics in the Mishnah* (Chicago, 1991: The University of Chicago Press), and *Judaism as Philosophy. The Method and Message of the Mishnah* (Columbia, 1991: University of South Carolina Press), presented the Mishnaic stratum adequately, but in disproportion to the presentation of the stratum formed by the Talmud of the Land of Israel, Genesis Rabbah, Leviticus Rabbah, and related writing. So I determined to right the balance, and I do so in this book. Any reader of the other work will benefit as well, which is why I conceived the project to be of general interest and to warrant publication in this form.

At the same time I hasten to add that the honors college students whom I taught did a valiant job with the course and proved superior in intellectual quality to most of their counterparts at Brown University, where I taught for twenty-two years. Comparing the poor and local students of the University of South Florida with the rich and privileged ones at Brown University reenforced my view that, while when God gives out money, the rich get more than the poor, when God gives out brains, everybody gets a rightful share; so the rich in the aggregate are dumber, the poor smarter. That working hypothesis called forth my best efforts when I came to USF, no one ever having taught me how to talk down to anybody, and the results validated it in the course that showed me the lacuna in my presentation of my theory of the formation of Judaism.

Summarizing the principal study and adding to the account of its historic context, I provide extensive presentations on the character of the sources of the religious system of Judaism described in the work, in Part Two, and then some episodic treatments of specific traits of the religious system of Judaism that emerged in the writings that reached closure in the age of the Christian emperors of Rome, in Part Three. These cover topics not treated adequately or at all in *Transformation*.

It is important at the outset to review the terms I have invented, on which in these pages all else depends. By a religious system (or "a Judaism" for the case at hand) I mean a theory of the social order that appeals for validation to supernatural authority and that comprises a worldview or philosophy, way of life or economics, and theory of the social entity or politics. These components of a theory of the social order formed under religious auspices may be represented by the words ethos, ethics, and ethnos. So much for the definition of religion that pertains here: a religious theory of the social order, accounting for the way in which (in theory at least) a social entity sees the world and conducts its affairs.

By (a) Judaism I mean a Judaic system, which is a cogent account of the social order, comprising a worldview, way of life, and theory of the social entity, "Israel," all together setting forth a response to a question deemed urgent and encompassing, providing an answer found self-evidently valid. The Jews' long history has witnessed the formation of a variety of such Judaic systems. In the first seven centuries of the Common Era (= A.D.) the canonical writings of one such system, the one that has predominated since that time, took shape.[1] That is the Judaic system the transformation of which is under discussion here. I describe that system as it is attested or adumbrated by the canonical writings produced by sages bearing the title "rabbis." I read those writings as accounts of the principal parts of the structure and system of society, with special attention to what seem to me essential: way of life or ethics,

---

[1] The definition of the system and the documentary evidence that permits describing it are set forth in a moment.

and, in secular social science, economics; world view or ethos, and, in secular language, philosophy (including science); and theory of the social entity that realizes the one and lives by the other, or ethnos.

By philosophy in these pages I mean very simply, a system of thought that, in the context of the same time and place, people generally deemed philosophers will have recognized as philosophical, with the proviso that there be no error as to the facts of the matter. In my book, *Judaism as Philosophy. The Method and Message of the Mishnah*,[2] I demonstrate that the Mishnah, the first canonical writing of Judaism after the Hebrew Scriptures of ancient Israel ("the Old Testament") in important ways is to be read as philosophy in accord with the generally accepted understanding of philosophy in the time, ca. A.D. 200, and place, the Greek-speaking Near East. By philosophy both in that study and here, therefore, I mean specifically the philosophical tradition of the Greco-Roman world of the Second Sophistic, in particular, as I shall explain at length, the method of Aristotle and the proposition important to Middle Platonism. But philosophy in a generic sense demands its place, and by philosophy in general I mean disciplined, rigorous thought, in accord with rules subject to application without limit as to topic, that intelligibly produces generalizations demonstrated on the basis of correct principles of thought concerning this-worldly facts to govern or explain a variety of circumstances. A philosophy forms a cogent system of rational thought that treats diverse cases by appeal to a limited set of internally coherent generalizations. Such a system, as to method, abstract and intelligible, subject to reasoned explanation, as to topic, concerning a variety of concrete cases or problems, defines what I mean by (a) philosophy and, consequently, philosophical.[3]

As is clear, in *Transformation*, I take the two sets of documents – the Mishnah and related Midrash compilations, the Talmud of the Land of Israel and associated Midrash collections – as evidence of systems to which they refer or attest, respectively, and it is the systems that I claim exhibit traits I can describe and connections – comparisons and contrasts – I can analyze and interpret. So this book forms an exercise in the study of category formation. What I show is two things. The first is how a continuous literary tradition – the Yerushalmi is represented as a (mere) continuation of, and commentary to, the Mishnah, and the several

---

[2](Columbia, 1991: University of South Carolina Press).

[3]I have further worked out in great detail an account of those passages in the entire Mishnah that are to be classified as philosophical, within the stated criterion, in my *The Philosophical Mishnah*. Volume I. *The Initial Probe;* Volume II. *The Tractates' Agenda. From Abodah Zarah to Moed Qatan;* Volume III. *The Tractates' Agenda. From Nazir to Zebahim;* and Volume IV. *The Repertoire* (Atlanta, 1989: Scholars Press for Brown Judaic Studies).

distinct groups of Midrash compilations are presented as (mere) commentary to Scripture – in fact attests to distinct religious systems. The second is how the categories that frame the initial system are received and dealt with in the successor system. This study then analyzes literary sources in such a way as to allow the description of religious systems by reference to the category formations characteristic of each, and it interprets those sources so as to carry out the comparison of the category formations of the one with those of the other.

With the decade of work completed in *Transformation* now receding over the last horizon, with much enjoyment I now proceed to accomplish the same work for the third and final stage in the formation of Judaism, from ca. 450 to ca. 600.[4] Some of the descriptive and analytical work is now complete, but a fair amount of descriptive study of texts and a still larger labor of analytical study of contexts stands between this work and the third and final interpretive enterprise I have in mind at this time, which is the passage from religion to theology. I hardly need say that – as is my way – the theoretical labor is now well underway for the final stage. In that study the work of comparison draws me to the latest stages in the writing down of the good religion of the worshippers of Mazda, which the world knows as "Zoroastrianism," and to the earliest stages in the formation of Islam, for it has become clear to me that the Talmud of Babylonia is to be read in the context of, compared with and contrasted to, the other massive religious systemic writings of that same era, commencing with the fall of the Zoroastrian empire of Iran, encompassing Babylonia, and the rise of the Muslim nation, also encompassing that same territory and its Jews. Catching up means another go-around in the literary evidence. As this work goes to press, my analytical translation of the Talmud of Babylonia is completed, so, too, the nearly score of monographs I have worked out to describe how that document works.

So to undertake systemic analysis on the strength of written evidence, I have systemically reread the classic documents of the Judaism that took shape in the first to the seventh centuries A.D. and that has predominated since then, the Judaism of the Dual Torah. These documents – the Mishnah, Midrash compilations, the two Talmuds – represent the collective statement and consensus of authorships (none is

---

[4]Michael G. Morony, "Teleology and the Significance of Change," in F. M. Clover and R. S. Humphreys, *Tradition and Innovation in Late Antiquity* (Madison, 1989: University of Wisconsin Press), pp. 21-27, seems to me right on target in his arguments on the character of the final centuries of late antiquity, and I should be inclined to accept his periodization. But I have not yet done my work on the sixth and seventh centuries.

credibly assigned to a single author and all are preserved because they are deemed canonical and authoritative) and show us how those authorships proposed to make a statement to their situation – and, I argue, upon the human condition. As I said at the outset, I generally write in my mind my major theoretical work, only afterward putting the whole down on paper – and catching up, in research, with the results of my abstraction, imagination, and sheer daydreaming. At this time the work of literary analysis is complete for the Midrash compilations of the third and final stage in the formation of Judaism, the late Midrash Rabbah collections, Ruth Rabbah, Lamentations Rabbati, Song of Songs Rabbah, and Esther Rabbah I.[5] To prepare for literary-analytical studies of the Talmud of Babylonia I have translated twenty-seven of the Bavli's thirty-seven tractates and supervised the translation of the other ten, so that the analytical system is complete for all of them. The planned studies now make excellent progress toward my goal, which is an account of how the religious system attested by the Talmud of the Land of Israel and related Midrash compilations yielded the theological system adumbrated in the final documents of the formative age of Judaism.[6]

---

[5]These are as follows: *Esther Rabbah I. An Analytical Translation* (Atlanta, 1989: Scholars Press for Brown Judaic Studies); *Ruth Rabbah. An Analytical Translation* (Atlanta, 1989: Scholars Press for Brown Judaic Studies); *Song of Songs Rabbah. An Analytical Translation.* Volume One. *Song of Songs Rabbah to Song Chapters One through Three* (Atlanta, 1990: Scholars Press for Brown Judaic Studies); *Song of Songs Rabbah. An Analytical Translation.* Volume Two. *Song of Songs Rabbah to Song Chapters Four through Eight* (Atlanta, 1990: Scholars Press for Brown Judaic Studies); *The Midrash Compilations of the Sixth and Seventh Centuries. An Introduction to the Rhetorical Logical, and Topical Program. I. Lamentations Rabbah* (Atlanta, 1990: Scholars Press for Brown Judaic Studies); *The Midrash Compilations of the Sixth and Seventh Centuries: An Introduction to the Rhetorical Logical, and Topical Program. II. Esther Rabbah I* (Atlanta, 1990: Scholars Press for Brown Judaic Studies); *The Midrash Compilations of the Sixth and Seventh Centuries: An Introduction to the Rhetorical Logical, and Topical Program. III. Ruth Rabbah* (Atlanta, 1990: Scholars Press for Brown Judaic Studies); *The Midrash Compilations of the Sixth and Seventh Centuries: An Introduction to the Rhetorical Logical, and Topical Program. IV. Song of Songs Rabbah* (Atlanta, 1990: Scholars Press for Brown Judaic Studies). See also *Translating the Classics of Judaism. In Theory and in Practice* (Atlanta, 1989: Scholars Press for Brown Judaic Studies).

[6]These studies may be described in the following way. [1] *The Bavli's One Voice: The Rules of Composition of the Talmud of Babylonia* (Atlanta, 1991: Scholars Press for South Florida Studies in the History of Judaism). The principal question here and in the next items is, how can I identify the statements of norms, and how can I demonstrate that these norms are cogent with one another? And precisely what do these norms set forth as a system, and why do I maintain that it is a theological system, within my definition of theology? This book asks the question, who is it who speaks through the Bavli? Is it the voice of the penultimate and ultimate authorship, or is it the voices of a variety of authors

It remains to express my thanks to my University for its long-term and exceptionally generous support of my research. What I find remarkable is that, in times of acute financial stress, my president, provost, dean, and chairman have insisted that I pursue my work without material concerns of any kind. I express my thanks also to my colleagues in the Department of Religious Studies, who have shown me the true meaning of the word collegiality.

JACOB NEUSNER

Distinguished Research Professor of Religious Studies
UNIVERSITY OF SOUTH FLORIDA
Tampa, St. Petersburg, Sarasota, Lakeland, Fort Myers

---

and authorships? If the former, then we can proceed to the next problem, which follows. [2] *The Bavli's One Statement: The Message of the Method of the Talmud of Babylonia.* What message can we derive from the methods of logical and cogent discourse that are paramount in the Bavli. [3] *The Transformation of Judaism. From Religion to Theology in the Talmud of Babylonia and the Late Midrash-Compilations.* Once I have established the method and message of the Bavli, I return to the already-completed work on the roughly-contemporary Midrash compilations. I compare the category-formations of the Yerushalmi and related writings with those of the Bavli and related writings and specify the category-structure of the final system of late antiquity. Do I find paramount the same categories or other categories? The principal question finally answered here is, since I identify the statements of norms, and I demonstrate that these norms are cogent with one another, what do these norms set forth as a system, and why do I maintain that it is a theological system, within my definition of theology? [4] *The Bavli and the Denkart: The Judaic and Zoroastrian Response to the Challenge of Nascent Islam.* Are the Zoroastrian sages writing on the same range of issues, or is this simply the collection and arrangement of inherited information, as the prior accounts of the 9th century Pahlavi books have maintained and as counterpart-accounts of Judaism, deriving from the same age, the early-Islamic, allege?

Part One

HISTORICAL CONSIDERATIONS

1

From Mishnaic Philosophy to Talmudic Religion: The Transformation of Judaism Between ca. 200 and 400

A Summary

I. The Philosophical Judaism of the Mishnah

The problem I address concerns the transformation, by continuator documents, of a Judaic system of the social order, one that was fully set forth in its initial document and both carried forward but also vastly recast by continuator documents.[1] That problem therefore directs attention to systemic description, analysis, and interpretation of documentary evidence, for by comparing one set of writings with another, we are able to contrast one system of a religion with another system within that same religion. The search for connections is both difficult and deceptively easy. It is easy because the second system is represented as a gloss upon the first; the connections therefore are formal

---

[1] The traits of mind of two sets of documents – the Mishnah, ca. A.D. 200, with its associated Midrash compilations, Sifra, Sifré to Numbers, and Sifré to Deuteronomy, and the Talmud of the Land of Israel (a.k.a. the Yerushalmi), a commentary to the Mishnah and associated Midrash collections, Genesis Rabbah, Leviticus Rabbah, and Pesiqta deRab Kahana, ca. A.D. 400-450 – permit us to undertake this exercise in the comparative study of category formation. A continuous literary tradition – the Yerushalmi is represented as a (mere) continuation of, and commentary to, the Mishnah, and the several distinct groups of Midrash compilations are presented as (mere) commentary to Scripture – in fact attests to two distinct religious systems.

and literary. It is difficult for that same reason: we have to be prepared to see as merely connected but in fact autonomous systems that generations have treated as continuous.

The foundation document is the Mishnah, a philosophical law code brought to closure at about ca. A.D. 200, which presents a theory of the social order that comprises a worldview or philosophy, way of life or economics, and an account of the social entity or politics. Why do I call the theory a philosophical one? By philosophy I mean very simply, a system of thought that, in the context of the same time and place, people generally deemed philosophers will have recognized as philosophical, with the proviso that there be no error as to the facts of the matter. The Mishnah, the first canonical writing of Judaism after the Hebrew Scriptures of ancient Israel ("the Old Testament") in important ways is to be read as philosophy in accord with the generally accepted understanding of philosophy in the time, ca. A.D. 200, and place, the Greek-speaking Near East. By philosophy both in that study and here, therefore, I mean specifically the philosophical tradition of the Greco-Roman world of the Second Sophistic, in particular the method of Aristotle and the proposition important to Middle Platonism. But philosophy in a generic sense demands its place, and by philosophy in general I mean disciplined, rigorous thought, in accord with rules subject to application without limit as to topic, that intelligibly produces generalizations demonstrated on the basis of correct principles of thought concerning this-worldly facts to govern or explain a variety of circumstances. A philosophy forms a cogent system of rational thought that treats diverse cases by appeal to a limited set of internally coherent generalizations. Such a system, as to method, abstract and intelligible, subject to reasoned explanation, as to topic, concerning a variety of concrete cases or problems, defines what I mean by (a) philosophy and, consequently, philosophical.[2]

Among the philosophers of the Greco-Roman philosophical tradition, the Mishnah's Judaic system can have been perceived as philosophical not merely in method but also in message. The Mishnah's method of hierarchical classification in important ways is like that of the natural history of Aristotle, and the central component of its message, congruent to that of neo-Platonism. Specifically, the Mishnah's Judaic

---

[2]I have further worked out in great detail an account of those passages in the entire Mishnah that are to be classified as philosophical, within the stated criterion, in my *The Philosophical Mishnah*. Volume I. *The Initial Probe*; Volume II. *The Tractates' Agenda. From Abodah Zarah to Moed Qatan*; Volume III. *The Tractates' Agenda. From Nazir to Zebahim*; and Volume IV. *The Repertoire* (Atlanta, 1989: Scholars Press for Brown Judaic Studies).

system sets forth in stupefying detail a version of one critical proposition of neo-Platonism, demonstrated through a standard Aristotelian method.³ The repeated proof through the Aristotelian method of hierarchical classification demonstrates in detail that many things – done enough times, *all* things – really form a single thing, many species, a single genus, many genera, an encompassing and well-crafted, cogent whole. Every time we speciate – and the Mishnah is a mass of speciated lists – we affirm that position; each successful labor of forming relationships among species, for example, making them into a genus, or identifying the hierarchy of the species, proves it again. Not only so, but when we can show that many things are really one, or that one thing yields many (the reverse and confirmation of the former), we say in a fresh way a single immutable truth, the one of this philosophy concerning the unity of all being in an orderly composition of all things within a single taxon. Accordingly, this Judaism's initial system, the Mishnah's, finds its natural place within philosophy because it appeals to the Aristotelian methods and medium of natural philosophy – classification, comparison and contrast, expressed in the forms of *Listenwissenschaft* – to register its position, which is an important one in Middle Platonism and later (close to a century after the closure of the Mishnah) would come to profound expression in Plotinus.

Let us dwell on the philosophical classification of the Mishnah's mode of thought. The Mishnah's method of inquiry is that of natural history, corresponding with that method of natural history characteristic of Aristotle. I do not claim that our sages of blessed memory read, or could have read, Aristotle or any other Greek philosopher. Aristotle's work on natural history, his reflections on scientific method, for example, the *Posterior Analytics*⁴ – these works speak in their own language to their own problems, and the Mishnah's authorship has written in a different language about incomparable problems. But when we compare our philosophers' method with that of Aristotle, who also, as a matter of fact, set forth a system that, in part, appealed to the right ordering of things

---

³And I need hardly add that the very eclecticism of the philosophy of Judaism places it squarely within the philosophical mode of its time. See J. M. Dillon and A. A. Long, eds., *The Question of "Eclecticism." Studies in Later Greek Philosophy* (Berkeley and Los Angeles, 1988: University of California Press). But these are only general observations, not meant to suggest direct connection or even to imply that an explanation drawn from "what was floating in the air" seems to me to pertain; I have no explanation.

⁴I consulted Jonathan Barnes, *Aristotle's Posterior Analytics* (Oxford, 1975: Clarendon Press).

through classification by correct rules[5] the simple fact becomes inescapable. Before us are different people, talking about different things, but in the same way.

The philosophical Judaism moreover utilized economics – the rational disposition of scarce resources – in order to set forth a systemic statement of fundamental importance. Entirely congruent with the philosophical economics of Aristotle, the Mishnah's economics answered the same questions concerning the definition of wealth, property, production and the means of production, ownership and control of the means of production, the determination of price and value and the like. And that fact signifies that the Judaic system to which the Mishnah attests is philosophical not only in method and message but in its very systemic composition. The principal components of its theory of the social order, its account of the way of life of its Israel and its picture of the conduct of the public policy of its social entity – all of these in detail correspond in their basic definitions and indicative traits with the economics and the politics of Greco-Roman philosophy in the Aristotelian tradition. Specifically, the Mishnah's economics, in general in the theory of the rational disposition of scarce resources and of the management and increase thereof, and specifically in its definitions of wealth and ownership, production and consumption, point by point corresponds to that of Aristotle.

The power of economics as framed by Aristotle, the only economic theorist of antiquity worthy of the name, was to develop the relationship between the economy and society as a whole.[6] And the framers of the Mishnah did the same when they incorporated issues of economics at a profound theoretical level into the system of society as a whole that they proposed to construct. That is why the authorship of the Mishnah will be seen as attacking the problem of man's livelihood within a system of sanctification of a holy people with a radicalism of which no later religious thinkers about utopias were capable. None has ever penetrated

---

[5] And, as to proposition about the hierarchical ordering of all things in a single way, the unity of all being in right order, while we cannot show and surely do not know that the Mishnah's philosophers knew anything about Plato, let alone Plotinus's neo-Platonism (which came to expression only in the century after the closure of the Mishnah!), we can compare our philosophers' proposition with that of neo-Platonism. For that philosophy, as we shall see, did seek to give full and rich expression to the proposition that all things emerge from one thing, and one thing encompasses all things, and that constitutes the single proposition that animates the system as a whole.

[6] Polanyi, "Aristotle Discovers the Economy," in Polanyi, Karl, Conrad M. Arensberg, and Harry W. Pearson, *Trade and Market in the Early Empires. Economies in History and Theory* (Glencoe, 1957: Free Press), p. 79.

deeper into the material organization of man's life under the aspect of God's rule. In effect, they posed, in all its breadth, the question of the critical, indeed definitive place occupied by the economy in society under God's rule. The points in common between Aristotle's and the Mishnah's economics in detail prove no less indicative. Both Aristotle and the Mishnah presented an anachronistic system of economics. The theory of both falls into the same classification of economic theory, that of distributive economics, familiar in the Near and Middle East from Sumerian times down to, but not including, the age of Aristotle (let alone that of the Mishnah five centuries later). But market economics had been well-established prior to Aristotle's time.[7] Aristotle's economics is distributive for systemic reasons, the Mishnah's replicates the received principles of the economics planned by the Temple priests and set forth in the Priestly Code of the Pentateuch, Leviticus in particular. The result – fabricated or replicated principles – was the same. Both systems – the Mishnah's and Aristotle's – in vast detail expressed the ancient distributive economics, in their theories of fixed value and conception of the distribution of scarce resources by appeal to other than the rationality of the market. The theory of money characteristic of Aristotle (but not of Plato) and of the Mishnah, for instance, conforms to that required by distributive economics; exchange takes place through barter, not through the abstract price setting mechanism represented by money. Consequently, the representation of the Mishnah as a philosophical Judaism derives from not only general characteristics but very specific and indicative traits held in common with the principal figure of the Greco-Roman philosophical tradition in economics.

---

[7]Let me briefly explain the difference between the two, which is a fundamental indicator in classifying economics. In market economics merchants transfer goods from place to place in response to the working of the market mechanism, which is expressed in price. In distributive economics, by contrast, traders move goods from point to point in response to political commands. In market economics, merchants make the market work by calculations of profit and loss. In distributive economics, there is no risk of loss on a transaction. In market economics, money forms an arbitrary measure of value, a unit of account. In distributive economics, money gives way to barter and bears only intrinsic value, as do the goods for which it is exchanged. It is something that people accept not for its inherent value in use but because of what it will buy. The idea of money requires the transaction to be complete in the exchange not of goods but of coins. The alternative is the barter transaction, in which, in theory at least, the exchange takes place when goods change hands. In distributive economics money is an instrument of direct exchange between buyers and sellers, not the basic resource in the process of production and distribution that it is in market economics.

There was a common social foundation for the economic theory of both systems.[8] Both Aristotle and the Mishnah's framers deemed the fundamental unit of production to be the household, and the larger social unit, the village, composed of households, marked the limits of the social entity. The Mishnah's economic tractates, such as the tractates on civil law, invariably refer to the householder, making him the subject of most predicates; where issues other than economics are in play, for example, in the political tractates such as Sanhedrin, the householder scarcely appears as a social actor. Not only so, but both Aristotle and the authorship of the Mishnah formed the conception of "true value," which maintained that something – an object, a piece of land – possessed a value extrinsic to the market and intrinsic to itself, such that, if a transaction varied from that imputed true value by (in the case of the Mishnah) 18 percent, the exchange was null. Not only so, but the sole definition of wealth for both Aristotle's and the Mishnah's economics was real estate: only land, however small. Since land does not contract or expand, of course, the conception of an increase in value through other than a steady state exchange of real value, "true value," between parties to a transaction lay outside of the theory of economics. Therefore all profit, classified as usury, was illegitimate and must be prevented.

The Mishnah's politics – its theory of the legitimate use of violence and the disposition of power in society – describes matters in a manner that is fundamentally philosophical in the Aristotelian context. Israel forms a political entity, fully empowered in an entirely secular sense, just as Scripture had described matters. To political institutions of the social order, king, priest, and court or civil administration, each in its jurisdiction, is assigned the right legitimately to exercise violence here on earth, corresponding to, and shared with, the same empowerment accorded to institutions of Heaven. These institutions moreover are conceived permanently to ration and rationalize the uses of that power. The picture, of course, is this-worldly, but, not distinguishing crime from sin, it is not secular, since the same system that legitimates king, high priest, and court posits in Heaven a corresponding politics, with God and the court on high exercising jurisdiction for some crimes or sins, the king, priesthood, or court down below for others. Three specific traits direct our attention toward the philosophical classification for the Mishnah's politics in framing a systemic composition even though, to be sure, the parallels prove structural and general, rather than detailed and doctrinal as was the case with economics.

---

[8]Though the politics of the Mishnah was disembedded from its economics, while the politics of Aristotle was embedded, so that the latter presents a political economy, the former does not.

First, like the politics of Plato and Aristotle, the Mishnah's politics describes only a utopian politics, a structure and system of a fictive and a fabricated kind: intellectuals' conception of a politics. Serving the larger purpose of system construction, politics of necessity emerges as invention, for example, by Heaven or in the model of Heaven, not as a secular revision and reform of an existing system. While in the middle second-century Rome incorporated their country, which they called the Land of Israel and the Romans called Palestine, into its imperial system, denying Jews access to their capital, Jerusalem, permanently closing their cult center, its Temple, the authorship of the Mishnah described a government of a king and a high priest and an administration fully empowered to carry out the law through legitimate violence. So the two politics – the Mishnah's, the Greco-Roman tradition represented by Plato's and Aristotle's – share in common their origins in intellectuals' theoretical and imaginative life and form an instance, within that life, of the concrete realization of a larger theory of matters. In strange and odd forms, the Mishnah's politics falls into the class of the *Staatsroman*, the classification that encompasses, also, Plato's *Republic* and Aristotle's *Politics*. But, admittedly, the same may be said for the strange politics of the Pentateuch.

Second and more to the point, the Mishnah's sages stand well within the philosophical mode of political thought that begins with Aristotle, who sees politics as a fundamental component of his system when he says, "political science...legislates as to what we are to do and what we are to abstain from"; and, as to the institutionalization of power, I cannot imagine a more ample definition of the Mishnah's system's utilization of politics than that.[9] While that statement, also, applies to the Pentateuchal politics, the systemic message borne by politics within the Pentateuchal system and that carried by politics in the Mishnah's system do not correspond in any important ways. Aristotle and the philosophers of the Mishnah utilize politics to make systemic statements that correspond to one another, in that both comparison and contrast prove apt and pointed. Both spoke of an empowered social entity; both took for granted that ongoing institutions legitimately exercise governance in accord with a rationality discerned by distinguishing among those empowered to inflict sanctions. Both see politics as a medium for accomplishing systemic goals, and the goals derive from the larger purpose of the social order, to which politics is subordinated and merely instrumental.

But, third, the comparison also yields a contrast of importance. Specifically, since political analysis comes only after economic analysis

---

[9]Cited by R. G. Mulgan, *Aristotle's Political Theory* (Oxford: Clarendon Press, 1977), p. 3.

and depends upon the results of that prior inquiry into a social system's disposition of scarce resources and theory of control of means of production, we have no choice but to follow up the results of the preceding chapter and compare the politics of Aristotle and the politics of the Mishnah, just as we did the economics of each system. For when we know who commands the means of production, we turn to inquire about who tells whom what to do and why: who legitimately coerces others even through violence. And here the Mishnah's system decisively parts company with that of the Pentateuch and also with that of Aristotle. As to the former, the distributive economics of the Pentateuch in the Priestly stratum at the foundations assigns both economic and political privilege to the same class of persons, the priesthood, effecting distributive economics and distributive politics. But that is not the way things are in the Mishnah's politics, which distinguishes the one in control of the means of production from the one control of the right legitimately to commit violence. The former, the householder, is not a political entity at all, and, dominant as the subject of most sentences in the economic tractates, he never appears in the political ones at all.

The point of difference from Aristotle is to be seen only within the context of the similarity that permits comparison and contrast. While the economics of Aristotle and the economics of Judaism commence with the consideration of the place and power of the person ("class," "caste," economic interest) in control of the means of production, the social metaphors that animate the politics of the two systems part company. Aristotle in his *Politics* is consistent in starting with that very same person ("class") when he considers issues of power, producing a distributive politics to match his distributive economics. But the Mishnah's philosophers build their politics with an altogether different set of building blocks. The simple fact is that the householder, fundamental to their economics, does not form a subject of political discourse at all and in no way constitutes a political class or caste. When the Mishnah's writers speak of economics, the subject of most active verbs is the householder; when they speak of politics, the householder never takes an active role or even appears as a differentiated political class. In this sense, the economics of the Mishnah is disembedded from its politics, and the politics from its economics. By contrast the economics and politics of Aristotle's system are deeply embedded within a larger and nurturing, wholly cogent theory of political economy.

II. Counterpart Categories

The successor system, represented by the Talmud of the Land of Israel and related writings, ca. 400-450, presented a theory of the social order lacking any theory of politics, philosophy, and economics of a conventional order. So while, as a matter of hypothesis, we must assume that a system formed in theory to describe the social order by definition attends to the way of life, worldview, and definition of the social entity, that that system puts forth, in practice that is not what happened. For by "way of life" – economics – or "worldview" – politics – the successor system did not mean – or even refer to – exactly the same category of data that initial system had adopted for itself. It is that fact that makes urgent for the study of world history the unfolding of the two distinct Judaisms, the one philosophical, the other, as I shall explain, religious. For herein we find a case in which establishing connections is complicated by the incongruency of categories.

The claim, "this is what functioned for this system in the way in which, in that system, that accomplished the (same) task," proves simply irrelevant. Such a claim forms an excuse, not a reason, for difference among systems, and, since what is at stake is establishing connections from society to society through systemic comparison, it hardly explains why one system sets forth its way of life by selecting data of one kind, while another one chooses data of a completely different order altogether for the same purpose. Not only so, but what we seek to describe, analyze, and interpret are systems, on their own and (in the case of systems that prove continuous in their canonical express) also in relationship with one another. So let me restate matters as I think a rigorous definition requires us to see them. A system selects its data to expose its systemic categories; defines its categories in accord with the systemic statement that it wishes to set forth; identifies the urgent question to which the systemic message compellingly responds. To understand a system, we begin with the whole and work our way inward toward the parts; the formation of categories then is governed by the system's requirements: the rationality of the whole dictates the structure of the categorical parts, and the structure of the parts then governs the selection of what fits into those categories.[10]

Now that we have seen the philosophical character of the initial system's worldview, way of life, and theory of the social entity, that is, its philosophy, economics, and politics, we ask how these same categories fared in the successor system's documentary evidence. As a matter of simple fact, while sharing the goal of presenting a theory of the social order, as to their categorical formations and structures, the initial, philosophical Judaic system and the successor system differ in a

---

[10]None of these points intersects with either relativism or functionalism; the issues are wholly other. At stake in systemic description, analysis, and interpretation, after all, ultimately is the comparative study of rationalities.

fundamental way. Stated very simply, what happened, as I shall explain, is that the successor system held up a mirror to the received categories and so redefined matters that everything was reversed. Left became right, down, up, and, as we shall see, in a very explicit transvaluation of values, power is turned into weakness, things of real value are transformed into intangibles. This transvaluation, yielding the transformation of the prior system altogether, is articulated and not left implicit; it is a specific judgment made concrete through mythic and symbolic revision by the later authorships themselves.[11] A free-standing document, received with reverence, served to precipitate the transvaluation of all of the values of that document's initial statement.

The categorical transformation that was underway, signaling the movement from philosophy to religion, comes to the surface when we ask a simple question. Precisely what do the authorships of the successor documents, speaking not about the Mishnah but on their own account, mean by economics, politics, and philosophy? That is to say, to what kinds of data do they refer when they speak of scarce resources and legitimate violence, and exactly how – as to the received philosophical method – do they define correct modes of thought and expression, logic and rhetoric, and even the topical program worthy of sustained inquiry? The components of the initial formation of categories were examined thoughtfully and carefully, paraphrased and augmented and clarified. But the received categories were not continued, not expanded, and not renewed. Preserved merely intact, as they had been handed on, the received categories hardly serve to encompass all of the points of emphasis and sustained development that characterize the successor documents – or, as a matter of fact, any of them. On the contrary, when the framers of the Yerushalmi, for one example, moved out from the exegesis of Mishnah passages, they also left behind the topics of paramount interest in the Mishnah and developed other categories altogether.[12] Here we find that, in these other categories, the framers of the successor system defined their own counterparts. These counterpart categories, moreover, redefined matters, following the main outlines of

---

[11] I underline that fact, since all that follows on the transvaluation of values through the formation of what I have invented as "counterpart categories" appeals to explicit statements, not a very general, post facto observation on my part.

[12] That fact is demonstrated in my *Talmud of the Land of Israel. A Preliminary Translation and Explanation. 35. Introduction. Taxonomy* (Chicago, 1983: University of Chicago Press). There I show that when Mishnah exegesis is concluded, a quite separate agendum takes centerstage, the emphases of which find no counterpart in the Mishnah. That seems to me to justify the consideration of counterpart categories, such as I introduce here.

From Mishnaic Philosophy to Talmudic Religion

the structure of the social order manifest in the initial system. The counterpart categories set forth an account of the social order just as did the ones of the Mishnah's framers. But they defined the social order in very different terms altogether. In that redefinition we discern the transformation of the received system, and the traits of the new one fall into the classification of not philosophy but religion.

For what the successor thinkers did was not continue and expand the categorical repertoire but, rather, set forth a categorically fresh vision of the social order – a way of life, worldview, and definition of the social entity – with appropriate counterpart categories. And what is decisive is that these served as did the initial categories within the generative categorical structure definitive for all Judaic systems. So there was a category corresponding to the generative component of worldview, but it was not philosophical; another corresponding to the required component setting forth a way of life, but in the conventional and accepted definition of economics it was not an economics; and, finally, a category to define the social entity, "Israel," that any Judaic system must explain, but in the accepted sense of a politics it was not politics.

Exactly how was this categorical reformation accomplished? To state matters first in the most abstract way, it was done by reversing the flow of language, specifically taking the predicate of a sentence and moving it to the position of the subject, that is, commencing not from subject but from predicate. From "[1] economics is [2] the rational disposition of scarce resources," the category of way of life was rephrased into, "[2] the rational disposition of scarce resources is [1] (their, in context, systemic) economics." The reverse reading therefore yields the counterpart category, defined by this sentence: *"a (any) theory of rational action with regard to scarcity..., then: is (for the system at hand) its economics."* The same procedure serves, too – *mutatis mutandis* – for discerning the later systems' politics and science or learning or philosophy. Precisely what the framers worked out as their economics, politics, and philosophy is laid out in this part of the book, and the result was a quite new system. This transvaluation of values, through not merely the re-formation but the utter transformation of categories, set forth an essentially fresh answer to a fundamentally new urgent question. But here, the answer is the main point of interest. To give a simple instance, when we say, "a (or any) theory of rational action with regard to scarcity *is* (an) economics," we mean, any account of what is deemed scarce and therefore to require rational action as to allocation, increase, and disposition, functions to define the category that is the counterpart, in the philosophical system of the Mishnah, to economics. It answers the same question, but it utterly recasts the terms of the question. True, standard topics such as as wealth and money, production and distribution, work and wage, ownership and conduct of economic entities play no role. But the issues of tangible wealth and materials goods do emerge, and, it follows, the system identifies something other than real wealth (real estate, capital, for instance) – but this "wealth in another form" also is claimed to put bread on the table.

That fact raises the question of how to deal with such accounts of the social order that, while answering the questions that pertain, nonetheless lack an economics or a politics or a philosophy in the familiar senses of these categories. To answer that question of method in the analysis of category formation, I have to discover and define what serves, in such a system, the task of economics in a philosophical system. To do so – as stated in abstract form just now – I propose the notion that, "[2] a (any) theory of rational action with regard to scarcity *is* [1] economics." Matters that hardly fall into the category of economic theory at all may yield points of congruency. As a matter of fact they may also validate those systemic comparisons and contrasts that permit us to trace the history of an ongoing system from its philosophical to its religious formulation. We know that we are right when we find, as we shall, that the authorships of the successor systems recognize and select the principal symbolic expression of a received category and turn it on its head: land becomes Torah learning, and that is made explicit, for one stunning instance. Then it is not merely my post-facto reading of one system as a reversal of a prior one that has yielded the counterpart category, but the documents themselves.

When we see that a category for an alien system and its rationality constitutes *its* economics and therefore forms a counterpart to economics as we understand that subject within our rationality, we learn how in a critical component to translate system to system. We may then make the statement, "In that system, within their rationality, that category of activity forms a component of economic theory, while in our system, within our rationality, we do not think of that category of activity as a component of economic theory at all." And this we do without assuming a posture of relativism, for example claiming that their economics, and, with it, their rationality, is pretty much the same, or as at least as valid, as ours. Framing the relativist judgment in that way, we see that it is simply not relevant to what is at stake. That kind of interpretation of matters is not pertinent to my exercise in translation and comparison carried out through the definition and examination of counterpart categories. We begin with the systemic counterpart to philosophy, then proceed to economics, and conclude with politics, following the order of Part One. Our first task is to follow the categorical formation of a new worldview generated by the received mode of thought, a worldview that fundamentally differed from the philosophical one at every point.

III. The Talmud's Categorical Reformation: Judaism as a Religion

What the philosophical Judaism kept apart, the religious Judaism portrayed by the Talmud of the Land of Israel and related writings now joined together, and it is just there, at that critical joining, that we identify the key to the system: its reversal of a received point of differentiation, its introduction of new points of differentiation altogether. The source of generative problems for the Mishnah's politics is simply not the same as the source that served the successor system's politics, and, systemic analysis being what it is, it is the union of what was formerly asunder that identifies for us in quite objective terms the critical point of tension, the sources of problems, the centerpiece of systemic concern throughout. Let me show how this process of reintegration was worked out in the categorical reformation underway in the Yerushalmi and related writings.

We begin with the shift from philosophy to Torah study, that is from abstract reflection to concrete text exegesis and digression out of sacred scripture; philosophy yields accurate and rational understanding of things; knowledge of the Torah, by contrast, yields power over this world and the next, capacity to coerce to the sage's will the natural and supernatural worlds alike, on that account. The Torah is thus transformed from a philosophical enterprise of the sifting and classification of the facts of this world into a gnostic process of changing persons through knowledge. It is on that basis that in the Yerushalmi and related writings I find in the Torah the counterpart category to philosophy in the Mishnah. Now we deal with a new intellectual category: Torah, meaning, religious learning *in place of* philosophical learning. What is the difference between the one and the other? First comes appeal to revealed truth as against perceived facts of nature and their regularities, second, the conception of an other-worldly source of explanation and the development of a propositional program focused upon not nature but Scripture, not the nations in general but Israel in particular, and third, the gnosticization of knowledge in the conception that knowing works salvation.

What was to change, therefore, was not the mode of thought. What was new, rather, was the propositions to be demonstrated philosophically, and what made these propositions new was the focus of interest, on the one side, and data assembled by way of demonstrating them, on the other. From a philosophical proposition within the framework of free-standing philosophy of religion and metaphysics that the Mishnah's system aimed to establish, we move to religious and even theological propositions within the setting of contingent exegesis of Scripture. Then how do we know that what was changing was not merely topical and propositional but *categorical* in character? The answer lies in the symbolic vocabulary that would be commonly used in the late fourth and fifth century writings but not at all, or not in the same way, in the late second century ones. When people select data not formerly taken into account and represent the data by appeal to symbols not formerly found evocative or expressive, or not utilized in the way in which they later on were used, then – so I claim – we are justified in raising questions about category formation and the development of new categories alongside, or instead, of the received ones. In the case at hand, the character of the transformation we witness is shown by the formation of a symbol serving to represent a category.

To signal what is to come, we shall find the quite bald statement that, in the weighing of the comparative value of capital, which in this time and place meant land or real property, and Torah, Torah was worthwhile, and land was not – a symbolic syllogism that is explicit, concrete, repeated, and utterly fresh for the documents we consider. On the basis of that quite explicit symbolic comparison I speak of transformation – symbolic and therefore *categorical* transformation, not merely thematic shifts in emphasis or even propositional change. And that is why I hold that we witness in the successor writings the formation of a system connected with, but asymmetrical to, the initial, philosophical one. Then for the worldview of the transformed Judaism, the counterpart category to philosophy is formulated by appeal to the symbolic medium for the theological message, and it is the category, the Torah, expressed, as a matter of fact, by the symbol of *Torah*.[13]

Philosophy sought the generalizations that cases might yield. So, too, did religion (and, in due course, theology would too). But the range of generalization vastly differed. Philosophy spoke of the nature of things, while theology represented the special nature of Israel in particular. Philosophy then appealed to the traits of things, while theology to the special indicative qualities of Israel. What of the propositional program that the document sets forth? The philosophical proposition of the Mishnah demonstrated from the facts and traits of things the hierarchical order of all being, with the obvious if merely implicit proposition that God stands at the head of the social order. The religious propositions of the successor documents speak in other words of other things, having simply nothing in common with the propositional program of the Mishnah's philosophy.

---

[13]Much that is said here alludes to the results of my *Torah: From Scroll to Symbol in Formative Judaism* (Philadelphia, 1985: Fortress; second printing: Atlanta, 1989: Scholars Press for Brown Judaic Studies).

The shift in economics is no less striking. Consideration of the transvaluation of value brings us to the successor system's counterpart category, that is, the one that in context forms the counterpart to the Mishnah's concrete, this-worldly, material and tangible definition of value in conformity with the familiar, philosophical economics. We have now to ask, what, in place of the received definition of value and the economics thereof, did the new system set forth? The transformation of economics involved the redefinition of scarce and valued resources in so radical a manner that the concept of value, while remaining material in consequence and character, nonetheless took on a quite different sense altogether. The counterpart category of the successor system concerned themselves with the same questions as did the conventional economics, presenting an economics in function and structure, but one that concerned things of value other than those identified by the initial system. So indeed we deal with an economics, an economics of something other than real estate.

But it was an economics just as profoundly embedded in the social order, just as deeply a political economics, just as pervasively a systemic economics, as the economics of the Mishnah and of Aristotle. Why so? Because issues such as the definition of wealth, the means of production and the meaning of control thereof, the disposition of wealth through distributive or other media, theory of money, reward for labor, and the like – all these issues found their answers in the counterpart category of economics, as much as in the received and conventional philosophical economics. The new "scarce resource" accomplished what the old did, but it was a different resource, a new currency. At stake in the category meant to address the issues of the way of life of the social entity, therefore, were precisely the same considerations as confront economics in its (to us) conventional and commonplace, philosophical sense. But since the definition of wealth changes, as we have already seen, from land to Torah, much else would be transformed on that account.

Land produced a living; so did Torah. Land formed the foundation of the social entity, so did Torah. The transvaluation of value was such that an economics concerning the rational management and increase of scarce resources worked itself out in such a way as to answer, for quite different things of value from real property or from capital such as we know as value, precisely the same questions that the received economics addressed in connection with wealth of a real character: land and its produce. Systemic transformation comes to the surface in articulated symbolic change. The utter transvaluation of value finds expression in a jarring juxtaposition, an utter shift of rationality, specifically, the substitution of Torah for real estate. We recall how in a successor document (but in none prior to the fifth century compilations) Tarfon thought wealth took the form of land, while Aqiba explained to him that wealth takes the form of Torah learning. That the sense is material and concrete is explicit: land for Torah, Torah for land. Thus, to repeat the matter of how Torah serves as an explicit symbol to convey the systemic worldview, let us note the main point of this passage:[14]

Leviticus Rabbah XXXIV:XVI

1. B. R. Tarfon gave to R. Aqiba six silver centenarii, saying to him, "Go, buy us a piece of land, so we can get a living from it and labor in the study of Torah together."
   C. He took the money and handed it over to scribes, Mishnah teachers, and those who study Torah.
   D. After some time R. Tarfon met him and said to him, "Did you buy the land that I mentioned to you?"
   E. He said to him, "Yes."
   F. He said to him, "Is it any good?"
   G. He said to him, "Yes."
   H. He said to him, "And do you not want to show it to me?"
   I. He took him and showed him the scribes, Mishnah teachers, and people who were studying Torah, and the Torah that they had acquired.
   J. He said to him, "Is there anyone who works for nothing? Where is the deed covering the field?"
   K. He said to him, "It is with King David, concerning whom it is written, 'He has scattered, he has given to the poor, his righteousness endures forever' (Ps. 112:9)."

The successor system has its own definitions not only for learning, symbolized by the word Torah but also for wealth, expressed in the same symbol. Accordingly, the category formation for worldview, Torah in place of philosophy, dictates, as a matter of fact, a still more striking category reformation, in which the entire matter of scarce resources is reconsidered, and a counterpart category set forth.

Philosophical politics tells who may legitimately do what to whom. When a politics wants to know who ought *not* to be doing what to whom, we find in hand the counterpart category to the received politics – anti-politics, a theory of the illegitimacy of power, the legitimacy of being

---

[14] While the attributions are to first century figures, the story appears in a document that reached closure in the fifth century, and I take the story to represent opinion deemed authoritative in the fifth century. For extensive explanation of what is at issue, see my *The Canonical History of Ideas. The Place of the So-called Tannaite Midrashim, Mekhilta Attributed to R. Ishmael, Sifra, Sifré to Numbers, and Sifré to Deuteronomy* (Atlanta, 1990: Scholars Press for South Florida Studies in the History of Judaism).

victim.[15] The received category set forth politics as the theory of legitimate violence, the counterpart category, politics as the theory of *illegitimate* violence. The received politics had been one of isolation and interiority, portraying Israel as sui generis and autocephalic in all ways. The portrait in the successor documents is a politics of integration among the nations; a perspective of exteriority replaces the inner-facing one of the Mishnah, which recognized no government of Israel but God's – and then essentially ab initio. The issues of power had found definition in questions concerning who legitimately inflicts sanctions upon whom within Israel. They now shift to give an account of who illegitimately inflicts sanctions upon ("persecutes") Israel. So the points of systemic differentiation are radically revised, and the politics of the successor system becomes not a revision of the received category but a formation that in many ways mirrors the received one: once more a counterpart category. Just as, in the definition of scarce resources, Torah study has replaced land, so now weakness forms the focus in place of strength, illegitimacy in place of legitimacy. Once more the mirror image of the received category presents the perspective of the counterpart category.

Now we find the answers to these questions: To whom is violence illegitimately done, and also, who may not legitimately inflict violence? With the move from the politics of legitimate to that of illegitimate power, the systemic interest now lies in defining not who legitimately does what, but rather, to whom, against whom, is power illegitimately exercised. And this movement represents not the revision of the received category, but its inversion. For thought on legitimate violence is turned on its head. A new category of empowerment is worked out alongside the old. The entity that is victim of power is at the center, rather than the entity that legitimately exercises power. That entity is now Israel *en masse*, rather than the institutions and agencies of Israel on earth, Heaven above – a very considerable shift in thought on the systemic social entity. Israel as disempowered, rather than king, high priest, and sage as Israel's media of empowerment, defines the new system's politics. The upshot is that the successor system has reconsidered not merely the contents of the received structure, but the composition of the structure itself. In place of its philosophy, we have now a new medium for the formulation of a worldview; in place of a way of life formulated as an economics, a new Valuation of value, in place of an account of the social entity framed as a politics, a new conception of legitimate violence. So much for the formation of counterpart categories.

---

[15]That is, of course, as much as, in the contrast of real wealth and true value, that is to say, land and Torah learning, we identify not a revised economics but a counterpart category to the familiar economics.

IV. From Philosophy to Religion: Systemic Integration

Points of integration, not of differentiation, guide us to the systemic problematic, and permit us to see the system as a whole. What holds the system together identifies the critical question that the system as a whole means to answer, its aspect of self-evidence. Seeing the whole all at once, we may then undertake that work of comparison and contrast that produces connections from system to system. How then may we characterize the shift from a philosophical to a religious system? The answer derives from our choice of the systemic center, for example, a symbol that captures the whole, that holds the whole together. Certainly, the integration of the philosophical system is readily stated in a phrase: the philosophical Judaism set forth a system of hierarchical classification. Having emphasized the succession – philosophy out, Torah in – I may ask whether for the religious system of Judaism, the systemic center is captured by the symbol of the Torah – focused on the holy man sanctified through mastery of revelation. The answer is negative, because, as a matter of fact, knowledge of the Torah forms a way-station on a path to a more distant, more central goal, it is a dependent variable, contingent and stipulative. Then wherein lies the systemic center? It is the quest for *zekhut*, properly translated as "the heritage of virtue and its consequent entitlements." It is the simple fact that Torah study is one means of attaining access to that heritage, of gaining *zekhut* – and there are other equally suitable means. The *zekhut* gained by Torah study is no different from the merit gained by acts of supererogatory grace. So we must take seriously the contingent status, the standing of a dependent variable, accorded to Torah study in such stories as the following:

Y. Taanit 3:11

IV. C. There was a house that was about to collapse over there [in Babylonia], and Rab set one of his disciples in the house, until they had cleared out everything from the house. When the disciple left the house, the house collapsed.

D. And there are those who say that it was R. Adda bar Ahbah.

E. Sages sent and said to him, "What sort of good deeds are to your credit [that you have that much merit]?"

F. He said to them, "In my whole life no man ever got to the synagogue in the morning before I did. I never left anybody there when I went out. I never walked four cubits without speaking words of Torah. Nor did I ever mention teachings of Torah in an inappropriate setting. I never laid out a bed and slept for a regular period of time. I never took great strides among the associates. I never called my fellow by a nickname. I never rejoiced in the embarrassment of my fellow. I never cursed my fellow when I was lying by myself in bed. I never walked over in the marketplace to someone who owed me money.

G. "In my entire life I never lost my temper in my household."

> H. This was meant to carry out that which is stated as follows: "I will give heed to the way that is blameless. Oh when wilt thou come to me? I will walk with integrity of heart within my house" (Ps. 101:2).

What I find striking in this story is that mastery of the Torah is only one means of attaining the *zekhut* that had enabled the sage to keep the house from collapsing. And Torah study is not the primary means of attaining *zekhut*. The question at E provides the key, together with its answer at F. For what the sage did to gain such remarkable *zekhut* is not to master such-and-so many tractates of the Mishnah. It was rather acts of courtesy, consideration, gentility, restraint. These produced *zekhut*, all of them acts of self-abnegation or the avoidance of power over others and the submission to the will and the requirement of self-esteem of others. Torah study is simply an item on a list of actions or attitudes that generate *zekhut*.

Here, in a moral setting, we find the politics replicated: the form of power that the system promises derives from the rejection of power that the world recognizes – legitimate violence replaced by legitimation of the absence of the power to commit violence or of the failure to commit violence. And, when we ask, whence that sort of power? the answer lies in the gaining of *zekhut* in a variety of ways, not in the acquisition of *zekhut* through the study of the Torah solely or even primarily. But, we note, the story at hand speaks of a sage in particular. He has gained *zekhut* by not acting the way sages are commonly assumed to behave but in a humble way.

In all three instances that follow, defining what the individual must do to gain *zekhut*, the point is that the deeds of the heroes of the story make them worthy of having their prayers answered, which is a mark of the working of *zekhut*. It is deeds beyond the strict requirements of the Torah, and even the limits of the law altogether, that transform the hero into a holy man, whose holiness served just like that of a sage marked as such by knowledge of the Torah The following stories should not be understood as expressions of the mere sentimentality of the clerks concerning the lower orders, for they deny in favor of a single action of surpassing power sages' lifelong devotion to what the sages held to be the highest value, knowledge of the Torah:

Y. Taanit 1:4

> I. F. A certain man came before one of the relatives of R. Yannai. He said to him, "Rabbi, attain *zekhut* through me [by giving me charity]."
> G. He said to him, "And didn't your father leave you money?"
> H. He said to him, "No."

I. He said to him, "Go and collect what your father left in deposit with others."

J. He said to him, "I have heard concerning property my father deposited with others that it was gained by violence [so I don't want it]."

K. He said to him, "You are worthy of praying and having your prayers answered."

The point of K, of course, is self-evidently a reference to the possession of entitlement to supernatural favor, and it is gained, we see, through deeds that the law of the Torah cannot require but must favor: what one does on one's own volition, beyond the measure of the law. Here I see the opposite of sin. A sin is what one has done by one's own volition beyond all limits of the law. So an act that generates *zekhut* for the individual is the counterpart and opposite: what one does by one's own volition that also is beyond all requirements of the law.

L. A certain ass driver appeared before the rabbis [the context requires: in a dream] and prayed, and rain came. The rabbis sent and brought him and said to him, "What is your trade?"

M. He said to them, "I am an ass driver."

N. They said to him, "And how do you conduct your business?"

O. He said to them, "One time I rented my ass to a certain woman, and she was weeping on the way, and I said to her, 'What's with you?' and she said to me, 'The husband of that woman [me] is in prison [for debt], and I wanted to see what I can do to free him.' So I sold my ass and I gave her the proceeds, and I said to her, 'Here is your money, free your husband, but do not sin [by becoming a prostitute to raise the necessary funds].'"

P. They said to him, "You are worthy of praying and having your prayers answered."

The ass driver clearly has a powerful lien on Heaven, so that his prayers are answered, even while those of others are not. What he did to get that entitlement? He did what no law could demand: impoverished himself to save the woman from a "fate worse than death."

Q. In a dream of R. Abbahu, Mr. Pentakaka ["Five sins"] appeared, who prayed that rain would come, and it rained. R. Abbahu sent and summoned him. He said to him, "What is your trade?"

R. He said to him, "Five sins does that man [I] do every day, [for I am a pimp:] hiring whores, cleaning up the theater, bringing home their garments for washing, dancing, and performing before them."

S. He said to him, "And what sort of decent thing have you ever done?"

T. He said to him, "One day that man [I] was cleaning the theater, and a woman came and stood behind a pillar and cried. I said to her, 'What's with you?' And she said to me, 'That woman's [my] husband is in prison, and I wanted to see what I can do to free him,'

From Mishnaic Philosophy to Talmudic Religion 23

U. so I sold my bed and cover, and I gave the proceeds to her. I said to her, 'Here is your money, free your husband, but do not sin.'"
U. He said to him, "You are worthy of praying and having your prayers answered."

Q moves us still further, since the named man has done everything sinful that one can do, and, more to the point, he does it every day. So the singularity of the act of *zekhut*, which suffices if done only one time, encompasses its power to outweigh a life of sin – again, an act of *zekhut* as the mirror image and opposite of sin. Here again, the single act of saving a woman from a "fate worse than death" has sufficed.

V. A pious man from Kefar Imi appeared [in a dream] to the rabbis. He prayed for rain and it rained. The rabbis went up to him. His householders told them that he was sitting on a hill. They went out to him, saying to him, "Greetings," but he did not answer them.
W. He was sitting and eating, and he did not say to them, "You break bread too."
X. When he went back home, he made a bundle of faggots and put his cloak on top of the bundle [instead of on his shoulder].
Y. When he came home, he said to his household [wife], "These rabbis are here [because] they want me to pray for rain. If I pray and it rains, it is a disgrace for them, and if not, it is a profanation of the Name of Heaven. But come, you and I will go up [to the roof] and pray. If it rains, we shall tell them, 'We are not worthy to pray and have our prayers answered.'"
Z. They went up and prayed and it rained.
AA. They came down to them [and asked], "Why have the rabbis troubled themselves to come here today?"
BB. They said to him, "We wanted you to pray so that it would rain."
CC. He said to them, "Now do you really need my prayers? Heaven already has done its miracle."
DD. They said to him, "Why, when you were on the hill, did we say hello to you, and you did not reply?"
EE. He said to them, "I was then doing my job. Should I then interrupt my concentration [on my work]?"
FF. They said to him, "And why, when you sat down to eat, did you not say to us 'You break bread too'?"
GG. He said to them, "Because I had only my small ration of bread. Why would I have invited you to eat by way of mere flattery [when I knew I could not give you anything at all]?"
HH. They said to him, "And why when you came to go down, did you put your cloak on top of the bundle?"
II. He said to them, "Because the cloak was not mine. It was borrowed for use at prayer. I did not want to tear it."
JJ. They said to him, "And why, when you were on the hill, did your wife wear dirty clothes, but when you came down from the mountain, did she put on clean clothes?"
KK. He said to them, "When I was on the hill, she put on dirty clothes, so that no one would gaze at her. But when I came home from the

hill, she put on clean clothes, so that I would not gaze on any other woman."

LL. They said to him, "It is well that you pray and have your prayers answered."

The pious man of V, finally, enjoys the recognition of the sages by reason of his lien upon Heaven, able as he is to pray and bring rain. What has so endowed him with *zekhut*? Acts of punctiliousness of a moral order: concentrating on his work, avoiding an act of dissimulation, integrity in the disposition of a borrowed object, his wife's concern not to attract other men and her equal concern to make herself attractive to her husband. None of these stories refers explicitly to *zekhut*; all of them tell us about what it means to enjoy not an entitlement by inheritance but a lien accomplished by one's own supererogatory acts of restraint.

Accordingly, *zekhut* integrates what has been differentiated. Holding together learning, virtue, and supernatural standing, by explaining how Torah study transforms the learning man, *zekhut* further makes implausible those points of distinction between economics, and politics that bore the systemic message of the initial philosophy. The Mishnah's philosophical theory of the social order, resting on hierarchical classification, with its demonstration of the upward reaching unity of all being, gives way to a different, religious proposition: the unity of all being within the heritage of *zekhut*, to be attained equally and without differentiation in all the principal parts of the social order. The definition of *zekhut* therefore carries us to the heart of the integrating and integrated religious system of Judaism.

Out of the integrating conception the several components of a theory of the social order are identified: theory of the social entity, way of life, worldview. Because *zekhut* is something one may receive as an inheritance, out of the distant past, *zekhut* imposes upon the definition of the social entity, "Israel," a genealogical meaning. It furthermore imparts a distinctive character to the definitions of way of life. So the task of the political component of a theory of the social order, which is to define the social entity by appeal to empowerment, and of the economic component, which is to identify scarce resources by specification of the rationality of right management, is accomplished in a single word, which stands for a conception, an attitude, a symbol, a social policy, and, of course, an unarticulated myth. All three components of this religious theory of the social order turn out to present specific applications, in context, for the general conception of *zekhut*. For the first source of *zekhut* derives from the definition of Israel as family; the entitlements of supernatural power deriving from virtue then care inherited from Abraham, Isaac, and Jacob. The second source is personal: the power one can gain for one's own heirs, moreover, by virtuous deeds. *Zekhut* deriving from either source is to be defined in context: What can you do if you have *zekhut* that you cannot do if you do not have *zekhut*, and to whom can you do it? The answer to that question tells the empowerment of *zekhut*.

Zekhut serves, in particular, that counterpart category that speaks of not legitimate but illegitimate violence, not power but weakness. In context, time and again, we observe that *zekhut* is the power of the weak. People who through their own merit and capacity can accomplish nothing, can accomplish miracles through what others do for them in leaving a heritage of *zekhut*. And, not to miss the stunning message of the triplet of stories cited above, *zekhut* also is what the weak and excluded and despised can do that outweighs in power what the great masters of the Torah have accomplished. In the context of a system that represents Torah as supernatural, that claim of priority for *zekhut* represents a considerable transvaluation of power, as much as of value. And, by the way, *zekhut* also forms the inheritance of the disinherited: what you receive as a heritage when you have nothing in the present and have gotten nothing in the past, that scarce resource that is free and unearned but much valued. So let us dwell upon the definitive character of the transferability of *zekhut* in its formulation, *zekhut abot*, the *zekhut* handed on by the ancestors, the transitive character of the concept and its standing as a heritage of entitlements.

So *zekhut* forms the political economy of the religious system of the social order put forward by the Talmud of the Land of Israel and related writings. Here we find the power that brought about the transvaluation of value, the reversal of the meaning of power and its legitimacy. *Zekhut* expresses and accounts for the economic Valuation of the scarce resource of what we should call moral authority. *Zekhut* stands for the political valorization of weakness, that which endows the weak with a power that is not only their own but their ancestors'. It enables the weak to accomplish goals through not their own power, but their very incapacity to accomplish acts of violence – a transvaluation as radical as that effected in economics. And *zekhut* holds together both the economics and the politics of this Judaism: it makes the same statement twice. *Zekhut* as the power of the powerless, the riches of the disinherited, the Valuation and valorization of the will of those who have no right to will.

In the context of Christian Palestine, Jews found themselves on the defensive. Their ancestry called into question by the claim that Christians are now Israel or heirs of the Israel to whom God revealed the Torah, the land now dotted with Christian shrines and peopled by Christians, now forming a majority, their supernatural standing thrown into doubt, their future denied, they called themselves "Israel," and the land, "the Land of Israel." But what power did they possess, legitimately, if need be through violence, to assert their claim to form "Israel"? And, with the Holy Land passing into the hands of others, what scarce resource did they own and manage to take the place of that measure of value that now no longer was subjected to their rationality? Asserting a politics in which all violence was illegitimate, an economics in which nothing tangible, even real property in the Holy Land, had value, the system through its counterpart categories made a single, simple, and sufficient statement. But those whom Judaism knows as "our sages of blessed memory" were not the only system builders, and theirs was not the only question about the social order framed in historical and theological, rather than analytical and philosophical terms.

Part Two

JUDAIC CLASSICS OF THE AGE OF CONSTANTINE

2

The Talmud of the Land of Israel in Literary Context

The Starting Point

To describe the Talmud (everywhere in this chapter: the Talmud of the Land of Israel), we first take up the whole and proceed to ask about its principal components. Looking at the Talmud whole, we notice two totally distinct sorts of materials: statements of law, then discussions of and excursus on those statements. We bring no substantial presuppositions to the text, if we declare these two sorts of materials to be, respectively, primary and constitutive, secondary and derivative. Calling the former the declaration of laws, the Mishnah passage, and the latter the exegesis of these laws, the Talmud proper, imposes no a priori judgment formed independently of the literary evidence in hand. We might as well call the two "the code" and "the commentary." The result would be no different.[1]

In fact, as we see everywhere, the Talmud is made up of two elements, each with its own literary traits and program of discussion. Since the Mishnah passage at the head of each set of Talmudic units of discourse defines the limits and determines the theme and, generally, the problematic of the whole, our attention is drawn to the traits of the Mishnah passages as a group. Here, of course, a certain measure of descriptive work has been done. But even if we for the first time saw these types of pericopes of the Mishnah (embedded as they are in the Talmud and separated from one another), we should discern that they adhere to a separate and quite distinctive set of literary and conceptual

---

[1]This chapter summarizes my *The Talmud of the Land of Israel. A Preliminary Translation and Explanation* (Chicago, 1983: University of Chicago Press) XXXV. Introduction. Taxonomy.

canons from what follows and surrounds them. Hence at the outset, with no appreciable attention to anything beyond the text, we should distinguish two "layers" of the Talmud and recognize that one "layer" is formed in one way, the other in another way. (I use "layer" for convenience only; it is not an apt metaphor.)

As I just said, if then we were to join together all the Mishnah pericopes, we should notice that they are stylistically and formally coherent and also different from everything else in the compilation before us. Accordingly, for stylistic reasons alone we are on firm ground in designating the "layer" before us as the base point for all further inquiry. For the Mishnah "layer" has been shown to be uniform, while the Talmud "layer" is not demonstrably so. Hence, itself undifferentiated, the former (the Mishnah "layer") provides the point of differentiation. The latter (the Talmud "layer") presents the diverse materials subject to differentiation. In the first stage in the work of making sense of the Talmud and describing it whole, what is the initial criterion through which the Talmud's diverse types of units of discourse are differentiated? It is the varied relationships, to the Mishnah's rule, exhibited by the Talmud's several, diverse units of discourse. Let me now expand on and qualify this point, for it is the principle of the opening initiative in this exercise of taxonomy and typology.

To amplify what I have said: since the Palestinian Talmud carries forward and depends upon the Mishnah, to describe that Talmud we have to begin with its relationship to the Mishnah, which is the Talmud's own starting point. While the Mishnah admits to no antecedents and neither alludes to nor cites anything prior to its own materials, a passage of the Talmud is often incomprehensible without knowledge of the passage of the Mishnah around which the Talmud's discourse centers. Yet in describing and defining the Talmud, we should grossly err if we were to say it is only, or mainly, a step-by-step commentary on the Mishnah, defined solely by the Mishnah's interests. We may not even say, though it is a step closer to the truth, that the Talmud before us is a commentary on or secondary development of, the Mishnah and important passages of the Tosefta. Units of discourse which serve these sorts of materials stand side by side with many which in an immediate sense do not. Accordingly, while a description of the Talmud requires attention to the interplay between the Talmud and the Mishnah and Tosefta, the diverse relationships between the Talmud and one or the other of those two documents constitute only one point of description and differentiation. For the Talmud is in full command of its own program of thought and inquiry. Its framers, responsible for the units of discourse, chose what in the Mishnah will be analyzed and what ignored. True, there could be no Talmud without the Mishnah and Tosefta. But

The Talmud of the Land of Israel in Literary Context

knowing only those two works, we could never have predicted in a systematic way the character of the Talmud's discourse at any point.

The Mishnah nonetheless permits us at the outset to gain perspective on the character of Yerushalmi. For the Mishnah does exhibit a remarkable unity of literary and redactional traits. By that standard our Talmud presents none. Accordingly, while whatever materials reached the framers of the Mishnah ca. 175-200 were revised by them in line with a single and simple literary and redactional program, the same is not the case for the Talmud of the Land of Israel. Whatever the stages of redaction of the document as a whole, let alone of its components, we may say with certainty that the people ultimately responsible for the document as we have it did not do to the materials in their hands what the framers of the Mishnah did to theirs. The ultimate redactors did not participate in the work of formulation. Units of discourse framed in some prior setting have been preserved as is (though we do not know to what extent as to detail). They were drawn together whole and complete with other such essentially fixed and final units of discourse.

Redaction and Formulation: Yerushalmi Contrasted with Mishnah

We now ask about the formulation and redaction of the Talmud of the Land of Israel as we know it, the end product in our hands – and not the formation, in earlier times, of ideas or whole discussions now contained within the document. The nature of the antecedent materials can only be determined when we have described what must be deemed the work of ultimate redaction. We shall first determine whether the process also included systematic formulation, or reformulation, of units of discourse already completed.

When I undertook to ask about the role of redaction in the formulation of the Mishnah, working on the division of Purities as my sample (roughly 25 percent of the entire Mishnah), I began from the outside and worked my way in. To review the process and its principal results, I began by asking this question: If all we had were a mass of words, how should we know where one thing stops and another starts? The first question is easy to answer definitively. We know that the mass of words is broken up (for Mishnah's division of Purities) into twelve principal divisions (tractates), uneven in length, because the subject of one long sequence of undifferentiated words ends and a new subject begins. There are, accordingly, lines of demarcation clearly drawn by the shift in theme or primary topic of discussion. What is blocked out, moreover, is consistent in its devotion to that given theme or primary topic, rarely dealing with a subject wholly irrelevant to the theme. It follows that the principal mode of organization is thematic. As is clear, the principal lines of division will be into tractates devoted to their respective, diverse topics. What is important is that that fact is shown on the basis of the internal character of the document, not merely of the post facto way in which exegetes, copyists, and printers organized matters.

Having proved that the Mishnah is organized, in its principal divisions, in accord with the unfolding of thematic and logical principles, I proceeded to ask about the delineation of the Mishnah's intermediate divisions. I avoided the word "chapters" because it can only yield confusion with the extant chapters, which are the work of copyists and printers, perhaps even of the earliest exegetes. These tell us nothing whatsoever about the original intent of the people who come before and stand behind the document, but only about the exegetical perceptions of the people who come afterward. How on the basis of internal evidence are intermediate divisions to be discerned? Having shown that the redactors not only organize their materials topically but also lay out the discussion of each topic in accord with its logically sequential parts, I am on firm ground in maintaining that one criterion for a demarcation line of undifferentiated columns of words of a Mishnah tractate, or principal division, will be a shift in topic or theme. What applies to, and emerges from, the whole surely must be asked to serve as criterion for what pertains also to the parts. There is, moreover, a second important criterion of delineation, and that is recurrent grammatical patterns or arrangements of words. This entails inquiry into the large-scale interplay between theme and form, between what is said and how it is said.

The first thing we notice when we study a Mishnah tractate from its opening sentence onward is that, when the subject changes, the formulary pattern shifts too. A given subtopic of a topical unit's principal division will be expressed in a distinctive pattern of syntax. These syntactical patterns, moreover, are divisible into two broad categories, tight and loose. The tight syntactical pattern will govern the layout of words for each concept, thought or rule devoted to a given subtopic. The loose pattern will not. Rather, it emerges chiefly at the commencement of every conceptual unit. The former is therefore called an "internally unitary formulary pattern," in that the paramount formulary pattern everywhere governs the internal construction and wording of what is expressed. The latter is named an "externally unitary formulary pattern," in that the formulary pattern is external to what is expressed, being imposed primarily upon the opening clauses of a conceptual unit, not on the later wording. The remainder of the unit then will proceed in unpatterned sentences or clauses. To put matters more descriptively, we are unable to discern, in sentences which follow the commencement of the matter, any systematic pattern at all.

These results impose the requirement of further definition, differentiation, and analysis of the recurrent patterns by which sentences are constructed. The reason is that, once we recognize intermediate divisions because of the congruence of form and theme within a group of sentences, we come to the stage of the analysis of form. The appropriate framework for form analysis is the redactionally sizable, intermediate unit. For it is within the setting of the intermediate unit that the patterning and formalization of language become self-evident. It ceases to be a subjective observation that things *seem* to be stereotyped only when we see that, within circumscribed but sizable sequences of sentences, things indeed *are* not random but recurrent. Within that same framework we discern precisely what patterning of language is undertaken, how thought is reduced not merely to words but to words laid out in distinctive, recurrent syntactical structures.

It is at this point that we must define the smallest unit of formal analysis, which for the Mishnah I call "the cognitive unit." A cognitive unit is the formal (and formalized) result of a single cogent process of cognition, that is, analysis of a situation and statement of a rule pertaining to it, or some other, similar intellectual process. The Mishnah's smallest whole and irreducible literary-conceptual units are the end result of a single sequence, or process, of thought. Formal or formulary traits of such a unit commonly occur at the outset or in the first element of the result of cognition to be set into words and given linguistically formal character. After that point in the unit, what follows commonly exhibits no equivalent formalization. The remainder of the cognitive unit will generally consist of simple declarative sentences exhibiting no recurrent pattern and lacking all syntactical distinctiveness. The cognitive unit rarely stands by itself but is grouped together with other such units, devoted to a single principle or theme and exhibiting a single, distinctive syntactical trait or preference. Accordingly, the form-analytical work yields the result that the cognitive unit is shaped within the processes of organization of the intermediate (and principal) divisions of the Mishnah. This means that the work of giving formalized verbal expression to cognitive units and the work of organizing them into groups go together and reciprocally govern one another's results.

To state the historical result simply: the Mishnah's formulation and its organization are the result of the work of a single generation of tradent-redactors, who formulate units of thought, and redactors, who organize aggregations of these units. The Mishnah is not the product of tradents *succeeded by* redactors. It is not possible upon the basis of objective, internal literary evidence revealed by the Mishnah itself to specify much in formulation which derives from the period before that of redaction itself.

We may now rapidly relate these results to the document at hand. In the case of the Palestinian Talmud, the principle of organization is provided by the Mishnah itself. Tractates begin and end where the Mishnah does. Accordingly, if all we had were a mass of words, we should know the beginning and end of a tractate of our Talmud precisely as we do in the case of the Mishnah, because the point of demarcation is identical. A glance at any volume of the translation will show that, in nearly all cases, the Talmud's discussion attached to a given pericope of the Mishnah runs through two or more completed units of discourse. In general, therefore, the principle of organizing a discussion is not supplied solely and completely by the logical, or other exegetical, requirements of a passage of the Mishnah. The principle by which a discussion is inaugurated, worked out, and concluded is different from that of the Mishnah in general. It also differs from that supplied by a given intermediate unit of the Mishnah in particular cases. Since the intermediate divisions of the Yerushalmi are not demarcated by the requirements of the Mishnah, we cannot attempt to relate the delineation of those units to formal traits of the Mishnah. Formal considerations do not come into play in the Talmud before us in so rigid and disciplined a way as they govern the formulation of the Mishnah's ideas. It must follow that the work of ultimate redaction of the Palestinian Talmud is wholly separate from the work of formulation of individual units of discourse. The upshot is that while the framers of the Talmud of the Land of Israel refer constantly to the Mishnah, they do not see themselves as bound by its patterns of formulation or even of redaction, let alone by its program and problems. They have in hand, or have created, diverse sorts of units of discourse, some of them essentially exegetical and tied to the Mishnah, others doing the same for Tosefta, still others of a quite separate literary character and substantive purpose. That is why, to describe the Talmud as a whole, we have to develop a taxonomy of its several types of units of discourse, in comparison and contrast to those of the Mishnah.

Yerushalmi's Redactional Program

To develop a taxonomy of the units of discourse contained within the Talmud of the Land of Israel, we begin by describing gross redactional traits. These are visible to the naked eye. The question then is simple: What kinds of units of discourse does the document exhibit and how are they arranged? The answer to this question should yield a first glimpse of the redactional program of the ultimate framers of the Talmud. Once we differentiate by type among the materials in the hands of the arrangers of the whole, we also may observe what principles, if any, guide their work of arrangement. For the present purpose, seeking the most general traits of the whole, a modest probe suffices. I review five tractates, a small one (Niddah), a very large one (Sanhedrin), an egregious one (Baba Mesia), and two medium ones (Nedarim and Sukkah).

By unit of discourse, as I said earlier, I mean simply a discussion on a single topic, beginning either at a pericope of the Mishnah or at the point at which that topic is raised, ending either at the next pericope of the Mishnah or at the point at which some other topic is introduced, respectively. These have been designated in my translation of the Talmud by Roman numerals. While the divisions are in some measure subjective, or may occasionally appear arbitrary, the relationship of a given set of materials ("unit of discourse") to the Mishnah will remain constant. I do not propose that quantitative numbers of units of discourse materially change matters, and, accordingly, the indications of units of discourse will not greatly affect the argument. What is more important from the redactional perspective is the sequence of these units. As we shall see in a moment, where there is direct analysis of the Mishnah, or, at the very least, inquiry into the Scriptural foundations of the pericope at hand, the unit of discourse presenting such analysis or inquiry normally is the opening one in a sequence, designated as I. Among 335 Mishnah pericopes enumerated in the tables presented in the book summarized here, only twenty-six units of discourse pertinent to the Mishnah rule at hand commence discussion of that rule other than as unit I, less than 8 percent of the whole. (I exclude reference to the handful of Mishnah pericopes in which there is no analysis of the Mishnah law at all; I also exclude reference to the passages in which Tosefta's complement to the Mishnah's rule stands at the commencement of the discussion.) Accordingly, it will become clear that the usual redactional practice was to take a unit of discourse closely pertinent to the Mishnah and to place it at the commencement of discourse on the passage of the Mishnah at hand.

Let me proceed to generalization. The redactional program of the men responsible for laying out the materials of Yerushalmi may now be described in simple terms. Most important, we see that there was such a program. There is nothing random. That is clear because, within the differentiation of units of discourse I have defined, diverse types of units of discourse are not mixed together promiscuously. There is a pronounced tendency to move from close reading of the Mishnah and then Tosefta to more general inquiry into the principles of a Mishnah passage and their interplay with those of some other, superficially unrelated passage, and, finally, to more general reflections on law not self-evidently related to the Mishnah passage at hand or to anthologies.

It follows that we may turn from redaction to formulation. Once more, with all due respect for variation and diversity, we seek gross and general traits, affecting the whole of the Talmud under study. Since the close interplay between redaction and formulation constitutes the sole firm result of our study of the Mishnah, we ask about the same matter for our Talmud. The issue is whether we can find evidence of systematic attention to formulating units of discourse in such a way as formally or syntactically to relate one to the next within a single redactional program or process. If there is such evidence, we must conclude that, even in the ultimate redactional stages of the formation of the Talmud, work went on not merely in minor correction, revision, or glossing of a passage. Such work pertained even to the very formulation of the statement of its main points, in the structure and wording by which those points would be expressed. It would then follow that, prior to the redaction of the whole, we are unable to posit the existence of units of discourse as we know them. If we find no points of correlation between redactional policies and problems of formulation of units of discourse, on the other hand, it must follow that, separate from (perhaps then, prior to) the redactional stages (though we do not know how long before) a process of formulation of units of discourse was underway.

Our question thus is, did the redactors work with essentially finished units of discourse? Or did they themselves participate in the formation of the completed units of discourse which they also organized and juxtaposed? The criterion for positive evidence for the second proposition, hence, also, negative evidence for the first, derives from comparison with the Mishnah. What we compare are units of discourse of our Talmud and the formulary traits of Mishnah pericopes. The latter indicate the hand of redaction and organization within the very phrasing of individual units of law of the Mishnah. Absence of equivalent traits then will signify for the Talmud a different relationship of redaction to formulation from that prevalent in the Mishnah. For the Mishnah, essential to the organization and layout of completed units of discourse is the very pattern of formulating those same units of discourse. The result, as I have now made clear, is proof, for the Mishnah, that redaction is prior and critical to formulation. In the Mishnah, redaction is not solely a process of joining together statements bearing no formal relationship to one another, hence existing before (we do not know how long before) the process of organization and layout we call redaction. A clear grasp of how the Mishnah works is then essential to a comparative inquiry into the Talmud's traits.

Now to spell out the interplay of formulation and redaction in the Mishnah. The principal result of my inquiry was to show constant and close relationship between the one and the other. Specifically, I found that when the Mishnah's redactors wished to indicate the formation of a unit of discourse (which I called, in that setting, "intermediate unit"), they would take up a distinctive formulary pattern or form, different from that which they had used beforehand and also from that which they would use in the following unit. They would carefully group their smallest whole statements ("smallest units of cognition") so that each one would repeat the same syntactic pattern, setting up (in general) groups of three or multiples of three, or groups of five or multiples of five, with such internally patterned statements of a single principle being applied to a single theme. This seemed to me definitive evidence that the whole could not have been formulated prior to the work of redaction, at which point, and not before, the larger program of arrangement of topics and principles expressed in connection with those topics was in hand. Only when the whole was fully in view was it possible to form the parts in the uniform way in which they were formed. There is no other economical way of explaining the facts I have discovered, since, as is clear, the whole was planned before the parts were laid out in their matching and distinctive syntactic patterns and in their little sets of three or five repetitions of such patterns.

The issue when we turn to the Talmud cannot of course be framed in the same way. But to begin with, we must ask ourselves whether we discern any formulary patterns at all, not merely those of a redactional type. When we speak of formulary patterns, to review, we mean recurrent arrangements of words in a given syntactic formula. Whether or not we may relate the use of such a pattern to a redactional plan is only second in line of inquiry. To present this matter as clearly as I can, I wish first of all to show, in three units selected at random, the Mishnah's formal traits. Then, for those same chapters, we shall look at the Talmud's formal or patterned language, if any. The former will be seen to exhibit patterned language at a gross and recurrent level. The latter will not.

I do not seek evidence from the recurrence of particles or rhetoric lacking more than merely conventional status in the formation of thought. That is, in context, syntactic structures matter, rhetorical patterns do not. The reason is that rhetorical patterns are not distinctive to the document at hand; they not only occur elsewhere but may well tell us merely how people said things. Consistent resort to a few, fixed syntactic structures, by contrast, tells us choices made by the framers of the document at hand. These choices furthermore may be shown to be deliberate, because of their recurrence in fixed patterns, and also particular to the document. Accordingly, the fact that the speech of the document contains fixed rhetorical patterns signifies something quite separate from the presence of patterns at the deep syntax of the document. The presence or absence of these other patterns of language, as distinct from mere rhetoric, alone testifies to the issue at hand. The fact, for example, that a Mishnah passage cited by the Talmud will ordinarily be introduced with a rhetorical pattern, "We have learned there...," does not seem to me to contain implications about the formulation of the construction in which such particles or rhetorical usages occur. They testify rather to the overall rhetorical conventions, independent of all redactional or formulary context. In the nature of our inquiry, it is distinctive context which concerns us. The fact is that I cannot find a single instance, in the twenty-nine tractates I have translated, where the unit of discourse is so formulated as to indicate an intention to relate what is formulated to its redactional context or to the larger needs of combining two or more completed units of thought into a principal redactional unit (a complete discussion of a Mishnah pericope, for instance).

I maintain a simple proposition. If the traits of the Mishnah indicate that central to the process of organizing materials was the work of formulating them, then the absence of the same traits in the Talmud indicates the opposite. The work of redaction of units of discourse in the Talmud therefore was distinct from, and later than, the work of formulation. Since there was a stage of discourse in which materials were laid out in accord with a few simple rules, governed by the relationship to the Mishnah exhibited by a given unit of discourse, the picture is clear. We have therefore to turn to the literary traits of the units of discourse with special attention to traits of form and formalization. Once we have found that the formation of the units of discourse of Yerushalmi is distinct from their arrangement and redaction into the larger document, the focus shifts to when and how these units themselves came into being. If we knew who bore responsibility for making things up as we now have them, we should have answers to the question of how we know the Yerushalmi tells us about any period before that of its own redaction.

That the Talmud of the Land of Israel reveals a clear-cut plan for organizing its component parts is beyond doubt. But knowing that fact helps very little in defining the work before us. No one need doubt that a repertoire of patterns governed the way in which language was shaped for the expression of ideas. But when the use of these patterns indicates a fact of social or historical significance is by no means clear. Sometimes a recurrent syntactic pattern shows us nothing more than how people said things "in general." We cannot discover from that fact anything consequential for the interpretation of the history of our document and the formation of its building blocks. Clearly, a brief probe into a single form turned up a few interesting facts. Most proved negative for our larger purpose. In all, the key issue for the use of the units of discourse for the study of important events in the history of Judaism in the third and fourth centuries in the Land of Israel has yet to be framed. If we want to know who is responsible for the formation of the units of discourse, all we now know is that it was not those who undertook redaction. Those at the point of formulation, on the one side, and in the framework of transmission and preservation to the time of redaction, on the other, stand behind the little "talmuds" of which our Talmud is composed.

Yerushalmi's units of discourse and their components were formulated sometime, somewhere, prior to the processes of ultimate closure and redaction. The work of formulation and original closure was essentially distinct from those processes. But, as I just said, that can have been earlier by a day, a year, or a century. It can have happened one house down the block. We have no evidence as to where or how the work was done. All we have is the result: what people said various authorities had earlier said.

The Mishnah in the Talmud of the Land of Israel

Using as a sample our selection of five tractates, we now probe ways in which the Talmud of the Land of Israel receives and deals with the Mishnah. What was the exegetical repertoire of the rabbis? The roughly 335 individual pericopes of the Mishnah within the present frame of inquiry are susceptible of categorization into just four categories. That is to say, the Talmud invariably does to the Mishnah one of these four things: (1) text criticism; (2) exegesis of the meaning of the Mishnah, including glosses and amplifications; (3) addition of Scriptural prooftexts of the Mishnah's central propositions; and (4) harmonization of one Mishnah passage with another such passage or with a statement of Tosefta. The first two of these four procedures remain wholly within the narrow frame of the Mishnah passage subject to discussion. The second pair take an essentially independent stance vis-à-vis the Mishnah pericope at hand.

We do not find a single usable category in which the Talmud treats the Mishnah as a whole, either viewing it as a complete document, or taking up entire tractates or at least entire chapters. The Mishnah is read by the Talmud as a composite of discrete and essentially autonomous rules, a set of atoms, not an integrated molecule, so to speak. In so doing, the most striking formal traits of the Mishnah are obliterated. More important, the Mishnah as a whole and complete statement of a viewpoint no longer exists. Its propositions are reduced to details. Then, on occasion, the details may be restated in generalizations encompassing a wide variety of other details across the gaps between one tractate and another. This immensely creative and imaginative approach to the Mishnah vastly expands the range of discourse. But, as I said, the first, and deepest, consequence is to deny to the Mishnah both its own mode of speech and its distinctive and coherent message.

Our Talmud deals with only thirty-nine of the Mishnah's sixty-two tractates, ignoring all of the Holy Things, on the Temple, and Purities, on cultic cleanness (with the sole exception of less than half of Niddah, on menstrual uncleanness). Even if, as is generally supposed, there never was a Talmud systematically composed for the twenty-three tractates of the Mishnah now lacking Yerushalmi, at this point we can go no further than observe a remarkable independence of spirit. What the Mishnah provided, therefore, was not received in a spirit of humble acceptance. Important choices were made about what to treat, hence what to ignore. The exegetical mode of reception did not have to obscure the main lines of the Mishnah's system. But it surely did so. The discrete reading of sentences, or, at most, paragraphs, denying all context, avoiding all larger generalizations except for those transcending the specific lines of tractates, this approach need not have involved the utter reversal of the paramount and definitive elements of the Mishnah's whole and integrated worldview (its "Judaism"). But doing these things did facilitate the revision of the whole into a quite different pattern. To use a different metaphor, they shifted the orbit of the Mishnah from one path to another. The Mishnah centers on the priesthood and the Temple. The Talmud took over and pushed the whole into an orbit around the rabbi and his relationship to the disciple, the rabbi and his activities in the court, the rabbi and his opinions in the school. The simplest way to overcome gravity is to reduce the critical mass of the whole. Chopping the Mishnah into bits and pieces accomplished just that.

The Talmud provides some indication of effort at establishing the correct text of various passages of the Mishnah. This nearly always is in the context of deciding the law. It is not a random search for a "perfect" text. It rather represents a deliberate and principled inquiry into the law as revealed by the phrasing of a passage. That is why, in the bulk of these passages, the legal consequences of one reading as opposed to another are carefully articulated, sometimes even tied to a range of other points subject to dispute.

Most, though by no means all, of the 335 pericopes under discussion are brought under close analysis. Approximately 227 of the 335 pericopes in the present sample are subjected to some sort of exegetical procedure. This shows that one principal interest among the framers of the Talmud's materials was simply to understand, essentially within its own terms and implicit meanings, the Mishnah's discrete passage at hand. That this close reading was primary is shown in the contrast presented at the fourth list. I count no more than fifty instances in which the systematic exegetical inquiry transcends the boundaries of a particular pericope. What that means is that in the main, when people read a passage of the Mishnah, they wanted to know mainly what that passage meant in its own terms and setting. They had only a limited interest, if our probe is suggestive, in how one passage related to some other. In gross terms, 66 percent of the units of our sample are subjected to some sort of limited, low-level exegesis, while no more than 15 percent of the units provoked wide-ranging search into underlying principles, points of conflict and their harmonization, and similar speculative inquiry. That is not to suggest the intent of the whole was to trivialize the Mishnah as a system or to reduce it to components available for reconstruction in some other way. But that is the effect.

Scripture, Mishnah, and Talmud

The Mishnah, as is well known, rarely finds it necessary to cite a Scriptural prooftext for its propositions. Just as the Mishnah ignores the Scriptural ways of stating propositions m general, and laws in particular, favoring instead its own highly distinctive and disciplined syntax and morphology and word choices, so the Mishnah rephrases whatever it borrows from Scripture into its own terms. It rarely invokes in behalf of its own ideas the authority of Scripture. That occurs more commonly in discussions of theological than narrowly legal matters. The Talmud of our probe, by contrast, finds it appropriate whenever possible to cite Scriptural prooftexts for the propositions of the Mishnah. I count ninety-four out of 335 instances, 28 percent of the sample in which the Talmud finds the Mishnah to require such prooftexts and supplies them. What is still more striking is that this inquiry, when we find it, appears to be systematic and not random. We notice long sequences of pericopes in tractates Sanhedrin, Nedarim, and Sukkah, in which prooftexts are adduced. It is tempting to suggest that whenever people could, they would supply Scriptural citations for the Mishnah. But that cannot be demonstrated. The best we can say is that the Talmud's approach to a given passage of the Mishnah, two out of three times, is to provide some sort of gloss or exegesis, and one out of three times a prooftext as well. The provision of exegetical remarks is hardly surprising. Given the traits of the Mishnah, we must find remarkable the interest in adding what the framers of the Mishnah, for their part, found unnecessary. For the Mishnah is hardly an independent code, totally autonomous of Scripture. On the contrary, viewed one by one, the tractates of the Mishnah exhibit diverse relationships to the facts presented in Scripture. While the various tractates of the Mishnah relate in different ways to Scripture, the view of the framers of the Talmud on the same matter is not differentiated. So far as they are concerned, prooftexts for Mishnaic rules are required. These will be supplied in substantial numbers. And that is the main point. The Mishnah now is systematically represented as not standing free and separate from Scripture, but dependent upon it. The authority of the Mishnah's laws then is reinforced. But the autonomy of the Mishnah as a whole is severely compromised. And that is the main point. Just as the Mishnah is represented in the Talmud as a set of rules, rather than as a philosophical essay, so it is presented, rule by rule, as a secondary and derivative development of Scripture.

So the undifferentiated effort to associate diverse Mishnah laws with Scripture is to be viewed together with the systematic breakup of the Mishnah into its diverse laws. The two quite separate activities produce a single effect. That is, they permit the Talmud to represent the state of affairs pretty much as the framers of the Talmud wish to do. Everything is continuous: Scripture, Mishnah, Talmud itself. Then all things, as now shaped by the rabbis of the Talmud, have the standing of Scripture and represent the authority of Moses (now called "our rabbi"). Accordingly, once the Mishnah enters the Talmud of the Land of Israel, it nowhere emerges intact. It is wholly preserved, but in bits and pieces, shaped and twisted in whatever ways the Talmud wishes. The sages of the Mishnah read the Scripture as closely and as honestly as can be imagined. To be sure, that is not to claim their results always, or even often, coincide with the original intent of the diverse writers and framers of the Scriptural law codes. It is only to allege that the trait of mind of the Mishnaic exegetes of Scripture was no different from our own: to do their best, in an honest and forthright way, to say what the passage meant, and therefore must continue to mean. The sages of the Talmud read the Mishnah in this same way. That simple fact is attested by the whole weight and character of the Talmud of the Land of Israel. But the framers of the Talmud made choices about what laws of Mishnah required discussion, and in carrying out these choices, they did to the Mishnah what Mishnah's sages did to the Scripture: they made it their own.

What Is Talmudic in the Talmud of the Land of Israel?

I have now to specify and characterize those passages in which the sages of the Talmud spoke essentially for themselves, not for, or about, the Mishnah. It is necessary to catalogue and describe the units of discourse that stand separate and independent of the Mishnah. We want to know two things. First, when does the Talmud speak for itself, not for the Mishnah? Second, what sorts of units of discourse contain such passages of "Talmudic" in the Talmud of the Land of Israel? As I argued at the outset, it is only in the present catalogue that to begin with we may hope to uncover evidence of the system of the Talmud as distinct from a mere extension and expansion of the system of the Mishnah. And only when these two systems have been separated from one another shall we be able to see how they are put together into a single entity, the Judaism of the Talmud of the Land of Israel.

What is striking is that once again we are able to take much data – 335 pericopes of the Mishnah – and discover no more than four taxa into which they may be divided. There is by no means a mass of random sayings, collected we know not how, for a purpose we cannot imagine, a mere anthology. Rather, when we collect all units of discourse, or larger parts of such units, in which exegesis of the Mishnah or expansion upon the law of the Mishnah is absent, we find at most four types, which in fact are only two.

1. *Theoretical questions of law not associated with a particular passage of the Mishnah.* There is some tendency to move beyond the legal boundaries set by the Mishnah's rules themselves. More general inquiries are taken up. These of course remain within the framework of the topic of one tractate or another, although there are some larger modes of thought characteristic of more than a single tractate. To explain what I mean, I point to the mode of thought in which the Scriptural basis of the law of the Mishnah will be investigated, without regard to a given tractate. Along these same lines, I may point to a general inquiry into the count under which one may be liable for a given act, comments on the law governing teaching and judging cases, and the like. But these items tend not to leave the Mishnah far behind.

2. *Exegesis of Scripture separate from the Mishnah.* It is under this rubric that we find the most important instances in which the Talmud presents materials essentially independent of the Mishnah. The repertoire produced by our probe is substantial and striking. While, as I said, many items on the foregoing list may be linked to a theme of the Mishnah, if not to a specific rule, virtually all of the items on this list stand totally separate from the Mishnah. They pursue problems or themes through what is said about a biblical figure, expressing ideas and values simply unknown to the Mishnah. Moreover, as we shall see in due course, most of what is said in response to verses of Scripture reveals right on the surface fundamental values of what we may call, for convenience's sake, Rabbinic Judaism.

3. *Historical statements.* The Talmud contains a fair number of statements that something happened, or narratives about how something happened. While many of these are replete with biblical quotations, in general they do not provide exegesis of Scripture, which serves merely as illustration or reference point.

4. *Stories about, and rules for, sages and disciples, separate from discussion of a passage of the Mishnah.* The Mishnah contains a tiny number of tales about rabbis. These serve principally as precedents for, or illustrations of, rules. The Talmud by contrast contains a sizable number of stories about sages and their relationships to other people. Like the items in the second and third lists, these, too, may be adduced as evidence of the values of the people who stand behind the Talmud, the things they thought important. These tales rarely serve to illustrate a rule or concept of the Mishnah. The main, though not the only, characteristic theme is the power of the rabbi, the honor due to the rabbi, and the tension between the rabbi and others, whether the patriarch, on the one side, the heretic on the second, or the gentile on the third.

The first thing we learn when we ask about those units of discourse (or large segments of such units) independent of the interests of the Mishnah is that they are not numerous. Varying in bulk from one tractate to the next, they are not apt to add up to much more than 10 percent of the whole. Furthermore, among the four lists before us, the items on the first do not move far from the principles and concerns of the Mishnah. I cannot point to many items that express conceptions essentially distinct from those of the Mishnah and outside of its modes of thought. The second thing we notice, complementary to the first, is that, where we do find extensive passages in which the Mishnah is left far behind, they normally are of two kinds: (1) exegesis of narrative or theological passages of Scripture, and (2) fables about heroes, lists 2 and 3. These latter are divided, artificially to be sure, into tales about rabbis and historical accounts. But there is no important distinction between the two lists, except that the former speaks of what rabbis said and did, while the latter tells about events on a more generous scale. Accordingly, when the Talmud presents us with ideas or expressions of a world related to, but fundamentally separate from, that of the Mishnah, that is, when the Talmud wishes to say something other than what the Mishnah says and means, it will take up one of two modes of discourse. Either we find exegesis of biblical passages, with the value system of the rabbis read into the Scriptural tales; or we are told stories about holy men and paradigmatic events, once again through tales told in such a way that a didactic and paranaetic purpose is served.

From Mishnah to Midrash: Yerushalmi as the Bridge

If, therefore, we want to point to what is Talmudic in the Talmud of the Land of Israel, it is the exegesis of Scripture, on the one side, and the narration of historical or biographical tales about holy men, on the other. Since much of the biblical exegesis turns upon holy men of biblical times, we may say that the Talmud speaks for itself alone, as distinct from addressing the problems of the Mishnah, when it tells about holy men now and then. But what is genuinely new in the Talmud, in comparison and contrast to the Mishnah, is the inclusion of extensive discourse on the meaning imputed to Scripture. Our Talmud therefore stands essentially secondary to two prior documents: Mishnah, on the one side, and Scripture, on the other. Mishnah is read in the Talmud pretty much within the framework of meaning established by the Mishnah itself. Scripture is read as an account of a world remarkably like that of the rabbis of the Talmud. When the rabbis speak for themselves, as distinct from the Mishnah, it is through exegesis of Scripture. (But any other mode of reading Scripture, to them, would have been unthinkable. They took for granted that they and Scripture's heroes and sages lived in a single timeless plane.)

It follows that the Talmud is a composite of three kinds of materials: exegeses of the Mishnah, exegeses of Scripture, and accounts of the men who provide both. Perhaps one might wish to see the Talmud as a reworking of its two antecedent documents: the Mishnah, lacking much reference to Scripture, and the Scripture itself. The Talmud brings the two together into a synthesis of its own making, both in reading Scripture into Mishnah, and in reading Scripture alongside of, and separate from, Mishnah. Further, since, as we know, the next major phase, beyond the Talmud, in the formation of the literature of Judaism, will be the making of compilations of Scriptural exegeses (midrashic collections), we may say that the Talmud forms the bridge from the formation of the Mishnah to the making of the earliest midrashic collections. Focused upon the Mishnah, it opens the way to the creation of compilations of midrashic passages. But the question of how to define and describe the Talmud's own system remains to be answered.

The System of the Talmud of the Land of Israel: An Overview

In fundamental taxonomic traits the Talmud of the Land of Israel presents a mirror image of the Mishnah. The Mishnah's tractates are distinct from one another. Consequently, we may take up and outline each one in its own classification and thereby present a picture of how the Mishnah as a whole treats a given topic. So a theme defines a tractate. The Talmud, by contrast, imposes upon all the tractates of the Mishnah treated by it, and upon all the individual statements of law presented by those tractates, a single and uniform approach. Types of exegesis of the whole define the taxa: the Talmud. While, therefore, it is possible to provide an introduction to a single tractate of the Mishnah, it would be pointless to attempt to do so for a single tractate of the Talmud by itself. All must be treated uniformly.

On the other hand, the work of uncovering the completed system of the Mishnah requires a patient accumulation of detail, followed by a sifting of the evidence for underlying unities of conception and mode of thought. The reason, again, is the same: the framers of the Mishnah organize their ideas around topics and the logical spelling out of the rules for those topics, item by item in order. The creators of the Talmud, by contrast, everywhere ask the same sort of questions. So the Mishnah centers upon content, the Talmud upon method; the one is a work of piecemeal exposition of facts, the other of systematic analysis of diverse facts through uniform modes of thought. When we seek to describe as a whole the system of the Talmud, we have first to separate the principal components of that system: the Mishnaic, the Talmudic; and then to describe the latter. Only after we have seen the parts in all their distinctiveness shall we return and ask how they fit together into a single, whole worldview and way of life, a kind of Judaism. It is to the description of the Talmudic component of the Talmud of the Land of Israel that we now turn.

The work once again begins as an exercise in taxonomy. We want to know the principal types of propositions presented by the sorts of discourse expressive solely of the Talmudic side of things. We now attend to the paramount and predominant themes, the matter of classifying overall content. But short of listing every pertinent item in the thirty-nine tractates, which would produce a mere paraphrase of the thirty-four volumes before this one, how are we to proceed? The answer is to exploit the two fundamental data of this study. First, as I have emphasized from the start, the Talmud of the Land of Israel is to be contrasted with the Mishnah. Second, the end product of the work of the framers of the Talmud from the end of the second century through the end of the fourth ca. A.D. 200-400 is a system of Judaism related to, but essentially distinct and different from, the system presented in the systematic construction of the Mishnah.

These two facts provide the key to the taxonomic work before us, just as they have defined the fundamental issues of the first three exercises: *In what way is the Talmud like, and not like, the Mishnah?* I have already specified the ways in which the Talmud is like, that is, continuous with, the Mishnah. I further identified the types of material units of discourse or major portions thereof apt to present discourse in which the Talmud is not like the Mishnah, but discontinuous and therefore fresh. Accordingly, for the present work, a statement of a common agendum in which the Talmud exhibits the opposite of the definitive traits of the

Mishnaic system should provide us with the principal elements of a taxonomy of the distinctively Talmudic program of Judaism.

In a probe of more than half of all tractates of our Talmud, we discover very little. There is not much in volume or in substance that is distinctively Talmudic. When, in particular, we use as our criterion of selection an element made up of a whole, or the greater part, of a unit of discourse, as distinct from isolated sayings, we gain sharper perspective still. For we see that less than 10 percent of the mass is made up of units of discourse, or the greater part of such units, wholly unrelated to the exposition of the Mishnah or the secondary expansion of its laws or exegesis. The bulk of the pertinent materials fall into two categories: exegesis of Scripture without regard to a problem or theme presented by the Mishnah, and stories about rabbis. These stories are to be subdivided for the present purpose into three categories: stories about the rabbi as a holy man, the rabbi in relationship to other people, and the distinctively rabbinical institution, the court-school. These three categories are set up for the sake of convenience only. In fact one can hardly distinguish the rabbi in his relationship to disciples, on the one side, to litigants, on the other, and to schools and courts, on the third. The prevailing conception of the rabbi as a holy man pertains as much to the school and court as it does to the graveyard or the place of worship or the time of trouble. Accordingly, cataloguing materials as we do differentiates among what in fact are closely related types of tales. What the two sorts of units of discourse have in common is simply that the issue of the message and meaning of the Mishnah is entirely absent.

The taxa for the present exercise are generated by the character of the materials themselves. In compiling these lists, I had little difficulty in finding a place for pretty much the entire corpus of non-Mishnaic units of discourse in the tractates subject to review. That is not to say that, within pertinent units of discourse, as much as within those units devoted to the Mishnah, I could not identify components, brief sayings, fragments of discourse, allusions to events or even stories belonging to some other type of category than the ones I have used. But these are fragmentary, unsustained, therefore not constitutive. If we ask about the gross and determinative traits of principal components of the Talmud seen whole, we may for the moment bypass bits and pieces of which these components themselves are made up. Then, as I said, we are able to classify the entire corpus of protracted statements of our Talmud in only two categories. Differentiation between these categories themselves yields, for the exegetical side, no consequential subdivisions, and for the rabbinical side, taxa serviceable essentially for the sake of convenience. The Talmud of the Land of Israel is made up of three types of material: (1) commentaries (in the broadest sense) on the Mishnah; (2) amplifications (of diverse types) of the Scriptures; and, finally, (3) a thin layer of tales about the men responsible for these commentaries and amplifications, thus substance and sponsorship.

So what is Talmudic in the Talmud of the Land of Israel? In sheer volume, there is very little. The Talmud of the Land of Israel centers mainly upon the Mishnah. Second, without reference to the Mishnah, the Talmud of the Land of Israel cannot be said to present us with a sustained, coherent, and cogent statement of a worldview. That is partly because the Talmud is organized around the Mishnah and in accord with the Mishnah's categories. But it is mainly because the Talmud does not present a systematic and well-articulated account of anything else. Elements of a Talmudic system, distinct from that of the Mishnah, appear as fragments. It is as if a whole world of reference lies outside, about which, to be sure, everyone within the document is well informed. Clearly, it was important to people to organize and transmit units of discourse on the meaning of Scripture and on the character of the rabbi as much as on the message of the Mishnah and its secondary amplification. On the other hand, once these units of discourse had come into being, no effort was made to group them and make of them something comparable to the sustained and systematic discussions of the Mishnah's rules and principles.

It follows that the catalogues I have constructed for the inquiry into what is Talmudic about the Talmud point toward, but do not ultimately define, the answer to that question. There was no provision in the fundamental structure of the Talmud for what, in fact, defined the very matrix and context of the Talmud: the rabbinic world, successor and heir to the world portrayed by the Mishnah. It would therefore appear that the entire legal program of the Talmud is defined by that of the Mishnah. Yet the contrary also turns out to be the case. The Talmud before us gives evidence of massive and fresh conceptions of both law and theology. The formation of the later compilations on legal topics, the so-called minor tractates of the Talmud on scribal rules and mourning, for instance, only confirmed what had been going on for some time. Legal initiatives were undertaken not only within the framework of the Mishnah but also quite separate and distinct from it. We cannot doubt that a layer of quite new theological ideas on fundamental issues treated in the Mishnah is spread over the whole frame of those tractates of the Mishnah treated by the Talmud. These ideas are blatant in the catalogues before us. The new viewpoints concern not merely matters of detail but issues at the very foundations of the structure of the document before us. Accordingly, our Talmud points toward a worldview separate from the Mishnah. But since this Talmud is essentially organized around the exposition of the Mishnah, whatever there is appears episodically and not sustainedly.

If, then, we want to know what is Talmudic in the Talmud of the Land of Israel, we have no choice but to examine what to begin with we treated as Mishnaic and therefore not Talmudic. For what is definitive is not merely recourse to Scripture, superficially absent from the Mishnah. It is not even the formation of a new sort of holy man, who stands at the center of a holy people differently defined, not a priest, and in the locus of a holy place of distinctive dimensions and boundaries, not the Temple. These new things on the face of it are symptoms of the deeper and definitive aspect of the whole. To get at that deeper aspect, we have now to turn back to the main part of the Talmud, which is the Mishnaic component. Specifically, we define not the conceptual or mythic result, but the mode of thought. From the *way* people analyzed old texts, I propose to uncover the adumbration of the new worldview they now labored to bring forth.

Talmudic within Mishnaic in the Talmud of the Land of Israel: Back to the Mishnaic Component of the Talmud

Because of the Talmud's essential character and mode of organizing both the whole and also the bulk of the parts (the units of discourse), it is when the Talmud speaks about the Mishnah that the Talmud reveals its system, nearly whole. The Talmud tells us about a different world from that of the Mishnah. The Talmud at its foundations presents a portrait of a world of rabbis making up laws for priests, law schools discussing the institution of the Temple. The Talmud's is a world facing Scripture when it talks about the Mishnah. So while the Mishnah and the Talmud share a common program and common categories of organization and structure the ones provided by the Mishnah at the very foundation, the Talmud is both part of, and also wholly separate from, the Mishnah.

The Mishnah describes a world and presents rules for it. So we may say, in simple language, that the Mishnah is about "life." The Mishnah describes the life of Israel, viewed from one now amply defined perspective. But the Talmud, for its part, is not so much about "life" in general as it is about the Mishnah in particular. Whatever the framers of the Talmud's units of discourse wish to say, they choose to say generally in relationship to something they find in the Mishnah. We now know that fact simply because we have reviewed the majority of the tractates and found a paltry mass of discrete materials in which redactors of a unit of discourse take as their organizing taxon something other than a problem of Mishnah exegesis.

The second point of difference is equally obvious, but more difficult to grasp: the Talmud's distinctive program of topics. At issue is what the Mishnah does not choose to treat, but which the Talmud for its part wishes to discuss. The principal example is not easy to state, for were we to propose a taxon defined by the issue of Israel's history, its form, direction, meaning, and end, we should find ourselves wholly outside of the Mishnah's frame of reference. On that protean topic the Mishnah offers no tractate, no chapter, scarcely a reference. We not only do not find attention to that classical issue of the Israelite worldview. We do not even know how we might find for discussion of the issue appropriate, specifically Mishnaic language or categories. The appropriate words elude us. Whatever discourse we do find in the Talmud pertinent to this formidable and urgent topic lies wholly outside the symbolic and even conceptual-linguistic framework of the Mishnah.

If, then, the Talmud principally deals with the Mishnah rather than with the exposition of ideas not to begin with generated by the Mishnah, we must now rigorously test the taxonomy required to encompass what the Talmud does choose to investigate: how the Talmud disposes of a given unit of the Mishnah. The charts at hand further allow us to inquire whether the Talmud ever departs from the basic task of exposition of what it finds at hand in the Mishnah. Do we require a taxon to encompass the points at which the Talmud uses the Mishnah as a pretext to make points of its own choosing? For (a modern reader might suppose) the Talmud surely imposes upon the various Scriptures it treats conceptions which are not self-evident, to the untutored mind, in those verses of Scriptures.

First, when we seek to define and describe what is both Mishnaic and Talmudic in the Talmud of the Land of Israel, we cannot turn chiefly to the substance of the document, the points at which the Talmud as we know it shares or does not share themes and conceptions found also in the Mishnah. Second, it does not suffice to allege, as I did above, that what is distinctively Mishnaic is identified in the discussion of the simple meaning of a Mishnah rule or an analysis of the interplay of two or more rules of the Mishnah. Third, when we catalogue issues essentially independent of the Mishnah, the result is a glimpse at a world definitive not of the Talmud as such but rather of the *context* of the Talmud as we know it. That is to say, lacking systematic tractates, chapters, or even an abundance of units of discourse, on the distinctively rabbinic themes and exercises, we cannot describe out of the resources of the Talmud itself a system we may call Talmudic, in contradistinction to the system we properly call Mishnaic. The materials are not sufficient. They are not represented as structurally definitive. They are episodic and hardly articulated.

Fourth and most decisive, what is Talmudic in our Talmud must be located, then defined and described, at that very point at which the distinctively Talmudic is itself Mishnaic. If, as we now know, the bulk of

The Talmud of the Land of Israel in Literary Context

the Talmud's materials focuses upon the Mishnah, it must follow that the system everywhere expressed within the Talmud *also* will be revealed when the Talmud addresses the Mishnah. Specifically we must once more seek to taxonomize and then catalogue those passages in which the Talmud's framers carry out that exercise that is paramount and predominant, defining the character of approximately 90 percent of the whole of the document: Mishnah exegesis. What we want now to know is how to describe the worldview of the framers of the document when at issue is the exegesis of the Mishnah. To phrase the questions from the top to the bottom: What do rabbis in particular do when they read the Mishnah? What are their modes of thought, their characteristic ways of analysis? Finally, what do we learn about their worldview from the ways in which they receive and interpret the worldview they have inherited in the Mishnah? These are the very questions, we now realize, that the Talmud answers. So when we wish to describe the Talmud's system as a whole, we must answer them.

The Talmudic exegetes of the Mishnah brought to the document no distinctive program of their own. At least, I perceive no hidden agenda. To state matters negatively, the exegetes did not know in advance of their approach to a law of the Mishnah facts about the passage not contained (even implicitly) within the boundaries of the language of the Mishnah passage itself (except only for facts contained within other units of the same document). Rejecting propositions that were essentially a priori, they proposed to explain and expand precisely the wording and the conceptions supplied by the document under study. I cannot point to a single instance in which the Talmudic exegetes appear to twist and turn the language and message of a passage, attempting to make the words mean something other than what they appear to say anyhow. Whether the exegetical results remain close to the wording of a passage of the Mishnah, or whether they leap beyond the bounds of the passage, the upshot is the same. There is no exegetical program revealed in the Talmud's reading of the Mishnah other than that defined, to begin with, by the language and conceptions of one Mishnah passage or another. That simple fact calls into question whether we may ever define what is Talmudic about the Talmud of the Land of Israel. That is hardly an operative category. For, at the end, the whole, seen whole, appears to be nothing more than a secondary development of the Mishnah. To be sure, the Talmud contains a merely episodic and negligible corpus of distinctively rabbinic, hence Talmudic, tales about rabbis and references to verses of Scripture read as rabbis read them. But that paltry and occasional set of "tacked-on" units of discourse merely underlines the main and definitive trait of the whole. The Talmud overall slavishly adheres to the program, canons of thought, and (so far as we may judge) "values" of the Mishnah itself. So that on the face of it appears to be the whole story: the Mishnah speaks about life, and the Talmud speaks about the Mishnah.

Nothing in Particular, Much in General

If there is nothing *in particular* that is Talmudic, there is much *in general* that is Talmudic. Distinguishing the Mishnaic from the Talmudic components of the Talmud of the Land of Israel shows us that the Talmudic sages' reading of the Mishnah, their hermeneutic, takes shape within the wording and contents of the Mishnah. For these set forth the problems to be solved and furthermore guided the exegete to the solutions of them. But the entire approach of the Talmud to the Mishnah is itself profoundly Talmudic, and this in several fundamental respects.

First, the Mishnah was set forth by Rabbi whole and complete, a profoundly unified, harmonious document. The Talmud insists upon obliterating the marks of coherence. It treats in bits and pieces what was originally meant to speak whole. That simple fact constitutes what is original, stunningly new and, by definition, Talmudic.

Second, the Mishnah, also by definition, delivered its message in the way chosen by Rabbi. That is to say, by producing the document as he did, Rabbi left no space for the very enterprises of episodic exegesis undertaken so brilliantly by his immediate continuators and heirs.

True, a rather limited process of explanation and gloss of words and phrases, accompanied by a systematic inquiry into the wording of one passage or another, got underway, probably at the very moment, and within the very process, of the Mishnah's closure. But insofar as the larger messages and meanings of the document are conveyed in the ways Rabbi chose through formalization of language, through contrasts, through successive instances of the same normally unspecified, general proposition, for example the need for exegesis was surely not generated by Rabbi's own program for the Mishnah. Quite to the contrary, Rabbi chose for his Mishnah a mode of expression and defined for the document a large-scale structure and organization, which, by definition, were meant to stand firm and autonomous. Rabbi's Mishnah speaks clearly and for itself.

For the Mishnah did not merely come to closure. At that moment it also formed a closed system, that is, a whole, complete statement. It does not require facts outside of its language and formulation, so makes no provision for commentary and amplification of brief allusions, as the Talmud's style assuredly does. The Mishnah refers to nothing beyond itself. It promises no information other than what is provided within its limits. It raises no questions for on-going discussion beyond its decisive,

The Talmud of the Land of Israel in Literary Context

final, descriptive statements of enduring realities and fixed relationships. The Talmud's single, decisive, irrevocable judgment is precisely opposite. The Talmud's first initiative is to reopen the Mishnah's closed system, almost at the moment of its completion and perfection. That at the foundations is what is Talmudic about the Talmud of the Land of Israel: its daring assertion that the concluded and completed demanded clarification and continuation. Once that assertion was made to stick, nothing else mattered very much.

What was to be clarified was obvious. What was to be continued must go forward along an essentially straight line from the starting point. No matter. The message was clear not solely in the character of the whole, still less in its contents, its assertions about the meaning of the Mishnah's laws. At every point, from the simplest gloss to the most far-ranging speculative inquiry, the message was the same. It was conveyed (we have learned to perceive) in the very medium of the Talmud: a new language, focused upon a new grid of discourse. The language was what it was: anything but patterned and thus anything but Mishnaic, even when (viewed redactionally) in Tosefta. The grid of discourse lay across, rather than within, the inner boundaries of the Mishnah itself, a profound and fundamental revolution in thought, as I have already stressed. Accordingly, the Talmud's distinctive traits, separate from those defined by the Mishnah for the age beyond the Mishnah's closure, lie not in the depths of what was said, but on the very surface, in the very literary formulation of the Talmud itself. Yet the judgment of the Talmud upon the Mishnah, that is, what is Talmudic in the Talmud of the Land of Israel, is not fully described when we have seen what lies scattered on the surface. When we return to the taxa just now found exhaustive, we discover a program of criticism of the Mishnah framed by independent and original minds. Let us bypass the obvious points of independent judgment, the matter of insistence that the very word choices of the Mishnah require clarification, therefore prove faulty. The meanings and amplification of phrases represent the judgment that Rabbi's formulation, while stimulating and provocative, left much to be desired. These indications of independence of judgment among people disposed not merely to memorize but to improve upon the text provided by Rabbi hardly represent judgments of substance.

Rather, let us turn to the two most striking lists: first, the provision of Scriptural prooftexts for the propositions of various passages of the Mishnah, a matter that has captured our attention many times; second, the rewriting, in the Mishnah's own idiom, if not in its redactional and disciplinary patterns, of much of the law, through the supplementary materials we call Tosefta, a matter treated here in only a preliminary way. As to the former, of course, the message is clear. The propositions of the Mishnah cannot stand by themselves but must be located within the larger realm of Scriptural authority. If Rabbi presented his Mishnah without prooftexts in the belief that such texts were either self-evident or unnecessary, his continuators and successors rejected his judgment on both counts. So far as the Mishnah was supposed to stand as a law code independent of the revelation of Torah to Moses at Mount Sinai, it was received by people to whom such a supposition was incredible. So far as Rabbi took for granted the Scriptural facticity of the facts of his law code, that was regarded as insufficient. What was implicit (if it was implicit) had to be made explicit. As to the latter, the Tosefta's numerous passages, serving as an exegetical complement to the Mishnah's corresponding passages, phrased in the way in which the Mishnah's sentences are written (as distinct from the utterly different way in which the Talmud's sentences are framed), show equivalent independence of mind. They indicate that, where sages of the time of the Talmud of the Land of Israel took up Mishnaic passages, they were not at all limited to the work of gloss and secondary expansion. They recognized and exercised a quite remarkable freedom of initiative. In the Tosefta they undertook to restate in their own words, but imitating the Mishnah's style, the propositions of the Mishnah passage at hand. That is, they both cite what the Mishnah had said and also continue, in imitation of the Mishnah's language, the discourse of the Mishnah passage itself.

These Toseftan complements to the Mishnah are Talmudic, just as much as the rhetorically unrelated passages listed in the other catalogues, in two senses. First, they come to expression in the period after the Mishnah had reached closure, as is clear from the fact that the exact language of the Mishnah is cited prior to the labor of extension expansion and revision. So they are the work of the Talmud's age and authority. Second, they self-evidently derive from precisely the same authorities responsible for the formation of the Talmud as a whole. That is the fact, by definition. Accordingly, both the insistence upon adducing prooftexts for passages Rabbi judged not to need, and the persistent revision and expansion of the Mishnah, even in clumsy imitation of the Mishnah's syntax, rhetoric, and word choices, tell us once more that simple truth we saw at the outset. The Talmud is distinctively Talmudic precisely when the Mishnah itself defines the Talmud's labor, dictates its ideas, displays its rhetoric, determines its results. The very shift in usable language, from "the Mishnah" (as a whole) to "the Mishnah passage" or "the Mishnaic law at hand" indicates the true state of affairs. On the surface, in all manner of details, the Talmud of the Land of Israel is little more than a secondary and derivative document, explaining the Mishnah itself in trivial ways, or expanding it in a casuistic and logic-chopping manner. But viewing that same surface from a different, more distant perspective and angle, we see things quite differently. In detail the Talmud changed nothing. Overall, the Talmud left nothing the same.

So, as I said at the outset, in the Talmud of the Land of Israel we find little to deem Talmudic in particular. But there is much that is Talmudic in general. The particular bits and pieces are Mishnaic. But the Talmud leaves nothing of the Mishnah whole and intact. Its work upon the whole presents an essentially new construction. Through the Mishnah, Rabbi contributed to the Talmud most of the bricks, but little of the mortar, and none of the joists and beams. The design of the whole bore no relationship to Rabbi's plan for the Mishnah. The sages of the Talmud of the Land of Israel did the rest. They alone imagined, then built, the building. They are the architects, theirs is the vision. The building is a monument to the authority of the sage above all.

I have left for last the single fact, spread over the whole, superficial beyond all others, thus indicative of the Talmudic sages' freedom of imagination: the exercise of free choice even among the Mishnah's tractates awaiting exegesis. We do not know why some tractates were chosen for Talmudic expansion and others left fallow. We may speculate that the omission of all reference to the entire division of Holy Things, on the everyday conduct of the Temple, and to most of the division of Purities, on the sources of uncleanness, objects subject to uncleanness, and modes of removing contamination, constitutes a radical revision of the law of Judaism. What for Rabbi was well over 40 percent of the whole story in volume, forming two of his six divisions in structure, for the Talmud's designers (I assume early as much as late), was of no importance. Interest in the division of Appointed Times involved extensive discussion of the conduct of the cult on extraordinary days. Perhaps at issue here was not what had to be omitted (the cult on appointed times) but what people wanted to discuss, the home and village on those same holy occasions. So the former came in the wake of the latter. Inclusion of the divisions of Women, on the family and the transfer of women from father to husband and back, and Damages, on civil law and institutions, is not hard to explain. The sages fully expected to govern the life of Israel, the Jewish people, in its material and concrete aspects. These divisions, as well as some of the tractates of the division on Appointed Times, demanded and received attention. Ample treatment of the laws in the first division, governing the priests' rations and other sacred segments of the agricultural produce of the Holy Land, is to be expected among authorities living not only in, but also off, the Holy Land.

Accordingly, when we describe the selection of divisions, at the very same moment we interpret the principle of selection: relevance to the setting of the nation of Israel in its Land. Here, too, as before, the details of how the Mishnah is received are only moderately interesting. But the central fact is stunning: whole divisions were dropped. There is evidently nothing in the particularity of the details to be regarded as definitive of the mind and imagination of the group behind our Talmud. But the Talmud as a whole tells us what we wish to know. Having labored in the underbrush of a document in form and substance totally subservient to its own principal focus, the Mishnah itself, we reach this simple conclusion. In accepting authority, in centering discourse upon the ideas of other men, in patiently listing even the names behind authoritative laws from olden times to their own day, the sages and framers of the Talmud accomplished exactly the opposite of what they apparently wished to do. They made a commentary. But they obliterated the text. They loyally explained the Mishnah. But they turned the Mishnah into something else than what it had been. They patiently hammered out chains of tradition, binding themselves to the authority of the remote and holy past. But it was, in the end, a tradition of their own design and choosing. That is, it was not tradition but a new creation. And so this Talmud of ours, so loyal and subservient to the Mishnah of Rabbi, turns out to be less a reworking of received materials than a work of remarkably independent judgment. The Talmud of the Land of Israel speaks humbly and subserviently about received truth, always in the name only of Moses and of sages of times past. But in the end it is truth not discovered and demonstrated, but determined and invented and declared.

The Starting Point

To describe the Talmud we first take up the whole and proceed to ask about its principal components. Looking at the Talmud whole, we notice two totally distinct sorts of materials: statements of law, then discussions of and excursus on those statements. We bring no substantial presuppositions to the text, if we declare these two sorts of materials to be, respectively, primary and constitutive, secondary and derivative. Calling the former the declaration of laws, the Mishnah passage, and the latter the exegesis of these laws, the Talmud proper, imposes no a priori judgment formed independently of the literary evidence in hand. We might as well call the two "the code" and "the commentary." The result would be no different.

In fact, as we see everywhere, the Talmud is made up of two elements, each with its own literary traits and program of discussion. Since the Mishnah passage at the head of each set of Talmudic units of discourse defines the limits and determines the theme and, generally, the problematic of the whole, our attention is drawn to the traits of the Mishnah passages as a group. Here, of course, a certain measure of descriptive work has been done. But even if we for the first time saw these types of pericopes of the Mishnah (embedded as they are in the Talmud and separated from one another), we should discern that they adhere to a separate and quite distinctive set of literary and conceptual canons from what follows and surrounds them. Hence at the outset, with no appreciable attention to anything beyond the text, we should distinguish two "layers" of the Talmud and recognize that one "layer" is formed in one way, the other in another way. (I use "layer" for convenience only; it is not an apt metaphor.)

If then we were to join together all the Mishnah pericopes, we should notice that they are stylistically and formally coherent and also different from everything else in the compilation before us. Accordingly, for stylistic reasons alone we are on firm ground in designating the "layer" before us as the base point for all further inquiry. For the Mishnah "layer" has been shown to be uniform, while the Talmud "layer" is not demonstrably so. Hence, itself undifferentiated, the former Mishnah "layer" provides the point of differentiation. The latter Talmud "layer" presents the diverse materials subject to differentiation. In the first stage in the work of making sense of the Talmud and describing it whole, what is the initial criterion through which the Talmud's diverse types of units of discourse are differentiated? It is the varied relationships to the Mishnah's rule, exhibited by the Talmud's several, diverse units of discourse. Let me now expand on and qualify this point, for it is the principle of the opening initiative in this exercise of taxonomy and typology.

Since the Palestinian Talmud carries forward and depends upon the Mishnah, to describe that Talmud we have to begin with its relationship to the Mishnah, which is the Talmud's own starting point. While the Mishnah admits to no antecedents and neither alludes to nor cites anything prior to its own materials, a passage of the Talmud is often incomprehensible without knowledge of the passage of the Mishnah around which the Talmud's discourse centers. Yet in describing and defining the Talmud, we should grossly err if we were to say it is only, or mainly, a step-by-step commentary on the Mishnah, defined solely by the Mishnah's interests. We may not even say, though it is a step closer to the truth, that the Talmud before us is a commentary on or secondary development of, the Mishnah and important passages of the Tosefta. Units of discourse which serve these sorts of materials stand side by side with many which in an immediate sense do not. Accordingly, while a description of the Talmud requires attention to the interplay between the Talmud and the Mishnah and Tosefta, the diverse relationships between the Talmud and one or the other of those two documents constitute only one point of description and differentiation. For the Talmud is in full command of its own program of thought and inquiry. Its framers, responsible for the units of discourse, chose what in the Mishnah will be analyzed and what ignored. True, there could be no Talmud without the Mishnah and Tosefta. But knowing only those two works, we could never have predicted in a systematic way the character of the Talmud's discourse at any point.

The Mishnah nonetheless permits us at the outset to gain perspective on the character of Yerushalmi. For the Mishnah does exhibit a remarkable unity of literary and redactional traits. By that standard our Talmud presents none. Accordingly, while whatever materials reached the framers of the Mishnah ca. 175-200 were revised by them in line with a single and simple literary and redactional program, the same is not the case for the Talmud of the Land of Israel. Whatever the stages of redaction of the document as a whole, let alone of its components, we may say with certainty that the people ultimately responsible for the document as we have it did not do to the materials in their hands what the framers of the Mishnah did to theirs. The ultimate redactors did not participate in the work of formulation. Units of discourse framed in some prior setting have been preserved as is (though we do not know to what extent as to detail). They were drawn together whole and complete with other such essentially fixed and final units of discourse.

It might be wise to present charts to prove the present proposition about the fundamental difference between the literary and redactional condition of the Mishnah and that of the Talmud. But the reader need only open to any passage of the Mishnah and set it side by side with any passage of the Talmud of the Land of Israel. Later we shall do just that. The contrast then will be clear. The former is constructed out of a severely limited repertoire of syntactic and rhetorical forms. The latter is diffuse and stylistically promiscuous. The former is tight, the latter loose; the former amply articulated, the latter remarkably elliptical; the former uniform and stylistically coherent, the latter diverse and formally incoherent. The former speaks in whole sentences; the latter in shorthand, abbreviated, notes toward discourse never amply articulated. Accordingly, it suffices to state as fact that what the Mishnah's redactors did to the Mishnah, Yerushalmi's redactors did not do to Talmud Yerushalmi. Our first task is to attempt to describe what they did do.

The redactional program of the men responsible for laying out the materials of Yerushalmi may now be described in simple terms. Most important, we see that there was such a program. There is nothing random. That is clear because, within the differentiation of units of discourse I have defined, diverse types of units of discourse are not mixed together promiscuously. There is a pronounced tendency to move from close reading of the Mishnah and then Tosefta to more general

The Talmud of the Land of Israel in Literary Context 59

inquiry into the principles of a Mishnah passage and their interplay with those of some other, superficially unrelated passage, and, finally, to more general reflections on law not self-evidently related to the Mishnah passage at hand or to anthologies intersecting only at a general topic. Now while that program may appear self-evident and logical, we must not assume there were no choices in how to lay things out. The program I have described exhibits sufficient variation to rule out the possibility that our Talmud's way is the better way of doing things. The redactors knew precisely how they wished to lay out the materials that they drew together into the Talmud. Accordingly, the work of redaction was active and followed a program. If therefore we now take as fact that the Talmud before us is the result of a generation, or several generations, of redaction, it is because we see the evidence of active participation in the formation of the document: a plan, a program. The contrary possibility, that this is just how things happened to come to hand, seems unlikely, given the disproportionate replication of a single logical, self-evident pattern. The second question flows from the first. If the redactors participated in the organization of units of discourse, did they also place their mark upon the formulation of those same units of discourse?

From Redaction to Formulation?

Since the close interplay between redaction and formulation constitutes the sole firm result of our study of the Mishnah, we ask about the same matter for our Talmud. The issue is whether we can find evidence of systematic attention to formulating units of discourse in such a way as formally or syntactically to relate one to the next within a single redactional program or process. If there is such evidence, we must conclude that, even in the ultimate redactional stages of the formation of the Talmud, work went on not merely in minor correction, revision, or glossing of a passage. Such work pertained even to the very formulation of the statement of its main points, in the structure and wording by which those points would be expressed. It would then follow that, prior to the redaction of the whole, we are unable to posit the existence of units of discourse as we know them. If we find no points of correlation between redactional policies and problems of formulation of units of discourse, on the other hand, it must follow that, separate from (perhaps then, prior to) the redactional stages (though we do not know how long before) a process of formulation of units of discourse was underway. Our question thus is, did the redactors work with essentially finished units of discourse? Or did they themselves participate in the formation of the completed units of discourse which they also organized and juxtaposed?

The criterion for positive evidence for the second proposition hence, also, negative evidence for the first, derives from comparison with the Mishnah. What we compare are units of discourse of our Talmud and the formulary traits of Mishnah pericopes. The latter indicate the hand of redaction and organization within the very phrasing of individual units of law of the Mishnah. Absence of equivalent traits then will signify for the Talmud a different relationship of redaction to formulation from that prevalent in the Mishnah. For the Mishnah, essential to the organization and layout of completed units of discourse is the very pattern of formulating those same units of discourse. The result is proof, for the Mishnah, that redaction is prior and critical to formulation. In the Mishnah, redaction is not solely a process of joining together statements bearing no formal relationship to one another, hence existing before (we do not know how long before) the process of organization and layout we call redaction. A clear grasp of how the Mishnah works is then essential to a comparative inquiry into the Talmud's traits.

Now to spell out the interplay of formulation and redaction in the Mishnah. The principal result of my inquiry was to show constant and close relationship between the one and the other. Specifically, I found that when the Mishnah's redactors wished to indicate the formation of a unit of discourse (which I called, in that setting, "intermediate unit"), they would take up a distinctive formulary pattern or form, different from that which they had used beforehand and also from that which they would use in the following unit. They would carefully group their smallest whole statements ("smallest units of cognition") so that each one would repeat the same syntactic pattern, setting up (in general) groups of three or multiples of three, or groups of five or multiples of five, with such internally patterned statements of a single principle being applied to a single theme. This seemed to me definitive evidence that the whole could not have been formulated prior to the work of redaction, at which point and not before the larger program of arrangement of topics and principles expressed in connection with those topics was in hand. Only when the whole was fully in view was it possible to form the parts in the uniform way in which they were formed. There is no other economical way of explaining the facts I have discovered, since, as is clear, the whole was planned before the parts were laid out in their matching and distinctive syntactic patterns and in their little sets of three or five repetitions of such patterns.

The issue when we turn to the Talmud cannot of course be framed in the same way. But to begin with, we must ask ourselves whether we discern any formulary patterns at all, not merely those of a redactional type. When we speak of formulary patterns to review we mean recurrent arrangements of words in a given syntactic formula. The fact is that I

The Talmud of the Land of Israel in Literary Context 61

cannot find a single instance, in the twenty-nine tractates of the Talmud of the Land of Israel that I have translated, where the unit of discourse is so formulated as to indicate an intention to relate what is formulated to its redactional context or to the larger needs of combining two or more completed units of thought into a principal redactional unit (a complete discussion of a Mishnah pericope, for instance). If the traits of the Mishnah indicate that central to the process of organizing materials was the work of formulating them, then the absence of the same traits in the Talmud indicates the opposite. The work of redaction of units of discourse in the Talmud therefore was distinct from, and later than, the work of formulation. Since we have seen ample evidence that there was a stage of discourse in which materials were laid out in accord with a few simple rules, governed by the relationship to the Mishnah exhibited by a given unit of discourse, the picture is clear.

Accordingly, the logically final question turns our attention to the way in which the framers of the Talmud of the Land of Israel express their ideas: the forms and patterns of their language. We seek to find out whether we can differentiate, on the basis of literary or syntactic traits of expression, any of the following: (1) units of discourse from one another, (2) tractates from one another, (3) specific authorities from one another, or (4) schools from one another. If such differentiation were to prove possible, then we might be able to answer elements of the question left unanswered at the end of the foregoing exercise: How do we know that the Yerushalmi provides us with any information at all concerning times before the period of its own redaction? For differentiating language characteristic of a given type of unit of discourse, tractate, authority, or school will permit further exercises of differentiation and yet further tests of falsification or validation. I phrase matters in rather general terms, since the net result of the probes undertaken in the present chapter is not heartening. At the end we shall have to draw the opposite conclusions from those exercises in historical and literary reasoning based on salient points characteristic of one thing and not some other.

By the criterion of use or neglect of our form, we may now differentiate one type of unit of discourse from another.

1. Among units of the first and second types, ten of the twenty-four instances (41 percent) occur; among those of the fifth and sixth types, nine (37 percent).

2. As to differentiation between or among tractates, there clearly is an important point of difference between Baba Mesia and Sanhedrin. More important: among the small tractates, of roughly equal size, the occurrences are random and right, two, three, and four, for Niddah, Nedarim, and Sukkah, respectively. (Why Baba Mesia should provide us

with no examples is a question to be raised in the larger study of the tractates of Caesarea; Lieberman's thesis once more is replicated.)

3. The issue of differentiating among schools by reference to forms used in one and neglected in another surely is not settled one way or the other. Perhaps Caesarean framers of units of tradition did not know the form in question, or knew it but did not find it useful. Perhaps those at Tiberias had a strong preference for it. But these are not questions we can settle, short of a far more extensive picture of both the statistics and aesthetics of the schools, the proportions of the whole Talmud contributed by each, the numbers of names of each center present in the entire Talmud, and the like. We restrict our question to the one at hand: Is there evidence in the literary traits of units of discourse to provide us with information on who stands behind a given unit, when and under what circumstances that unit was framed? So long as we define our purpose carefully within that question, these questions are not apt to demand our sustained attention.

But even if they were, the data would be no different. In fact the point of differentiation among the mass of formal material is one only: names of authorities mentioned in a unit of discourse. We cannot reach the schools or centers of learning through any other route. Without the evidence supplied by a given name, we have nothing whatsoever. So even if our question were a literary one only, we should have to take up the same basic problem, namely, evaluating the historical value of materials assigned in a given authority's name. This we cannot do in an exercise of taxonomy.

The Yerushalmi's Distinctive Traits

That the Talmud of the Land of Israel reveals a clear-cut plan for organizing its component parts is beyond doubt. But knowing that fact helps very little in defining the work before us. For all we have accomplished is to differentiate the redaction from the formulation of the Talmud's units of discourse. No one need doubt that a repertoire of patterns governed the way in which language was shaped for the expression of ideas. But when the use of these patterns indicates a fact of social or historical significance is by no means clear. Sometimes a recurrent syntactic pattern shows us nothing more than how people said things "in general." We cannot discover from that fact anything consequential for the interpretation of the history of our document and the formation of its building blocks. Clearly, a brief probe into a single form turned up a few interesting facts. Most proved negative for our larger purpose. In all, the key issue for the use of the units of discourse for the study of important events in the history of Judaism in the third and fourth centuries in the Land of Israel has yet to be framed. If we want to know who is responsible for the formation of the units of discourse, all we now know is that it was not those who undertook redaction. Those at the point of formulation, on the one side, and in the framework of transmission and preservation to the time of redaction, on the other, stand behind the little "talmuds" of which our Talmud is composed.

It looks to me as if the point of formulation of a sizable proportion of units of discourse in particular, those containing the names of two or more authorities can be no earlier than the moment at which the opinions of those authorities were made to intersect and form the foundations of a larger inquiry. For the sake of convenience, we may say, therefore, that if two members of the same generation, not in constant association with one another, are represented in a unit of discourse as disputing a common point, that representation must be the work of people who flourished somewhat later than the moment at which the two authorities expressed themselves on the common point, on the one side, and at which interest in drawing together diverse views on that same point had developed, on the other. So, obviously, this is "afterward." But how long? It can have been a day later, or a century later. The *terminus a qua* given authority's lifetime is not very helpful for our needs. We require a *terminus ad quem*, a point prior to which the unit of discourse as we know it, or a principal component thereof, simply must have reached its present formulation.

On the basis of literary analysis, so far as I am able to accomplish it, I can say no more than this: Yerushalmi's units of discourse and their components were formulated sometime, somewhere, prior to the processes of ultimate closure and redaction. The work of formulation and original closure was essentially distinct from those processes. But, as I just said, that can have been earlier by a day, a year, or a century. It can have happened one house down the block. We have no evidence as to where or how the work was done. All we have is the result: what people said various authorities had earlier said.

The Mishnah speaks about uncleanness and holiness, priests and their rations, holy days and appointed times in the Temple, ordinary, everyday rites at the altar. The Mishnah's picture of Israelite government presents a portrait of a king and a high priest in charge of everything. Its conception of civil law aims at preserving the perfect stability of the status quo, all in the name of the sanctification of Israel. While the Mishnah names sages, called rabbis, it does not present a system of Judaism characterized by those traits definitive, later on, of Rabbinic Judaism. That is, its principal concerns are those of priests, not sages. Its focus of interest is in the Temple and its cult, not in the schoolhouse and its ritual learning. Its conception of the civil life rests upon an orderly world in majestic stasis, and does not deal with that disorderly detritus of ordinary life to which, later on, the rabbis address themselves in their small claims courts. Above all, the Mishnah provides no place at all for the upheavals of history public or personal and the ordering and end to be effected by the Messiah. Rabbinic Judaism, fully exposed, would rest its claim upon its supernatural power to bring the Messiah: do things our way and he will come. So the *persona* of the Mishnah may be described as a priest, facing the destroyed Temple and the now-forbidden city of Jerusalem. The system of Yerushalmi, ca. A.D. 400, to emerge within two centuries after the closure of the Mishnah in A.D. 200, addressed the everyday life of Israel in the towns and villages of the Holy Land. Its *persona* is a rabbi, walking with his disciples through the streets and marketplaces of the country and abroad as well. The contrast between the Mishnah's priestly system of an Israelite world laid out in lines of structure focused upon and emanating from the Temple, and the Talmud's striking reshaping of that system through the grafting on of a separate value system, is captured within the Mishnah itself. M. Horayot 3:5 states: A priest takes precedence over a Levite, Levite over an Israelite, and Israelite over a *mamzer*, a *mamzer* over a *natin*, a *natin* over a proselyte, a proselyte over a freed slave. This scale of social standing places the priest at the head of Israelite society.

But, the same passage proceeds: Under what circumstances [is this the case]? When all of them are equivalent [in other respects]. But if a *mamzer* was a disciple of a sage and a high priest was an ignoramus, the *mamzer* who is a disciple of a sage takes precedence over the high priest who is an ignoramus. The allegation of the priority of learning over genealogy presents the very core of Rabbinic Judaism, of which our Talmud and the Babylonian one form the first, and principal, monuments. A quite separate scale, supplied in our Talmud, underlines what is at issue, by introducing the (typically) more practical claim to the priority of the king (in the time of the Talmud: the *nasi*, or patriarch) and stating that the sage stands above him. Here is Yerushalmi's comment on the cited passage of the Mishnah (Y. Hor. 3:5.I.A-D):

> [A] A sage takes precedence over a king, a king over a high priest, a high priest over a prophet; a prophet takes precedence over a priest anointed for war; a priest anointed for war takes precedence over the head of a priestly watch; the head of a priestly watch takes precedence over the head of a household [of priests]; the head of a household of priests takes precedence over the superintendent of cashiers;
>
> [B] **The superintendent of cashiers takes precedence over the Temple treasurer; the Temple treasurer takes precedence over an ordinary priest [T. Hor. 2:10F-H];**

The Talmud of the Land of Israel in Literary Context 65

[C] *An ordinary priest takes precedence over a Levite; a Levite takes precedence over an Israelite; an Israelite takes precedence over a mamzer; a mamzer takes precedence over a natin; a natin takes precedence over a proselyte; a proselyte takes precedence over a freed slave. Under what circumstances? When all of them are equivalent. But if the mamzer was a disciple of a sage, and a high priest was an ignoramus, then the mamzer who is the disciple of a sage takes precedence over a high priest who is an ignoramus [M. Hor. 3:5A-D].*

[D] A sage takes precedence over a king.

[E] [For if] a sage dies, we have none who is like him.

[F] [If] a king dies, any Israelite is eligible to mount the throne [T. Hor. 2:8].

Speaking out of its immaterial world of theory, the Mishnah does not introduce the concrete claim, therefore political presence, of the patriarch (king). The Talmud's restatement is down-to-earth. A sage takes precedence over a king, because anyone can be king, but not anyone can be a sage. I cannot think of a more stunning shift in focus from theory to practice, and from a hyperbolic claim of cosmic order to a modest, but practical and concrete, judgment of what can be done. We see how the Mishnah may be said to define the starting point in the formation of Rabbinic Judaism. We also perceive why the Mishnah cannot be described as at heart a Rabbinic document. From the perspective of the third and fourth centuries, the Mishnah speaks about the wrong things, in behalf of the wrong group of people, turning toward the wrong time and the wrong place: sanctification, Temple, and cult, for the priests, in the ever more distant past, of the forbidden city of Jerusalem. The Talmud, viewed whole and complete, testifies to a different vision for Israel. It speaks of learning, in behalf of sages, living in the present, and located everywhere that Israel now is found. The Mishnah scarcely speaks of a messiah. Whoever is anointed bears, at best, a particular status, not a general power over Israel's history. The Talmud, at the end, ties itself tightly to the messianic fervor of Israel, promising that when Israel does what sages teach, the Messiah will come. The Mishnah scarcely alludes to the end of time or the world to come. The Talmud will present a road map of how to get there. As I pointed out in the beginning, what has just been said, however, does not emerge from inductive sifting of evidence. Let us return to the mode of inquiry practiced in this study: merely sifting evidence and classifying it.

The Mishnah's Language and the Talmud's: Contrasts

The contrast is to be drawn between the mode of expression dominant in the Mishnah and that characteristic of the Talmud, reviewed above. Let us dwell for a moment on the stylistic traits of the Mishnah, specifically, the acute formalization of its syntactical structure, and its carefully framed sequences of formalized language, specifically, its intermediate divisions, so organized that the limits of a theme correspond to those of a formulary pattern. The balance and order of the Mishnah are particular to the Mishnah. The Talmud knows no reason to follow suit.

Just as the Mishnah portrays a utopia, a destroyed Temple in a forbidden city, a calendar for a lunar cycle of sacrifices no one can follow, a government-in-exile no one can now obey, a caste everyone must feed but from whom none now derives sacerdotal benefit, so its language is remote from the material sensibilities of sound and speech and consequence. This is shown, in particular, in its mnemonic traits. A sense for the deep, inner logic of word patterns, of grammar and syntax, rather than for their external similarities, governs the Mishnaic mnemonic. Even though the Mishnah is to be memorized and handed on orally, it expresses a mode of thought attuned to abstract relationships, rather than concrete and substantive forms. The formulaic, not the formal, character of the Mishnaic rhetoric yields a picture of a subculture of the sages who made up the book which speaks of immaterial, and not material, things. In this subculture the *relationship*, rather than the thing or person which is related, is primary. The way things come together constitutes the principle of reality. The thing in itself is less than the thing in cathexis with other things; so, too, the person: you are what you do in social context. It is self-evident that the repetition of form creates form. But what is repeated is not external or superficial. Rather we find formulary patterns of deep syntax, patterns effected through persistent grammatical or syntactical relationships and affecting an infinite range of diverse objects and topics. Form and structure emerge not from concrete, formal things but from abstract and unstated, but ubiquitous and powerful relationships.

This fact the creation of pattern through grammatical relationship of syntactical elements more than through concrete sounds tells us that the people who memorized conceptions reduced to these particular forms were capable of extraordinarily abstract cognition and perception. Hearing peculiarities of word order in diverse cognitive contexts, their ears and minds perceived regularities of grammatical arrangement. They could catch repeated functional variations of utilization of diverse words. They grasped from such subtleties syntactical patterns not expressed by recurrent external phenomena such as sounds, rhythms, or key words, and independent of particular meanings. What they heard, it is clear, were not only abstract relationships among parts of speech. They could bring to the surface principles conveyed along with and through these relationships. For what was memorized was a recurrent and fundamental notion, expressed in diverse *examples* but in fixed, recurrent rhetorical-syntactical *patterns*. Accordingly, what the memorizing student of a sage could and did hear was what lay far beneath the surface of the rule: the unstated principle within the unsounded pattern of contrast or repetition. This means that the prevalent mode of thought was attuned to what lay beneath the surface; minds and ears perceived what was not said behind what was said and how it was said. They sought that ineffable and metaphysical reality, concealed within but conveyed through spoken and palpable material reality.

Social interrelationships within the community of Israel are left behind in the ritual speech of the Mishnah, just as, within the laws, natural realities are made to give form and expression to supernatural or metaphysical regularities. The Mishnah speaks of Israel, but the speakers are a group apart. The Mishnah talks of this-worldly things, but the things stand for and speak of another world entirely, a destroyed Temple in a forbidden city. The language of the Mishnah and its formalized grammatical rhetoric create a world of discourse quite separate from the concrete realities of a given time, place, or society. The exceedingly limited repertoire of grammatical patterns by which all things on all matters are said gives symbolic expression to the notion that beneath the accidents of life are a few comprehensive relationships. Unchanging and enduring patterns lie deep in the inner structure of reality and impose structure upon the accidents of the world. This means, as I have implied, that reality for Mishnaic rhetoric consists in the grammar and syntax of language: consistent and enduring patterns of relationship among diverse and changing concrete things or persons. What lasts is not the concrete thing but the abstract interplay governing any and all sorts of concrete things. We turn now to the language of the Talmud.

The Talmud is phrased so differently that a comparison of the syntax of the Mishnah with that of the Talmud is incongruous. We do not know whether the Talmud phrases attributed statements in accordance with how people actually said things. We do know that, unlike the Mishnah, the Talmud reveals no effort to systematize sayings in larger constructions, to impose a pattern upon all individual sayings. If the Mishnah is framed to facilitate memorization, then we must say that the Talmud's materials are not framed with mnemonics in mind. If the Mishnah focuses upon subsurface relationships in syntax, the Talmud in the main looks like notes of a discussion. These notes may serve to recreate the larger patterns of argument and reasoning, a summary of what was thought and perhaps also said. The Talmud preserves and expresses concrete ideas, reducing them to brief but usually accessible and obvious statements. The Mishnah speaks of concrete things in order to hint at abstract relationships, which rarely are brought to the surface and fully exposed.

The Mishnah hides. The Talmud spells out. The Mishnah hints. The Talmud repeats, *ad nauseam*. The Mishnah is subtle, the Talmud obvious; the one restrained and tentative, the other aimed at full and exhaustive expression of what is already clear. The sages of the Mishnah rarely represent themselves as deciding cases. Only on unusual occasions do they declare the decided law, at best reticently spelling out what underlies their positions. The rabbis of the Talmud harp on who holds which opinion and how a case is actually decided, presenting a rich corpus of precedents. They seek to make explicit what is implicit in the law. The Mishnah is immaterial and spiritual, the Talmud earthy and social. The Mishnah deals in the gossamer threads of philosophical principle, the Talmud in the coarse rope that binds this one and that one into a social construction.

So the comparison and contrast of the Mishnah to the Talmud once more presents us with a set of opposites, captured in this simple contrast between exemplifying a pattern as against providing a precedent, speculating on the implications of principles as against deciding the law and declaring whose opinion counts. My interpretation of the matter beyond the evidence is this: the Mishnah speaks of stasis and eternity to whom it may concern. The Talmud addresses Israel in the here and now of ever-changing times, the gross matter of disorder and history. Clearly, the central traits of the Mishnah, revealed in the document at its time of closure in ca. A.D. 200, were revised and transformed into those definitive of the Talmud at its time of closure in ca. A.D. 400. But whatever changes emerged from the two centuries of Mishnah study contained in the Talmud took place in such a subtle and unarticulated way that on the surface there is little trace of how they occurred. We know only that when we compare the Mishnah to the Talmud we find two intertwined documents, quite different from one another both in style and in values. Yet they are so tightly joined that the Talmud appears in the main to provide mere commentary and amplification for the Mishnah. Indeed, the critical problem in the study of Judaism as revealed in the Palestinian Talmud will be to find out how the obvious happened when in the document itself nothing at all remarkable was taking place. And that is the question that is answered in the study of category formation presented in *Transformation of Judaism*.

3
Leviticus Rabbah and the Hebrew Scriptures

While the world at large treats Judaism as "the religion of the Old Testament," the fact is otherwise. Judaism inherits and makes the Hebrew Scriptures its own, just as does Christianity. But just as Christianity rereads the entire heritage of ancient Israel in the light of "the resurrection of Jesus Christ," so Judaism understands the Hebrew Scriptures as only one part, the written one, of "the one whole Torah of Moses, our rabbi." Ancient Israel no more testified to the Oral Torah, now written down in the Mishnah and later rabbinic writings, than it did to Jesus as the Christ. In both cases, religious circles within Israel of later antiquity reread the entire past in the light of their own conscience and convictions. Accordingly, while the framers of Judaism as we know it received as divinely revealed ancient Israel's literary heritage, they picked and chose as they wished what would serve the purposes of the larger system they undertook to build. Since the Judaism at hand first reached literary expression in the Mishnah, a document in which Scripture plays a subordinate role, the founders of that Judaism clearly made no pretense at tying up to scriptural prooftexts or at expressing in the form of scriptural commentary the main ideas they wished to set out. Accordingly, Judaism only asymmetrically rests upon the foundations of the Hebrew Scriptures, and Judaism is not alone or mainly "the religion of the Old Testament."

Since Judaism is not "the religion of the Old Testament," we cannot take for granted or treat as predictable or predetermined the entry of the Hebrew Scriptures into the system of Judaism at hand. That is why we must ask exactly how the Scriptures did enter the framework of Judaism. In what way, when, and where, in the unfolding of the canon of Judaism, were they absorbed and recast, and how did they find the distinctive role they were to play from late antiquity onward?

I. The Importance of Leviticus Rabbah

If we wish to know in detail how the framers of Judaism confronted the challenge of Scripture, we logically turn to the books they wrote in which they expressed their ideas by making use of verses of Scripture. Some of these are organized around the structure of the Mishnah, others around that of Scripture. Clearly, the latter bring us closer to the answer, since in them the confrontation with Scripture proves immediate and ever-present. The issue of the Tosefta and the Talmud is the Mishnah, however, to which Scripture forms a merely critical component, but not the definitive issue. The issue of Sifra, the two Sifrés, Genesis Rabbah, and Leviticus Rabbah is Scripture, specifically, the re-reading of Scripture in the light of the rabbis' established system. All the texts, both those formed around the Mishnah and those ordered in accord with a book of Scripture, find a place within, and point toward, a larger matrix of values and convictions, the rabbinic system as a whole. Each one testifies in its own way. Sifra and the two Sifrés address the Mishnah through Scripture. They explain how the Mishnah relates to Scripture. In Genesis Rabbah and Leviticus Rabbah the issue is not the Mishnah but Scripture itself.

But how do rabbis propose to speak within, about, and through Scripture, when the Mishnah is not a principal issue? And what modes of discourse do they find useful when the exegesis of the Mishnah or the accommodation of the Mishnah to Scripture does not dictate the appropriate redactional and rhetorical forms? Only Genesis Rabbah and Leviticus Rabbah provide evidence of the answers to these questions.

The former, however, stands altogether too close to its predecessors – the Tosefta, Sifra, the two Sifrés. How so? Just as they take shape essentially around the phrase-by-phrase exegesis of an established text, so, too, does Genesis Rabbah. The group that focuses upon the Mishnah adopts a rhetoric of word-for-word or phrase-by-phrase exegesis. The largest arena of discourse then is defined by a complete sentence or two, not a topic or a problem. In this regard, Genesis Rabbah takes only one step away from established conventions. It organizes ideas around a book other than a Mishnah tractate, the book of Genesis. That is stunning and original. But then the framers express their ideas in exactly the same rhetorical pattern – exegesis of words and phrases – that had long predominated in the study and amplification of the Mishnah. There are no large-scale discursive constructions on themes or problems, no evidences of a philosophical reading of Scripture such as Philo or Origen accomplished. It is only when we reach Leviticus Rabbah that we come to an essentially new situation.

II. A Sample of Leviticus Rabbah

Leviticus Rabbah deals with a biblical book, not a Mishnah tractate. But it approaches that book with a fresh plan, one in which exegesis does not dictate rhetoric, and in which amplification of an established text (whether Scripture or Mishnah) does not supply the underlying logic by which sentences are made to compose paragraphs, completed thoughts. To state matters affirmatively, the framers of Leviticus Rabbah treat topics, not particular verses. They make generalizations which are free-standing. They express cogent propositions through extended compositions, not episodic ideas. Earlier, things people wished to say were attached to predefined statements based on an existing text, constructed in accord with an organizing logic independent of the systematic expression of a single, well-framed idea. Now the authors so collect and arrange their materials that an abstract proposition emerges. That proposition is not expressed only or mainly through episodic restatements, assigned, as I said, to an order established by a base-text. Rather it emerges through a logic of its own. In this book I claim to uncover that logic that transforms exegesis of a biblical text into syllogistic, propositional discourse about the vivid issues of Israel's life, that is, that moves from Scripture to Judaism.

Before proceeding, let us consider a complete parashah of Leviticus Rabbah, taking account of the traits of its individual units and noting how it develops its large ideas. The translation is my own, based on the critical text and commentary of M. Margulies, Midrash Wayyikra Rabbah. A Critical Edition based on Manuscripts and Genizah Fragments, with Variants and Notes (Jerusalem, 1953). My individual comments on each unit of thought of the parashah should not obscure our main interest, which is to see how the plan of the framer of the document pursues a theme, rather than verse-by-verse exegesis of individual verses. The theme, moreover, does not impose an order based on the sequence of specific verses of Scripture. So the mode of organizing and laying out comments on Mishnah tractates, familiar in the Talmud of the Land of Israel and of Babylonia, and biblical books, well known in such exercises as Sifra on Leviticus, Sifré on Numbers, Sifré on Deuteronomy, and Genesis Rabbah, is abandoned. A quite different mode is at hand.

Parashah One I.I

1.   A.   "The Lord called Moses [and spoke to him from the tent of meeting, saying, 'Speak to the children of Israel and say to them, "When any

		man of you brings an offering to the Lord, you shall bring your offering of cattle from the herd or from the flock"']."

B. R. Tanhum bar Hinilai opened [discourse by citing the following verse:] "'Bless the Lord, you his messengers, you mighty in strength, carrying out his word, obeying his word' (Ps. 103:20).

C. "Concerning whom does Scripture speak?

D. "If [you maintain that] Scripture speaks about the upper world's creatures, [that position is unlikely, for] has not [Scripture in the very same passage already referred to them, in stating], 'Bless the Lord, all his hosts [his ministers, who do his word]' (Ps. 103:21)?

E. "If [you maintain that] Scripture speaks about the lower world's creatures, [that position, too, is unlikely,] for has not [Scripture in the very same passage already referred to them, in stating], 'Bless the Lord, [you] his messengers' (Ps. 103:20)? [Accordingly, concerning whom does Scripture speak?]

F. "[We shall now see that the passage indeed speaks of the lower ones.] But, since the upper world's creatures are perfectly able to fulfill the tasks assigned to them by the Holy One, blessed be He, therefore it is said, 'Bless the Lord, all of his hosts.' But as to the creatures of the lower world [here on earth], who cannot fulfill the tasks assigned to them by the Holy One, blessed be He, [the word all is omitted, when the verse of Scripture states,] 'Bless the Lord, [you] his messengers' – but not all of his messengers."

2. A. Another matter: Prophets are called messengers [creatures of the lower world], in line with the following passage, "And he sent a messenger and he took us forth from Egypt" (Num. 20:16).

B. Now was this a [heavenly] messenger, [an angel]? Was it not [merely] Moses [a creature of the lower world]?

C. Why then does [the verse of Scripture, referring to what Moses did,] call him a "messenger?"

D. But: It is on the basis of that usage that [we may conclude] prophets are called "messengers" [in the sense of creatures of the lower world].

E. "Along these same lines, 'And the messenger of the Lord came up from Gilgal to Bochim' (Judg. 2:1). Now was this a [heavenly] messenger, [an angel]? Was it not [merely] Phineas?

F. "Why then does [the verse of Scripture, referring to Phineas], call him a 'messenger?'"

G. Said R. Simon, "When the holy spirit rested upon Phineas, his face burned like a torch."

H. [There is better proof of the allegation concerning Phineas, deriving from an explicit reference, namely:] rabbis said, "What did Manoah's wife say to him [concerning Phineas]? 'Lo, a man of God came to me, and his face was like the face of a messenger of God' (Judg. 13:6).

I. [Rabbis continue,] "She was thinking that he was a prophet, but he was in fact a [heavenly] messenger [so the two looked alike to her]."

3. A. Said R. Yohanan, "From the passage that defines their very character, we derive evidence that the prophets are called 'messengers,' in line with the following passage: Then said

Leviticus Rabbah and the Hebrew Scriptures

		Haggai, the messenger of the Lord, in the Lord's agency, to the people, "I am with you, says the Lord" (Hag. 1:13).'
	B.	"Accordingly, you must reach the conclusion that on the basis of the passage that defines their very character, we prove that the prophets are called 'messengers.'"
4.	A.	[Reverting to the passage cited at the very outset,] "You mighty in strength, carrying out his word [obeying his word]" (Ps. 103:20).
	B.	Concerning what [sort of mighty man or hero] does Scripture speak?
	C.	Said R. Isaac, "Concerning those who observe the restrictions of the Seventh Year [not planting and sowing their crops in the Sabbatical Year] does Scripture speak.
	D.	"Under ordinary conditions a person does a religious duty for a day, a week, a month. But does one really do so for all of the days of an entire year?
	E.	"Now [in Aramaic:] this man sees his field lying fallow, his vineyard lying fallow, yet he pays his anona-tax [a share of the crop] and does not complain.
	F.	"[In Hebrew:] Do you know of a greater hero than that!"
	G.	Now if you maintain that Scripture does not speak about those who observe the Seventh Year, [I shall bring evidence that it does].
	H.	"Here it is stated, 'Carrying out his word' (Ps. 103:20) and with reference to the Seventh Year, it is stated, 'This is the word concerning the year of release' (Deut. 15:2).
	I.	"Just as the reference to 'word' stated at that passage applies to those who observe the Seventh Year, so reference to 'word' in the present passage applies to those who observe the Seventh Year."
5.	A.	[Continuing discussing of the passage cited at the outset:] "Carrying out his word" (Ps. 103:20):
	B.	R. Huna in the name of R. Aha: "It is concerning the Israelites who stood before Mount Sinai that Scripture speaks, for they first referred to doing [what God would tell them to do], and only afterward referred to hearing [what it might be], accordingly stating 'Whatever the Lord has said we shall carry out and we shall hear' (Ex. 24:7)."
6.	A.	[Continuing the same exercise:] "Obeying his word" (Ps. 103:20):
	B.	Said R. Tanhum bar Hinilai, "Under ordinary circumstances a burden which is too heavy for one person is light for two, or too heavy for two is light for four.
	C.	"But is it possible to suppose that a burden that is too weighty for six hundred thousand can be light for a single individual?
	D.	"Now the entire people of Israel were standing before Mount Sinai and saying, 'If we hear the voice of the Lord our God any more, then we shall die' (Deut. 5:22). But, [for his part], Moses heard the voice of God himself and lived.
	E.	"You may find evidence that that is the case, for, among all [the Israelites], the [Act of] Speech [of the Lord] called only to Moses, on which account it is stated, 'The Lord called Moses' (Lev. 1:1)."

Lev. 1:1 intersects with Ps. 103:20 to make the point that Moses was God's messenger par excellence, the one who blesses the Lord, is mighty

in strength, carries out God's word, obeys God's word. This point is made first at No. 1 by proving that the verse speaks of earthly, not heavenly, creatures. Then it is made explicit at No. 6. No. 1 presents two sets of proofs, 1.A-F and G-M. The second may stand by itself. It is only the larger context that suggests otherwise. No. 2-3 is continuous with 1.G-M, No. 3 is equally continuous with 1.G-M, to which explicit reference is made. No. 4 and No. 5 refer back to the cited verse, Ps. 103:20, but not to the context of Lev. 1:1. So we have these units:

1. A-F		Ps. 103:20 refers to earthly creatures.
1. G-M, 2, 3		Prophets are called messengers.
4		Ps. 103:20 refers to a mighty man who observes the Sabbatical Year.
5		Ps. 103:20 refers to the Israelites before Mount Sinai
6		Ps. 103:20 refers to Moses.

If then we ask what is primary to the redaction resting on Lev. 1:1, it can only be 1.A-F and 6. 1.A-F does not refer to Moses at all, but only sets up the point made at No. 6. No. 6 does not require No. 1. It makes its point without No. 1's contribution. Furthermore, No. 1, for its part, is comprehensible by itself as a comment on Ps. 103:20, and hardly requires linkage to Lev. 1:1. If, therefore, I may offer a thesis on the history of the passage, it would begin with Lev. 1:1 + No. 6. Reference to Ps. 103:20 then carried in its wake Nos. 1.A-F, G-M, 2, 3, 4, and 5 – all of them to begin with autonomous sayings formed into a kind of handbook on Ps. 103:20. So first came the intersection of Lev. 1:1 and Ps. 103:20 presented by No. 6, and everything else followed in the process of accretion and aggregation, mostly of passages in Ps. 103:20.

I:II

1. A. R. Abbahu opened [discourse by citing the following verse]: "'They shall return and dwell beneath his shadow, they shall grow grain, they shall blossom as a vine, their fragrance shall be like the wine of Lebanon' (Hos. 14:7).
    B. "'They shall return and dwell beneath his shadow' – these are proselytes who come and take refuge in the shadow of the Holy One, blessed be He.
    C. "'They shall grow grain' – they are turned into [part of] the root, just as [any other] Israelite.
    D. "That is in line with the following verse: 'Grain will make the young men flourish, and wine the women' (Zech. 9:17).
    E. "'They shall blossom as a vine' – like [any other] Israelite.
    F. "That is in line with the following verse: 'A vine did you pluck up out of Egypt, you did drive out the nations and plant it' (Ps. 80:9)."

2. A. Another item [= Genesis Rabbah 66:3]: "They shall grow grain" – in Talmud.
   B. "They shall blossom as a vine" – in lore.
3. A. "Their fragrance shall be like the wine of Lebanon [and Lebanon signifies the altar]" –
   B. Said the Holy One, blessed be He, "The names of proselytes are as dear to me as the wine-offering that is poured out on the altar before me."
4. A. And why [is that mountain called "Lebanon"?
   B. In line with [the following verse]: "That goodly mountain and the Lebanon" (Deut. 3:25).
   C. R. Simeon b. Yohai taught [= Sifré Deut. 6, 28], "Why is it called Lebanon (LBNN)? Because it whitens (MLBYN) the sins of Israel like snow.
   D. "That is in line with the following verse: 'If your sins are red as scarlet, they shall be made white (LBN) as snow' (Isa. 1:18)."
   E. R. Tabyomi said, "It is [called Lebanon (LBNN)] because all hearts (LBB) rejoice in it.
   F. "That is in line with the following verse of Scripture: 'Fair in situation, the joy of the whole world, even Mount Zion, at the far north' (Ps. 48:3)."
   G. And rabbis say, "It is [called Lebanon] because of the following verse: 'And my eyes and heart (LB) shall be there all the days' (1 Kgs. 9:3)."

So far as we have a sustained discourse, we find it at Nos. 1, 3. No. 2 is inserted whole because of its interest in the key verse, Hos. 14:7. Reference at that verse to "Lebanon" explains the set-piece treatment of the word at No. 4. These units may travel together, but the present location seems an unlikely destination. But someone clearly drew together this anthology of materials on, first, Hos. 14:7, and, by the way, second, the word Lebanon. Why the two sets were assembled is much clearer than how they seemed to the compositor of the collection as a whole to belong to the exposition of Lev. 1:1. Margulies' thesis that the theme of the righteous proselyte intersects with the personal biography of Moses through Pharaoh's daughter (a proselyte!) on the surface seems farfetched. So, in all, the construction of the passage surely is prior to any consideration of its relevance to Lev. 1:1, and the point of the construction certainly is the exegesis of Hos. 14:7 – that alone. Whether the materials shared with other collections – Nos. 2, 5 – fit more comfortably in those compositions than they do here is not a pressing issue, since, as is self-evident, there is no link to Lev. 1:1 anyhow.

I:III

1. A. R. Simon in the name of R. Joshua b. Levi, and R. Hama, father of R. Hoshaiah, in the name of Rab: "The Book of Chronicles was revealed only for the purposes of exegetical exposition."

2. A. "And his wife Hajehudijah bore Jered, the father of Gedor, and Heber, the father of Soco, and Jekuthiel the father of Zanoah – and these are the sons of Bithiah, the daughter of Pharaoh, whom Mered took" (1 Chr. 4:17).
   B. "And his wife, Hajehudijah [= the Judah-ite]" – that is Jochebed.
   C. Now was she from the tribe of Judah, and not from the tribe of Levi? Why then was she called Hajehudijah [the Judah-ite]?
   D. Because she kept Jews (Jehudim) alive in the world [as one of the midwives who kept the Jews alive when Pharaoh said to drown them].
3. A. "She bore Jered" – that is Moses.
   B. R. Hanana bar Papa and R. Simon:
   C. R. Hanana said, "He was called Jered (YRD) because he brought the Torah down (HWRYD) from on high to earth."
   D. "Another possibility: 'Jered' – for he brought down the Presence of God from above to earth."
   E. Said R. Simon, "The name Jered connotes only royalty, in line with the following verse: 'May he have dominion (YRD) from sea to sea, and from the river to the end of the earth' (Ps. 72:8).
   F. "And it is written, 'For he rules (RWDH) over the entire region on this side of the River' (1 Kgs. 5:4)."
4. A. "Father of Gedor" –
   B. R. Huna in the name of R. Aha said, "Many fence-makers (GWDRYM) stood up for Israel, but this one [Moses] was the father of all of them."
5. A. "And Heber" –
   B. For he joined (HBR) Israel to their father in Heaven.
   C. Another possibility: "Heber" – for he turned away punishment from coming upon the world.
6. A. "The father of Soco" –
   B. This one was the father of all the prophets, who perceive (SWKYN) by means of the holy spirit.
   C. R. Levi said, "It is an Arabic word. In Arabic they call a prophet 'sakya.'"
7. A. "Jekuthiel" (YQWTY'L) –
   B. R. Levi and R. Simon:
   C. R. Levi said, "For he made the children hope (MQWYN) in their Father in Heaven."
   D. Said R. Simon, "When the children sinned against God in the incident of the Golden Calf...."
   E. "'The father of Zanoah' –
   F. "Moses came along and forced them to give up (HZNYHN) that transgression.
   G. "That is in line with the following verse of Scripture: '[And he took the calf which they had made and burned it with fire and ground it to powder] and strewed it upon the water' (Ex. 32:20)."
8. A. "And these are the sons of Bithiah, the daughter of Pharaoh" –
   B. R. Joshua of Sikhnin in the name of R. Levi: "The Holy One, blessed be He, said to Bithiah, the daughter of Pharaoh, 'Moses was not your child, but you called him your child. So you are not my

Leviticus Rabbah and the Hebrew Scriptures

		daughter, but I shall call you my daughter' [thus BT\YH, daughter of the Lord]."
9.	A.	"These are the sons of Bithiah...whom Mered took" –
	B.	[Mered] is Caleb.
	C.	R. Abba bar Kahana and R. Judah bar Simon:
	D.	R. Abba bar Kahana said, "This one [Caleb] rebelled [MRD] against the counsel of the spies, and that one rebelled [MRDH] against the counsel of her father [Pharaoh, as to murdering the babies]. Let a rebel come and take as wife another rebellious spirit."
	E.	[Explaining the link of Caleb to Pharaoh's daughter in a different way], R. Judah b. R. Simon said, "This one [Caleb] saved the flock, while that one [Pharaoh's daughter] saved the shepherd [Moses]. Let the one who saved the flock come and take as wife the one who saved the shepherd."
10.	A.	Moses [thus] had ten names [at 1 Chr. 4:17]: Jered, Father of Gedor, Heber, Father of Soco, Jekuthiel, and Father of Zanoah [with the other four enumerated in what follows].
	B.	R. Judah bar Ilai said, "He also was called [7] Tobiah, in line with the following verse: 'And she saw him, that he was good (TWB)' (Ex. 2:2). He is Tobiah."
	C.	R. Ishmael bar Ami said, "He also was called [8] Shemaiah."
11.	A.	R. Joshua bar Nehemiah came and explained the following verse: "'And Shemaiah, the son of Nethanel the scribe, who was of the Levites, wrote them in the presence of the king and the princes and Zadok the priest and Ahimelech the son of Abiathar' (1 Chr. 24:6).
	B.	"[Moses was called] Shemaiah because God heard his prayer.
	C.	"[Moses was called] the son of Nethanel because he was the son to whom the Torah was given from hand to hand.
	D.	"'The scribe,' because he was the scribe of Israel.
	E.	"'Who was of the Levites,' because he was of the tribe of Levi.
	F.	"'Before the king and the princes' – this refers to the King of kings of kings, the Holy One, blessed be He, and his court.
	G.	"'And Sadoq the priest' – this refers to Aaron the priest.
	H.	"'Ahimeleh' – because [Aaron] was brother ('H) of the king.
	I.	"'The son of Abiathar' ('BYTR) – the son through whom the Holy One, blessed be He, forgave (WYTR) the deed of the Golden Calf."
12.	A.	R. Tanhuma in the name of R. Joshua b. Qorhah, and R. Menehemiah in the name of R. Joshua b. Levi: "He also was called [9] Levi after his eponymous ancestor: 'And is not Aaron, your brother, the Levite' (Ex. 4:14)."
	B.	And [he of course was called] [10] Moses – hence [you have] ten names.
	C.	Said the Holy One, blessed be He, to Moses, "By your life! Among all the names by which you are called, the only one by which I shall ever refer to you is the one which Bithiah, the daughter of Pharaoh, gave to you: 'And she called his name Moses' (Ex. 2:10)," so God called Moses.
	D.	So: "He called Moses" (Lev. 1:1).

Now we see some slight basis for Margulies' view of the relevance of I:II, that the daughter of Pharaoh named Moses, and she was a proselyte.

But the passage at hand stands fully by itself, leading to the climax at the very end, at which the opening words of the opening verse of the book of Leviticus are cited. The point of the entire, vast construction is the inquiry into the various names of Moses. From that standpoint we have a strikingly tight composition. But still, the unit is a composite, since it draws together autonomous and diverse materials. The first passage, No. 1, is surely independent, yet it makes for a fine superscription to the whole. Then the pertinent verse, at No. 2.A, 1 Chr. 4:17, is cited and systematically spelled out, Nos. 2, 3, 4, 5, 6, 7, 8, 9. Not only so, but at No. 10, we review the matter and amplify it with an additional, but completely appropriate, set of further names of Moses, Nos. 10 + 12, to be viewed, in line with No. 12, as a unified construction. No. 11 is inserted and breaks the thought. Then 12.C tells us the point of it all, and that brings us back to Lev. 1:1, on the one side, and to No. 8. But, as we have seen, we cannot refer to No. 8 without drawing along the whole set, Nos. 2-9. So the entire passage forms a single, sustained discussion, in which diverse materials are determinedly drawn together into a cogent statement. We notice that No. 7 presents a text problem, since Levi's statement is not matched by Simon's. Levi speaks of Jekuthiel and Simon of "the father of Zanoah." But the only problem is at 7.B. If we omit that misleading superscription – which served perfectly well at 3.B + C-F – and have 7.D and E change places, we get a perfectly fine autonomous statement.

I:IV

1. A. R. Abin in the name of R. Berekhiah the Elder opened [discourse by citing the following verse]: "'Of old you spoke in a vision to your faithful one, saying, "I have set the crown upon one who is mighty, I have exalted one chosen from the people" (Ps. 89:20).'
   B. "[The Psalmist] speaks of Abraham, with whom [God] spoke both in word and in vision.
   C. "That is in line with the following verse of Scripture: 'After these words the word of God came to Abram in a vision, saying...' (Gen. 15:1).
   D. "'...To your faithful one' – 'You will show truth to Jacob, faithfulness to Abraham' (Mic. 7:20).
   E. "'...Saying, "I have set the crown upon one who is mighty" – for [Abraham] slew four kings in a single night.'
   F. "That is in line with the following verse of Scripture: 'And he divided himself against them by night...and smote them' (Gen. 14:15)."
2. A. Said R. Phineas, "And is there a case of someone who pursues people already slain?
   B. "For it is written, 'He smote them and he [then] pursued them' (Gen. 14:15)!

Leviticus Rabbah and the Hebrew Scriptures

	C.	"But [the usage at hand] teaches that the Holy One, blessed be He, did the pursuing, and Abraham did the slaying.
3.	A.	[Abin continues,] "'I have exalted one chosen from the people' (Ps. 89:20).
	B.	"'It is you, Lord, God, who chose Abram and took him out of Ur in Chaldea' (Neh. 9:7).''
4.	A.	["I have exalted one chosen from the people" (Ps. 89:20)] speaks of David, with whom God spoke both in speech and in vision.
	B.	That is in line with the following verse of Scripture: "In accord with all these words and in accord with this entire vision, so did Nathan speak to David" (2 Sam. 7:17).
	C.	"To your faithful one" (Ps. 89:20) [refers] to David, [in line with the following verse:] "Keep my soul, for I am faithful" (Ps. 86:2).
	D.	"...Saying, 'I have set the crown upon one who is mighty" (Ps. 89:20) –
	E.	R. Abba bar Kahana and rabbis:
	F.	R. Abba bar Kahana said, "David made thirteen wars."
	G.	And rabbis say, "Eighteen."
	H.	But they do not really differ. The party who said thirteen wars [refers only to those that were fought] in behalf of the need of Israel [overall], while the one who held that [he fought] eighteen includes five [more, that David fought] for his own need, along with the thirteen [that he fought] for the need of Israel [at large].
	I.	"I have exalted one chosen from the people" (Ps. 89:20) – "And he chose David, his servant, and he took him..." (Ps. 78:70).
5.	A.	["Of old you spoke in a vision to your faithful one..."] speaks of Moses, with whom [God] spoke in both speech and vision, in line with the following verse of Scripture: "With him do I speak mouth to mouth [in a vision and not in dark speeches]" (Num. 12:8).
	B.	"To your faithful one" – for [Moses] came from the tribe of Levi, the one concerning which it is written, "Let your Thummim and Urim be with your faithful one" (Deut. 33:8).
	C.	"...Saying, 'I have set the crown upon one who is mighty'" –
	D.	The cited passage is to be read in accord with that which R. Tanhum b. Hanilai said, "Under ordinary circumstances a burden which is too heavy for one person is light for two, or too heavy for two is light for four. But is it possible to suppose that a burden that is too weighty for six hundred thousand can be light for a single individual? Now the entire people of Israel were standing before Mount Sinai and saying, 'If we hear the voice of the Lord our God any more, then we shall die' (Deut. 5:22). But, for his part, Moses heard the voice of God himself and lived" [= I:I.6.B-D].
	E.	You may know that that is indeed the case, for among them all, the act of speech [of the Lord] called only to Moses, in line with that verse which states, "And [God] called to Moses" (Lev. 1:1).
	F.	"I have exalted one chosen from the people" (Ps. 89:20) – "Had not Moses, whom he chose, stood in the breach before him to turn his wrath from destroying them" [he would have destroyed Israel] (Ps. 106:23).

The whole constitutes a single, beautifully worked out composition, applying Ps. 89:20 to Abraham, David, then Moses, at Nos. 1, 3 (Abraham), 4 (David), and 5 (Moses). No. 2 is a minor interpolation, hardly spoiling the total effect. No. 5.D is jarring and obviously inserted needlessly. That the purpose of the entire construction was to lead to the climactic citation of Lev. 1:1 hardly can be doubted, since the natural chronological (and eschatological) order would have dictated Abraham, Moses, David. That the basic construction, moreover, forms a unity is shown by the careful matching of the stichs of the cited verse in the expositions of how the verse applies to the three heroes. If we had to postulate an "ideal form," it would be simply the juxtaposition of verses, A illustrated by X, B by Y, etc., with little or no extraneous language. But where, in the basic constituents of the construction, we do find explanatory language or secondary development, in the main it is necessary for sense. Accordingly, we see as perfect a construction as we are likely to find: whole, nearly entirely essential, with a minimum of intruded material. To be sure, what really looks to be essential is the notion of God's communicating by two media to the three great heroes. That is the clear point of the most closely corresponding passages of the whole. In that case, the reorganization and vast amplification come as an afterthought, provoked by the construction of a passage serving Lev. 1:1. Since 5.E contradicts the message of the rest, that must be regarded as a certainty. Then the whole, except 5.E (hence, 5.D, too) served Ps. 89:20, and 5.F is the original conclusion, with 5.D-E inserted by the redactor.

I:V

1. A. R. Joshua of Sikhnin in the name of R. Levi opened [discourse by citing the following] verse: "'For it is better to be told, "Come up here," than to be put lower in the presence of the prince' (Prov. 25:7)."
   B. R. Aqiba repeated [the following tradition] in the name of R. Simeon b. Azzai, "Take a place two or three lower and sit down, so that people may tell you, 'Come up,' but do not go up [beyond your station] lest people say to you, 'Go down.' It is better for people to say to you, 'Come up, come up,' than that they say to you, 'Go down, go down.'"
   C. And so did Hillel say, "When I am degraded, I am exalted, but when I am exalted, I am degraded."
   D. What is the pertinent biblical verse? "He who raises himself is to be made to sit down, he who lowers himself is to be [raised so that he is] seen" (Ps. 113:5).
   E. So, too, you find that, when the Holy One, blessed be He, revealed himself to Moses from the midst of the bush, Moses hid his face from him.
   F. That is in line with the following verse of Scripture: "Moses hid his face" (Ex. 3:6).

2. A. Said to him the Holy One, blessed be He, "And now, go (LKH), I am sending you to Pharaoh" (Ex. 3:10).
   B. Said R. Eleazar, "[Taking the word 'Go,' LK, not as the imperative, but to mean, 'to you,' and spelled LKH, with an H at the end, I may observe that] it would have been sufficient to write, 'You (LK),' [without adding] an H at the end of the word. [Why then did Scripture add the H?] To indicate to you, 'If you are not the one who will redeem them, no one else is going to redeem them.'
   C. "At the Red Sea, Moses stood aside. Said to him the Holy One, blessed be He, 'Now you, raise your rod and stretch out your hand [over the sea and divide it]' (Ex. 14:16).
   D. "This is to say, 'If you do not split the sea, no one else is going to split it.'
   E. "At Sinai Moses stood aside. Said to him the Holy One, blessed be He, 'Come up to the Lord, you and Aaron' (Ex. 24:1).
   F. "This is to say, 'If you do not come up, no one else is going to come up.'
   G. "At the [revelation of the instructions governing sacrifices at] the tent of meeting, [Moses] stood to the side. Said to him the Holy One, blessed be He, 'How long are you going to humble yourself? For the times demand only you.'
   H. "You must recognize that that is the case, for among them all, the speech of God called only to Moses, as it is written, 'And [God] called to Moses' (Lev. 1:1)."

We have once more to work backward from the end to find out what, at the outset, is necessary to make the point of the unit as a whole. It obviously is the emphasis upon how the humble man is called to take exalted position and leadership, that is, No. 2. Then what components of No. 1 are thematically irrelevant? None, so far as I can see. We may regard 1.A as standing by itself, a suitable introduction to a statement on the theme at hand, namely, it is better to be called upon, as at Lev. 1:1. Then Nos. 1.B, C-D, E-F illustrate the same theme, leading to the introduction of the figure of Moses. E-F are so formulated ("so, too, you find") as to continue the foregoing, but, of course, they form a bridge to what follows, No. 2. Accordingly, a rather deft editorial hand has drawn together thematically pertinent materials. I find it difficult to imagine that the composition was not worked out essentially within a unitary framework, with the exegetical program of the whole, expressed at No. 2, fully in hand before the anthology of No. 1 was gathered. But the fact is that Nos. 1.B, C-D, do come from already-framed materials.

I:VI

1. A. R. Tanhuma opened [discourse by citing the following verse:] "'There are gold and a multitude of rubies, but lips [that speak] knowledge are the [most] valuable ornament' (Prov. 20:15).

	B.	"Under ordinary circumstances [if] a person has gold, silver, precious stones, pearls, and all sorts of luxuries, but has no knowledge – what profit does he have?
	C.	"In a proverb it says, 'If you have gotten knowledge, what do you lack? But if you lack knowledge, what have you gotten?'"
2.	A.	"There is gold" – all brought their freewill-offering of gold to the tabernacle.
	B.	That is in line with the following verse of Scripture: "And this is the offering [which you shall take from them, gold]..." (Ex. 25:3).
	C.	"And a multitude of rubies" – this refers to the freewill-offering of the princes.
	D.	That is in line with the following verse of Scripture: "And the rulers brought [onyx stones and the stones to be set]" (Ex. 35:27).
	E.	"But lips [that speak] knowledge are the [most] valuable ornament" (Prov. 20:15).
	F.	Now Moses was sad, for he said, "Everyone has brought his freewill-offering for the tabernacle, but I have not brought a thing!"
	G.	Said to him the Holy One, blessed be He, "By your life! Your words [of address to the workers in teaching them how to build the tabernacle] are more precious to me than all of these other things."
	H.	You may find proof for that proposition, for among all of them, the Word [of God] called only to Moses, as it is written, "And [God] called to Moses" (Lev. 1:1).

Once more we see a complete construction, with a seemingly irrelevant introduction, No. 1, serving to cite a verse in no way evoked by the passage at hand. The exposition of the verse, further, does not appear to bring us closer to the present matter. But at No. 2, both the cited verse and the exposition of the verse are joined to the verse before us. If we may venture a guess at the aesthetic jeu d'esprit involved, it is this: how do we move from what appears to be utterly irrelevant to what is in fact the very heart of the matter? The aesthetic accomplishment is then to keep the hearer or reader in suspense until the climax, at which the issue is worked out, the tension resolved. It must follow, of course, that we deal with unitary composition.

I:VII

1.	A.	What subject matter is discussed just prior to the passage at hand? It is the passage that deals with the building of the tabernacle [in which each pericope concludes with the words,] "As the Lord commanded Moses" (cf. Ex. 38:22; 39:1, 5, 7, 21, 26, 29, 31, 32, 42, 43; 40:16, 19, 21, 23, 25, 27, 29, 32).
	B.	To what may this matter be compared? To a king who commanded his servant, saying to him, "Build a palace for me."
	C.	On everything that [the employee] built, he wrote the name of the king. When he built the walls, he inscribed the name of the king, when he set up the buttresses, he wrote the name of the king on them, when he roofed it over, he wrote the name of the king on [the roof]. After some days, the king came into the palace, and

Leviticus Rabbah and the Hebrew Scriptures 83

	everywhere he looked, he saw his name inscribed. He said, "Now my employee has paid me so much respect, and yet I am inside [the building he built], while he is outside!" He called him to enter.
D.	So when the Holy One, blessed be He, called to Moses, "Make a tabernacle for me," on [every] thing that Moses made, he inscribed, "...as the Lord commanded Moses."
E.	Said the Holy One, blessed be He, "Now Moses has paid me so much respect, and yet I am inside, while he is outside!"
F.	He called him to come in, on which account it is said, "And [God] called Moses" (Lev. 1:1).

The passage begins with the imputation to the verb QR' of the sense of invitation. The focus of exegesis shifts from Moses to God's calling him. The exegetical resource is the repeated reference, as indicated, to Moses' doing as God had commanded him. But this is now read as Moses' inscribing God's name everywhere on the tabernacle as he built it, and the rest follows.

I:VIII

1.	A.	R. Samuel bar Nahman said in the name of R. Nathan, "Eighteen times are statements of [God's] commanding written in the passage on the building of the tabernacle, corresponding to the eighteen vertebrae in the backbone.
	B.	"Correspondingly, sages instituted eighteen statements of blessing in the Blessings of the Prayer, eighteen mentions of the divine name in the recitation of the Shema, eighteen mentions of the divine name in the Psalm, 'Ascribe to the Lord, you sons of might' (Ps. 29)."
	C.	Said R. Hiyya bar Ada, "[The counting of the eighteen statements of God's commandment to Moses] excludes [from the count the entry prior to the one in the verse], 'And with him was Oholiab, son of Ahisamach of the tribe of Dan' (Ex. 38:23), [thus omitting reference to Ex. 38:22, 'And Bezalel, son or Uri son of Hur of the tribe of Judah, made all that the Lord commanded Moses']. [But the counting then includes all further such references to the end of the book [of Exodus]."
2.	A.	To what is the matter comparable? To a king who made a tour of a province, bringing with him generals, governors, and lesser officers, and, [in watching the procession], we do not know which one among them is most favored. But [when we see] to whom the king turns and speaks, we know that he is the favorite.
	B.	So everyone surrounded the tabernacle, Moses, Aaron, Nadab and Abihu, and the seventy elders, so we do not know which one of them is the favorite. But now, since the Holy One, blessed be He, called to Moses and spoke to him, we know that he was the favorite of them all.
	C.	On that account it is said, "And [God] called Moses" (Lev. 1:1).
3.	A.	To what may the matter be compared? To a king who made a tour of a province. With whom will he speak first? Is it not with the market inspector, who oversees the province? Why? Because he bears responsibility for the very life of the province.

84   *Sources of the Transformation of Judaism*

      B.   So Moses bears responsibility for Israel's every burden,
      C.   saying to them, "This you may eat" (Lev. 11:2), "And this you may not eat" (Lev. 11:4), "This you may eat of whatever is in the water" (Lev. 11:9), and this you may not eat, "This you shall treat as an abomination among fowl" (Lev. 11:13), and so these you shall treat as an abomination, and others you need not abominate, "And these are the things that are unclean for you" (Lev. 11:29), so these are unclean, and those are not unclean.
      D.   Therefore it is said, "And [God] called Moses" (Lev. 1:1).

No. 1 bears no relationship to what follows. It continues I:VII, with its interest in the repetitions of the statement about Moses' having done as God had commanded him. 1.A-B however stand completely outside the present frame of reference, Lev. 1:1. 1.C harmonizes the number of times the cited phrase actually occurs with the number of vertebrae in the backbone. No. 1 further occurs at B. Ber. 28b, Y. Ber. 4:3, so we may be certain the passage was tacked on because of the interest in the verse at the center of the preceding item.

No. 2 and No. 3 match one another, making essentially the same point and leading up to the citation of the verse by establishing the same connotation, "called" in the sense of "recognized, gave preference to." 3.C is wildly out of place, since, as it is now composed, the emphasis is on the fact that, if Scripture says you may not eat a certain thing, whatever is not covered in the negative statement then may be eaten. That is why the language of the verse is repeated, "...not this...but then that is permitted." In fact, we should move from 3.A-B to D. The passage as a whole then is a composite of three distinct items.

I:IX

1.   A.   "And [the Lord] called to Moses" (Lev. 1:1) [bearing the implication, to Moses in particular].
      B.   Now did he not call Adam? [But surely he did:] "And the Lord God called Adam" (Gen. 3:9).
      C.   [He may have called him, but he did not speak with him, while at Lev. 1:1, the Lord "called Moses and spoke to him"], for is it not undignified for a king to speak with his tenant farmer [which Adam, in the Garden of Eden, was]?
      D.   "...And the Lord spoke to him" (Lev. 1:1) [to him in particular].
      E.   Did he not speak also with Noah? [But surely he did:] "And God speak to Noah" (Gen. 8:15).
      F.   [He may have spoken to him, but he did not call him,] for is it not undignified for a king to speak with [better: call] his ship's captain [herding the beasts into the ark]?
      G.   "And [the Lord] called to Moses" (Lev. 1:1) [in particular].
      H.   Now did he not call Abraham? [But surely he did:] "And the angel of the Lord called Abraham a second time from heaven" (Gen. 22:15).

Leviticus Rabbah and the Hebrew Scriptures

	I.	[He may have called him, but he did not speak with him,] for is it not undignified for a king to speak with his host [Gen. 18:1]?
	J.	"And the Lord spoke with him" (Lev. 1:1) [in particular].
	K.	And did he not speak with Abraham? [Surely he did:] "And Abram fell on his face, and [God] spoke with him" (Gen. 17:3).
	L.	But is it not undignified for a king to speak with his host?
2.	A.	"And the Lord called Moses" (Lev. 1:1), but not as in the case of Abraham.
	B.	[How so?] In the case of Abraham, it is written, "And an angel of the Lord called Abraham a second time from heaven" (Gen. 22:15). The angel did the calling, the the Word [of God] then did the speaking.
	C.	"Here, [by contrast,]" said R. Abin, "the Holy One, blessed be He, said, 'I am the one who does the calling, and I am the one who does the speaking.'
	D.	"'I, even I, have spoken, yes, I have called him, I have brought him and he shall prosper in his way' (Isa. 48:15)."

The point of No. 1 is clear, but the text is not. What is demanded is three instances in which God called someone but did not speak with him, or spoke with him but did not call him, in contrast with the use of both verbs, "call" and "speak," in regard to Moses at Lev. 1:1. If that is what is intended, then the pattern does not work perfectly for all three: Adam, Noah, and Abraham. 1.A-D and E-G are smooth. With Abraham, however, the exposition breaks down, since the point should be that he called Abraham but did not actually speak with him, and it is only No. 2 that makes that point. We can readily reconstruct what is needed, of course, in the model of the passages for Adam and Noah.

No. 2 of course is independent of No. 1, and handsomely worked out. But No. 2 cannot have served the form selected by the framer of the triplet at No. 1.

My guess is that No. 1 fails as it does because of yet another problem. F does have God speaking with Noah, while G says that that is undignified, and the same problem recurs with Abraham. In all, No. 2 is a success, and No. 1 is not. Here it is difficult to claim that someone deliberately worked up the entire unit, leading to the climax at the very end. Two existing sets have been combined, and the first of the two turns out to be flawed.

I:X

1.	A.	"[And the Lord called Moses and spoke to him] from the tent of meeting" (Lev. 1:1).
	B.	Said R. Eleazar, "Even though the Torah [earlier] had been given to Israel at Sinai as a fence [restricting their actions], they were liable to punishment on account of [violating] it only after it has been repeated for [taught to] them in the tent of meeting.

- C. "This may be compared to a royal decree, that had been written and sealed and brought to the province. The inhabitants of the province became liable to be punished on account of violating the decree only after it had been spelled out for them in a public meeting in the province.
- D. "Along these same lines, even though the Torah had been given to Israel at Sinai, they bore liability for punishment on account of violating it[s commandments] only after it had been repeated for them in the tent of meeting.
- E. "That is in line with the following verse of Scripture: 'Until I had brought him into my mother's house and into the chamber of my teaching [lit.: parent]' (Song 3:4).
- F. "'...Into my mother's house' refers to Sinai.
- G. "'...And into the chamber of my teaching' refers to the tent of meeting, from which the Israelites were commanded through instruction [in the Torah]."

The passage is formally perfect, running from the beginning, a general proposition, 1.B, through a parable, C, explicitly linked to the original proposition, D, and then joined to the exposition of a seemingly unrelated verse of Scripture, which turns out to say exactly what the general proposition has said. So the original statement, B, is worked out in two separate and complementary ways, first, parabolic, second, exegetical.

I cannot see any problem but one: What has the stated proposition to do with the present context? In fact, the theme is the tent of meeting, that alone. We may expect an anthology of materials on the tent of meeting, none of which bears any distinctive relationship to what happens there, so far as Lev. 1:1ff. will tell us. In other words, the redaction of materials following the order of verses of Scripture in the present instance imposes no thesis upon what will be said about those materials, what is important in them. Rather we have nothing more than a list of topics, each to be treated through the formation of an anthology of materials relevant to a topic, not through the unpacking of a problematic indicated by the substance and the context at hand.

I:XI

1.
   - A. Said R. Joshua b. Levi, "If the nations of the world had known how valuable the tent of meeting was to them, they would have sheltered it with tents and ballustrades.
   - B. "[How so?] You note that before the tabernacle was erected, the nations of the world could hear the noise of [God's] speech and [fearing an earthquake(?)] they would rush out of their dwellings.
   - C. "That is in line with the following verse of Scripture: 'For who is there of all flesh, who has heard the voice of the living God [speaking out of the midst of the first as we have, and lived]?' (Deut. 5:23)."

2. A. Said R. Simon, "The word [of God] went forth in two modes, for Israel as life, for the nations of the world as poison.
   B. "That is in line with the following verse of Scripture: '...As you have, and lived' (Deut. 4:33).
   C. "You hear [the voice of God] and live, while the nations of the world hear and die."
   D. That is in line with what R. Hiyya taught [= Sifra Dibura dinedabah 2:10], "'...from the tent of meeting' (Lev. 1:1) teaches that the sound was cut off and did not go beyond the tent of meeting."

Nos. 1 and 2 go over the same ground but are unrelated. For the sense of 1.B, I follow Margulies. But then the relevance of the verse cited at 1.C is not clear. I should have thought that the nations of the world would benefit from the possibility of hearing God's speech, which would then have warned them about an impending earthquake, for example, getting them out of their houses in time. But 1.C and No. 2 make the point that the tent of meeting prevented the gentiles from hearing God's voice, and this was good for them, since the Torah was life for Israel and death for the gentiles. Accordingly, the sense of 1.B as Margulies reads it seems incongruous to the meaning required by its context. Israelstam (p. 14) gives: "...rushed in fright out of their camps." I cannot suggest anything better. As noted above, the larger context of Lev. 1:1 makes no impact upon the exegesis of the passage, which is focused upon the theme, the tent of meeting, and not on the meaning of the place or tent in this setting.

I:XII

1. A. Said R. Isaac, "Before the tent of meeting was set up, prophecy was common among the nations of the world. Once the tent of meeting was set up, prophecy disappeared from among them. That is in line with the following verse of Scripture: 'I held it' [the holy spirit, producing], 'and would not let it go [until I had brought it...into the chamber of her that conceived me]' (Song 3:4)."
   B. They said to him, "Lo, Balaam [later on] practiced prophecy!"
   C. He said to them, "He did so for the good of Israel: 'Who has counted the dust of Jacob' (Num. 23:10). 'No one has seen iniquity in Jacob' (Num. 23:21). 'For there is no enchantment with Jacob' (Num. 23:23). 'How goodly are your tents, O Jacob' (Num. 24:5). 'There shall go forth a star out of Jacob' (Num. 24:17). 'And out of Jacob shall one have dominion' (Num. 24:19)."

"The chamber" of 1.A is the tent of meeting, as before. In fact the passage at hand is continuous with the foregoing. As we shall see, the established theme then moves forward in what follows. The construction is of course unitary. "They said to him" of B simply sets up discourse; it is not meant to signify an actual conversation, rather it serves as a convention of rhetoric. B then allows C to string out the relevant verses.

We now continue the same matter of Balaam, prophet of the gentiles, and Israel.

I:XIII

1. A. What is the difference between the prophets of Israel and those of the nations [= Gen. R. 52:5]?
   B. R. Hama b. R. Haninah and R. Issachar of Kepar Mandi:
   C. R. Hama b. R. Hanina said, "The Holy One, blessed be He, is revealed to the prophets of the nations of the world only in partial speech, in line with the following verse of Scripture: 'And God called [WYQR, rather than WYQR', as at Lev. 1:1] Balaam' (Num. 23:16). On the other hand, [he reveals himself] to the prophets of Israel in full and complete speech, as it is said, 'And [the Lord] called (WYQR') to Moses' (Lev. 1:1)."
   D. Said R. Issachar of Kepar Mandi, "Should that [prophecy, even in partial form] be [paid to them as their] wage? [Surely not, in fact there is no form of speech to gentile prophets, who are frauds]. [The connotation of] the language, 'And [God] called (WYQR) to Balaam' (Num. 23:16) is solely uncleanness. That is in line with the usage in the following verse of Scripture: 'That is not clean, by that which happens (MQRH) by night' (Deut. 23:11). [So the root is the same, with the result that YQR at Num. 23:16 does not bear the meaning of God's calling to Balaam. God rather declares Balaam unclean.]
   E. "But the prophets of Israel [are addressed] in language of holiness, purity, clarity, in language used by the ministering angels to praise God. That is in line with the following verse of Scripture: 'And they called (QR') one to another and said' (Isa. 6:3)."
2. A. Said R. Eleazar b. Menahem, "It is written, 'The Lord is far from the evil, but the prayer of the righteous does he hear' (Prov. 5:29).
   B. "'The Lord is far from the wicked' refers to the prophets of the nations of the world.
   C. "'But the prayer of the righteous does he hear' refers to the prophets of Israel.
   D. "You [furthermore] find that the Holy One, blessed be He, appears to the prophets of the nations of the world only like a man who comes from some distant place.
   E. "That is in line with the following verse of Scripture: 'From a distant land they have come to me, from Babylonia' (Isa. 39:3).
   F. "But in the case of the prophets of Israel [he is always] near at hand: 'And he [forthwith] appeared [not having come from a great distance]' (Gen. 18:1), 'and [the Lord] called' (Lev. 1:1)."
3. A. Said R. Yose b. Biba, "The Holy One, blessed be He, is revealed to the prophets of the nations of the world only by night, when people leave one another: 'When men branch off, from the visions of the night, when deep sleep falls on men' (Job 4:13), 'Then a word came secretly to me' (Job 4:12). [Job is counted among the prophets of the gentiles.]"
4. A. R. Hanana b. R. Pappa and rabbis [= Gen. R. 74:7]:
   B. R. Hanana b. R. Pappa said, "The matter may be compared to a king who, with his friend, was in a hall, with a curtain hanging down

		between them. When [the king] speaks to his friend, he turns back the curtain and speaks with his friend."
	C.	And rabbis say, "[The matter may be compared] to a king who had a wife and a concubine. When he walks about with his wife, he does so in full public view. When he walks about with his concubine, he does so discreetly. So, too, the Holy One, blessed be He, is revealed to the prophets of the nations of the world only at night, in line with that which is written: 'And God came to Abimelech in a dream by night' (Gen. 29:3). 'And God came to Laban, the Aramean, in a dream by night' (Gen. 22:24). 'And God came to Balaam at night' (Num. 22:20).
	D.	"To the prophets of Israel, however, [he comes] by day: '[And the Lord appeared to Abraham...] as he sat at the door of his tent in the heat of the day' (Gen. 18:1). 'And it came to pass by day that the Lord spoke to Moses in the land of Egypt' (Ex. 6:28). 'On the day on which he commanded the children of Israel' (Lev. 6:38). 'These are the generations of Aaron and Moses. God spoke to Moses by day on Mount Sinai' (Num. 3:1)."

Once the topic of comparing Israel's receiving of revelation to that of the nations of the world has arisen, at I:XII, we pursue it further, and, as we shall see, I:XIV adds still more pertinent material. We have a fine superscription, 1.A, with three independent items strung together, 1.B-D, 2, 3, and 4. Nos. 1.B-D, 4, follow an obvious, simple pattern, and Nos. 2, 3 simply assign a protracted saying to a given name. We have no reason to suppose the entire set has come from a single hand. Since the same points are made by two or more authorities, it is likely that a redactor has chosen pertinent materials out of what he had available.

I:XIV

1.	A	What is the difference between Moses and all the other [Israelite] prophets?
	B.	R. Judah b. R. Ilai and rabbis:
	C.	R. Judah said, "All the other prophets saw [their visions] through nine mirrors [darkly], in line with the following verse of Scripture: 'And the appearance of the vision which I saw was like the vision that I saw when I came to destroy the city; and the visions were like the vision that I saw by the River Chebar, and I fell on my face' (Ex. 43:3) [with the root R'H occurring once in the plural, hence two, and seven other times in the singular, nine in all].
	D.	"But Moses saw [his vision] through a single mirror: 'In [one vision] and not in dark speeches' (Num. 12:8)."
	E.	Rabbis said, "All other [Israelite] prophets saw [their visions] through a dirty mirror. That is in line with the following verse of Scripture: 'And I have multiplied visions, and by the ministry of the angels I have used similitudes' (Hos. 12:11).
	F.	"But Moses saw [his vision] through a polished mirror: 'And the image of God does he behold' (Num. 12:8)."
2.	A.	R. Phineas in the name of R. Hoshaia: "[The matter may be compared] to a king who makes his appearance to his courtier in his

informal garb [as an intimate] [Lieberman in Margulies, p. 870 to p. 32].

B. "For in this world the Indwelling Presence makes its appearance only to individuals [one by one], while concerning the age to come, what does Scripture say? 'The glory of the Lord shall be revealed, and all flesh shall see [it together, for the mouth of the Lord has spoken]' (Isa. 40:5)."

The continuous discourse continues its merry way, ignoring not only the passage at hand – Lev. 1:1 – but the several topics provoked by exposition of the theme under discussion in connection with the tent of meeting. Having compared Balaam to Israelite prophets, we proceed to compare Israelite prophets to Moses, with the predictable result. No. 1 preserves the matter. But No. 2 on the surface is wildly out of place, since Moses now is forgotten, and the contrast is between prophecy in this age and in the time to come – a subject no one has hitherto brought up. But the messianic finis is a redactional convention.

Note that Margulies rejects as spurious I:XV, in the standard printed text. This passage is absent in all manuscript evidence of Lev. R. except for one and was added in the earliest printed texts (p. 32 n. to 1.5).

III. Judaism and Scripture

To state the outcome at the very beginning, when Judaism had defined its matrix of myth and rite – a system of worldview and way of life focused on a particular social group – then Judaism attained its independent voice, its inner structure and logic. At that moment Scripture would reenter and assume its proper position as source of truth and proof for all (autonomously framed, independently reached) propositions. Scripture became paramount when it no longer provided a source of prooftexts for the Mishnah but began to dominate discourse and define rhetoric. But Scripture succeeded the Mishnah as the focus of discourse only when discourse itself had expressed determinants autonomous of both the Mishnah and also Scripture – determinants, or propositions, prior to all else. To revert to the operative myth, it is only when the Torah had reached full expression as an autonomous entity of logic that the (mere) components of Torah – Scripture, the Mishnah and associated writings alike – found their proper place and proportion.

Accordingly, when we listen to the framers of Leviticus Rabbah, we see how statements in the document at hand thus become intelligible not contingently, that is, on the strength of an established text, but a priori, that is, on the basis of a deeper logic of meaning and an independent principle of rhetorical intelligibility. How so? Leviticus Rabbah is topical, not exegetical. Each of its thirty-seven parashiyyot pursues its given topic and develops points relevant to that topic. It is logical, in that (to repeat) discourse appeals to an underlying principle of composition and intelligibility, and that logic inheres in what is said. Logic is what joins one sentence to the next and forms the whole into paragraphs of meaning, intelligible propositions, each with its place and sense in a still larger, accessible system. Because of logic one mind connects to another, public discourse becomes possible, debate on issues of general intelligibility takes place, and an anthology of statements about a single subject becomes a composition of theorems about that subject. In this sense, after the Mishnah, Leviticus Rabbah constitutes the next major logical composition in the rabbinic canon. Accordingly, with Leviticus Rabbah rabbis take up the problem of saying what they wish to say not in an exegetical, but in a syllogistic and freely discursive logic and rhetoric. It follows that just as much as the Mishnah marks a radical break from all prior literature produced by Jews, so Leviticus Rabbah marks a stunning departure from all prior literature produced by a particular kind of Jews, namely, rabbis. Since these same rabbis defined Judaism as we have known it from their time to ours, we rightly turn to the book at hand for evidence about how the Scripture entered into, was absorbed by, and reached full status as the foundation document of, the Judaism taking shape at just this time.

IV. What is New in Leviticus Rabbah

To seek, through biblical exegesis, to link the Mishnah to Scripture, detail by detail, represented a well-trodden and firmly-packed path. Sifra shows what could be done. Scripture exegesis by rabbis also was a commonplace, as Genesis Rabbah indicates. One document opened a new road to Scripture, and that is Leviticus Rabbah. How so? Leviticus Rabbah is the first major rabbinic composition to propose to make topical and discursive statements. Not merely a phrase-by-phrase or verse-by-verse exegesis of a document, whether the Mishnah or Scripture itself, Leviticus Rabbah takes a new road. The framers of that composition undertook to offer propositions, declarative sentences (so to speak), in which, not through the exegesis of verses of Scripture in the order of Scripture but through an order dictated by their own sense of the logic of syllogistic composition, they would say what they had in mind. To begin with, they laid down their own topical program, related to, but essentially autonomous of, that of the book of Leviticus. Second, in expressing their ideas on these topics, they never undertook simply to cite a verse of Scripture and then to claim that that verse states precisely what they had in mind to begin with. Accordingly, through rather distinctive modes of expression, the framers said what they wished to say in their own way – just as had the authors of the Mishnah itself.

True, in so doing, the composers of Leviticus Rabbah treated Scripture as had their predecessors. That is to say, to them as to those who had gone before, Scripture provided a rich treasury of facts.

V. The Mode of Thought of Leviticus Rabbah

The paramount and dominant exegetical construction in Leviticus Rabbah is the base-verse/intersecting verse exegesis. Parashah I:I provides an ample instance. In this construction, a verse of Leviticus is cited (hence: base-verse), and another verse, from such books as Job, Proverbs, Qohelet, or Psalms, is then cited. The latter, not the former, is subjected to detailed and systematic exegesis. But the exegetical exercise ends up by leading the intersecting verse back to the base-verse and reading the latter in terms of the former. In such an exercise, what in fact do we do? We read one thing in terms of something else. To begin with, it is the base-verse in terms of the intersecting verse. But it also is the intersecting verse in other terms as well – a multiple layered construction of analogy and parable. The intersecting verse's elements always turn out to stand for, to signify, to speak of, something other than that to which they openly refer. If water stands for Torah, the skin disease for evil speech, the reference to something for some other thing entirely, then the mode of thought at hand is simple. One thing symbolizes another, speaks not of itself but of some other thing entirely.

How shall we describe this mode of thought? It seems to me we may call it an as-if way of seeing things. That is to say, it is as if a common object or symbol really represented an uncommon one. Nothing says what it means. Everything important speaks metonymically, elliptically, parabolically, symbolically. All statements carry deeper meaning, which inheres in other statements altogether. The profound sense, then, of the base-verse emerges only through restatement within and through the intersecting verse – as if the base-verse spoke of things that, on the surface, we do not see at all.

Accordingly, if we ask the single prevalent literary construction to testify to the prevailing frame of mind, its message is that things are never what they seem. All things demand interpretation. Interpretation begins in the search for analogy, for that to which the thing is likened, hence the deep sense in which all exegesis at hand is parabolic. It is a quest for that for which the thing in its deepest structure stands.

Exegesis as we know it in Leviticus Rabbah (and not only there) consists in an exercise in analogical thinking – something is like something else, stands for, evokes, or symbolizes that which is quite outside itself. It may be the opposite of something else, in which case it conforms to the exact opposite of the rules that govern that something else. The reasoning is analogical or it is contrastive, and the fundamental logic is taxonomic. The taxonomy rests on those comparisons and contrasts we should call, as I said, metonymic and parabolic. In that case what lies on the surface misleads. What lies beneath or beyond the surface – there is the true reality, the world of truth and meaning. To revert to the issue of taxonomy, the tracts that allow classification serve only for that purpose. They signify nothing more than that something more.

How shall we characterize people who see things this way? They constitute the opposite of ones who call a thing as it is. Self-evidently, they have become accustomed to perceiving more – or less – than is at hand. Perhaps that is a natural mode of thought for the Jews of this period (and not then alone), so long used to calling themselves God's first love, yet now seeing others with greater worldly reason claiming that same advantaged relationship. Not in mind only, but still more, in the politics of the world, the people that remembered its origins along with the very creation of the world and founding of humanity, that recalled how it alone served, and serves, the one and only God, for more than three hundred years had confronted a quite different existence. The radical disjuncture between the way things were and the way Scripture said things were supposed to be – and in actuality would some day become – surely imposed an unbearable tension. It was one thing for the slave born to slavery to endure. It was another for the free man sold into slavery to accept that same condition. The vanquished people, the nation that had lost its city and its temple, that had, moreover, produced another nation from its midst to take over its Scripture and much else could not bear too much reality. That defeated people will then have found refuge in a mode of thought that trained vision to see other things otherwise than as the eyes perceived them. Among the diverse ways by which the weak and subordinated accomodate to their circumstance, the one of iron-willed pretense in life is most likely to yield the mode of thought at hand: things never are, because they cannot be, what they seem.

VI. The Role of Scripture in Leviticus Rabbah: Renewal and Reconstruction

Everyone has always known that Jews read Scripture. Every system of Judaism has done so. But why did they do so? What place did Scripture take in the larger systems of reality presented by various Judaisms? Why one part of Scripture rather than some other, and why read it in one way rather than another? These questions do not find ready answers in the mere observation that Jews read Scripture and construct Judaisms out of it. Nor is that observation one of a predictable and necessary pattern, since some of the documents of the rabbinic canon did not focus upon Scripture or even find it necessary to quote Scripture a great deal. The Mishnah, Tosefta, and important units of discourse of both Talmuds, for example, did not express their ideas in the way in which people who "read Scripture" ought to. They make use of Scripture sparingly, only with restraint adducing proofs for propositions even when these are based upon scriptural statements. So the paramount and dominant place accorded to Scripture in Leviticus Rabbah and documents like it cannot pass without comment and explanation.

Exactly what can we say for the position of Scripture in this composition in particular, and what did Scripture contribute? We ask first about the use of Scripture in the mode of thought at hand: Where, why, and how did Scripture find its central place in the minds of people who thought in the way in which the framers of our document did? The answer is that Scripture contributed that other world that underlay this one. From Scripture came that other set of realities to be discovered in the ordinary affairs of the day. Scripture defined the inner being, the mythic life, that sustained Israel. The world is to be confronted as if things are not as they seem, because it is Scripture that tells us how things always are – not one-time, in the past only, not one-time, in the future only, but now and always. So the key to the system is what happens to, and through, Scripture. The lock that is opened is the deciphering of the code by which people were guided in their denial of one thing and recognition and affirmation of the presence of some other. It was not general, therefore mere lunacy, but specific, therefore culture.

To spell this out: the mode of thought pertained to a particular set of ideas. People did not engage ubiquitously and individually in an ongoing pretense that things always had to be other than they seemed. Had they done so, the Jewish nation would have disintegrated into a collectivity of pure insanity. The insistence on the as-if character of reality collectively focused upon one, and only one, alternative existence. All parties (so far as we know) entered into and shared that same and single interior universe. It was the one framed by Scripture.

What happens in Leviticus Rabbah (and, self-evidently, in other documents of the same sort)? Reading one thing in terms of something else, the builders of the document systematically adopted for themselves the reality of the Scripture, its history and doctrines. They transformed that history from a sequence of one-time events, leading from one place to some other, into an ever-present mythic world. No longer was there one Moses, one David, one set of happenings of a distinctive and never-to-be-repeated character. Now whatever happens, of which the thinkers propose to take account, must enter and be absorbed into that established and ubiquitous pattern and structure founded in Scripture. It is not that biblical history repeats itself. Rather, biblical history no longer constitutes history as a story of things that happened once, long ago, and pointed to some one moment in the future. Rather it becomes an account of things that happen every day – hence, an ever-present mythic world, as I said.

A rapid glance at Leviticus Rabbah (and its fellows) tells us that Scripture supplies the document with its structure, its content, its facts, its everything. But a deeper analysis also demonstrates that Scripture never provides the document with that structure, contents, and facts, that it now exhibits. Everything is reshaped and reframed. Whence the paradox?

Scripture as a whole does not dictate the order of discourse, let alone its character. Just as the Talmudic authors destroyed the wholeness of the Mishnah and chose to take up its bits and pieces, so the exegetical writers did the same to Scripture. In our document they chose in Leviticus itself a verse here, a phrase there. These then presented the pretext for propositional discourse commonly quite out of phase with the cited passage. Verses that are quoted ordinarily shift from the meanings they convey to the implications they contain, speaking – as I have made clear – about something, anything, other than what they seem to be saying. So the as-if frame of mind brought to Scripture brings renewal to Scripture, seeing everything with fresh eyes.

And the result of the new vision was a re-imagining of the social world envisioned by the document at hand, I mean, the everyday world of Israel in its Land in that difficult time. For what the sages now proposed was a reconstruction of existence along the lines of the ancient design of Scripture as they read it. What that meant was that, from a sequence of one-time and linear events, everything that happened was turned into a repetition of known and already experienced paradigms, hence, once more, a mythic being. The source and core of the myth, of course, derive from Scripture – Scripture reread, renewed, reconstructed along with the society that revered Scripture.

So, to summarize, the mode of thought that dictated the issues and the logic of the document, telling the thinkers to see one thing in terms of something else, addressed Scripture in particular and collectively. And thinking as they did, the framers of the document saw Scripture in a new way, just as they saw their own circumstance afresh, rejecting their world in favor of Scripture's, reliving Scripture's world in their own terms.

That, incidentally, is why they did not write history, an account of what was happening and what it meant. It was not that they did not recognize or appreciate important changes and trends reshaping their nation's life. They could not deny that reality. In their apocalyptic reading of the dietary and leprosy laws, they made explicit their close encounter with the history of the world as they knew it. But they had another mode of responding to history. It was to treat history as if it were already known and readily understood. Whatever happened had already happened. How so? Scripture dictated the contents of history, laying forth the structures of time, the rules that prevailed and were made known in events. Self-evidently, these same thinkers projected into Scripture's day the realities of their own, turning Moses and David into rabbis, for example. But that is how people think in that mythic, enchanted world in which, to begin with, reality blends with dream, and hope projects onto future and past alike how people want things to be.

The upshot is that the mode of thought revealed by the literary construction under discussion constitutes a rather specific expression of a far more general and prevailing way of seeing things. The literary form in concrete ways says that the entirety of the biblical narrative speaks to each circumstance, that the system of Scripture as a whole not only governs, but comes prior to, any concrete circumstance of that same Scripture. Everything in Scripture is relevant everywhere else in Scripture. It must follow, the Torah (to use the mythic language of the system at hand) defines reality under all specific circumstances. Obviously we did not have to come to the specific literary traits of the document at hand to discover those prevailing characteristics of contemporary and later documents of the rabbinic canon. True, every exercise in referring one biblical passage to another expands the range of discourse to encompass much beyond the original referent. But that is a commonplace in the exegesis of Scripture, familiar wherever midrash exegesis was undertaken, in no way particular to rabbinic writings.

VII. The System of Leviticus Rabbah

The message of Leviticus Rabbah comes to us from the ultimate framers. It is delivered through their selection of materials already available as well as through their composition of new ones. What we now require is a clear statement of the major propositions expressed in Leviticus Rabbah. That will emerge through classification of the statements, with the notion that the principal themes, and the messages on those themes, should coalesce into a few clear statements.

The recurrent message may be stated in a single paragraph. God loves Israel, so gave them the Torah, which defines their life and governs their welfare. Israel is alone in its category (sui generis), as in Parashah One, so what is a virtue to Israel is a vice to the nation, life-giving to Israel, poison to the gentiles. True, Israel sins, but God forgives that sin, having punished the nation on account of it. Such a process has yet to come to an end, but it will culminate in Israel's complete regeneration. Meanwhile, Israel's assurance of God's love lies in the many expressions of special concern, for even the humblest and most ordinary aspects of the national life: the food the nation eats, the sexual practices by which it procreates. These life-sustaining, life-transmitting activities draw God's special interest, as a mark of his general love for Israel. Israel then is supposed to achieve its life in conformity with the marks of God's love. These indications moreover signify also the character of Israel's difficulty, namely, subordination to the nations in general, but to the fourth kingdom, Rome, in particular. Both food laws and skin diseases stand for the nations. There is yet another category of sin, also collective and generative of collective punishment, and that is social. The moral character of Israel's life, the treatment of people by one another, the practice of gossip and small-scale thuggery – these, too, draw down divine penalty. The nation's fate therefore corresponds to its moral condition. The moral condition, however, emerges not only from the current generation. Israel's richest hope lies in the merit of the ancestors, thus in the Scriptural record of the merits attained by the founders of the nation, those who originally brought it into being and gave it life.

The world to come upon the nation is so portrayed as to restate these same propositions. Merit overcomes sin, and doing religious duties or supererogatory acts of kindness will win merit for the nation that does them. Israel will be saved at the end of time, and the age, or world, to follow will be exactly the opposite of this one. Much that we find in the account of Israel's national life, worked out through the definition of the liminal relationships, recurs in slightly altered form in the picture of the world to come.

VIII. Salvation and Sanctification

The message of Leviticus Rabbah attaches itself to the book of Leviticus, as if that book had come from prophecy and addressed the issue of salvation. But it came from the priesthood and spoke of sanctification. The paradoxical syllogism – the as-if reading, the opposite of how things seem – of the composers of Leviticus Rabbah therefore reaches simple formulation. In the very setting of sanctification we find the promise of salvation. In the topics of the cult and the priesthood we uncover the national and social issues of the moral life and redemptive hope of Israel. The repeated comparison and contrast of priesthood and prophecy, sanctification and salvation, turn out to produce a complement, which comes to most perfect union in the text at hand.

The basic mode of thought – denial of what is at hand in favor of a deeper reality – proves remarkably apt. The substance of thought confronts the crisis too.

Are we lost for good to the fourth empire, now-Christian Rome? No, we may yet be saved.

Has God rejected us forever? No, aided by the merit of the patriarchs and matriarchs and of the Torah and religious duties, we gain God's love.

What must we do to be saved? We must do nothing, we must be something: sanctified.

That status we gain through keeping the rules that make Israel holy. So salvation is through sanctification, all embodied in Leviticus read as rules for the holy people.

The Messiah will come not because of what a pagan emperor does, nor, indeed, because of Jewish action either, but because of Israel's own moral condition. When Israel enters the right relationship with God, then God will respond to Israel's condition by restoring things to their proper balance. Israel cannot, but need not, so act as to force the coming of the Messiah. Israel can so attain the condition of sanctification, by forming a moral and holy community, that God's response will follow the established prophecy of Moses and the prophets. So the basic doctrine of Leviticus Rabbah is the metamorphosis of Leviticus. Instead of holy caste, we deal with holy people. Instead of Holy Place, we deal with holy community, in its Holy Land. The deepest exchange between reality and inner vision, therefore, comes at the very surface: the rereading of Leviticus in terms of a different set of realities from those to which the book, on the surface, relates. No other biblical book would have served so well; it had to be Leviticus. Only through what the framers did on that particular book could they deliver their astonishing message and vision.

The complementary points of stress in Leviticus Rabbah – the age to come will come, but Israel must reform itself beforehand – address that context defined by Julian, on the one side, and by the new anti-Judaic Christian policy of the later fourth and fifth centuries, on the other. The repeated reference to Esau and Edom and how they mark the last monarchy before God's through Israel underlines the same point. These truly form the worst of the four kingdoms. But they also come at the end. If only we shape up, so will history. As I said, that same message will hardly have surprised earlier generations and it would be repeated afresh later on. But it is the message of our document, and it does address this context in particular. We therefore grasp an astonishing correspondence between how people are thinking, what they wish to say, and the literary context – rereading a particular book of Scripture in terms of a set of values different from those expressed in that book – in which they deliver their message. Given the mode of thought, the crisis that demanded reflection, the message found congruent to the crisis, we must find entirely logical the choice of Leviticus and the treatment accorded to it. So the logic and the doctrine – the logos and topos of our opening discussion – prove remarkably to accord with the society and politics that produced and received Leviticus Rabbah.

IX. Scripture in Judaism

Scripture proves paramount on the surface, but subordinated in the deep structure of the logic of Leviticus Rabbah. Why so? Because Scripture enjoys no autonomous standing, for example, as the sole source of facts. It does not dictate the order of discussion. It does not (by itself) determine the topics to be taken up, since its verses, cited one by one in sequence, do not tell us how matters will proceed. Scripture, moreover, does not allow us to predict what proposition a given set of verses will yield. On the contrary, because of the insistence that one verse be read in light of another, one theme in light of another, augmentative one, Leviticus Rabbah prohibits us from predicting at the outset, merely by reading a given verse of Scripture, the way in which a given theme will be worked out or the way in which a given proposition will impart a message through said theme.

So, in all, the order of Scripture does not govern the sequence of discourse, the themes of Scripture do not tell us what themes will be taken up, the propositions of Scripture about its stated themes, what Scripture says, in its context, about a given topic, do not define the propositions of Leviticus Rabbah about that topic. The upshot is simple. Scripture contributes everything and nothing. It provides the decoration, the facts, much language. But whence the heart and soul and spirit? Where the matrix, where source? The editors, doing the work of selection, making their points through juxtaposition of things not otherwise brought into contact with one another – they are the ones who speak throughout. True, the voice is the voice of Scripture. But the hand is the hand of the collectivity of the sages, who are authors speaking through Scripture.

If, moreover, Scripture contributes facts, so, too, do the ones who state those ineluctable truths that are expressed in parables, and so, too, do the ones who tell stories, also exemplifying truths, about great heroes and villains. No less, of course, but, in standing, also no more than these, Scripture makes its contribution along with other sources of social truth.

Greek science focused upon physics. Then the laws of Israel's salvation serve as the physics of the sages. But Greek science derived facts and built theorems on the basis of other sources besides physics; the philosophers also, after all, studied ethnography, ethics, politics, and history. For the sages at hand, along these same lines, parables, exemplary tales, and completed paragraphs of thought deriving from other sources (not to exclude the Mishnah, Tosefta, Sifra, Genesis Rabbah and such literary compositions that had been made ready for the Talmud of the Land of Israel) – these, too, make their contribution of data subject to analysis. All of these sources of truth, all together, were directed toward the discovery of philosophical laws for the understanding of Israel's life, now and in the age to come.

So to state the main conclusion, standing paramount and dominant, Scripture contributed everything but the main point. That point comes to us from the framers of Leviticus Rabbah – from them alone. So far as Leviticus Rabbah transcends the book of Leviticus – and that means, in the whole of its being – the document speaks for the framers, conveys their message, pursues their discourse, makes the points they wished to make. For they are the ones who made of Leviticus, the book, Leviticus Rabbah, that greater Leviticus, the document that spoke of sanctification but, in its augmented version at hand, meant salvation. As closely related to the book of Leviticus as the New Testament is to the Old, Leviticus Rabbah delivers the message of the philosophers of Israel's history.

I have emphasized that Leviticus Rabbah carries a message of its own, which finds a place within, and refers to, a larger system. The method of thought and mode of argument act out a denial of one reality in favor of the affirmation of another. That dual process of pretense at the exegetical level evokes the deeper pretense of the mode of thought of the larger system, and, at the deepest layer, the pretense that fed Israel's soul and sustained it. Just as one thing evokes some other, so does the rabbinic system overall turn into aspects of myth and actions of deep symbolic consequence what to the untutored eye were commonplace deeds and neutral transactions. So, too, the wretched nation really enjoyed God's special love. So, as I stated at the outset, what is important in the place and function accorded to Scripture derives significance from the host and recipient of Scripture, that is to say, the rabbinic system itself.

But so far as Leviticus Rabbah stands for and points toward that larger system, what are the commonplace traits of Scripture in this other, new context altogether?

1. Scripture, for one thing, forms a timeless present, with the affairs of the present day read back into the past and the past

into the present, with singular events absorbed into Scripture's paradigms.
2. Scripture is read whole and atomistically. Everything speaks to everything else, but only one thing speaks at a time.
3. Scripture is read as an account of a seamless world, encompassing present and past alike, and Scripture is read atemporally and ahistorically.

All of these things surprise no one; they have been recognized for a very long time. What is new here is the claim to explain why these things are so, I mean, the logic of the composition that prevails, also, when Scripture comes to hand.

1. Scripture is read whole, because the framers pursue issues of thought that demand all data pertain to all times and all contexts. The authors are philosophers, looking for rules and their verification. Scripture tells stories, to be sure. But these exemplify facts of social life and national destiny: the laws of Israel's life.
2. Scripture is read atomistically, because each of its components constitutes a social fact, ever relevant to the society of which it forms a part, with that society everywhere uniform.
3. Scripture is read as a source of facts pertinent to historical and contemporary issues alike, because the issues at hand when worked out will indicate the prevailing laws, the rules that apply everywhere, all the time, to everyone of Israel.

Accordingly, there is no way for Scripture to be read except as a source of facts about that ongoing reality that forms the focus and the center of discourse, the life of the unique social entity, Israel. But, as we have seen, the simple logic conveyed by the parable also contributes its offering of facts. The simple truth conveyed by the tale of the great man, the exemplary event of the rabbinic sage, the memorable miracle – these, too, serve as well as facts of Scripture. The several truths therefore stand alongside and at the same level as the truths of Scripture, which is not the sole source of rules or cases. The facts of Scripture stand no higher than those of the parable, on the one side, or of the tale of the sage, on the other. Why not? Because to philosophers and scientists, facts are facts, whatever their origin or point of application.

What we have in Leviticus Rabbah, therefore, is the result of the mode of thought not of prophets or historians, but of philosophers and scientists. The framers propose not to lay down, but to discover, rules governing Israel's life. I state with necessary emphasis: as we find the rules of nature by identifying and classifying facts of natural life, so we find rules of society by identifying and classifying the facts of Israel's social life. In both modes of inquiry we make sense of things by bringing together like specimens and finding out whether they form a species, then bringing together like species and finding out whether they form a genus – in all, classifying data and identifying the rules that make possible the classification. That sort of thinking lies at the deepest level of listmaking, which is, as I said, work of offering a proposition and facts (for social rules) as much as a genus and its species (for rules of nature). Once discovered, the social rules of Israel's national life of course yield explicit statements, such as that God hates the arrogant and loves the humble. The readily assembled syllogism follows: if one is arrogant, God will hate him, and if he is humble, God will love him. The logical status of these statements, in context, is as secure and unassailable as the logical status of statements about physics, ethics, or politics, as these emerge in philosophical thought. What differentiates the statements is not their logical status – as sound, scientific philosophy – but only their subject matter, on the one side, and distinctive rhetoric, on the other.

So Leviticus Rabbah is anything but an exegetical exercise. We err if we are taken in by the powerful rhetoric of our document, which resorts so ubiquitously to the citation of biblical verses and, more important, to the construction, out of diverse verses, of a point transcendent of the cited verses. At hand is not an exegetical composition at all, nor even verses of Scripture read as a corpus of prooftexts. We have, rather, a statement that stands by itself, separate from Scripture, and that makes it points only secondarily, along the way, by evoking verses of Scripture to express and exemplify those same points. We miss the main point if we posit that Scripture plays a definitive or even central role in providing the program and agenda for the framers of Leviticus Rabbah. Their program is wholly their own. But of course Scripture then serves their purposes very well indeed.

So, too, their style is their own. Scripture merely contributes to an aesthetic that is at once pleasing and powerful for people who know Scripture pretty much by heart. But in context the aesthetic, too, is original. The constant invocation of Scriptural verses compares with the place of the classics in the speech and writing of gentlefolk of an earlier age, in which the mark of elegance was perpetual allusion to classical writers. No Christian author of the age would have found alien the aesthetic at hand. So while the constant introduction of verses of Scripture provides the wherewithal of speech, these verses serve only as do the colors of the painter. The painter cannot paint without the oils. But the colors do not make the painting. The painter does. As original and astonishing as is the aesthetic of the Mishnah, the theory of persuasive rhetoric governing Leviticus Rabbah produces a still more amazing result.

X. Conclusion

We may say that Leviticus Rabbah provides an exegesis of the book of Leviticus just as much as the school of Matthew provides an exegesis of passages cited in the book of Isaiah. Yet, I must reiterate at the end, Leviticus serves as something other than a source of prooftexts. It is not that at all. And that is the important fact I mean to prove. What is new in Leviticus Rabbah's encounter with Scripture emerges when we realize that, for former Israelite writers, Scriptures do serve principally as a source of prooftexts. That certainly is the case for the school of Matthew, for one thing, and also for the Essene writers whose library survived at Qumran, for another. The task of Scripture for the authors of the Tosefta, Sifra, Genesis Rabbah, and the Talmud of the Land of Israel emerged out of a single need. That need was to found the creations of the new age upon the authority of the old. Thus the exegetical work consequent upon the Mishnah demanded a turning to Scripture. From that necessary and predictable meeting, exegetical work on Scripture itself got underway, with the results so self-evident in most of the exegetical compositions on most of the Pentateuch, including Leviticus, accomplished in the third and fourth centuries. None of this in fact defined how Scripture would reach its right and proper place in the Judaism of the Talmuds and exegetical compositions. It was Leviticus Rabbah that set the pattern, and its pattern would predominate for a very long time. How so? The operative rules would be these:

1. From Leviticus Rabbah onward, Scripture would conform to paradigms framed essentially independent of Scripture.
2. From then onward, Scripture was made to yield paradigms applicable beyond the limits of Scripture.

In these two complementary statements we summarize the entire argument. The heart of the matter lies in laying forth the rules of life – of Israel's life and salvation. These rules derive from the facts of history, as much as the rules of the Mishnah derive from the facts of society (and, in context, the rules of philosophy derive from the facts of nature). Scripture then never stands all by itself. Its exalted position at the center of all discourse proves contingent, never absolute. That negative result of course bears an entirely affirmative complement.

Judaism is not the religion of the Old Testament because Judaism is Judaism. Scripture enters Judaism because Judaism is the religion of "the one whole Torah of Moses, our rabbi," and part of that Torah is the written part, Scripture. But that whole Torah, viewed whole, is this: God's revelation of the rules of life: creation, society, history alike.

Obviously, every form of Judaism would be in some way a scriptural religion. But the sort of scriptural religion a given kind of Judaism would reveal is not to be predicted on the foundations of traits of Scripture in particular. One kind of Judaism laid its distinctive emphasis upon a linear history of Israel, in a sequence of unique, one-time events, all together yielding a pattern of revealed truth, from creation, through revelation, to redemption. That kind of Judaism then would read Scripture for signs of the times and turn Scripture into a resource for apocalyptic speculation. A kind of Judaism interested not in one-time events of history but in all-time rules of society, governing for all time, such as the kind at hand, would read Scripture philosophically and not historically. That is, Scripture would yield a corpus of facts conforming to rules. Scripture would provide a source of paradigms, the opposite of one-time events.

True enough, many kinds of Judaism would found their definitive propositions in Scripture and build upon them. But while all of Scripture was revealed and authoritative, for each construction of a system of Judaism only some passages of Scripture would prove to be relevant. Just as the framers of the Mishnah came to Scripture with a program of questions and inquiries framed essentially among themselves, one which turned out to be highly selective, so did their successors who made up Leviticus Rabbah. What they brought was a mode of thought, a deeply philosophical and scientific quest, and an acute problem of history and society. In their search for the rules of Israel's life and salvation, they found answer not in the one-time events of history but in paradigmatic facts, social laws of salvation. It was in the mind and imagination of the already-philosophical authors of Leviticus Rabbah that Scripture came to serve, as did nature, as did everyday life and its parables, all together, to reveal laws everywhere and always valid – if people would only keep them.

4

From Exegesis to Syllogism

How Leviticus Rabbah Makes Intelligible Statements: Listmaking and Classifying Facts

Leviticus Rabbah deals with a biblical book, not a Mishnah tractate. But it approaches that book with a fresh plan, one in which exegesis does not dictate rhetoric, and in which amplification of an established text (whether Scripture or Mishnah) does not supply the underlying logic by which sentences are made to compose paragraphs, and paragraphs completed thoughts. To state matters affirmatively, the framers of Leviticus Rabbah treat topics, not particular verses. They make generalizations which are free-standing. They express cogent propositions through extended compositions, not episodic ideas. Earlier, things people wished to say were attached to predefined statements based on an existing text, constructed in accord with an organizing logic independent of the systematic expression of a single, well-framed idea. Now the authors so collect and arrange their materials that an abstract proposition emerges. That proposition is not expressed only or mainly through episodic restatements, assigned, as I said, to an order established by a base-text. Rather it emerges through a logic of its own. Let me explain with some care what I think is new in Leviticus Rabbah. What is new is the move from an essentially exegetical mode of logical discourse to a fundamentally philosophical one. It is the shift from discourse framed around an established (hence old) text to syllogistic argument organized around a proposed (hence new) theorem or proposition. What changes, therefore, is the way in which cogent thought takes place, as people move from discourse contingent on some prior principle of organization to discourse autonomous of a ready-made program inherited from an earlier paradigm.

Accordingly, when we listen to the framers of Leviticus Rabbah, we see how statements in the document at hand thus become intelligible not contingently, that is, on the strength of an established text, but a priori, that is, on the basis of a deeper logic of meaning and an independent principle of rhetorical intelligibility. How so? Leviticus Rabbah is topical, not exegetical. Each of its thirty-seven parashiyyot pursues its given topic and develops points relevant to that topic. It is logical, in that (to repeat) discourse appeals to an underlying principle of composition and intelligibility, and that logic inheres in what is said. Logic is what joins one sentence to the next and forms the whole into paragraphs of meaning, intelligible propositions, each with its place and sense in a still larger, accessible system. Because of logic one mind connects to another, public discourse becomes possible, debate on issues of general intelligibility takes place, and an anthology of statements about a single subject becomes a composition of theorems about that subject. In this sense, after the Mishnah, Leviticus Rabbah constitutes the next major logical composition in the rabbinic canon. Accordingly, with Leviticus Rabbah rabbis take up the problem of saying what they wish to say not in an exegetical, but in a syllogistic and freely discursive logic and rhetoric.

I. Defining The Syllogism of Rabbinic Discourse

The task of making sense of a book begins with the simple question: Precisely what is this book? By that I mean to ask for a definition of how the book is so constructed as to become intelligible in its context (and in ours). Only when we can see the whole are we ready to investigate the parts. Seeing the whole demands that we explain what holds it together, what makes the whole whole. For, at the very outset I have claimed that the document at hand constitutes not a mere collection of unrelated or random statements, but a set of related and purposeful ones. Then, to prove my thesis, I must explain what defines the relationship, and how we shall make sense of the purpose. To answer that question I must uncover the fundamental logic of organization and topic: the logos of both intellect and aesthetics that account for the whole; the topics that render the book as we have it a sustained syllogism.

II. The Composition of Logic and Topic

My thesis is that Leviticus Rabbah falls into the classification of syllogistic compositions, not of exegetical collections. The proposition is that Leviticus Rabbah constitutes not a compilation of random sentences but a purposeful and sustained composition, comparable to the Mishnah in its principles of organization and aggregation of materials. On what basis do I claim that the document in hand constitutes a single and systematic statement? I shall state matters both negatively and positively. What would constitute adequate proof that we have an anthology or a typical compilation, lacking a logic of either form or topic? What would constitute decisive proof that we have a sustained composition, exhibiting in detail an inner, animating, and encompassing logic? If we cannot falsify, we also cannot validate or proposition. Accordingly, I lay forth what I conceive to be evidence and argumentation to guide us on whether we are right or wrong.

The negative: if we wished to demonstrate that a text in the rabbinic canon comprised nothing more than a compilation of discrete sentences, in no way constituting paragraphs, chapters, propositions and syllogisms, we should begin with these questions: (1) Can we show that no external, formal pattern governed the formulation of sentences? It would then follow that the sentences were made up with no interest in composing a stylistically balanced and formally cogent paragraph or chapter. (2) Can we demonstrate that no single issue or problem occupied the mind of the authors of the sentences at hand? It would then follow that the compilation of sentences in no way flowed from a single generative problematic or addressed a cogent problem or proposition. On that basis, we should stand on firm ground in alleging that at hand was a topical anthology, a compilation of this-and-that, and not a sustained and cogent composition.

True, someone made the compilation as we have it. No one alleges that, crawling across the far reaches of rabbinical tradents, random sentences somehow made their way to a given pericope on their own. Every document reached closure and entered circulation in something very like the condition in which we now have it (making provision for enormous variations in the wording of sentences). But the person who made the compilation followed a simple principle in selecting the aggregation of materials that he gave us: shared topic, common theme. Whether or not through the shared topic he wished to deliver anything more than simply the aggregation of sentences, in no clear logical order and making no obvious single point, we cannot say. Why not? Because the parts do not add up to more than the sum of the whole. The decisive criterion is simple: the order of sentences of such an anthology makes no intelligible difference, because one could have arranged the sentences in any other sequence and gained as little, or as much, meaning from the compilation as a whole.

The positive: beginning the account of the criteria by which we identify a composition as distinct from a compilation, a purposeful essay in contrast to an anthology on a single topic, we begin with this same point, the order of sentences. In a syllogistic paragraph, the order of sentences matters a great deal. It would not be possible to arrange matters other than in the sequence in which they occur, for each sentence depends upon the other for sense and meaning, one standing fore, the other aft, of the statement at hand. Such an orderly composition in no way serves as a mere anthology of diverse sayings on a single topic. Quite the opposite, the sentences gain their full sense and meaning only in the order dictated by the logic of the syllogism at hand.

In the rabbinic canon, moreover, sentences that are meant to be coherent with one another very commonly follow a single syntactic formula and resort to shared forms of rhetoric. The Mishnah, I have demonstrated, joins form to meaning. When a given topic is at hand, the sentences that spell out the rules on that topic will prove cogent not only in theme and even in detailed principle but also in syntax and rhetoric. When, then, the subject changes, the syntactical and rhetorical pattern and form will also change. So we shall talk about one thing in some one way, then the next thing in some other.

While the logic of a syllogism therefore comes to detailed expression in both aesthetic, or formal, and literary ways, and also in intellectual, or substantive, ones, the shortest path into the center of a syllogism lies through form. How so? In the literature at hand, if we discern patterns of formal expression, we may reasonably look for patterns of substantive discourse as well. If we find no effort at formalization, we may find it more difficult, also, to demonstrate the intent of delivering cogent and substantive propositions. (Self-evidently, repeated recourse to a single form may also produce gibberish, as in the Hekhalot writings. But that fact is inconsequential in this context, since I make no claim that patterned language all by itself proves we have in hand syllogistic propositions too.) So the way forward lies through the discovery of the logic of Leviticus Rabbah, logic of expression, logic of composition, logic of proposition.

Let me now link what has been said about formal cogency to the larger claim that Leviticus Rabbah expresses a cogent logic, a logic of form and a logic of substance, a logic of context as well. What has formal cogency to do with logic? The question may be reframed as follows: How shall we recognize – and so demonstrate the presence of – logic? Since logic constitutes what orders and renders intelligible a set of sentences or propositions so laying down the principle of composition for discourse and the rules by which discourse takes place, we look throughout for regularities. Our perception of order emerges from our discovery of repeated choices, first of form, and only second, of proposition. If we can demonstrate a single program of formal choices, we may also try to show that the author or authors of the document – the people who in the end made it what it now is – did some one thing, rather than some other. Then through systematic classification we may describe what they chose to do. That taxonomic description constitutes the statement of the formal logic of the document as a whole.

By contrast, if we can discover in a text of the character of this one no repeated patterns in the way people express their ideas – no sustained logic of rhetoric and syntax, for example – we have slight warrant for supposing that in substance or in topical program we deal with a composition, a proportioned statement, a cogent syllogism. We shall have then to concede that what we have in hand is what people generally suppose we have – a composite, not a composition. We shall have to agree that Leviticus Rabbah is a collection of diverse and episodic sentences, this-and-that about what-not, not a coherent syllogism, a statement and intelligible judgment addressed to the age in which the composition reached closure. Leviticus Rabbah, located by the scholarly consensus at ca. A.D. 400-450, contends with the context of its age, addresses Israel's condition with syllogisms of substance and meaning, not merely with ad hoc sayings equally relevant – because of their very discrete and episodic character – everywhere but also nowhere in particular.

In Leviticus Rabbah, we have a composition in which outsiders, not the authors but other people, provided "completed units of thought" which are whole paragraphs, and in which the authors also provided "completed units of thought," also whole paragraphs. When we speak of these "completed units of thought" and invoke the analogy of the sentence, therefore, in fact we refer not to atomic but to molecular units of thought, that is to say, composites which, all together, make a single point or statement.

What then forms the arena for analysis, and where do I claim to locate the boundaries of discourse? The answer is simple. I speak of the parashah as the proposition. Then there are thirty-seven of them. My entire mode of analysis is to claim that each parashah constitutes not merely an assembly of relevant materials about a topic, but something much more cogent and purposive, that is, a composition that makes a specific polemical point about a topic. I further propose that the main points of the polemic on the bulk, though not all, of the parashiyyot and their topics, cohere and add up to a single proposition concerning Israel's salvation. So the parts make points and the whole makes a point. And, in the nature of things (since I claim to contribute to the study of the history of the formation of the ideas of Judaism) the point that is made concerns the world to which the framers speak.

The burden of proof lies on the one who alleges we deal with a composition and not a composite. Either a document is exegetical and so depends upon some other for its cogency and order, or it is syllogistic and therefore provides its own inner connections and relations.

The former sort of document, by definition, constitutes a timeless exegesis out of all distinctive historical and social context. It depends upon, therefore it meant to amplify, some other document, of some other age, hence provides an exegesis of something other than itself.

The latter sort of document, by definition, constitutes a timely syllogism, a free-standing statement made intelligible in two complementary ways. These are, first, by its own inner correspondences and proportions, a set of relationships joined from within and, second, by a socially defined logic, a cogent address directed to a given world by a specific intellect and therefore meant to be intelligible at some one time (if, also, for all time, too).

III. The Mode of Thought of Leviticus Rabbah

Elsewhere I have shown a deep cogency to the formulary and redactional systems of Leviticus Rabbah. What of that logic – that mode of thought, of formulating and answering questions, of deciding what is fit and right and proportionate – that inheres in the whole and emerges in each of that parts? Surely we have reason to ask whether the formal traits of discourse correspond to the substantive purposes. So far as style and aesthetic dictate one mode, rather than some other, of saying what the author wants, do they also signal limits to what one may appropriately say in that mode? I ask the question, but in phrasing matters this way, I also dictate the selection of data to lead us to the answer of a still more encompassing inquiry into the mode of thought, the manner of the construction, in mind, of reality out there. Accordingly, I shall try to find a route to the fundamental layers of the intellect that animates and generates the accessible layers of formal expression of doctrine and deliberation.

Since I hypothesize that form and substance cohere, I start back with the points of formal cogency of the document. It is there, at the repeated literary structures, that I should be able to point to the evidences of a fundamentally coherent way of seeing things, a mode of thought expressed thoughout. What people wished to say and the way in which they chose to say it together constituted the document as we now know it. So, as is clear, we turn to the one to teach us how to analyze the other.

We begin, then, once more with the paramount and dominant exegetical construction, the base-verse/intersecting verse exegesis characteristic of our document. In such an exercise, what in fact do we do? We read one thing in terms of something else. To begin with, it is the base-verse in terms of the intersecting verse. But, as the reader will observe in the text itself, it also is the intersecting verse in other terms as well – a multiple layered construction of analogy and parable. The intersecting verse's elements always turn out to stand for, to signify, to speak of, something other than that to which they openly refer. If water stands for Torah, the skin disease for evil speech, the reference to something for some other thing entirely, then the mode of thought at hand is simple. One thing symbolizes another, speaks not of itself but of some other thing entirely.

How shall we describe this mode of thought? It seems to me we may call it an as-if way of seeing things. That is to say, it is as if a common object or symbol really represented an uncommon one. Nothing says what it means. Everything important speaks metonymically, elliptically, parabolically, symbolically. All statements carry deeper meaning, which inheres in other statements altogether. The profound sense, then, of the base-verse emerges only through restatement within and through the intersecting verse – as if the base-verse spoke of things that, on the surface, we do not see at all.

Accordingly, if we ask the single prevalent literary construction to testify to the prevailing frame of mind, its message is that things are never what they seem. All things demand interpretation. Interpretation begins in the search for analogy, for that to which the thing is likened, hence the deep sense in which all exegesis at hand is parabolic. It is a quest for that for which the thing in its deepest structure stands.

Exegesis as we know it in Leviticus Rabbah (and not only there) consists in an exercise in analogical thinking – something is like something else, stands for, evokes, or symbolizes that which is quite outside itself. It may be the opposite of something else, in which case it conforms to the exact opposite of the rules that govern that something else. The reasoning is analogical or it is contrastive, and the fundamental logic is taxonomic. The taxonomy rests on those comparisons and contrasts we should call, as I said, metonymic and parabolic. In that case what lies on the surface misleads. What lies beneath or beyond the surface – there is the true reality, the world of truth and meaning. To revert to the issue of taxonomy, the tracts that allow classification serve only for that purpose. They signify nothing more than that something more.

How shall we characterize people who see things this way? They constitute the opposite of ones who call a thing as it is. Self-evidently, they have become accustomed to perceiving more – or less – than is at hand. Perhaps that is a natural mode of thought for the Jews of this period (and not then alone), so long used to calling themselves God's first love, yet now seeing others with greater worldly reason claiming that same advantaged relationship. Not in mind only, but still more, in the politics of the world, the people that remembered its origins along with the very creation of the world and founding of humanity, that recalled how it alone served, and serves, the one and only God, for more than three hundred years had confronted a quite different existence. The radical disjuncture between the way things were and the way Scripture said things were supposed to be – and in actuality would some day become – surely imposed an unbearable tension. It was one thing for the slave born to slavery to endure. It was another for the free man sold into slavery to accept that same condition. The vanquished people, the nation that had lost its city and its temple, that had, moreover, produced another nation from its midst to take over its Scripture and much else could not bear too much reality. That defeated people will then have found refuge in a mode of thought that trained vision to see other things otherwise than as the eyes perceived them. Among the diverse ways by which the weak and subordinated accomodate to their circumstance, the one of iron-willed pretense in life is most likely to yield the mode of thought at hand: things never are, because they cannot be, what they seem.

IV. History and Syllogism

If we now ask about further recurring themes or topics in Leviticus Rabbah, there is one so commonplace that we should have to list the majority of paragraphs of discourse in order to provide a complete list. It is the list of events in Israel's history, meaning, in this context, Israel's history solely in scriptural times, down through the return to Zion. The one-time events of the generation of the flood, Sodom and Gomorrah, the patriarchs and the sojourn in Egypt, the exodus, the revelation of the Torah at Sinai, the golden calf, the Davidic monarchy and the building of the Temple, Sennacherib, Hezekiah, and the destruction of northern Israel, Nebuchadnezzar and the destruction of the Temple in 586, the life of Israel in Babylonian captivity, Daniel and his associates, Mordecai and Haman – these events occur over and over again. They turn out to serve as paradigms of sin and atonement, steadfastness and divine intervention, and equivalent lessons. We find, in fact, a fairly standard repertoire of scriptural heroes or villains, on the one side, and conventional lists of Israel's enemies and their actions and downfall, on the other. The boastful, for instance, include (VII:VI) the generation of the flood, Sodom and Gomorrah, Pharaoh, Sisera, Sennacherib, Nebuchadnezzar, the wicked empire (Rome) – contrasted to Israel, "despised and humble in this world." The four kingdoms recur again and again, always ending, of course, with Rome, with the repeated message that after Rome will come Israel. But Israel has to make this happen through its faith and submission to God's will. Lists of enemies ring the changes on Cain, the Sodomites, Pharaoh, Sennacherib, Nebuchadnezzar, Haman.

Accordingly, the mode of thought brought to bear upon the theme of history remains exactly the same as in the Mishnah: listmaking, with data exhibiting similar taxonomic traits drawn together into lists based on common monothetic traits or definitions. These lists then through the power of repetition make a single enormous point or prove a social law of history. The catalogues of exemplary heroes and historical events serve a further purpose. They provide a model of how contemporary events are to be absorbed into the biblical paradigm. Since biblical events exemplify recurrent happenings, sin and redemption, forgiveness and atonement, they lose their one-time character. At the same time and in the same way, current events find a place within the ancient, but eternally present, paradigmatic scheme. So no new historical events, other than exemplary episodes in lives of heroes, demand narration because, through what is said about the past, what was happening in the times of the framers of Leviticus Rabbah would also come under consideration. This mode of dealing with biblical history and contemporary events produces two reciprocal effects. The first is the mythicization of biblical stories, their removal from the framework of ongoing, unique patterns of history and sequences of events and their transformation into accounts of things that happen all the time. The second is that contemporary events, too, lose all of their specificity and enter the paradigmatic framework of established mythic existence. So (1) the Scripture's myth happens every day, and (2) every day produces re-enactment of the Scripture's myth.

In seeking the substance of the mythic being invoked by the exegetes at hand, who read the text as if it spoke about something else and the world as if it lived out the text, we uncover a simple fact. At the center of the pretense, that is, the as-if mentality of Leviticus Rabbah and its framers, we find a simple proposition. Israel is God's special love. That love is shown in a simple way. Israel's present condition of subordination derives from its own deeds. It follows that God cares, so Israel may look forward to redemption on God's part in response to Israel's own regeneration through repentance. When the exegetes proceeded to open the scroll of Leviticus, they found numerous occasions to state that proposition in concrete terms and specific contexts. The sinner brings on his own sickness. But God heals through that very ailment. The nations of the world govern in heavy succession, but Israel's lack of faith guaranteed their rule and its moment of renewal will end it. Israel's leaders – priests, prophets, kings – fall into an entirely different category from those of the nations, as much as does Israel. In these and other concrete allegations, the same classical message comes forth.

Accordingly, at the foundations of the pretense lies the long-standing biblical-Jewish insistence that Israel's sorry condition in no way testifies to Israel's true worth – the grandest pretense of all. All of the little evasions of the primary sense in favor of some other testify to this, the great denial that what is, is what counts. Leviticus Rabbah makes that statement with art and imagination. But it is never subtle about saying so.

V. Salvation and Sanctification

Nearly all of the parashiyyot of Leviticus Rabbah turn out to deal with the national, social condition of Israel, and this in three contexts: (1) Israel's setting in the history of the nations, (2) the character of the inner life of Israel itself, (3) the future history of Israel. So the biblical book that deals with the holy Temple now is shown to address the holy people. Leviticus really discusses not the consecration of the cult but the sanctification of the nation – its conformity to God's will, laid forth in the Torah, and God's rules.

So when we review the document as a whole and ask what is that something else that the base-text is supposed to address, it turns out that the sanctification of the cult stands for the salvation of the nation. So the nation now is like the cult then, the ordinary Israelite now like the priest then. The holy way of life lived now, through acts to which merit accrues, corresponds to the holy rites then. The process of metamorphosis is full, rich, complete. When everything stands for something else, the something else repeatedly turns out to be the nation. This is what our document spells out in exquisite detail, yet never missing the main point.

VI. The Logic of the Composition in Context

The authors of Leviticus Rabbah express their ideas, first, by selecting materials already written for other purposes and using them for their own, second, by composing materials, and third, by arranging both in parashiyyot into an order through which propositions may reach expression. As we sifted and resifted traits of organization and topics of discourse, we reached two complementary conclusions.

From Exegesis to Syllogism

The formal conclusion was that the principal mode of thought required one thing to be read in terms of another, one verse in light of a different verse (or topic, theme, symbol, idea), one situation in light of another.

The substantive conclusion was that the principal subject of our composition is the moral condition of Israel, on the one side, and the salvation of Israel, on the other.

The single unifying proposition – the syllogism at the document's deepest structure – was that Israel's salvation depends upon its moral condition.

In these three statements we are able to account for the literary character and the topical contents of the document and further to express its single paramount proposition. The context in which the work of selection, arrangement, and composition went on, of course, is one (if not uniquely) in which Israel's salvation framed the issue of the times.

At the outset I alleged that we have at hand a syllogistic statement, by which I mean a statement of logical, not merely rhetorical, coherence. I promised to specify the logic that defines the underlying principle to account for the unity and cogency of the whole. The logic in substance has now been identified. My reason for maintaining that Leviticus Rabbah constitutes not merely diverse thoughts but a single, sustained composition, is fully exposed. But the question remains, in the context of logical discourse, what sort of syllogism do we have in hand? It is to this matter that we now turn. The question demands attention, because when we answer it, we shall know how the framers communicate. We shall claim to understand how, through selecting existing materials and including compositions of new ones, they develop their points and establish a discourse sufficiently cogent and logical to make an important point.

Since I claim that the authors do state propositions, I have at the end to make that claim stick by showing how they do so. It is, in a word, through a rich tapestry of unstated propositions that only are illustrated, delineated at the outset, by the statement of some propositions that also are illustrated. It is, in a word, a syllogism by example – that is, by repeated appeal to facts – rather than by argument alone. For in context, an example constitutes a fact. The source of many examples or facts is Scripture, the foundation of all reality. Accordingly, in the context of Israelite life and culture, in which Scripture recorded facts, we have a severely logical, because entirely factual, statement of how rightly organized and classified facts sustain a proposition. In context that proposition is presented as rigorously and critically as the social rules of discourse allowed.

Precisely what sort of syllogism does our document set forth? In my view, it is a perfectly simple one (which biblical historians and prophets used all the time as at Leviticus 26-27): if X, then Y; if not X, then not Y. If Israel carries out its moral obligations, then God will redeem Israel. If Israel does not, then God will punish Israel. This simple statement is given innumerable illustrations, for example, Israel in times past repented, therefore God saved them. Israel in times past sinned, therefore God punished them. Other sorts of statements follow suit. God loves the humble and despises the haughty. Therefore God saves the humble and punishes the haughty. In the same terms, if he is humble, then God will save him, and if one is haughty, then God will punish him. Accordingly, if one condition is met, then another will come about. And the opposite also is the fact. True, the document does not express these syllogisms in the form of arguments at all. Rather they come before us as statements of fact, and the facts upon which numerous statements rest derive from Scripture. So, on the surface, there is not a single statement in the document that a Greco-Roman logician would have understood, since the formal patterns of Greco-Roman logic do not make an appearance. Yet once we translate the statements the authors do make into the language of abstract discourse, we find exact correspondences between the large-scale propositions of the document and the large-scale syllogisms of familiar logic.

Along these same lines, we may find numerous individual examples in which, in exquisite detail, the syllogistic mode at hand – if X, then Y; if not X, then not Y – defines the pattern of discourse. The logic at hand, at its deepest layers, accords with the formal logic of the Stoic logic of propositions (described by Berchman in Appendix One). We find both brief and simple propositions that make sense of large-scale compositions, for example, on humility and arrogance, and also an overall scheme of proposition and argument, a micro- and a macro-syllogistic discourse, with the small and the large corresponding to one another.

The place of Scripture in such a logical system now requires explanation. To understand how Scripture functions, we have clearly to grasp the larger logical matrix.

In light of the account of the syllogistic possibilities at hand, we may identify the theorems of argumentation operative in our document (and not alone here, of course). What is important is that the logic at hand proves subject to verification on grounds other than those supplied by the prooftexts alone. How so? The appeal is to an autonomous realm, namely, reason confirmed by experience. The repeated claim is not that things are so merely because Scripture says what it says, but that things happened as they happened in accord with laws we may verify or test (as

Scripture, among other sources of facts, tells us). The emphasis is on the sequence of events, the interrelationship exhibited by them. How does Scripture in particular participate? It is not in particular at all. Scripture serves as a source of information, much as any history of the world or of a nation would provide sources of information: facts. Who makes use of these facts? In our own time it is the social scientist, seeking the rules that social entities are supposed to exhibit. In the period at hand it was the rabbinical philosopher, seeking the rules governing Israel's life. So far as people seek rules and regularities, the search is one of logic, of philosophy. It follows that our document rests upon logical argumentation. Its framers, rabbis, served as philosophers in the ancient meaning of the term. And, in consequence, Scripture for its part is transformed into the source of those facts that supply both the problem, chaos, and the solution, order, rule, organized in lists. So Scripture in the hands of the rabbis of our document corresponds to nature in the hands of the great Greek philosophers.

The Mishnah makes its principal points by collecting three or five examples of a given rule. The basic rule is not stated, but it is exemplified through the several statements of its application. The reader then may infer the generalization from its specific exemplifications. Sometimes, but not often, the generalization will be made explicit. The whole then constitutes an exercise in rhetoric and logic carried out through list-making. And the same is true in Leviticus Rabbah. But it makes lists of different things from those of the Mishnah: events, not everyday situations. The framers of Leviticus Rabbah revert to sequences of events, all of them exhibiting the same definitive traits and the same ultimate results, for example, arrogance, downfall, not one time but many; humility, salvation, over and over again, and so throughout. Indeed, if I had to select a single paramount trait of argument in Leviticus Rabbah, it would be the theorem stated by the making of a list of similar examples. The search for the rules lies through numerous instances that, all together, yield the besought rule.

In context, therefore, we have in the parashiyyot of Leviticus Rabbah the counterpart to the list-making that defined the labor of the philosophers of the Mishnah. Through composing lists of items joined by a monothetic definitive trait, the framers produce underlying or overriding rules always applicable. Here too, through lists of facts of history, the foundations of social life rise to the surface. All of this, we see, constitutes a species of a molecular argument, framed in very definite terms, for example, Nebuchadnezzar, Senacherib, David, Josiah did so-and-so with such-and-such result. So, as I said, the mode of argument at hand is the assembly of instances of a common law. The argument derives from the proper construction of a statement of that law in something close to a syllogism. The syllogistic statement often, though not invariably, occurs at the outset, all instances of so-and-so produce such-and-such a result, followed by the required catalogue.

A final point is in order. The conditional syllogisms of our composition over and over again run through the course of history. The effort is to demonstrate that the rule at hand applies at all times, under all circumstances. Why so? It is because the conditional syllogism must serve under all temporal circumstances. The recurrent listing of events subject to a single rule runs as often as possible through the course of all of human history, from creation to the fourth monarchy (Rome), which, everyone knows, is the end of time prior to the age that is coming. Accordingly, the veracity of rabbinic conditional arguments depends over and over again on showing that the condition holds at all times.

To summarize the proposition: the proposition of the syllogistic argument at hand derives from clear statements of Scripture, the conditional part: if X, then Y; if not X, then not Y. Leviticus 26 (which occupies strikingly slight attention in our composition) states explicitly that if the Israelites keep God's rules, they will prosper, and if not, they will suffer. The viewpoint is commonplace, but its appearance at Leviticus in particular validates the claim that it is topically available to our authors. The two further stages in the encompassing logic of the document do represent a step beyond the simple and commonplace theorem. The first is the construction of the molecular argument, encompassing a broad range of subjects. The second, and the more important of the two, is the insistence of the temporal character of the list. That is why the recurrent reference to sequences of figures, events, or actions, all listed in accord with a monothetic definitive trait, forms so central a component in the argument of the document as a whole.

What Leviticus Rabbah does not contribute is the basic proposition at hand. Why not? Because, as I said, it is one that would not have surprised most of the framers of the important components of Scripture itself. What the authors of the document do originate (along with authors in the Talmud of the Land of Israel) is the proof through review of examples deriving from a wide range of times and places. That logical contribution explains why our document differs from all but one of its contemporaries and all of its predecessors, except, of course, for one. As I explained, the Mishnah, too, composes its arguments through the laying down of basic principles – syllogisms – sustained by lists of specific instances in the validation and clarification of those principles. So, too, the authors of Leviticus Rabbah collect and arrange, since they do not propose to invent facts, but to interpret them by discovering the rules the facts obey. The facts with which they work are indifferently Scriptural or contemporary (though mostly the former). The

From Exegesis to Syllogism

propositions they propose to demonstrate through these facts, however, are eternal.

So, in a word, Leviticus Rabbah takes up the modes of thought and argumentation characteristic of the Mishnah and accomplishes the logically necessary task of applying them to society. Speaking of society, the authors turn to, among other records, the history book, Scripture, which provides examples of the special laws governing Israel, the physics of Israel's fate. In Scripture, but not only there, the authors find rules and apply them to their own day.

Greek science focused upon physics. Then the laws of Israel's salvation serve as the physics of the sages. But Greek science derived facts and built theorems on the basis of other sources besides physics; the philosophers also, after all, studied ethnography, ethics, politics, and history. For the sages at hand, along these same lines, parables, exemplary tales, and completed paragraphs of thought deriving from other sources (not to exclude the Mishnah, Tosefta, Sifra, Genesis Rabbah and such literary compositions that had been made ready for the Talmud of the Land of Israel) – these, too, make their contribution of data subject to analysis. All of these sources of truth, all together, were directed toward the discovery of philosophical laws for the understanding of Israel's life, now and in the age to come.

What we have in Leviticus Rabbah, therefore, is the result of the mode of thought not of prophets or historians, but of philosophers and scientists. The framers propose not to lay down, but to discover, rules governing Israel's life. I state with necessary emphasis: as we find the rules of nature by identifying and classifying facts of natural life, so we find rules of society by identifying and classifying the facts of Israel's social life. In both modes of inquiry we make sense of things by bringing together like specimens and finding out whether they form a species, then bringing together like species and finding out whether they form a genus – in all, classifying data and identifying the rules that make possible the classification. That sort of thinking lies at the deepest level of list-making, which is, as I said, work of offering a proposition and facts (for social rules) as much as a genus and its species (for rules of nature). Once discovered, the social rules of Israel's national life of course yield explicit statements, such as that God hates the arrogant and loves the humble. As we have seen, the readily-assembled syllogism follows: if one is arrogant, God will hate him, and if he is humble, God will love him. The logical status of these statements, in context, is as secure and unassailable as the logical status of statements about physics, ethics, or politics, as these emerge in philosophical thought. What differentiates the statements is not their logical status – as sound, scientific philosophy – but only their subject matter, on the one side, and distinctive rhetoric, on the other.

5

Genesis Rabbah and the History of Israel

Genesis Rabbah presents the first complete and systematic Judaic commentary to the book of Genesis. In normative and classical Judaism, that is, the Judaism that reached its original expression in the Mishnah, ca. A.D. 200, and came to final and full statement in the Talmud of Babylonia, ca. A.D. 600, Genesis Rabbah therefore takes an important position. Specifically, this great rabbinic commentary to Genesis, generally thought to have been closed ("redacted") at ca. A.D. 400, provides a complete and authoritative account of how Judaism proposes to read and make sense of the first book of the Hebrew Scriptures. Who speaks to us here? Genesis Rabbah is a composite document, as I said, generally regarded as the work of compilers of the period ca. A.D. 400. Much of the material in the compilation, however, can be shown to have been put together before that material was used for the purposes of the late fourth century compilers. Many times we shall see, for example, that a comment entirely apposite to a verse of Genesis has been joined to a set of comments in no way pertinent to the verse of Genesis at hand. Proof for a given syllogism, furthermore, will derive from a verse of Genesis as well as from verses of other books of the Bible. Such a syllogistic argument therefore has not been written for exegetical purposes particular to the verse at hand. The ones who selected that completed composition made the decision of what to include. Hence they are the ones who speak through their selection. We find in the work of redaction, and only in that aspect of the text before us, our point of entry into the mind and imagination of the compositors of Genesis Rabbah. So if we want to know about the mind and imagination of fourth-century rabbis in the Land of Israel, we have to pay close attention to what the sages at hand have selected, to how they have arranged the document at hand, and to the points of stress and emphasis they repeatedly locate in the verses that are subject to their explanation.

Here therefore we venture into the inner life, the worldview, of Israel's sages in the Land of Israel in a critical age. For at the time at which our document reached closure, the Roman empire in general, and the Land of Israel in particular, went from pagan to Christian rule. The political situation of the Jews and of the Judaism presented by the sages of the document at hand and of the canon of which it forms a part radically changed. Now we see how Israel's sages proposed to read the book of Genesis for purposes important in their circumstance and context. When we know the answer to that question, we may gain entry into the way in which the sages at hand thought about, and responded to, the world in which they lived. And understanding how they read Scripture as a statement in particular to them and their age, we gain access, also, to Scripture as a statement to us and ours.

Method and Message:
How the Sages Read the Book of Genesis, What They Found There

Once we understand the method that tells the sages how to approach a verse or a story, we know how they derive meaning from the message of the Torah. So the proper route directs us first to the literary-critical question: Exactly what does a sage see when he looks at a verse of Scripture? Only then shall we turn to questions of meaning, that is, sages' results in the explanation and amplification of a text. The fundamental method of sages is simple and familiar: they persistently see one thing in terms of another thing, one story in the light of another.

By method I mean a very simple thing: What tells a sage to ask one sort of question, rather than some other? How does a sage know what to look for? What will strike the sage as noteworthy? For example, a sage may want to know about the connection between one story and some other story, because the sage takes for granted that stories form a connected narrative and so relate to one another. So one point of method will be the sages' interest in tying tightly the threads of narrative and the strands of a story.

To take another, more telling example, the sage takes for granted that Scripture speaks to the life and condition of Israel, the Jewish people. God repeatedly says exactly that to Abraham and to Jacob. The entire narrative of Genesis is so formed as to point toward the sacred history of Israel, the Jewish people: its slavery and redemption; its coming Temple in Jerusalem; its exile and salvation at the end of time. The powerful message of Genesis proclaims that the world's creation commenced a single, straight line of events, leading in the end to the salvation of Israel

Genesis Rabbah and the History of Israel

and through Israel all humanity. Therefore a given story will bear a deeper message about what it means to be Israel, on the one side, and what in the end of days will happen to Israel, on the other. So another point of method will be the sages' persistent search in Scripture for meaning for their own circumstance and for the condition of their people.

Sages read Genesis as the history of the world with emphasis on Israel. So the lives portrayed, the domestic quarrels and petty conflicts with the neighbors, all serve to yield insight into what was to be. While many times up to this point we have come across that simple truth, we now turn to a detailed examination of how sages spelled out the historical law at hand. For, as we have seen, just as the deeds of the patriarchs taught lessons on how the children were to act, so the lives of the patriarchs signaled the history of Israel. These propositions really laid down the same judgment, one for the individual and the family, the other for the community and the nation. Every detail of the narrative therefore served to prefigure what was to be, and Israel found itself, time and again, in the revealed facts of the history of the creation of the world, the decline of humanity down to the time of Noah, and, finally, its ascent to Abraham, Isaac, and Israel.

Sages read Genesis as history. What in fact does that mean? It was literally and in every detail a book of facts. Genesis constituted an accurate and complete testimony to things that really happened just as the story is narrated. While, therefore, sages found in Genesis deeper levels of meaning, uncovering the figurative sense underlying a literal statement, they always recognized the literal facticity of the statements of the document. The following picture of the way in which facts of Scripture settled claims of living enemies makes the matter clear. To sages Genesis reported what really happened. But, as we see throughout, Genesis also spelled out the meanings and truth of what happened.

LXI

VII.1   A. "But to the sons of his concubines, Abraham gave gifts, and while he was still living, he sent them away from his son Isaac, eastward to the east country" (Gen. 25:6):

B. In the time of Alexander of Macedonia the sons of Ishmael came to dispute with Israel about the birthright, and with them came two wicked families, the Canaanites and the Egyptians.

C. They said, "Who will go and engage in a disputation with them."

D. Gebiah b. Qosem [the enchanter] said, "I shall go and engage in a disputation with them."

E. They said to him, "Be careful not to let the Land of Israel fall into their possession."

F. He said to them, "I shall go and engage in a disputation with them. If I win over them, well and good. And if not, you may say, 'Who is this hunchback to represent us?'"

G. He went and engaged in a disputation with them. Said to them Alexander of Macedonia, "Who lays claim against whom?"

H. The Ishmaelites said, "We lay claim, and we bring our evidence from their own Torah: 'But he shall acknowledge the firstborn, the son of the hated' (Deut. 21;17). Now Ishmael was the firstborn. [We therefore claim the land as heirs of the firstborn of Abraham.]"

I. Said to him Gebiah b. Qosem, "My royal lord, does a man not do whatever he likes with his sons?"

J. He said to him, "Indeed so."

K. "And lo, it is written, 'Abraham gave all that he had to Isaac' (Gen. 25:2)."

L. [Alexander asked,] "Then where is the deed of gift to the other sons?"

M. He said to him, "'But to the sons of his concubines, Abraham gave gifts, [and while he was still living, he sent them away from his son Isaac, eastward to the east country]' (Gen. 25:6)."

N. [The Ishmaelites had no claim on the land.] They abandoned the field in shame.

O. The Canaanites said, "We lay claim, and we bring our evidence from their own Torah. Throughout their Torah it is written, 'the land of Canaan.' So let them give us back our land."

P. Said to him Gebiah b. Qosem, "My royal lord, does a man not do whatever he likes with his slave?"

Q. He said to him, "Indeed so."

R. He said to him, "And lo, it is written, 'A slave of slaves shall Canaan be to his brothers' (Gen. 9:25). So they are really our slaves."

S. [The Cannanites had no claim to the land and in fact should be serving Israel.] They abandoned the field in shame.

T. The Egyptians said, "We lay claim, and we bring our evidence from their own Torah. Six hundred thousand of them left us, taking away our silver and gold utensils: 'They despoiled the Egyptians' (Ex. 12:36). Let them give them back to us."

U. Gebiah b. Qosem said, "My royal lord, six hundred thousand men worked for them for two hundred and ten years, some as silversmiths and some as goldsmiths. Let them pay us our salary at the rate of a *denar* a day."

V. The mathematicians went and added up what was owing, and they had not reached the sum covering a century before the Egyptians had to forfeit what they had claimed. They abandoned the field in shame.

W. [Alexander] wanted to go up to Jerusalem. The Samaritans said to him, "Be careful. They will not permit you to enter their most holy sanctuary."

X. When Gebiah b. Qosem found out about this, he went and made for himself two felt shoes, with two precious stones worth twenty-thousand pieces of silver set in them. When he got to the mountain of the house [of the Temple], he said to him, "My royal lord, take off

Genesis Rabbah and the History of Israel

	your shoes and put on these two felt slippers, for the floor is slippery, and you should not slip and fall."
Y.	When they came to the most holy sanctuary, he said to him, "Up to this point, we have the right to enter. From this point onward, we do not have the right to enter."
Z.	He said to him, "When we get out of here, I'm going to even out your hump."
AA.	He said to him, "You will be called a great surgeon and get a big fee."

VII.2 A. "[But to the sons of his concubines, Abraham gave gifts, and while he was still living,] he sent them away from his son Isaac, eastward to the east country]" (Gen. 25:6):
B. He said to them, "Go as far to the east as you can, so as not to be burned by the flaming coal of Isaac."
C. But because Esau came to make war with Jacob, he took his appropriate share on his account: "Is this your joyous city, whose feet in antiquity, in ancient days, carried her afar off to sojourn? Who has devised this against Tyre, the crowning city" (Isa. 23:7).
D. Said R. Eleazar, "Whenever the name of Tyre is written in Scripture, if it is written out [with all of the letters], then it refers to the province of Tyre. Where it is written without all of its letters [and so appears identical to the word for enemy], the reference of Scripture is to Rome. [So the sense of the verse is that Rome will receive its appropriate reward.]"
E. [As to the sense of the word for] "the crowning city,"
F. R. Abba bar Kahana said, "It means that they surrounded the city like a crown."
G. R. Yannai, son of R. Simeon b. R. Yannai, said, "They surrounded it with a fence of thorns."

No. 1 is deposited here because of the case of the Ishmaelites, Abraham's children, deprived as they were of their inheritance. That issue pressed on the consciousness of the exegete compositors. No. 2 carries forward the eschatological reading of the incident. Israel's later history is prefigured in the gift to Isaac and the rejection of the other sons. The self-evidence that Esau's reward will be recompense for his evil indicates that the passage draws upon sarcasm to make its point. Sages essentially looked in the facts of history for the laws of history. We may compare them to social scientists or social philosophers, trying to turn anecdotes into insight and to demonstration how we may know the difference between impressions and truths. Genesis provided facts. Careful sifting of those facts will yield the laws that dictated why things happened one way, rather than some other. The language, as much as the substance, of the narrative provided facts demanding careful study. We understand why sages thought so if we call to mind their basic understanding of the Torah. To them (as to many today, myself included) the Torah came from God and in every detail contained revelation of God's truth. Accordingly, just as we study nature and derive facts demanding explanation and yielding law, so we study Scripture and find facts susceptible of explanation and yielding truth. Let us now turn to a sustained reading of how the biblical patriarchs prefigured the history of Israel in the age of Constantine.

The Case of Abraham

LVI

IX.1 A. "And Abraham lifted up his eyes and looked, and behold, behind him was a ram, [caught in a thicket by his horns. And Abraham went and took the ram and offered it up as a burnt-offering instead of his son]" (Gen. 22:13):

B. What is the meaning of the word for "behind"?

C. Said R. Yudan, "'Behind' in the sense of 'after,' that is, after all that happens, Israel nonetheless will be embroiled in transgressions and perplexed by sorrows. But in the end, they will be redeemed by the horns of a ram: 'And the Lord will blow the horn' (Zech. 9:14)."

D. Said R. Judah bar Simon, "'After' all generations Israel nonetheless will be embroiled in transgressions and perplexed by sorrows. But in the end, they will be redeemed by the horns of a ram: 'And the Lord God will blow the horn' (Zech. 9:14)."

E. Said R. Hinena bar Isaac, "All through the days of the year Israelites are embroiled in transgressions and perplexed by sorrows. But on the New Year they take the ram's horn and sound it, so in the end, they will be redeemed by the horns of a ram: 'And the Lord God will blow the horn' (Zech. 9:14)."

F. R. Abba bar R. Pappi, R. Joshua of Siknin in the name of R. Levi: "Since our father, Abraham, saw the ram get himself out of one thicket only to be trapped in another, the Holy One, blessed be He, said to him, 'So your descendants will be entangled in one kingdom after another, struggling from Babylonia to Media, from Media to Greece, from Greece to Edom. But in the end, they will be redeemed by the horns of a ram: 'And the Lord God will blow the horn...the Lord of Hosts will defend them' (Zech. 9:14-5)."

IX.2 A. "[...And Abraham went and took the ram and offered it up as a burnt-offering instead of his son]" (Gen. 22:13):

B. R. Yudan in the name of R. Benaiah: "He said before him, 'Lord of all ages, regard the blood of this ram as though it were the blood of Isaac, my son, its innards as though they were the innards of Isaac my son.'"

C. That [explanation of the word "instead"] accords with what we have learned in the Mishnah: "Lo, this is instead of that, this is in exchange for that, this is in place of that" – lo, such is an act of exchanging [one beast for another in the sacrificial rite, and both beasts then are held to be sanctified] [M. Tem. 5:5].

D. R. Phineas in the name of R. Benaiah: "He said before him, 'Lord of all ages, regard it as though I had offered up my son, Isaac, first, and afterward had offered up the ram in his place.'"

E. That [sense of the word "instead"] is in line with this verse: "And Jothan his son reigned in his stead" (2 Kgs. 15:7).

Genesis Rabbah and the History of Israel

> F. That accords with what we have learned in the Mishnah: [If one says, "I vow a sacrifice] like the lamb," or "like the animals of the Temple stalls" [it is a valid vow] [M. Ned. 1:3].
> G. R. Yohanan said, "That is in the sense of 'like the lamb of the daily whole-offering.'" [One who made such a statement has vowed to bring a lamb.]
> H. R. Simeon b. Laqish said, "...'Like the ram of Abraham, our father.'" [One who has made such a statement has vowed to bring a ram.]
> I. There they say, "...'Like the offspring of a sin-offering.'"
> J. Bar Qappra taught on Tannaite authority, "...'Like a lamb which has never given suck [thus, a ram].'"

The power of No. 1 is to link the life of the private person, affected by transgression, and the history of the nation, troubled by its wandering among the kingdoms. From the perspective of the Land of Israel, the issue is not Exile but the rule of foreigners. In both cases the power of the ram's horn to redeem the individual and the nation finds its origin in the Binding of Isaac. The exegetical thrust, linking the lives of the patriarchs to the life of the nation, thus brings the narrative back to the paradigm of individual being, so from patriarch to nation to person. The path leads in both directions, of course, in a fluid movement of meaning. No. 2 works on the language of "instead," a technical term in the cult, and so links the Binding of Isaac to the Temple cult.

LVI

> XII.1 A. "And the angel of the Lord called to Abraham a second time from Heaven and said, 'By myself I have sworn, [says the Lord, because you have done this thing, and have not withheld your son, your only son, I will indeed bless you and I will multiply your descendants as the stars of Heaven and as the sand which is on the seashore. And your descendants shall possess the gate of their enemies, and by your descendants shall all the nations of the earth bless themselves, because you have obeyed my voice']" (Gen. 22:15-17):
> B. What need was there for taking such an oath?
> C. He said to him, "Take an oath to me that you will never again test me or Isaac my son."
> XII.2 A. What need was there for taking such an oath?
> B. R. Levi in the name of R. Hama bar Hanina, "He said to him, 'Take an oath to me that you will never again test me.'
> C. "The matter may be compared to the case of a king who was married to a noble lady. She produced a first son from him, and then he divorced her, [remarried her, so she produced] a second son, and he divorced her again, a third son, and he divorced her again. When she had produced a tenth son, all of them got together and said to him, 'Take an oath to us that you will never again divorce our mother.'
> D. "So when Abraham had been tested for the tenth time, he said to him, 'Take an oath to me that you will never again test me.'"

XII.3 A. Said R. Hanan, "'...Because you have done this thing...'! It was the tenth trial and he refers to it as '...this [one] thing...'? But this also is the last, since it outweighs all the rest.
B. "For if he had not accepted this last trial, he would have lost the merit of all that he had already done."

XII.4 A. "...I will indeed bless you [and I will multiply your descendants as the stars of Heaven and as the sand which is on the seashore. And your descendants shall possess the gate of their enemies, and by your descendants shall all the nations of the earth bless themselves, because you have obeyed my voice]" (Gen. 22:17):
B. [Since the Hebrew makes use of the verb, "bless," two times, translated "indeed bless," we explain the duplicated verb to mean] a blessing for the father, a blessing for the son.
C. [Similarly, the duplicated verb for "multiply" means] myriads for the father and myriads for the son.

XII.5 A. "...And your descendants shall possess the gate of their enemies...":
B. Rabbi said, "This refers to Palmyra. Happy is he who will witness the fall of Palmyra, since it participated in both destructions of the Temple."
C. R. Yudan and R. Hanina:
D. One of them said, "At the destruction of the first Temple it provided eighty thousand archers."
E. The other said, "At the destruction of the Temple it supplied eight thousand archers."

XII.6 A. "So Abraham returned to his young men [and they arose and went together to Beersheba and Abraham dwelt at Beersheba]" (Gen. 22:19):
B. And where was Isaac?
C. R. Berekhiah in the name of Rabbis over there [in Babylonia]: "He had sent him to Shem to study Torah with him. [Why the emphasis on Torah study?]
D. "The matter may be compared to the case of a woman who got rich from her spinning. She said, 'Since it is from this spindle that I got rich, it will never leave my hand.'"
E. R. Yose bar Haninah said, "He sent him away by night, on account of the evil eye."
F. For from the moment that Hananiah, Mishael, and Azariah came up out of the fiery furnace, their names are not mentioned again in the narrative. So where had they gone?
G. R. Eleazar said, "They died in spit."
H. R. Yose bar Haninah said, "They died on account of the evil eye."
I. R. Joshua b. Levi said, "They changed their residence and went to Joshua b. Yehosedeq to study Torah, in line with this verse: 'Hear now, O Joshua the high priest, you and your fellows that sit before you, for they are men that are a sign' (Zech. 3:8)."
J. R. Tanhum bar Abina in the name of R. Hinena: "It was on that stipulation that Hananiah, Mishael, and Azariah descended to the fiery furnace."

Isaac and Jacob and Israel's History

While Abraham founded Israel, Isaac and Jacob carried forth the birthright and the blessing. This they did through the process of selection, ending in the assignment of the birthright to Jacob alone. The lives of all three patriarchs flowed together, each being identified with the other as a single long life. This immediately produces the proposition that the historical life of Israel, the nation, continued the individual lives of the patriarchs. The theory of who is Israel, therefore, rested on genealogy: Israel is one extended family, all being children of the same fathers and mothers, the patriarchs and matriarchs of Genesis. This theory of Israelite society, and of the Jewish people in the time of the sages of Genesis Rabbah, made of the people a family, and of genealogy, a kind of ecclesiology. The importance of that proposition in countering the Christian claim to be a new Israel cannot escape notice. Israel, sages maintained, is Israel after the flesh, and that in a most literal sense. But the basic claim, for its part, depended upon the facts of Scripture, not upon the logical requirements of theological dispute. Here is how those facts emerged in the case of Isaac.

LXIII

III.1 A. "These are the descendants of Isaac, Abraham's son: Abraham was the father of Isaac" (Gen. 25:19):

B. Abram was called Abraham: "Abram, the same is Abraham" (1 Chr. 1:27).

C. Isaac was called Abraham: "'These are the descendants of Isaac, Abraham's son, Abraham."

D. Jacob was called Israel, as it is written, "Your name shall be called no more Jacob but Israel" (Gen. 32:29).

E. Isaac also was called Israel: "And these are the names of the children of Israel, who came into Egypt, Jacob and his" (Gen. 46:8).

F. Abraham was called Israel as well.

G. R. Nathan said, "This matter is deep: 'Now the time that the children of Israel dwelt in Egypt' (Ex. 12:40), and in the land of Canaan and in the land of Goshen 'was four hundred and thirty years' (Ex. 12:40)." [Freedman, p. 557, n. 6: They were in Egypt for only 210 years. Hence their sojourn in Canaan and Goshen must be added, which means, from the birth of Isaac. Hence the children of Israel commence with Isaac. And since he was Abraham's son, it follows that Abraham was called Israel.]

The polemic at hand, linking the patriarchs to the history of Israel, claiming that all of the patriarchs bear the same names, derives proof, in part, from the base verse. But the composition in no way rests upon the exegesis of the base verse. Its syllogism transcends the case at hand. The importance of Isaac in particular derived from his relationship to the two nations that would engage in struggle, Jacob, who was and is Israel, and

Esau, who stood for Rome. By himself, as a symbol for Israel's history, Isaac remained that same shadowy figure whom we encountered earlier. Still, Isaac plays his role in setting forth the laws of Israel's history.

LXV

XIII.1   A.   "[He said, 'Behold I am old; I do not know the day of my death.] Now then take your weapons, [your quiver and your bow, and go out to the field and hunt game for me, and prepare for me savory food, such as I love, and bring it to me that I may eat; that I may bless you before I die']" (Gen. 27:2-4):

     B.   "Sharpen your hunting gear, so that you will not feed me carrion or an animal that was improperly slaughtered.

     C.   "Take your *own* hunting gear, so that you will not feed me meat that has been stolen or grabbed."

XIII.2   A.   "Your quiver":

     B.   [Since the word for "quiver" and the word for "held in suspense" share the same consonants, we interpret the statement as follows:] he said to him, "Lo, the blessings [that I am about to give] are held in suspense. For the one who is worthy of a blessing, there will be a blessing."

XIII.3   A.   Another matter: "Now then take your weapons, your quiver and your bow and go out to the field":

     B.   "Weapons" refers to Babylonia, as it is said, "And the weapons he brought to the treasure house of his god" (Gen. 2:2).

     C.   "Your quiver" speaks of Media, as it says, "So they suspended Haman on the gallows" (Est. 7:10). [The play on the words is the same as at No. 2.]

     D.   "And your bow" addresses Greece: "For I bend Judah for me, I fill the bow with Ephraim and I will story up your sons, O Zion, against your sons, O Javan [Greece]" (Zech. (9:13).

     E.   "and go out to the field" means Edom: "Unto the land of Seir, the field of Edom" (Gen. 32:4).

XIII.4   A.   "And prepare for me savory food":

     B.   R. Eleazar in the name of R. Yose b. Zimra: "Three statements were made concerning the tree, that it was good to eat, a delight to the eyes, and that it added wisdom,

     C.   "and all of them were stated in a single verse:

     D.   "'So when the woman saw that the tree was good for food,' on which basis we know that it was good to eat;

     E.   "'and that it was a delight to the eyes,' on which basis we know that it was a delight for the eyes,

     F.   "'and that the tree was to be desired to make one wise,' on which basis we know that it added to one's wisdom.

     G.   "That is in line with the following verse of Scripture: 'A song of wisdom of Ethan the Ezrahite' (Ps. 89:l)" [and the root for "song of wisdom" and that for "to make one wise" are the same].

     H.   "So did Isaac say, '"And prepare for me savory food." I used to enjoy the appearance [of food], but now I get pleasure only from the taste.'

Genesis Rabbah and the History of Israel

I. "And so did Solomon say, 'When goods increase, those who eat them are increased, and what advantage is there to the owner thereof, saving the beholding of them with his eyes' (Qoh. 5:10).

J. "The one who sees an empty basket of bread and is hungry is not equivalent to the one who sees a full basket of bread and is satisfied."

XIII.5 A. "And Rebecca was listening when Isaac spoke to his son Esau. So when Esau went to the field to hunt for game and bring it..." (Gen. 27:5):

B. If he found it, well and good.

C. And if not, "...to bring it" even by theft or violence.

No. 1 begins with the imputation of some deeper meanings for Isaac's statement, showing him to be more perspicacious than the narrative before us. No. 2 broadens the range of meaning, making the matter of the blessing more conditional than the narrative suggests. Isaac now is not sure who will get the blessing; his sense is that it will go to whoever deserves it. No. 3 then moves from the moral to the national, making the statement a clear reference to the history of Israel (as though, by this point, it were not obvious). What the author of the item at hand contributes, then, is the specific details. What the compositor does is move the reader's mind from the philological to the moral to the national dimension of exegesis of the statements at hand. No. 4 works out the meaning of the request for tasty food; the main point is that Isaac wants highly spiced food, since he cannot see what he is eating. If one knows he has something to eat, that often satisfies; not seeing is not knowing. No. 5 contributes a familiar motif. Esau steals, but Jacob takes only what is lawful. Isaac foresaw the entire history of Israel.

LXV

XXIII.1 A. ["See the smell of my son is as the smell of a field which the Lord has blessed" (Gen. 27:27):] Another matter: This teaches that the Holy One, blessed be He, showed him the house of the sanctuary as it was built, wiped out, and built once more.

B. "See the smell of my son": This refers to the Temple in all its beauty, in line with this verse: "A sweet smell to me shall you observe" (Num. 28:2).

C. "...Is as the smell of a field": This refers to the Temple as it was wiped out, thus: "Zion shall be ploughed as a field" (Mic. 3:12).

D. "...Which the Lord has blessed": This speaks of the Temple as it was restored once more in the age to come, as it is said, "For there the Lord commanded the blessing, even life for ever" (Ps. 133:3).

The conclusion explicitly links the blessing of Jacob to the Temple throughout its history. The concluding prooftext presumably justifies the entire identification of the blessing at hand with what was to come.

LXVI

II.1 A. R. Berekhiah opened [discourse by citing the following verse:] "'Return, return, O Shulamite, return, return that we may look upon you' (Song 7:1):

B. "The verse at hand refers to 'return' four times, corresponding to the four kingdoms in which Israel enters in peace and from which Israel comes forth in peace.

C. "'O Shulamite': The word refers to the nation who every day is blessed with a blessing ending with peace [which shares the consonants of the word at hand], as it is said, 'And may he give you peace' (Num. 7:26).

D. "It is the nation in the midst of which dwells the peace of the ages, as it is said, 'And let them make me a sanctuary that I may dwell among them' (Ex. 25:8).

E. "It is the nation to which I am destined to give peace: 'And I will give peace in the land' (Lev. 26:6).

F. "It is the nation over which I am destined to spread peace: 'Behold, I will extend peace to her like a river' (Isa. 66:12)."

G. R. Samuel bar Tanhum, R. Hanan bar Berekiah in the name of R. Idi: "It is the nation that makes peace between me and my world. For if it were not for that nation, I would destroy my world."

H. R. Hana in the name of R. Aha: "'When the earth and all the inhabitants thereof are dissolved' (Ps. 75:4), as in the statement, 'All the inhabitants of Canaan are melted away' (Ex. 15:15).

I. "'I' (Ps. 75:4), that is, when they accepted upon themselves [the Ten Commandments, beginning,] 'I am the Lord your God' (Ex. 20:2), 'I established the pillars of it' (Ps. 75:4), and the world was set on a solid foundation."

J. Said R. Eleazar bar Merom, "This nation preserves [makes whole] the stability of the world, both in this age and in the age to come."

K. R. Joshua of Sikhnin in the name of R. Levi: "This is the nation on account of the merit of which whatever good that comes into the world is bestowed. Rain comes down only for their sake, that is, 'to you' [as in the base verse], and the dew comes down only 'to you.'

L. "May God give you of the dew of Heaven."

The point of this rather sizable composition comes at the end, but the intersecting verse is worked out in its own terms. We have a philosophy of Israel among the nations, stating in one place every component. We begin with a reference to the four kingdoms, but then we move out of that item to the name of the Shulamite, and, third, we proceed to work on the theme of Israel as the nation of peace. Once the praise of Israel forms the focus, we leave behind the issue of peace and deal with the blessings that come to the world on Israel's account. Only at that point does the base verse prove relevant. I could not begin to speculate on the origins of this complex composition – unitary or incremental. What is important to us is the reason for its selection and inclusion on the part of those responsible for the document before us, and their interest is self-

Genesis Rabbah and the History of Israel

evident. But whether they took existing materials and tacked on their point, or whether the composition existed in this form prior to its selection and inclusion, we cannot now know. Whatever future history finds adumbration in the life of Jacob derives from the struggle with Esau. Israel and Rome – these two contend for the world. Still, Isaac plays his part in the matter. Rome does have a legitimate claim, and that claim demands recognition – an amazing, if grudging concession on the part of sages that Christian Rome at least is Esau.

LXVII

IV.1 A "When Esau heard the words of his father, he cried out with an exceedingly great and bitter cry [and said to his father, 'Bless me, even me also, O my father!']" (Gen. 27:34):

B. Said R. Hanina, "Whoever says that the Holy One, blessed be He, is lax, may his intestines become lax. While he is patient, he does collect what is coming to you.

C. "Jacob made Esau cry out one cry, and where was he penalized? It was in the castle of Shushan: 'And he cried with a loud and bitter cry' (Est. 4:1)."

IV.2 A. "But he said, 'Your brother came with guile and he has taken away your blessing'" (Gen. 33:35):

B. R. Yohanan said, "[He came] with the wisdom of his knowledge of the Torah."

IV.3 A. "Esau said, 'Is he not rightly named Jacob? [For he has supplanted me these two times. He took away my birthright and behold, now he has taken away my blessing.' Then he said, 'Have you not reserved a blessing for me?']" (Gen. 27:36):

B. "'He took away my birthright, and I kept silence, and now he has taken away my blessing.'"

IV.4 A. "Then he said, 'Have you not reserved a blessing for me?'" (Gen. 27:36):

B. Even an inferior one?

The stunning concession for Christianity should not be missed. Rome really is Israel's brother. The history of the two brothers forms a set of counterpoints, the rise of one standing for the decline of the other. The ultimate end, Israel's final glory, will permanently mark the subjugation of Esau. The point of No. 1 is to link the present passage to the history of Israel's redemption later on. In this case, however, the matter concerns Israel's paying recompense for causing anguish to Esau. No. 2 introduces Jacob's knowledge of Torah in place of Esau's view of Jacob as full of guile. The remainder of the entries provides minor glosses.

Joseph, the Tribal Fathers, and Israel's History

Along with Abraham, Isaac, and Jacob, Joseph take up an important role in the revelation of Israel's history. His brothers, founders of the tribes bearing their names, obviously give their testimony, too, to what will happen in the time to come. Since Jacob, in Genesis 49, and Moses, in Deuteronomy 32, treat the brothers of Joseph, founders of the tribes, as precursors of what was to happen in the future history of Israel as well as at the end of days, none of these modes of reading the book of Genesis presents surprises. Since both Jacob and Moses explicitly spoke of the sons of Jacob as paradigms of history, the sages understood the text precisely as the Torah itself told them to understand it. That is, the sages simply took seriously and at face value the facts in hand, as any scientist or philosopher finds facts and reflects upon their meaning and the implications and laws deriving from them. So sages' mode of reading derived from an entirely inductive and scientific, philosophical mode of thought. The laws of history begin with the principle that the merit of the founders sustains the children to come. The model for the transaction in merit – which underlines and explains the theory of genealogy as the foundation of Israel's social entity – comes to expression in the life of Joseph. Joseph both derived benefit from the merit of his ancestors and handed on merit to his descendants.

LXXXIV

V.2 A. "These are the generations of the family of Jacob. Joseph [being seventeen years old, was shepherding the flock with his brothers]" (Gen. 37:2):

B. These generations came along only on account of the merit of Joseph.

C. Did Jacob go to Laban for any reason other than for Rachel?

D. These generations thus waited until Joseph was born, in line with this verse: "And when Rachel had borne Joseph, Jacob said to Laban, 'Send me away'" (Gen. 30:215).

E. Who brought them down to Egypt? It was Joseph.

F. Who supported them in Egypt? It was Joseph.

G. The sea split open only on account of the merit of Joseph: "The waters saw you, O God" (Ps. 77:17). "You have with your arm redeemed your people, the sons of Jacob and Joseph" (Ps. 77:16).

H. R. Yudan said, "Also the Jordan was divided only on account of the merit of Joseph."

No. 2 asks why only Joseph is mentioned as the family of Jacob. The inner polemic is that the merit of Jacob and Joseph would more than suffice to overcome Esau/Rome. Joseph's life, as much as Abraham's or Jacob's, represents the history of Israel and its meaning.

LXXXVII

VI.1 A. "And although she spoke to Joseph [day after day, he would not listen to her, to lie with her or to be with her. But one day, when he went into the house to do his work and none of the men of the house was there in the house, she caught him by his garment,

Genesis Rabbah and the History of Israel

saying, 'Lie with me.' But he left his garment in her hand and fled and got out of the house]" (Gen. 39:10-13):

B. R. Yudan in the name of R. Benjamin bar Levi: "As to the sons of Levi, the trials affecting them were the same, and the greatness that they achieved was the same.

C. "...The trials affecting them were the same: 'And although she spoke to Joseph [day after day.' 'Now it came to pass, when they spoke to him day by day'; (Est. 3:4). [Mordecai, descended from Benjamin, was nagged every day.] 'He would not listen to her.' 'And he did not listen to them' (Est. 3:4).

D. "...And the greatness that they achieved was the same: 'And Pharaoh took off his signet ring from his hand and put it upon Joseph's hand' (Gen. 41:42). 'And the king took off his ring, which he had taken from Haman and gave it to Mordecai' (Est. 8:2).

E. "'And arrayed him in fine linen clothing and put a gold chain about his neck' (Gen. 41:42). 'And Mordecai went forth from the presence of the king in royal apparel of blue and white, and with a great crown of gold and with a robe of fine linen and purple' (Est. 8:15).

F. "'And he made Joseph ride in the second chariot which he had' (Gen. 41:43). 'And cause Mordecai to ride on horseback through the street of the city' (Est. 6:9).

G. "'And they cried before him, Abrech' (Gen. 41:43). 'And proclaimed before Mordecai, "Thus shall it be done to the man"' (Est. 6:11)."

VI.2 A. "...He would not listen to her, to lie with her or to be with her":

B. "...To lie with her" in this world, that he would not have children with her.

C. "...Or to be with her" in the world to come.

VI.3 A. "...He would not listen to her, to lie with her or to be with her":

B. "...To lie with her": Even lying without sexual relations.

VI.4 A. A noble lady as R. Yose, "Is it possible that Joseph, at the age of seventeen, in his full vigor, could have done such a thing?"

B. He produced for her a copy of the book of Genesis. He began to read the story of Reuben and Judah. He said to her, "If these, who were adults and in their father's domain, were not protected by the Scripture [but were revealed by Scripture in all their lust], Joseph, who was a minor and on his own, all the more so [would have been revealed as lustful, had he done what the lady thought he had]."

The parallel drawn between Joseph and Benjamin = Mordecai permits the exegete to draw a parallel between the life of Joseph and the history of Israel. No. 2 expands on the base verse, and No. 3 presents an argument in favor of its authenticity, at the same time linking the present story to the two that have preceded.

LXXXVIII

V.1 A. ["So the chief butler told his dream to Joseph and said to him, 'In my dream there was a vine before me, and on the vine there were three branches; as soon as it budded, its blossoms shot forth, and the clusters ripened into grapes. Pharaoh's cup was in my hand, and I took the grapes and pressed them into Pharaoh's cup and placed the cup in Pharaoh's hand. And I took the grapes and pressed them into Pharaoh's cup and placed the cup in Pharaoh's hand'" (Gen. 49:11-13)]. "'...There was a vine before me'": This refers to Israel: "You plucked up a vine out of Egypt" (Ps. 80:9).

B. "'...And on the vine there were three branches'": This refers to Moses, Aaron, and Miriam.

C. "'...As soon as it budded, its blossoms shot forth'": Specifically, the blossoming of the redemption of Israel.

D. "'...And the clusters ripened into grapes'": As soon as the vine budded, it blossomed, and as soon as the grapes blossomed, the clusters ripened.

V.2 A. "'Pharaoh's cup was in my hand, and I took the grapes and pressed them into Pharaoh's cup and placed the cup in Pharaoh's hand. And I took the grapes and pressed them into Pharaoh's cup and placed the cup in Pharaoh's hand.'...' You shall place Pharaoh's cup in his hand'":

B. On what basis did sages ordain that there should be four cups of wine for Passover?

C. R. Hunah in the name of R. Benaiah: "They correspond to the four times that redemption is stated with respect to Egypt: 'I will bring you out...and I will deliver you...and I will redeem you...and I will take you' (Ex. 6:6-7)."

D. R. Samuel b. Nahman said, "They correspond to the four times that 'cups' are mentioned here: 'Pharaoh's *cup* was in my hand, and I took the grapes and pressed them into Pharaoh's *cup* and placed the *cup* in Pharaoh's hand. And I took the grapes and pressed them into Pharaoh's *cup*.'"

E. R. Levi said, "They correspond to the four kingdoms."

F. R. Joshua b. Levi said, "They correspond to the four cups of fury that the Holy One, blessed be He, will give the nations of the world to drink: 'For thus says the Lord, the God of Israel, to me, "Take this cup of the wine of fury"' (Jer. 25:15). 'Babylon has been a golden cup in the Lord's hand' (Jer. 51:7). 'For in the hand of the Lord there is a cup' (Ps. 75:9). 'And burning wind shall be the portion of their cup' (Ps. 11:6).

G. "And in response to these, the Holy One, blessed be He, will give Israel four cups of salvation to drink in the age to come: 'O Lord, the portion of my inheritance and of my cup, you maintain my lot' (Ps. 16:5). 'You prepare a table before me in the presence of my enemies, you have anointed my head with oil, my cup runs over' (Ps. 23:5). 'I will lift up the cup of salvations and call upon the name of the Lord' (Ps. 116:13).

H. "What is said is not 'cup of salvation' but 'cup of salvations,' one in the days of the Messiah, the other in the time of Gog and Magog."

V.3 A. Joseph said to him, "[Since the dream refers to Israel's coming redemption,] you have brought me a good gospel, so I shall now give you a good gospel: 'within three days Pharaoh will lift up your head and restore you to your office.'"

V.4 A. "But remember me, when it is well with you, and do me the kindness, I pray you, to make mention of me to Pharaoh, and so get me out of this house. For I was indeed stolen out of the land of the

Genesis Rabbah and the History of Israel 137

		Hebrews, and here also I have done nothing that they should put me into the dungeon' (Gen. 40:14-15)":
	B.	Said R. Aha, "On the basis of the use of the verb 'stolen' twice [in the statement, 'indeed stolen,'] we learn that he was stolen twice."
V.5	A.	"...That they should put me into the dungeon":
	B.	Said R. Abin, "The meaning is that they put [One] with me in prison. [Freedman, p. 817, n. 4: The Divine Presence accompanied me.]"

No. 1 reads the vision in light of the story of Israel's redemption from Egypt. No. 2 then brings the point home, by linking Israel's redemption specifically to aspects of the language of the vision. Obviously, our base verse plays only a modest role in the grand vision of No. 2. No. 3 carries forward No. 2 and therefore cannot be understood without it. If, as it would appear, No. 2 is an independent composition, then No. 3 surely was added afterward, at the level of redactional composition, to link the whole still more tightly to our context and to exploit in the service of that context the enormous conceptions introduced in No. 2. Nos. 4, 5 provide minor glosses.

LXXXIX

I.1	A.	"At it came to pass at the end of two years, [Pharaoh dreamed that he was standing by the Nile]" (Gen. 41:1):
	B.	"He sets an end to darkness...the stones of thick darkness and the shadow of death" (Job 28:3):
	C.	A span of time has been assigned to the world, decreeing how many years it would spend in darkness.
	D.	What is the scriptural evidence? "He sets an end to darkness...the stones of thick darkness and the shadow of death" (Job 28:3).
	E.	For all that time that the impulse to do evil is in the world, darkness and gloom are in the world. When the impulse to do evil is uprooted from the world, darkness and deep gloom will pass from the world.
I.2	A.	Another interpretation of the verse: "He sets an end to darkness...the stones of thick darkness and the shadow of death" (Job 28:3):
	B.	A span of time was assigned to the Joseph, decreeing how many years he would spend in prison.
	C.	Once the end came, Pharaoh had his dream: "At it came to pass at the end of two years, [Pharaoh dreamed that he was standing by the Nile]" (Gen. 41:1).

The cited verse introduces at No. 1 the theme of the prevailing interpretation of Joseph's life, which has emphasized his power to sin and his regeneration. So the underlying point is that Joseph's impulse to do evil reached the end of its allotted span of time, at which point the end of his period of suffering also came. Since Joseph's story has repeatedly been linked to Israel's history, with strong emphasis on the links between Joseph and Mordecai, the deeper message addresses Israel's condition and links its impulse to sin with its degraded condition.

XCVIII

II.4   A.   "Then Jacob called his sons and said, 'Gather yourselves together, that I may tell you what shall befall you in days to come'":

B.   "Gather yourselves together" from the Land of Israel, "and assemble and hear" in Raameses.

C.   "Gather yourselves together" the ten tribes.

D.   "And assemble and hear" the tribes of Judah and Benjamin.

E.   He commanded them to treat the tribes of Judah and Benjamin with honor.

II.5   A.   R. Aha said, "'Gather together' means 'purify' in line with this verse: 'And they gathered themselves together...and they purified themselves' (Neh. 12:28)."

II.6   A.   Rabbis say, "It means that he commanded themselves about dissension. He said to them, 'All of you should form a single gathering.'

B.   "That is in line with this verse: 'And you, son of man, take one stick and write upon it, "For Judah and for the children of Israel his companions" (Ezek. 37:16).'

C.   "What is written is 'his companion,' meaning, that when the children of Israel form a single assembly, then they prepare themselves for redemption.

D.   "For what is written afterward? 'And I will make them one nation in the land' (Ezek. 37:22)."

II.7   A.   "Then Jacob called his sons and said, 'Gather yourselves together, that I may tell you what shall befall you in days to come'":

B.   R. Simon said, "He showed them the fall of Gog, in line with this usage: 'It shall be in the end of days...when I shall be sanctified through you, O Gog' (Ezek. 38:165). 'Behold, it shall come upon Edom' (Isa. 34:5)."

C.   R. Judah said, "He showed them the building of the house of the sanctuary: 'And it shall come to pass in the end of days that the mountain of the Lord's house shall be established' (Isa. 2:2)."

D.   Rabbis say, "He came to reveal the time of the end to them, but it was hidden from him."

E.   R. Judah in the name of R. Eleazar bar Abina: "To two men the secret of the time of the end was revealed, but then it was hidden from them, and these are they: Jacob and Daniel.

F.   "Daniel: 'But you, O Daniel, shut up the words and seal the book' (Dan. 12:4).

G.   "Jacob: 'Then Jacob called his sons and said, "Gather yourselves together, that I may tell you what shall befall you in days to come. Assemble and hear, O sons of Jacob, and hearken to Israel, your father. Reuben, you are my firstborn."'

H.   "This teaches that he came to reveal the time of the end to them, but it was hidden from him."

I.   The matter may be compared to the case of the king's ally, who was departing this world, and his children surrounded his bed. He said to them, "Come and I shall tell you the secrets of the king." Then he

Genesis Rabbah and the History of Israel   139

                 looked up and saw the king. He said to them, "Be most meticulous about the honor owing to the king."
- J.   So our father Jacob looked up and saw the Presence of God standing over him. He said to them, "Be most meticulous about the honor owing to the Holy One, blessed be He."

No. 4 interprets the language at hand both in its immediate context and in the larger setting of Israel's history. No. 5 goes over the same language, and No. 6 introduces, in the identical context, an eschatological dimension. No. 7 successfully carries forward this final theme, which surely is invited by the base verse, so that the personal history of the individual, dealt with at the opening compositions, gives way to the national history of Israel.

XCIX

II.1
- A. "For the Lord God will do nothing unless he reveals his secret to his servants the prophets" (Amos 3:7).
- B. Jacob linked two of his sons, corresponding to two of the monarchies, and Moses linked two of the tribes, corresponding to two of the monarchies.
- C. Judah corresponds to the kingdom of Babylonia, for this is compared to a lion and that is compared to a lion. This is compared to a lion: "Judah is a lion's whelp" (Gen. 49:9), and so, too, Babylonia: "The first was like a lion" (Dan. 7:4).
- D. Then by the hand of which of the tribes will the kingdom of Babylonia fall? It will be by the hand of Daniel, who comes from the tribe of Judah.
- E. Benjamin corresponds to the kingdom of Media, for this is compared to a wolf and that is compared to a wolf. This is compared to a wolf: "Benjamin is a ravenous wolf, in the morning devouring the prey, and at evening dividing the spoil." And that is compared to a wolf: "And behold, another beast, a second, like a wolf" (Dan. 7:5).
- F. R. Hanina said, "The word for 'wolf' in the latter verse is written as 'bear.' It had been called a bear."
- G. That is the view of R. Yohanan, for R. Yohanan said, "'Wherefore a lion of the forest slays them' (Jer. 5:6) refers to Babylonia, and 'a wolf of the deserts spoils them' refers to Media."
- H. [Reverting to E:] Then by the hand of which of the tribes will the kingdom of Media fall? It will be by the hand of Mordecai, who comes from the tribe of Benjamin.
- I. Levi corresponds to the kingdom of Greece. This is the third tribe in order, and that is the third kingdom in order. This is written with a word that is made up of three letters, and that is written with a word which consists of three letters. This one sounds the horn and that one sounds the horn, this one wears turbans and that one wears helmets, this one wears pants and that one wears knee cuts.
- J. To be sure, this one is very populous, while that one is few in numbers. But the many came and fell into the hand of the few.

140   *Sources of the Transformation of Judaism*

> K. On account of merit deriving from what source did this take place? It is on account of the blessing that Moses bestowed: "Smiter through the loins of them that rise up against him": (Deut. 33:11).
> L. Then by the hand of which of the tribes will the kingdom of Greece fall? It will be by the hand of sons of the Hasmoneans, who come from the tribe of Levi.
> M. Joseph corresponds to the kingdom of Edom [Rome], for this one has horns and that one has horns. This one has horns: "His firstling bullock, majesty is his, and his horns are the horns of the wild ox" (Deut. 33:17). And that one has horns: "And concerning the ten horns that were on its head" (Dan. 7:20). This one avoided kept away from fornication while that one cleaved to fornication. This one paid respect for the honor owing to his father, while that one despised the honor owing to his father. Concerning this one it is written, "For I fear God" (Gen. 42:18), while in regard to that one it is written, "And he did not fear God" (Deut. 25:18). [So the correspondence in part is one of opposites.]
> N. Then by the hand of which of the tribes will the kingdom of Edom fall? It will be by the hand of the anointed for war, who comes from the tribe of Joseph.
> O. R. Phineas in the name of R. Samuel b. Nahman: "There is a tradition that Esau will fall only by the hand of the sons of Rachel: 'Surely the least of the flock shall drag them away' (Jer. 49:20). Why the least? Because they are the youngest of the tribes."

This impressive theory of Israel's history finds a place here only because of E. Yet the larger relevance – Jacob's predictions of the future – justifies including the composition.

XCIX

> III.1 A. "Benjamin is a ravenous wolf, in the morning devouring the prey, and at evening dividing the spoil" (Gen. 49:27):
> B. The verse speaks of the judge that comes from Benjamin, that is, Ehud.
> C. Just as a wolf seizes, so Ehud seized the heart of Eglon: "And Ehud came to him and he was sitting by himself alone in his cool upper chamber" (Judg. 3:20).
> D. "And he said, I have a secret errand for you, O king" (Judg. 3:19):
> E. He said to him, "Thus has the master of the world said to me, 'Take a sword and thrust it into his belly.'"
> F. "And the dirt came out" (Judg. 3:22):
> G. This refers to his shit.
> H. "Then Ehud went out onto the porch" (Judg. 3:23):
> I. R. Yudan said, "Out into the public square."
> J. R. Berekhiah said, "There the ministering angels sat all in a row."
> III.2 A. Another matter: "Benjamin is a ravenous wolf, in the morning devouring the prey, and at evening dividing the spoil" (Gen. 49:27):
> B. The verse speaks of the king that comes from Benjamin, [that is, Saul].
> C. Just as the wolf seizes, so Saul seized the monarchy, as it is said, "So Saul took the kingdom over Israel" (1 Sam. 14:47).

Genesis Rabbah and the History of Israel   141

	D.	"...In the morning devouring the prey": "And he fought against his enemies on all sides" (1 Sam. 14:47).
	E.	"...And at evening dividing the spoil": "So Saul died, and his three sons" (1 Sam. 31:6).
III.3	A.	Another matter: "Benjamin is a ravenous wolf, in the morning devouring the prey, and at evening dividing the spoil" (Gen. 49:27):
	B.	The verse speaks of the queen [that comes from Benjamin, [that is, Esther].
	C.	Just as the wolf seizes, so Esther seized the monarchy: "Esther was taken into the king's house" (Est. 2:8).
	D.	"...In the morning devouring the prey": "On that day did the king Ahasuerus give the house of Haman the Jews' enemy to Esther the queen" (Est. 8:1).
	E.	"...And at evening dividing the spoil": "And Esther set Mordecai over the house of Haman" (Est. 8:2).
III.4	A.	Another matter: "Benjamin is a ravenous wolf, in the morning devouring the prey and at evening dividing the spoil" (Gen. 49:27):
	B.	The verse speaks of the land that belongs to Benjamin, [that is, Jericho].
	C.	Just as the wolf seizes, so the land of Benjamin seizes its crops [making them ripen fast].
	D.	"...In the morning devouring the prey: This speaks of Jericho, where the produce ripens first.
	E.	"...And at evening dividing the spoil": this speaks of Beth El, where the produce ripens last.
III.5	A.	["Benjamin is a ravenous wolf, in the morning devouring the prey, and at evening dividing the spoil":] R. Phineas interpreted the verse to speak of the altar: "Just as a wolf seizes, so the altar would seize the offerings.
	B.	"'...In the morning devouring the prey': 'The one lamb you shall offer in the morning' (Num. 28:4).
	C.	"'...And at evening dividing the spoil': 'And the other lamb you shall offer in the evening' (Num. 28:45)."

The systematic reading of the reference to Benjamin links the blessing to successive events in the later history of Israel, the judge of Benjamin, then the king that Benjamin produced, then the queen, then the land, and, finally, the Temple, located as it was in Benjamin's territory. The clear intent of the compositors, to read Jacob's blessing in the light of future history, has attained realization time and again.

Rome in Particular

Why Rome in the form it takes in Genesis Rabbah? And how come the obsessive character of sages disposition of the theme of Rome? Were their picture merely of Rome as tyrant and destroyer of the Temple, we should have no reason to link the text to the problems of the age of redaction and closure. But, as we have repeatedly observed, now it is Rome as Israel's brother, counterpart, and nemesis, Rome as the one thing standing in the way of Israel's, and the world's, ultimate salvation. So the stakes are different, and much higher. It is not a political Rome but a messianic Rome that is at issue: Rome as surrogate for Israel, Rome as obstacle to Israel. Why? It is because Rome now confronts Israel with a crisis, and, I argue, Genesis Rabbah constitutes a response to that crisis. Rome in the fourth century became Christian. Sages respond by facing that fact quite squarely and saying, "Indeed, it is as you say, a kind of Israel, an heir of Abraham as your texts explicitly claim. But we remain the sole legitimate Israel, the bearer of the birthright – we and not you. So you are our brother: Esau, Ishmael, Edom." And the rest follows.

Genesis Rabbah reached closure, people generally agree, toward the end of the fourth century. That century marks the beginning of the West as we have known it. Why so? Because in the fourth century, from the conversion of Constantine and over the next hundred years, the Roman empire became Christian – and with it, the West. So the fourth century marks the first century of the history of the West in that form in which the West would flourish for the rest of time, to our own day. Accordingly, we should not find surprising sages' recurrent references, in the reading of Genesis, to the struggle of two equal powers, Rome and Israel, Esau and Jacob, Ishmael and Isaac. The world historical change, marking the confirmation in politics and power of the Christians' claim that Christ was king over all humanity, demanded from sages an appropriate, and, to Israel, persuasive. response.

By rereading the story of the beginnings, sages discovered the answer and the secret of the end. Rome claimed to be Israel, and, indeed, sages conceded, Rome shared the patrimony of Israel. That claim took the form of the Christians' appropriation of the Torah as "the Old Testament," so sages acknowledged a simple fact in acceding to the notion that, in some way, Rome, too, formed part of Israel. But it was the rejected part, the Ishmael, the Esau, not the Isaac, not the Jacob. The advent of Christian Rome precipitated the sustained, polemical, and, I think, rigorous and well-argued rereading of beginnings in light of the end. Rome then marked the conclusion of human history as Israel had known it. Beyond? The coming of the true Messiah, the redemption of Israel, the salvation of the world, the end of time. So the issues were not inconsiderable, and when the sages spoke of Esau/Rome, as they did so often, they confronted the life or death decision of the day.

Let us begin with a simple example of how ubiquitous is the shadow of Ishmael/Esau/Edom/Rome. Wherever sages reflect on future history, their minds turn to their own day. They found the hour difficult, because Rome, now Christian, claimed that very birthright and blessing that they understood to be theirs alone. Christian Rome posed a threat without precedent. Now another dominion, besides Israel's, claimed the

Genesis Rabbah and the History of Israel

rights and blessings that sustained Israel. Wherever in Scripture they turned, sages found comfort in the iteration that the birthright, the blessing, the Torah, and the hope – all belonged to them and to none other. Here is a striking statement of that constant proposition.

LIII

XII.1 A. "[So she said to Abraham, 'Cast out this slave woman with her son, for the son of this slave woman shall not be heir with my son Isaac.'] And the thing was very displeasing to Abraham on account of his son" (Gen. 21:11):

B. That is in line with this verse: "And shuts his eyes from looking upon evil" (Isa. 33:15). [Freedman, p. 471, n. 1: He shut his eyes from Ishmael's evil ways and was reluctant to send him away.]

XII.2 A. "But God said to Abraham, 'Be not displeased because of the lad and because of your slave woman; whatever Sarah says to you, do as she tells you, for through Isaac shall your descendants be named' (Gen. 21:12)":

B. Said R. Yudan bar Shillum, "What is written is not 'Isaac' but 'through Isaac.' [The matter is limited, not through all of Isaac's descendants but only through some of them, thus excluding Esau.]"

XII.3 A. R. Azariah in the name of Bar Hutah: "The use of the B, which stands for two, indicates that he who affirms that there are two worlds will inherit both worlds [this age and the age to come]."

B. Said R. Yudan bar Shillum, "It is written, 'Remember his marvelous works that he has done, his signs and the judgments of his mouth' (Ps. 105:5). I have given a sign, namely, it is one who gives the appropriate evidence through what he says. Specifically, he who affirms that there are two worlds will be called 'your seed.'

C. "And he who does not affirm that there are two worlds will not be called 'your seed.'"

No. 1 makes "the matter" refer to Ishmael's misbehavior, not Sarah's proposal, so removing the possibility of disagreement between Abraham and Sarah. Nos. 2, 3 interpret the limiting particle, "in," that is, *among* the descendants of Isaac will be found Abraham's heirs, but not all the descendants of Isaac will be heirs of Abraham. No. 2 explicitly excludes Esau, that is Rome, and No. 3 makes the matter doctrinal in the context of Israel's inner life.

As the several antagonists of Israel stand for Rome in particular, so the traits of Rome, as sages perceived them, characterized the biblical heroes. Esau provided a favorite target. From the womb Israel and Rome contended.

LXIII

VI.1 A. "And the children struggled together [within her, and she said, 'If it is thus, why do I live?' So she went to inquire of the Lord. And the Lord said to her, 'Two nations are in your womb, and two peoples,

144   *Sources of the Transformation of Judaism*

		born of you, shall be divided; the one shall be stronger than the other, and the elder shall serve the younger']" (Gen. 25:22-23):
	B.	R. Yohanan and R. Simeon b. Laqish:
	C.	R. Yohanan said, "[Because the word, 'struggle,' contains the letters for the word, 'run,'] this one was running to kill that one and that one was running to kill this one."
	D.	R. Simeon b. Laqish: "This one releases the laws given by that one, and that one releases the laws given by this one."
VI.2	A.	R. Berekhiah in the name of R. Levi said, "It is so that you should not say that it was only after he left his mother's womb that [Esau] contended against [Jacob].
	B.	"But even while he was yet in his mother's womb, his fist was stretched forth against him: 'The wicked stretch out their fists [so Freedman] from the womb' (Ps. 58:4)."
VI.3	A.	"And the children struggled together within her":
	B.	[Once more referring to the letters of the word "struggled," with special attention to the ones that mean, "run,"] they wanted to run within her.
	C.	When she went by houses of idolatry, Esau would kick, trying to get out: "The wicked are estranged from the womb" (Ps. 58:4).
	D.	When she went by synagogues and study houses, Jacob would kick, trying to get out: "Before I formed you in the womb, I knew you" (Jer. 1:5).
VI.4	A.	"...And she said, 'If it is thus, why do I live?'"
	B.	R. Haggai in the name of R. Isaac: "This teaches that our mother, Rebecca, went around to the doors of women and said to them, 'Did you ever have this kind of pain in your life?'"
	C.	"[She said to them,] '"If thus": If this is the pain of having children, would that I had not gotten pregnant.'"
	D.	Said R. Huna, "If I am going to produce twelve tribes only through this kind of suffering, would that I had not gotten pregnant."
VI.5	A.	It was taught on Tannaite authority in the name of R. Nehemiah, "Rebecca was worthy of having the twelve tribes come forth from her. That is in line with this verse:
	B.	"'"Two nations are in your womb, and two peoples, born of you, shall be divided; the one shall be stronger than the other, and the elder shall serve the younger." When her days to be delivered were fulfilled, behold, there were twins in her womb. The first came forth red, all his body like a hairy mantle, so they called his name Esau. Afterward his brother came forth...' (Gen. 25:23-24).
	C.	"'Two nations are in your womb': Thus two.
	D.	"'And two peoples': Thus two more, hence four.
	E.	"'...The one shall be stronger than the other': Two more, so six.
	F.	"'...And the elder shall serve the younger': Two more, so eight.
	G.	"'When her days to be delivered were fulfilled, behold, there were twins in her womb': Two more, so ten.
	H.	"'The first came forth red': Now eleven.
	I.	"'Afterward his brother came forth': Now twelve."
	J.	There are those who say, "Proof derives from this verse: 'If it is thus, why do I live?' Focusing on the word for 'thus,' we note that

Genesis Rabbah and the History of Israel 145

		the two letters of that word bear the numerical value of seven and five respectively, hence, twelve in all."
VI.6	A.	"So she went to inquire of the Lord":
	B.	Now were there synagogues and houses of study in those days [that she could go to inquire of the Lord]?
	C.	But is it not the fact that she went only to the study of Eber?
	D.	This serves to teach you that whoever receives an elder is as if he receives the Presence of God.

Nos. 1-3 take for granted that Esau represents Rome, and Jacob, Israel. Consequently the verse underlines the point that there is natural enmity between Israel and Rome. Esau hated Israel even while he was still in the womb. Jacob, for his part, revealed from the womb those virtues that would characterize him later on, eager to serve God as Esau was eager to worship idols. The text invites just this sort of reading. No. 4 and No. 5 relate Rebecca's suffering to the birth of the twelve tribes. No. 6 makes its own point, independent of the rest and tacked on.

LXIII

VII.2	A.	"Two nations are in your womb, [and two peoples, born of you, shall be divided; the one shall be stronger than the other, and the elder shall serve the younger]" (Gen. 25:23):
	B.	There are two proud nations in your womb, this one takes pride in his world, and that one takes pride in his world.
	C.	This one takes pride in his monarchy, and that one takes pride in his monarchy.
	D.	There are two proud nations in your womb.
	E.	Hadrian represents the nations, Solomon, Israel.
	F.	There are two who are hated by the nations in your womb. All the nations hate Esau, and all the nations hate Israel.
	G.	[Following Freedman's reading:] The one whom your creator hates is in your womb: "And Esau I hated" (Mal. 1:3).
VII.3	A.	"And two peoples, born of you, shall be divided":
	B.	Said R. Berekhiah, "On the basis of this statement we have evidence that [Jacob] was born circumcized."
VII.4	A.	"...The one shall be stronger than the other, [and the elder shall serve the younger]" (Gen. 25:23):
	B.	R. Helbo in the name of the house of R. Shila: "Up to this point there were Sabteca and Raamah, but from you will come Jews and Romans." [Freedman, p. 561, n. 8: "Hitherto even the small nations such as Sabteca and Raamah counted; but henceforth all these will pale into insignificance before the two who will rise from you."]
VII.5	A.	"...And the elder shall serve the younger" (Gen. 25:23):
	B.	Said R. Huna, "If he has merit, he will be served, and if not, he will serve."

The syllogism invokes the base verse as part of its repertoire of cases. No. 2 augments the statement at hand, still more closely linking it to the history of Israel. Nos. 3, 4, and 5 gloss minor details. The same polemic proceeds in what follows.

LXIII

VIII.3   A.   "The first came forth red":
- B. R. Haggai in the name of R. Isaac: "On account of the merit attained by obeying the commandment, 'You will take for yourself on the first day...' (Lev. 23:40),
- C. "I shall reveal myself to you as the First, avenge you on the first, rebuild the first, and bring you the first.
- D. "I shall reveal myself to you the First: 'I am the first and I am the last' (Isa. 44:6).
- E. "...Avenge you on the first: Esau, 'The first came forth red.'
- F. "...Rebuild the first: That is the Temple, of which it is written, 'You throne of glory, on high from the first, you place of our sanctuary' (Jer. 17:12).
- G. "...And bring you the first: That is, the messiah-king: 'A first unto Zion will I give, behold, behold them, and to Jerusalem' (Isa. 41:27)."

LXIII

X.1   A.   "[When the boys grew up,] Esau was a skillful hunter, [a man of the field, while Jacob was a quiet man, dwelling in tents]" (Gen. 25:27):
- B. He hunted people through snaring them in words [as the Roman prosecutors do:] "Well enough, you did not steal. But who stole with you? You did not kill, but who killed with you?"

X.2   A.   R. Abbahu said, "He was a trapper and a fieldsman, trapping at home and in the field.
- B. "He trapped at home: 'How do you tithe salt?' [which does not, in fact, have to be tithed at all!]
- C. "He trapped in the field: 'How do people give tithe for straw?' [which does not, in fact, have to be tithed at all!]"

X.3   A.   R. Hiyya bar Abba said, "He treated himself as totally without responsibility for himself, like a field [on which anyone tramples].
- B. "Said the Israelites before the Holy One, blessed be He, 'Lord of all ages, is it not enough for us that you have subjugated us to the seventy nations, but even to this one, who is subjected to sexual intercourse just like a woman?'
- C. "Said to them the Holy One, blessed be He, 'I, too, will exact punishment from him with those same words: "And the heart of the mighty men of Edom at that day shall be as the heart of a woman in her pangs"' (Jer. 49:22)."

X.4   A.   "...While Jacob was a quiet man, dwelling in tents" (Gen. 25:27):
- B. There is a reference to two tents, that is, the schoolhouse of Shem and the schoolhouse of Eber.

X.5   A.   "Now Isaac loved Esau, because he ate of his game":
- B. It was first-rate meat and wine for Isaac's eating.

X.6   A.   "...But Rebecca loved Jacob" (Gen. 25:28):
- B. The more she heard his voice, the more she loved him.

Nos. 1-3 deal with the description of Esau, explaining why he was warlike and aggressive. Nothing Esau did proved sincere. He was a hypocrite, even when he tried to please his parents.

LXV

I.1 A. "When Esau was forty years old, he took to wife Judith, the daughter of Beeri, the Hittite, and Basemath the daughter of Elon the Hittite; and they made life bitter for Isaac and Rebecca" (Gen. 26:34-35):
B. "The swine out of the wood ravages it, that which moves in the field feeds on it" (Ps. 80:14).
C. R. Phineas and R. Hilqiah in the name of R. Simon: "Among all of the prophets, only two of them spelled out in public [the true character of Rome, represented by the swine], Asaf and Moses.
D. "Asaf: 'The swine out of the wood ravages it.'
E. "Moses: 'And the swine, because he parts the hoof' (Deut. 14:8).
F. "Why does Moses compare Rome to the swine? Just as the swine, when it crouches, puts forth its hoofs as if to say, 'I am clean,' so the wicked kingdom steals and grabs, while pretending to be setting up courts of justice.
G. "So Esau, for all forty years, hunted married women, ravished them, and when he reached the age of forty, he presented himself to his father, saying, 'Just as father got married at the age of forty, so I shall marry a wife at the age of forty.'
H. "'When Esau was forty years old, he took to wife Judith, the daughter of Beeri, the Hittite, and Basemath the daughter of Elon the Hittite.'"

The exegesis of course once more identifies Esau with Rome. The round-about route linking the fact at hand, Esau's taking a wife, passes through the territory of Roman duplicity. Whatever the government does, it claims to do in the general interest. But it really has no public interest at all. Esau for his part spent forty years pillaging women and then, at the age of forty, pretended, to his father, to be upright. That, at any rate, is the parallel clearly intended by this obviously unitary composition. The issue of the selection of the intersecting verse does not present an obvious solution to me; it seems to me only the identification of Rome with the swine accounts for the choice. The contrast between Israel and Esau produced the following anguished observation. But here the Rome is not yet Christian, so far as the clear reference is concerned.

LXV

XXI.3 A. Said R. Judah bar Ilai, "Rabbi would give the following exposition:
B. "'"The voice is Jacob's voice," that is, the voice of Jacob crying out on account of what "the hands of Esau" have done to him.'"
C. Said R. Yohanan, "It is the voice of Hadrian, may his bones be pulverized, killing in Betar eighty thousand myriads of people."

The insistence upon reading the history of Israel into the biography of Jacob stands behind No. 3. The question then arises, why the enmity?

LXVII

VIII.1 A. "Now Esau hated Jacob [because of the blessing with which his father had blessed him, and Esau said to himself, 'The days of mourning for my father are approaching; then I will kill my brother Jacob]' (Gen. 27:41)":

B. Said R. Eleazar b. R. Yose, "He turned into a vengeful and vindictive enemy of his, just as even today they are called 'senators' in Rome [with the word for 'senator' bearing the consonants that appear in the words for enemy and vindictive]."

LXXV

I.1 A. "And Jacob sent messengers before him [to Esau his brother in the land of Seir, the country of Edom, instructing them, Thus shall you say to my lord Esau, 'Thus says your servant Jacob, 'I have sojourned with Laban and stayed until now. And I have oxen, asses flocks, menservants and maidservants; and I have sent to tell my lord, in order that I may find favor in your sight''']" (Gen. 32:4):

B. R. Phineas in the name of R. Reuben opened discourse by citing the following verse: "Arise, O Lord, confront him" (Ps. 17:13).

C. R. Phineas in the name of R. Reuben said, "There are five passages in the first book of Psalms in which David asks the Holy One, blessed be He, to rise: 'Arise O Lord, save me O my God' (Ps. 3:8); 'Arise, O Lord, in your anger' (Ps. 7:7); 'Arise, O Lord, O God, lift up your hand' (Ps. 10:12); 'Arise, O Lord, let not man prevail' (Ps. 9:20).

D. "'Arise, O Lord, confront him':

E. "Said the Holy One, blessed be He, to him, 'David, my son, even if you ask me to rise a thousand times, I shall not arise. When shall I arise? When you see the poor oppressed and the needy groaning.'

F. "'For the oppression of the poor, for the sighing of the needy, now I will arise, says the Lord' (Ps. 12:6)."

I.2 A. ["For the oppression of the poor, for the sighing of the needy, now I will arise, says the Lord":] R. Simeon b. Jonah said, "'Now I will arise.' As long as [Jerusalem] wallows in the dust, as it were. But when that day comes, concerning which it is written, 'Shake yourself from the dust, arise, and sit down, O Jerusalem' (Isa. 52:2), at that time, 'Be silent, all flesh, before the Lord' (Zech. 2:17).

B. "Why so? 'For he is aroused out of his holy habitation' (Zech. 2:17)."

C. Said R. Aha, "Like a chicken that shakes itself out of the dust."

I.3 A. "[Arise, O Lord,] confront him" (Ps. 17:13):

B. Confront the wicked before he confronts you.

C. "Cast him down" (Ps. 17:13):

D. Into the scale of guilt.

E. "Break him," in line with this verse: "They are bowed down and fallen" (Ps. 20:9).

F. "Deliver my soul from the wicked, your sword" (Ps. 17:13):

Genesis Rabbah and the History of Israel

		G.	From the wicked person who comes with the power of the sword. "And by your sword shall you live" (Gen. 27:40).
I.4	A.		Another interpretation of "Your sword":
	B.		"[Esau] is your sword, because with it you punish the world."
I.5	A.		R. Joshua of Sikhnin in the name of R. Levi: "Save my soul from that wicked man who is destined to fall by your sword: 'For my sword has drunk its fill in heaven, behold, it shall come down upon Edom' (Isa. 34:5).
	B.		"Said the Holy One, blessed be He, to Jacob, 'Esau was walking along his solitary way, and you had to go and send word to him and say to him, "Thus says your servant Jacob."'" [Freedman, p. 690, n. 1: "You would have had nothing to fear had you not drawn his attention to you, and the same applies to Jacob's descendants in their relations with Rome."]

No. 1 makes one point, No. 2 a different one. No. 1 stresses that God will rouse himself only to aid the poor and oppressed. No. 2 then maintains that God rouses himself to save Jerusalem at the end of time. These are distinct motifs. No. 3 works on the theme of the sword, in line with Gen. 27:40. No. 4 carries forward that same point of intersection. No. 5 makes the point articulated by Freedman, and that seems to me the upshot of the entire composition.

LXXV

II.1	A.	R. Judah b. R. Simon opened discourse by citing the following verse: "'As a troubled fountain and a corrupted spring, so is a righteous man who gives way before the wicked' (Prov. 25:26):
	B.	"Just as it is impossible for a fountain to be forever muddied and for a spring to be forever spoiled, so it is impossible for a righteous man to be forever humbled before a wicked one.
	C.	"And like a fountain that is muddied or a spring that is spoiled, so is a righteous man who is humbled before a wicked man.
	D.	"Said the Holy One, blessed be He, to him, 'Esau was walking along his solitary way, and you had to go and send word to him and say to him, "Thus says your servant Jacob."'"

The same message is underlined, now interwoven with a different intersecting verse. Jacob should not have taken an initiative in dealing with Esau. The message of passivity in response to Rome, which Freedman underlined above, can be seen as the subterranean polemic.

LXXV

IV.2	A.	"And Jacob sent messengers before him":
	B.	To this one [Esau] whose time to take hold of sovereignty would come before him [namely, before Jacob, since Esau would rule, then Jacob would govern].
	C.	R. Joshua b. Levi said, "Jacob took off the purple robe and threw it before Esau, as if to say to him, 'Two flocks of starlings are not going to sleep on a single branch' [so we cannot rule at the same time]."

IV.3   A.   "...To Esau his brother":
       B.   Even though he was Esau, he was still his brother.

IV.4   A.   "...In the land of Seir, the country of Edom":
       B.   He was red, his food was red, his land was red, his mighty men were red, their clothing was red, his avenger will be red, and dressed in red. [Red symbolizes war.]
       C.   He was red: "And the first came forth ruddy" (Gen. 25:25).
       D.   ...His food was red: "'Let me swallow some of that red pottage, for I am famished'" (Gen. 25:30).
       E.   ...His land was red: "To Esau his brother to the land of Seir, the field of red" (Gen. 32:4).
       F.   ...His mighty men were red: "The shield of his mighty men is made red" (Nahum 2:4).
       G.   ...Their clothing was red: "The valiant men are in scarlet" (Nahum 2:4).
       H.   ...His avenger will be red: "My beloved is white and ruddy" (Song 5:10).
       I.   ...And dressed in red: "Wherefore is your apparel red" (Isa. 63:2).

No. 1 pursues a question important to the compositors, namely, the status of the "messenger" wherever such occurs. The point is that if angels served lesser figures, they surely accompanied Jacob. Nos. 2, 3 make a stunning point. It is that Esau remains Jacob's brother, and that Esau rules before Jacob will. The application to contemporary affairs cannot be missed, both in the recognition of the true character of Esau – a brother! – and in the interpretation of the future of history. No. 4 is familiar and simply works out the meaning of the color, red, of the land of Edom, the word meaning red. In what follows Rome is identified with Esau in a less negative context. Rabbi Judah the Patriarch, called simply "Rabbi" or "our holy master," and a Roman "emperor" called Antoninus are said to have maintained cordial relationships with one another. In that context the following story shows that Esau and Jacob still provided the generative paradigm.

LXXV

V.1   A.   "...Instructing them, 'Thus shall you say to my lord Esau, "Thus says your servant Jacob, 'I have sojourned with Laban and stayed until now'"'":
       B.   Our master [Judah the Patriarch] said to R. Efes, "Write a letter in my name to our lord, King Antoninus."
       C.   He went and wrote, "From Judah the Patriarch to our lord, King Antoninus."
       D.   Rabbi took it, read it, tore it up, and had him write, "To our lord, the king, from Judah your servant."
       E.   He said to him, "My lord, why do you treat your own honor with contempt?"
       F.   He said to him, "Am I any better than my forefather? Did he not instruct them: 'Thus shall you say to my lord Esau, "Thus says your

Genesis Rabbah and the History of Israel

servant Jacob, 'I have sojourned with Laban and stayed until now'"'?"

V.2   A.   "I have sojourned with Laban and stayed until now":
       B.   "Laban, the master of deceit, did I keep in my sleeve [having got the better of him (Freedman)], and as to you, how much the more so!"

V.3   A.   "And why is it the case that 'I have stayed until now'?"
       B.   Because the adversary of Satan had not yet been born.
       C.   For R. Phineas in the name of R. Samuel bar Nahman: "It is a tradition that Esau will fall only by the hand of the descendants of the children of Rachel: 'Surely the youngest of the flock shall drag them away' (Jer. 49:20).
       D.   "[And why does Scripture call them 'the youngest of the flock'? Because they are] the youngest of the tribes."

No. 1 cites the base verse for its own purposes, thus showing how the patriarch followed the example of the patriarch, Jacob. No. 2 gives Jacob a more ominous message than does the biblical narrative. No. 3 goes over familiar ground. Esau, meaning Rome, will fall by the hand of the Messiah.

LXXV

IX.1   A.   Someone else commenced discourse by citing this verse: "Do not grant, O Lord, the desires of the wicked, do not advance his evil plan" (Ps. 140:9).
       B.   "Lord of all ages, do not give to the wicked Esau what his heart has devised against Jacob."
       C.   What is the meaning of, "Do not advance his evil plan"?
       D.   He said before him, "Lord of the ages, Make a bit for the mouth of the wicked Esau, so that he will not get full pleasure [from anything he does]." [The word for "evil plan" and for "bit" use the same consonants.]
       E.   What sort of bit did the Holy One, blessed be He, make for Esau?
       F.   Said R. Hama bar Haninah, "These are the barbarian nations, the Germans whom the Edomites fear."

Sages clearly followed the news of the day and drew their own conclusions from the Romans' political problems.

LXXV

XI.1   A.   Another explanation of the statement, "And Jacob sent...":
       B.   Why did he send out messengers to him?
       C.   This is what he was thinking, "I shall send messengers to him, perhaps he will return in repentence."
       D.   And he said to them, "This is what to say to him: 'Do not suppose that the way that Jacob went forth from the house of his father is the way he is coming back.'"
       E.   For it is said, "For with my staff I passed over this Jordan" (Gen. 32:11).
       F.   [Reverting to Jacob's message:] "'For he did not take anything from his father. But it was for "my salary [the messengers are to repeat

		to Esau] that I have acquired all of these properties, through my own strength."'"
	G.	For it is said, "And now I have become two camps" (Gen. 32:11).
XI.2	A.	At the moment that Jacob referred to Esau as "my lord," the Holy One, blessed be He, said to him, "You have lowered yourself and called Esau 'my Lord' no fewer than eight times.
	B.	"I shall produce out of his descendants eight kings before your children [have any]: 'And these are the kings that reigned in the land of Edom before any king ruled the children of Israel' (Gen. 36:31)."
XI.3	A.	In his message to Esau, Jacob said to him,] "If you are ready for peace, I shall be your counterpart, and if you are ready for war, I shall be your counterpart.
	B.	"I have heroic, powerful troops, for I say something before the Holy One, blessed be He, and he grants what I ask: 'He will fulfill the desire of those who fear him' (Ps. 145:19)."
	C.	Therefore David came to give praise and glory before the Holy One, blessed be He, for he helped him when he fled from Saul, as it is said, "For lo, the wicked bend the bow" (Ps. 11:2), then, "When the foundations are destroyed, what has the righteous done" (Ps. 11:3).
	D.	He said to him, "Lord of the age, if you had been angry with Jacob and had forsaken him and not helped him, and he was pillar and foundation of the world, in line with this verse, 'But the righteous is the foundation of the world' (Prov. 10:25), then 'what has the righteous done' (Ps. 11:3)?"
	E.	Concerning that moment it is said: "Some in chariots, some in horses, but we shall call on the name of the Lord our God" (Ps. 20:8). [Freedman, p. 697, n. 4: Jacob discomfited Esau by mentioning God, and David was saved from Saul by his trust in God.]

No. 1 supplies a message for the messengers in place of that given at Gen. 32:3-4. No. 2 responds to the statement, Gen. 32:3: "Thus you shall say to my lord Esau." The effect is to link Jacob's encounter with Esau to Israel's history with Edom/Rome. There are no surprises here. No. 3 works out a parallel between Jacob and David, as made explicit by Freedman.

LXXV

VII.1	A.	"And the messengers returned to Jacob, saying, 'We came to your brother Esau' (Gen. 32:6)":
	B.	[They said to him,] "You treat him as a brother, but he treats you as Esau."
VII.2	A.	"...And he is coming to meet you, and four hundred men with him" (Gen. 32:6):
	B.	R. Simeon b. Laqish said, "'With him' means people equivalent to him himself.
	C.	"Just as he has four hundred men with him, so each of them has four hundred men with him."

> D. R. Levi said, "He had gone and bought the right to collect duties. He thought to himself, 'If I can overcome him, well and good, and if not, I shall tax him and in doing so I shall kill him.'"

Here again sages refer to contemporary considerations in interpreting the sense of Scripture.

LXXVI

> VI.1 A. "'Deliver me, I pray you, from the hand of my brother, from the hand of Esau, for I fear him'":
> B. "From the hand of my brother, who comes against me with the strength of Esau" [which was the sword] (Gen. 27:40).
> C. That is in line with this verse: "I considered the horns, and behold, there came up among them another horn, a little one" (Dan. 7:8).
> D. This refers to Ben Neser [Odenathus of Palmyra].
> E. "Before which three of the first horns were plucked up by the roots" (Dan. 7:8).
> F. This refers to Macrinus, Carinus, and Cyriades.
> G. "And behold, in this horn were eyes like the eyes of a man and a mouth speaking great things" (Dan. 7:8).
> H. This speaks of the wicked realm, which imposes taxes on all the nations of the world.
> I. Said R. Yohanan, "It is written, 'And as for the ten horns, out of this kingdom shall ten kings arise' (Dan. 7:24), that is, the ten sons of Esau.
> J. "'I considered the horns, and behold, there came up among them another horn, a little one,' meaning, the wicked realm.
> K. "'Before which three of the first horns were plucked up by the roots' speaks of the first three monarchies [Babylonia, Media, Greece].
> L. "'And behold, in this horn were eyes like the eyes of a man' alludes to the wicked realm, which looks enviously on someone's wealth, saying, 'Since Mr. So-and-so has a lot of money, we shall elect him magistrate,' 'Since Mr. So-and-so has a lot of money, we shall elect him councillor.'"
>
> VI.2 A. "'...Lest he come and slay us all, the mothers with the children. But you did say, "I will do you good and make your descendants as the sand of the sea, which cannot be numbered for multitude" (Gen. 32:12)'":
> B. "But you did say, 'You will not take the dam with the fledglings' (Deut. 22:6)."
> C. Another matter: "'...Lest he come and slay us all, the mothers with the children. But you did say, "And whether it be cow or ewe, you shall not kill it and its young both in one day (Lev. 22:28).""'

The explicit allusion at No. 1 to Rome in the time of Odenathus is puzzling, because, of course, Odenathus at Palmyra was an independent chief, not ruler of Rome (!). The reading of Daniel has three Roman generals fall before Palmyra. Now what this has to do with the power of one's brother, the power of the sword, I take it, is simple. Jacob is made to refer to wanting to be saved from someone who exercises the sort of

154   *Sources of the Transformation of Judaism*

power that Esau exercises, namely, from Palmyra. The message to Israel is that Palmyra, no less than Rome, exercises a kind of power from which Israel is to be delivered, not power Israel is itself to aspire to wield. Then the sense of Yohanan's statement is that the cited verse speaks of Rome, not Palmyra, and that at issue is Rome as successor to the first three monarchies. So Yohanan reads Daniel in the way in which rabbis generally did, and in his view, there is no point of contact with our base verse. It is a rather interesting construction therefore, in which a dispute on the meaning of Daniel has taken shape, only afterward to be brought into juxtaposition with our base verse. The reason the compositor chose the completed statement of course is the opening allusion, but that alone. No. 2 goes over familiar ground, drawing upon the setting of Jacob's address to call to God's attention the requirement of the Torah. The one who gave the Torah must see to it that its rule applies.

LXXVIII

XII.1 A. "Jacob said, 'No, I pray you, if I have found favor in your sight, then accept my present from my hand, for truly to see your face is like seeing the face of God, [with such favor have you received me. Accept, I pray you, my gift that is brought to you, because God has dealt graciously with me, and because I have enough.' Thus he urged him, and he took it]" (Gen. 33:10-11):
       B. "Just as the face of God is judgment, so your face is judgment.
       C. "Just as the face of God involves this statement: 'You will not see my face empty-handed' (Ex. 23:15), so as to you: I will not see your face empty-handed." [That is the meaning of the comparison Jacob has made.]
XII.2 A. "Accept, I pray you, my gift that is brought to you, because God has dealt graciously with me, and because I have enough":
       B. He said to him, "How much I suffered, how hard I worked, before this gift came to me, but to you it comes on its own."
       C. What is written is not "which I have brought" but "[on its own] is brought to you."
XII.3 A. "...Thus he urged him, and he took it" (Gen. 33:11):
       B. He acted as if to decline, but he put on his hands.
       C. R. Judah b. Rabbi said, "'Every one submitting himself with pieces of silver' (Ps. 68:31) means, [Freedman:] 'he opens his hand and would be appeased with silver.' [Freedman, p. 723, n. 4: Esau meaning Rome demands money for appeasement.]"
XII.4 A. R. Simeon b. Laqish went up to pay his respects to our master [Judah the Patriarch]. He said to him, "Pray for me, because this kingdom is very wicked."
       B. He said to him, "Do not take anything from anybody, and you will not have to give anything to anyone. [Stop collecting taxes.]"
       C. While they were in session, a woman came along carrying a salver and a knife on it. He took the knife and gave her back the salver.
       D. A royal representative came along, saw it, liked it, and took it.

	E.	In the evening, R. Simeon b. Laqish went up to pay his respects to our master [Judah the Patriarch]. He saw him sitting and laughing.
	F.	He said to him, "Why are you laughing?"
	G.	He said to him, "That knife that you saw – a royal representative came along and took it away."
	H.	He said to him, "Didn't I tell you, 'Do not take anything from anybody, and you will not have to give anything to anyone.'"
XII.5	A.	A commoner said to R. Hoshaiah, "If I say something good to you, will you repeat it in my name in public?"
	B.	He said to him, "What is it?"
	C.	He said to him, "All the gifts that our father, Jacob, gave to Esau are the nations of the world destined to restore to the king-messiah in the age to come.
	D.	"What is the verse of Scripture that indicates it? 'The kings of Tashish and of the isles shall return tribute' (Ps. 72:10).
	E.	"What is said is not, 'bring,' but 'return.'"
	F.	He said to him, "By your life, that indeed is a good thing that you have said, and in your name I shall repeat it."

No. 1 amplifies Jacob's statement. No. 2 subjects the cited verse to an acute reading, producing the indicated exegesis. No. 3 is important because of its more general comment on Esau's rule, following Freedman, another instance of drawing from Jacob's life a lesson for the life of the people, Israel. I take it that No. 4 is tacked on because it underlines the judgment of No. 3 about Roman rule. No. 5 reverts to the theme of the gifts of Jacob to Esau, joins the tale to Israel's history, and imparts to it an eschatological dimension.

LXXXIII

I.1	A.	"These are the kings who reigned in the land of Edom before any king reigned over the Israelites: Bela the son of Beor reigned in Edom, the name of his city being Dinhabah" (Gen. 36:31-32):
	B.	R. Isaac commenced discourse by citing this verse: "Of the oaks of Bashan they have made your oars" (Ezek. 27:6).
	C.	Said R. Isaac, "The nations of the world are to be compared to a ship. Just as a ship has its mast made in one place and its anchor somewhere else, so their kings: 'Samlah of Masrekah' (Gen. 36:36), 'Shaul of Rehobot by the river' (Gen. 36:27), and: 'These are the kings who reigned in the land of Edom before any king reigned over the Israelites.'"
I.2	A.	["An estate may be gotten hastily at the beginning, but the end thereof shall not be blessed" (Prov. 20:21)]: "An estate may be gotten hastily at the beginning": 'These are the kings who reigned in the land of Edom before any king reigned over the Israelites."
	B.	"...But the end thereof shall not be blessed": "And saviors shall come up on mount Zion to judge the mount of Esau" (Obad. 1:21).

No. 1 contrasts the diverse origin of Roman rulers with the uniform origin of Israel's king in the house of David. No. 2 makes the same point still more forcefully. How so? Freedman makes sense of No. 2 as follows: Though Esau was the first to have kings, his land will eventually be overthrown (Freedman, p. 766, n. 3). So the point is that Israel will have kings after Esau no longer does, and the verse at hand is made to point to the end of Rome, a striking revision to express the importance in Israel's history to events in the lives of the patriarchs.

LXXXIII

II.1   A.   "These are the kings who reigned in the land of Edom before any king reigned over the Israelites: Bela the son of Beor reigned in Edom, the name of his city being Dinhabah" (Gen. 36:31-32):

       B.   Said R. Aibu, "Before a king arose in Israel, kings existed in Edom: 'These are the kings who reigned in the land of Edom before any king reigned over the Israelites.'" [Freedman, p. 766, n. 4: "1 Kgs. 22:48 states, 'There was no king in Edom, a deputy was king.' This refers to the reign of Jehoshaphat. Subsequently in Jehoram's reign, Edom revolted and 'made a king over themselves' (2 Kgs. 8:20). Thus from Saul to Jehoshaphat, in which Israel had eight kings, Edom had no king but was ruled by a governor of Judah. Aibu observes that this was to balance the present period, during which Edom had eight kings while Israel had none. For that reason, Aibu employs the word for deputy when he wishes to say 'existed' thus indicating a reference to the verse in the book of Kings quoted above."]

       C.   R. Yose bar Haninah said, "[Alluding to a mnemonic, with the first Hebrew letter for the word for kings, judges, chiefs, and princes:] When the one party [Edom] was ruled by kings, the other party [Israel] was ruled by judges, when one side was ruled by chiefs, the other side was ruled by princes."

       D.   Said R. Joshua b. Levi, "This one set up eight kings and that one set up eight kings. This one set up Bela, Jobab, Husham, Samlah, Shaul, Hadad, Baalhanan, and Hadar. The other side set up Saul, Ishbosheth, David Solomon, Rehoboam, Abijah, Asa, and Jehoshaphat.

       E.   "Then Nebuchadnezzar came and overturned both: 'That made the world as a wilderness and destroyed the cities thereof' (Isa. 14:17).

       F.   "Evil-Merodach came and exalted Jehoiakin, Ahasuerus came and exalted Haman."

The passage once more stresses the correspondence between Israel's and Edom's governments, respectively. The reciprocal character of their histories is then stated in a powerful way, with the further implication that, when the one rules, the other waits. So now Israel waits, but it will rule. The same point is made in what follows, but the expectation proves acute and immediate.

LXXXIII

IV.3   A.   "Magdiel and Iram: these are the chiefs of Edom, that is Esau, the father of Edom, according to their dwelling places in the land of their possession" (Gen. 36:42):

Genesis Rabbah and the History of Israel

	B.	On the day on which Litrinus came to the throne, there appeared to R. Ammi in a dream this message: "Today Magdiel has come to the throne."
	C.	He said, "One more king is required for Edom [and then Israel's turn will come]."
IV.4	A.	Said R. Hanina of Sepphoris, "Why was he called Iram? For he is destined to amass [a word using the same letters] riches for the king-messiah."
	B.	Said R. Levi, "There was the case of a ruler in Rome who wasted the treasuries of his father. Elijah of blessed memory appeared to him in a dream. He said to him, 'Your fathers collected treasures and you waste them.'
	C.	"He did not budge until he filled the treasuries again."

Nos. 3 presents once more the theme that Rome's rule will extend only for a foreordained and limited time, at which point the Messiah will come. No. 4 explains the meaning of the name Iram. The concluding statement also alleges that Israel's saints even now make possible whatever wise decisions Rome's rulers make. That forms an appropriate conclusion to the matter. Ending in the everyday world of the here and the now, we note that sages attribute to Israel's influence anything good that happens to Israel's brother, Rome.

Part Three

PRINCIPLES OF JUDAISM IN THE
AGE OF CONSTANTINE

6

When Did Judaism Become a Messianic Religion?

Within the Judaism born in the centuries after 70, the distinct traditions of priest, sage, and messianist, were joined in a new way. In the person of the rabbi, holy man, Torah incarnate, avatar and model of the son of David, rabbinic Judaism found its sole overarching system. So the diverse varieties of Judaic piety present in Israel before 70 came to be bonded over the next several centuries in a wholly unprecedented way, with each party to the union imposing its logic upon the other constituents of the whole. The ancient categories remained. But they were so profoundly revised and transformed that nothing was preserved intact. Judaism as we know it, the Judaism of Scripture and Mishnah, Midrash and Talmud, thereby effected the ultimate transvaluation of all the values, of all the kinds of Judaism that had come before, from ancient Israel onward. Through the person and figure of the rabbi, the whole burden of Israel's heritage was taken up, renewed, and handed on from late antiquity to the present day.

The character of the Israelite Scriptures, with their emphasis upon historical narrative as a mode of theological explanation, leads us to expect all Judaisms to evolve as deeply messianic religions. With all prescribed actions pointed toward the coming of the Messiah at the end of time, and all interest focused upon answering the historical salvific questions ("how long?"), Judaism from late antiquity to the present day presents no surprises. Its liturgy evokes historical events to prefigure salvation; prayers of petition repeatedly turn to the speedy coming of the messiah; and the experience of worship invariably leaves the devotee expectant and hopeful. Just as rabbinic Judaism is a deeply messianic religion, secular extensions of Judaism have commonly proposed secularized versions of the focus upon history and have shown interest in the purpose and denouement of events. Teleology again appears as an eschatology embodied in messianic symbols.

Yet, for a brief moment, a vast and influential document presented a kind of Judaism in which history did not define the main framework by which the issue of teleology took a form other than the familiar eschatological one and in which historical events were absorbed, through their trivialization in taxonomic structures, into an ahistorical system. In the kind of Judaism in this document, messiahs played a part. But these "anointed men" had no historical role. They undertook a task quite different from that assigned to Jesus by the framers of the Gospels. They were merely a species of priest, falling into one classification rather than another.

That document is the Mishnah, a strange corpus of normative statements which we may, though with some difficulty, classify as a law code or a school book for philosophical jurists. By ca. A.D. 600 a system of Judaism emerged in which the Mishnah as foundation document would be asked to support a structure at best continuous with, but in no way fully defined by the outlines of, the Mishnah itself.

Coming at the system from the asymmetrical endpoint, we ask the Mishnah to answer the questions at hand. What of the Messiah? When will he come? To whom, in Israel, will he come? And what must, or can, we do while we wait to hasten his coming? If we now reframe these questions and divest them of their mythic cloak, we ask about the Mishnah's theory of the history and destiny of Israel and the purpose of the Mishnah's own system in relationship to Israel's present and end: the implicit teleology of the philosophical law at hand.

Answering these questions out of the resources of the Mishnah is not possible. The Mishnah presents no large view of history. It contains no reflection whatever on the nature and meaning of the destruction of the Temple in A.D. 70, an event which surfaces only in connection with some changes in the law explained as resulting from the end of the cult. The Mishnah pays no attention to the matter of the end time. The word "salvation" is rare, "sanctification" commonplace. More strikingly, the framers of the Mishnah are virtually silent on the teleology of the system; they never tell us why we should do what the Mishnah tells us, let alone explain what will happen if we do. Incidents in the Mishnah are preserved either as narrative settings for the statement of the law, or, occasionally, as precedents. Historical events are classified and turned into entries on lists. But incidents in any case come few and far between. True, events do make an impact. But it always is for the Mishnah's own purpose and within its own taxonomic system and rule-seeking mode of thought. To be sure, the framers of the Mishnah may also have had a theory of the Messiah and of the meaning of Israel's history and destiny.

When Did Judaism Become a Messianic Religion?

But they kept it hidden, and their document manages to provide an immense account of Israel's life without explicitly telling us about such matters.

The Messiah in the Mishnah does not stand at the forefront of the framers' consciousness. The issues encapsulated in the myth and person of the Messiah are scarcely addressed. The framers of the Mishnah do not resort to speculation about the Messiah as a historical supernatural figure. So far as that kind of speculation provides the vehicle for reflection on salvific issues, or in mythic terms, narratives on the meaning of history and the destiny of Israel, we cannot say that the Mishnah's philosophers take up those encompassing categories of being: Where are we heading? What can we do about it? That does not mean questions found urgent in the aftermath of the destruction of the Temple and the disaster of Bar Kokhba failed to attract the attention of the Mishnah's sages. But they treated history in a different way, offering their own answers to its questions. To these we now turn.

By "history" I mean not merely events, but how events serve to teach lessons, reveal patterns, tell us what we must do and what will happen to us tomorrow. In that context, some events contain richer lessons than others; the destruction of the Temple of Jerusalem teaches more than a crop failure, being kidnapped into slavery more than stubbing one's toe. Furthermore, lessons taught by events – "history" in the didactic sense – follow a progression from trivial and private to consequential and public. The framers of the Mishnah explicitly refer to very few events, treating those they do mention with a focus quite separate from the unfolding events themselves. They rarely create narratives; historical events do not supply organizing categories or taxonomic classifications. We find no tractate devoted to the destruction of the Temple, no complete chapter detailing the events of Bar Kokhba nor even a sustained celebration of the events of the sages' own historical lives. When things that have happened are mentioned, it is neither to narrate nor to interpret and draw lessons from the events. It is either to illustrate a point of law or to pose a problem of the law – always en passant, never in a pointed way.

The Mishnah absorbs into its encompassing system all events, small and large. With them the sages accomplish what they accomplish in everything else: a vast labor of taxonomy, an immense construction of the order and rules governing the classification of everything on earth and in Heaven. The disruptive character of history – one-time events of ineluctable significance – scarcely impresses the philosophers. They find no difficulty in showing that what appears unique and beyond classification has in fact happened before and so falls within the range of trustworthy rules and known procedures. Once history's components, one-time events, lose their distinctiveness, then history as a didactic intellectual construct, as a source of lessons and rules, also loses all pertinence.

So lessons and rules come from sorting things out and classifying them from the procedures and modes of thought of the philosopher seeking regularity. To this labor of taxonomy, the historian's way of selecting data and arranging them into patterns of meaning to teach lessons proves inconsequential. One-time events are not important. The world is composed of nature and supernature. The laws that count are those to be discovered in Heaven and, in Heaven's creation and counterpart, on earth. Keep those laws and things will work out. Break them, and the result is predictable: calamity of whatever sort will supervene in accordance with the rules. But just because it is predictable, a catastrophic happening testifies to what has always been and must always be, in accordance with reliable rules and within categories already discovered and well explained. That is why the lawyer-philosophers of the mid second century produced the Mishnah – to explain how things are. Within the framework of well-classified rules, there could be messiahs, but no single Messiah.

If the end of time and the coming of the Messiah do not serve to explain, for the Mishnah's system, why people should do what the Mishnah says, then what alternative teleology does the Mishnah's first apologetic, Abot, provide? Only when we appreciate the clear answers given in that document, brought to closure at ca. 250, shall we grasp how remarkable is the shift, which took place in later documents of the rabbinic canon, to a messianic framing of the issues of the Torah's ultimate purpose and value. Let us see how the framers of Abot, in the aftermath of the creation of the Mishnah, explain the purpose and goal of the Mishnah: an ahistorical, non-messianic teleology.

The first document generated by the Mishnah's heirs took up the work of completing the Mishnah's system by answering questions of purpose and meaning. Whatever teleology the Mishnah as such would ever acquire would derive from Abot, a collection of sayings by authorities who flourished in the generation after Judah the Patriarch; in all likelihood the document is of the mid-third-century rabbinic estate of the Land of Israel. Abot presents statements to express the ethos and ethic of the Mishnah, and so provides a kind of theory.

Abot agreed with the other sixty-two tractates: history proved no more important here than it had been before. With scarcely a word about history and no account of events at all, Abot manages to provide an ample account of how the Torah – written and oral, thus in later eyes, Scripture and Mishnah – came down to its own day. Accordingly, the passage of time as such plays no role in the explanation of the origins of the document, nor is the Mishnah presented as eschatological.

When Did Judaism Become A Messianic Religion?

Occurrences of great weight ("history") are never invoked. How then does the tractate tell the story of Torah, narrate the history of God's revelation to Israel, encompassing both Scripture and Mishnah? The answer is that Abot's framers manage to do their work of explanation without telling a story or invoking history at all. They pursue a different way of answering the same question, by exploiting a non-historical mode of thought and method of legitimation. And that is the main point: teleology serves the purpose of legitimation, and hence is accomplished in ways other than explaining how things originated or assuming that historical fact explains anything.

Disorderly historical events entered the system of the Mishnah and found their place within the larger framework of the Mishnah's orderly world. But to claim that the Mishnah's framers merely ignored what was happening would be incorrect. They worked out their own way of dealing with historical events, the disruptive power of which they not only conceded but freely recognized. Further, the Mishnah's authors did not intend to compose a history book or a work of prophecy or apocalypse. Even if they had wanted to narrate the course of events, they could hardly have done so through the medium of the Mishnah. Yet the Mishnah presents its philosophy in full awareness of the issues of historical calamity confronting the Jewish nation. So far as the philosophy of the document confronts the totality of Israel's existence, the Mishnah by definition also presents a philosophy of history.

The Mishnah's subordination of historical events contradicts the emphasis of a thousand years of Israelite thought. The biblical histories, the ancient prophets, the apocalyptic visionaries all had testified that events themselves were important. Events carried the message of the living God. Events constituted history, pointed toward, and so explained, Israel's destiny. An essentially ahistorical system of timeless sanctification, worked out through construction of an eternal rhythm which centered on the movement of the moon and stars and seasons, represented a life chosen by few outside of the priesthood. Furthermore, the pretense that what happens matters less than what is testified against palpable and memorable reality. Israel had suffered enormous loss of life. The Talmud of the Land of Israel takes these events seriously and treats them as unique and remarkable. The memories proved real. The hopes evoked by the Mishnah's promise of sanctification of a world in static perfection did not. For they had to compete with the grief of an entire century of mourning.

The most important change is the shift in historical thinking adumbrated in the pages of the Talmud of the Land of Israel, a shift from focus upon the Temple and its supernatural history to close attention to the people Israel and its natural, this-worldly history. Once Israel, holy

Israel, had come to form the counterpart to the Temple and its supernatural life, that other history – Israel's – would stand at the center of things. Accordingly, a new sort of memorable event came to the fore in the Talmud of the Land of Israel. Let me give this new history appropriate emphasis: it was the story of Israel's suffering, remembrance of that suffering, on the one side, and an effort to explain events of such tragedy, on the other. So a composite "history" constructed out of the Yerushalmi's units of discourse which were pertinent to consequential events would contain long chapters on what happened to Israel, the Jewish people, and not only, or mainly, what had earlier occurred in the Temple.

The components of the historical theory of Israel's sufferings were manifold. First and foremost, history taught moral lessons. Historical events entered into the construction of a teleology for the Yerushalmi's system of Judaism as a whole. What the law demanded reflected the consequences of wrongful action on the part of Israel. So, again, Israel's own deeds defined the events of history. Rome's role, like Assyria's and Babylonia's, depended upon Israel's provoking divine wrath as it was executed by the great empire. This mode of thought comes to simple expression in what follows.

Y. Erubin 3:9

IV. B. R. Ba, R. Hiyya in the name of R. Yohanan: "'Do not gaze at me because I am swarthy, because the sun has scorched me. My mother's sons were angry with me, they made me keeper of the vineyards; but, my own vineyard, I have not kept!' (Song 1:6). What made me guard the vineyards? It is because of not keeping my own vineyard.

C. What made me keep two festival days in Syria? It is because I did not keep the proper festival day in the Holy Land.

D. "I imagined that I would receive a reward for the two days, but I received a reward only for one of them.

E. "Who made it necessary that I should have to separate two pieces of dough-offering from grain grown in Syria? It is because I did not separate a single piece of dough-offering in the Land of Israel."

Israel had to learn the lesson of its history to also take command of its own destiny.

But this notion of determining one's own destiny should not be misunderstood. The framers of the Talmud of the Land of Israel were not telling the Jews to please God by doing commandments in order that they should thereby gain control of their own destiny. To the contrary, the paradox of the Yerushalmi's system lies in the fact that Israel can free itself of control by other nations only by humbly agreeing to accept God's rule. The nations – Rome, in the present instance – rest on one side

When Did Judaism Become a Messianic Religion?

of the balance, while God rests on the other. Israel must then choose between them. There is no such thing for Israel as freedom from both God and the nations, total autonomy and independence. There is only a choice of masters, a ruler on earth or a ruler in Heaven.

With propositions such as these, the framers of the Mishnah will certainly have concurred. And why not? For the fundamental affirmations of the Mishnah about the centrality of Israel's perfection in stasis – sanctification – readily prove congruent to the attitudes at hand. Once the Messiah's coming had become dependent upon Israel's condition and not upon Israel's actions in historical time, then the Mishnah's system will have imposed its fundamental and definitive character upon the Messiah myth. An eschatological teleology framed through that myth then would prove wholly appropriate to the method of the larger system of the Mishnah. When this fact has been fully and completely spelled out in the final chapter, we shall then have grasped the distinctive history of the myth of the Messiah in the formative history of Judaism.

What, after all, makes a messiah a false messiah? In this Talmud, it is not his claim to save Israel, but his claim to save Israel without the help of God. The meaning of the true Messiah is Israel's total submission, through the Messiah's gentle rule, to God's yoke and service. So God is not to be manipulated through Israel's humoring of Heaven in rite and cult. The notion of keeping the commandments so as to please Heaven and get God to do what Israel wants is totally incongruent to the text at hand. Keeping the commandments as a mark of submission, loyalty, humility before God is the rabbinic system of salvation. So Israel does not "save itself." Israel never controls its own destiny, either on earth or in Heaven. The only choice is whether to case one's fate into the hands of cruel, deceitful men, or to trust in the living God of mercy and love. We shall now see how this critical position is spelled out in the setting of discourse about the Messiah in the Talmud of the Land of Israel.

Bar Kokhba, above all, exemplifies arrogance against God. He lost the war because of that arrogance. In particular, he ignored the authority of sages:

Y. Taanit 4:5

X. J. Said R. Yohanan, "Upon orders of Caesar Hadrian, they killed eight hundred thousand in Betar."

K. Said R. Yohanan, "There were eighty thousand pairs of trumpeteers surrounding Betar. Each one was in charge of a number of troops. Ben Kozeba was there and he had two hundred thousand troops who, as a sign of loyalty, had cut off their little fingers.

L. "Sages sent word to him, 'How long are you going to turn Israel into a maimed people?'

M. "He said to them, 'How otherwise is it possible to test them?'
N. "They replied to him, 'Whoever cannot uproot a cedar of Lebanon while riding on his horse will not be inscribed on your military rolls.'
O. "So there were two hundred thousand who qualified in one way, and another two hundred thousand who qualified in another way."
P. When he would go forth to battle, he would say, "Lord of the world! Do not help and do not hinder us! 'Hast thou not rejected us, O God? Thou dost not go forth, O God, with our armies' (Ps. 60:10)."
Q. Three and a half years did Hadrian besiege Betar.
R. R. Eleazar of Modiin would sit on sackcloth and ashes and pray every day, saying "Lord of the ages! Do not judge in accord with strict judgment this day! Do not judge in accord with strict judgment this day!"
S. Hadrian wanted to go to him. A Samaritan said to him, "Do not go to him until I see what he is doing, and so hand over the city [of Betar] to you. [Make peace...for you.]"
T. He got into the city through a drain pipe. He went and found R. Eleazar of Modiin standing and praying. He pretended to whisper something in his ear.
U. the townspeople say [the Samaritan] do this and brought him to Ben Kozeba. They told him, "We saw this man having dealings with your friend."
V. [Bar Kokhba] said to him, "What did you say to him, and what did he say to you?"
W. He said to [the Samaritan], "If I tell you, then the king will kill me, and if I do not tell you, then you will kill me. It is better that the king kill me, and not you.
X. "[Eleazar] said to me, 'I should hand over my city.' ['I shall make peace...']."
Y. He turned to R. Eleazar of Modiin. He said to him, "What did this Samaritan say to you?"
Z. He replied, "Nothing."
AA. He said to him, "What did you say to him?"
BB. He said to him, "Nothing."
CC. [Ben Kozeba] gave [Eleazar] one good kick and killed him.
DD. Forthwith an echo came forth and proclaimed the following verse:
EE. "'Woe to my worthless shepherd, who deserts the flock! May the sword smite his arm and his right eye! Let his arm be wholly withered, his right eye utterly blinded!' (Zech. 11:17).
FF. "You have murdered R. Eleazar of Modiin, the right arm of all Israel, and their right eye. Therefore may the right arm of that man wither, may his right eye be utterly blinded!"
GG. Forthwith Betar was taken, and Ben Kozeba was killed.

We notice two complementary themes. First, Bar Kokhba treats Heaven with arrogance, asking God merely to keep out of the way. Second, he treats an especially revered sage with a parallel arrogance. The sage had the power to preserve Israel. Bar Kokhba destroyed Israel's one protection. The result was inevitable.

The Messiah, the centerpiece of salvation history and hero of the tale, emerged as a critical figure. The historical theory of this Yerushalmi passage is stated very simply. In their view Israel had to choose between wars, either the war fought by Bar Kokhba or the "war for Torah." "Why had they been punished? It was because of the weight of the war, for they had not wanted to engage in the struggles over the meaning of the Torah" (Y. Ta. 3:9 XVI I). Those struggles, which were ritual arguments about ritual matters, promised the only victory worth winning. Then Israel's history would be written in terms of wars over the meaning of the Torah and the decision of the law.

True, the skins are new, but the wine is very old. For while we speak of sages and learning, the message is the familiar one. It is Israel's history that works out and expresses Israel's relationship with God. The critical dimension of Israel's life, therefore, is salvation, the definitive trait, a movement in time from now to then. It follows that the paramount and organizing category is history and its lessons. In the Yerushalmi we witness, among the Mishnah's heirs, a striking reversion to biblical convictions about the centrality of history in the definition of Israel's reality. The heavy weight of prophecy, apocalyptic, and biblical historiography, with their emphasis upon salvation and on history as the indicator of Israel's salvation, stood against the Mishnah's quite separate thesis of what truly mattered. What, from their viewpoint, demanded description and analysis and required interpretation? It was the category of sanctification, for eternity. The true issue framed by history and apocalypse was how to move toward the foreordained end of salvation, how to act in time to reach salvation at the end of time. The Mishnah's teleology beyond time and its capacity to posit an eschatology without a place for a historical Mishnah take a position beyond that of the entire antecedent sacred literature of Israel. Only one strand, the priestly one, had ever taken so extreme a position on the centrality of sanctification and the peripheral nature of salvation. Wisdom had stood in between, with its own concerns, drawing attention both to what happened and to what endured. But to wisdom what finally mattered was not nature or supernature, but rather abiding relationships in historical time.

The Talmud of Babylonia, at the end, carried forward the innovations we have seen in the talmud of the Land of Israel. In the view expressed here, the principal result of Israel's loyal adherence to the Torah and its religious duties will be Israel's humble acceptance of God's rule. The humility, under all conditions, makes God love Israel.

B. Hullin 89a

"It was not because you were greater than any people that the Lord set his love upon you and chose you" (Deut. 7:7). The Holy One, blessed be He, said to Israel, "I love you because even when I bestow greatness upon you, you humble yourselves before me. I bestowed greatness upon Abraham, yet he said to me, 'I am but dust and ashes' (Gen. 18:27); upon Moses and Aaron, yet they said, 'But I am a worm and no man' (Ps. 22:7). But with the heathens it is not so. I bestowed greatness upon nimrod, and he said, 'Come, let us build us a city' (Gen. 11:4); upon Pharaoh, and he said, 'Who are they among all the gods of the counties?' (2 Kgs. 18:35); upon Nebuchadnezzar, and he said, 'I will ascend above the heights of the clouds' (Isa. 14:14); upon Hiram, king of Tyre, and he said, 'I sit in the seat of God, in the heart of the seas' (Ezek. 28:2)."

So the system emerges complete, each of its parts stating precisely the same message as is revealed in the whole. The issue of the Messiah and the meaning of Israel's history framed through the Messiah myth convey in their terms precisely the same position that we find everywhere else in all other symbolic components of the rabbinic system and canon. The heart of the matter then is Israel's subservience to God's will, as expressed in the Torah and embodied in the teachings and lives of the great sages. When Israel fully accepts God's rule, then the Messiah will come. Until Israel subjects itself to God's rule, the Jews will be subjugated to pagan domination. Since the condition of Israel governs, Israel itself holds the key to its own redemption. But this it can achieve only by throwing away the key!

The paradox must be crystal clear: Israel acts to redeem itself through the opposite of self-determination, namely, by subjugating itself to God. Israel's power lies in its negation of power. Its destiny lies in giving up all pretense at deciding its own destiny. So weakness is the ultimate strength, forbearance the final act of self-assertion, passive resignation the sure step toward liberation. (The parallel is the crucified Christ.) Israel's freedom is engraved on the tablets of the commandments of God: to be free is freely to obey. That is not the meaning associated with these words in the minds of others who, like the sages of the rabbinical canon, declared their view of what Israel must do to secure the coming of the Messiah.

The passage, praising Israel for its humility, completes the circle begun with the description of Bar Kokhba as arrogant and boastful. Gentile kings are boastful; Israelite kings are humble. So, in all, the Messiah myth deals with a very concrete and limited consideration of the national life and character. The theory of Israel's history and destiny as it was expressed within that myth interprets matters in terms of a single criterion. What others within the Israelite world had done or in the future would do with the conviction that, at the end of time, God would send a (or the) Messiah to "save" Israel, it was a single idea for the sages of the Mishnah and the Talmuds and collections of scriptural exegesis. And that conception stands at the center of their system; it shapes and is shaped by their system. In context, the Messiah expresses the system's meaning and so makes it work.

When constructing a systematic account of Judaism – that is, the worldview and way of life for Israel presented in the Mishnah – the philosophers of the Mishnah did not make use of the Messiah myth in the construction of a teleology for their system. They found it possible to present a statement of goals for their projected life of Israel which was entirely separate from appeals to history and eschatology. Since they certainly knew, and even alluded to, long-standing and widely held convictions on eschatological subjects, beginning with those in Scripture, the framers thereby testified that, knowing the larger repertoire, they made choices different from others before and after them. Their document accurately and ubiquitously expresses these choices, both affirmative and negative.

Second, the appearance of a messianic eschatology fully consonant with the larger characteristic of the rabbinic system – with its stress on the viewpoints and prooftexts of Scripture, its interest in what was happening to Israel, its focus upon the national historical dimension of the life of the group – indicates that the encompassing rabbinic system stands essentially autonomous of the prior, mishnaic system. True, what had gone before was absorbed and fully assimilated. but the rabbinic system first appearing in the Talmud of the Land of Israel, is different in the aggregate from the mishnaic system. It represents more, however, than a negative response to its predecessor. The rabbinic system of the two Talmuds took over the fundamental convictions of the Mishnaic worldview about the importance of Israel's constructing for itself a life beyond time. The rabbinic system then transformed the Messiah myth in its totality into an essentially ahistorical force. If people wanted to reach the end of time, they had to rise above time, that is, history, and stand off at the side of great movements of political and military character. That is the message of the Messiah myth as it reaches full exposure in the rabbinic system of the two Talmuds. At its foundation it is precisely the message of teleology without eschatology expressed by the Mishnah and its associated documents. Accordingly, we cannot claim that the rabbinic or talmudic system in this regard constitutes a reaction against the mishnaic one. We must conclude, quite to the contrary, that in the Talmuds and their associated documents we see the restatement in classical mythic form of the ontological convictions that had informed the minds of the second-century philosophers. The new medium contained the old and enduring message: Israel must turn away from time and change, submit to whatever happens, so as to win for itself the only government worth having, that is, God's rule, accomplished through God's anointed agent, the Messiah.

7

What, Exactly, Do We Mean by "An Event" in Judaism? History in the Formation of Judaism

In an exact sense, "event" has no meaning at all in Judaism, since Judaism forms culture through other than historical modes of organizing existence. Without the social construction of history, there also is no need for the identification of events, that is, individual and unique happenings that bear consequence, since, within the system and structure of Judaism, history forms no taxon, assuredly not the paramount one, and, it must follow, no happening is unique, and, on its own, no event bears consequence. These statements rest upon modes of the analysis of history as the fabrication of culture, including a religious culture, and require us to review the recent formation of thought on history as culturally ordered, and on the event as "contingent realization of the cultural pattern," for it is only in that context that we may make sense, also, of the representation of both history and its raw materials, events, in Judaism in its definitive canon.

Until modes of historical thinking of a social scientific character got underway – beginning, as a matter of fact, in this most distinguished collegium – narrative history, ordinarily a paraphrastic chronicle, served as a medium for organizing and explaining perceived experience. That kind of history enjoyed the status of objective truth, a principle of explanation of self-evident validity. Its generative data, events, meaning, happenings of (self-evident) consequence, defined the foci of learning, an episteme ultimately formulated as the search for precisely what happened. When people contemplated the past, it was because they proposed through such precise knowledge to explain whatever mattered in the present. What they chose to interpret in the present then defined their curiosity about the past. They then identified out of the unlimited agenda of the past those things that mattered, and these they called events, occasions of consequence, as distinct from undifferentiated and unperceived happenings – from eating breakfast to losing one's keys – which of course bear no material consequence in the explanation of the world.

Now it hardly mattered, in the long era during which historical study predominated as the medium for the explanation of the social order, that the received manner of doing history as a mode of organizing and explaining experience involved a series of logical fallacies. Explaining the outcome by reference to a sequence of ordered events, after all, formed an intellectually legitimate way of appel to the intellectually illegitimate argument, *post hoc, ergo propter hoc.* So too, explanation without verification through a process of generalization, interpretation without a process of comparison and contrast, analysis as mere paraphrase of received accounts – these traits of historical learning did not attract attention. Historical explanation of the world, specific and ad hoc and episodic, found no competition and enjoyed the standing of self-evident truth. The notion that the mere paraphrase of "happenings," identified by ourselves as a matter of fact as events, could account for the perceived present demands for credulity an innocence so childlike that we must wonder how historical explanation of society and culture served for as long as it did. All the more reason to admire the towering intellects, so many of them collected in this one place, whose independence of mind impelled them to ask, why so? when everyone held, indeed, why not? and how otherwise? But they persisted. In consequence we now understand that the very notion of an "event," and with it the vast superstructure of the ordering of intellect and the explanation of society built upon historical explanation of sequences of events, then to now, there to here, all rational, all obvious, all self-evidence, come to us as the gifts of naive credulity.

It would carry us far afield to trace the long history of historical explanation of the social order by appeal to the definition, selection, and sequence of events. Chronicles and other exercises in *Listenwissenschaft*, of course, go back to remote antiquity. But history as arbiter of truth, history as mediator of sensibility and source of explanation – these honored roles in the court of intellect came to history only in the formative centuries of our own civilization. We should, after all, have to trace the path back to the Protestant Reformation, with its insistence on the priority of historical fact, deriving from a mythic age of perfection, in dictating the legitimacy of social reality in the present moment. Cutting through the detritus and sediment of the long centuries of increment and accumulation, therefore appealing not to *Listenwissenschaft*, but to a different, more autonomous kind of judgment altogether, for the logic of their discourse, the Reformation theologians identified history, the record of what happened (in this case) in Scripture, as the instrument for the validation of reform. Reform then would accomplish the renewal of times past, times perfect, appealing therefore to the court of appeal formed by history.

But history of a particular order, events of a very specific character, reaching their definition in the second way station, beyond the Reformation, in our quest for the self-evidence of history as a medium of social explanation. And that, of course, is the nineteenth century with its interest in historical explanation of not merely the life of faith but the reality of society, above all, the formation of the nation. Here again, I stand in the right place to speak of the appeal to history, once more with its canon of well-chosen events, in explanation of the social order, this time, the "we" of the nation, the other-ness of other peoples. If history with its prooftexts in self-evidently probative events served the purpose of religious reform, it provided a still more abundant source for explaining the self-evidence of the nation state. No wonder, then, that in the American State of Texas, once an independent nation, all school children must study Texas history in three sequences, but American history in only one. No wonder, too, that Zionism precipitated the massive rewriting of the histories of Jews as a single, unitary Jewish history, with a beginning, middle, and end, with the self-evident message of Zionism as its ubiquitous proposition. The State of Texas and the State of Israel exemplify the uses that for so long guaranteed for history a principal place in the academy, for both appeal to facts to validate the claims of social ideology.

Now it is only in the recent past that we have begun to recognize that history forms a discourse of contemporary taste and judgment, events become eventful only because we make them so, and, in all, history is culturally ordered, and events are defined and identified as statements of an intensely contemporary perception. It follows, we now understand, that all histories are the creation of an eternal present, that is, those moments in which histories are defined and distinguished, in which events are identified and assigned consequence, and in which sequences of events, "this particular thing happened here and therefore...," are strung together, pearls on a string, to form ornaments of intellect. And, with that understanding well in hand, fully recognizing that history is one of the grand fabrications of the human intellect, facts not discovered but invented, explanations that themselves form cultural indicators of how things are in the here and now, we find ourselves no longer historians of ideas of history, or analysts of the history of culture, let alone practitioners of the dread narrative history that makes of historical writing a work of elegant imagination. We find ourselves, rather, archaeologists, working from the surface, that is known, through the detritus of the unknown, in quest of a material understanding of a reality that is not known but for its artifacts, not susceptible of explanation and understanding except in categories and terms that are defined by those same artifacts. And that quest is, we all recognize, not a very smooth one.

The metaphor of archaeology for historical study, chosen for obvious reasons, is jarring, because, after all, nearly all historical evidence is in writing, and we are used to thinking of archaeology in terms of the pick and the shovel. But it is an apt metaphor, nonetheless, for it teaches us how to examine the written evidence on which most of us work in our cultural analysis of we know not what. The archaeologist (in theory at least) peels back from the surface to the underneath, and so must we. The archaeologist knows no categories other than the boundaries of the dig and the strata of the dig, knows no categories, imposes no categories, invents no categories that are not there. Then the things dug up define the categories and impose their own questions, their location in situ defining their "text," by which I mean, their circumstance, their relationships with other artifacts in situ defining their context, their stratum in situ dictating the matrix of interpretation. For us, the site is the document, and our task is to treat the document as not a candidate for paraphrase, that is, for descriptive historical study within the premise of explaining how things were and how they got to be the way they are. For us the task is to treat the document – as we have all learned from the faculty of this college – as a cultural artifact, as evidence for the working out of a social order in small detail.

Now if these remarks have suggested in your mind, however generous your spirit, that I have come to Paris to reinvent the intellectual wheel that, after all, has already been invented here, then consider how fresh and remarkable are the initial results of the anti-historicistic revolution you have sparked. For the consequences for hermeneutics, which I have outlined in the analogy of the archaeology of knowledge, are such that just now we cannot have too many examples of what only recently has become obvious. In sustaining the self-evidence of a new order of learning, I mean to take part in the task of rereading cases and reconsidering problems long thought settled. In the present instance at stake is the proposition that the definition of events forms an acutely concrete statement of the larger systemic principles, and when we understand how a system defines events, we grasp the working of that system.

The task is important, even though narrative history in the academy no longer enjoys immediate recognition as how things must be done. For still, as a matter of fact, in the English language at least, the annual lists of new historical writings devote the larger part of the catalogue to narratives of how things were, explaining how they now are. Analytical history does not yet predominate, and the anthropology of history has achieved its greatest successes in the study of not Europe and its overseas dependencies in North America but the Pacific. And it is equally true that we are trying to teach ourselves to regard written evidence as a cultural artifact, no less than the broken sherd dug up in the field. But as a matter of fact, in entire ranges of learning the urgent question remains, did it really happen? And the urgency of the question derives from the conviction that, if so, certain important consequences must follow. The self-evidence of a connection between past and present competes with the view of the systemic character of culture, and we who propose to hold the whole together in a different way from the historical may not yet claim to hold the field. Consequently, we do not waste our energy by exercises in the rehearsal of other modes of reading the writing of prior ages than the historical-historicistic ones.

One fresh way of reviewing old things is to ask how the historical invention of history defines and identifies its raw materials. I mean to say, when we know what literary site presents to us as its artifacts, and when we can read those artifacts in our vocation as archaeologists of knowledge, rather than as historians of how things were (perhaps then theologians or storytellers of how things are connected and so what they mean), then we gain perspective on the new way by contrast to the old. No more telling indicator of the shift in the processes of understanding than the definition of an event comes to hand. For the event is to the composition of history as the atom is to the molecule, the thread to the fabric, or the steel beam to the building. And yet, these diverse metaphors reverse matters. The molecule defines the atoms that it wants (to impute teleology to the inanimate, in the manner of historians), the fabric requires that thread and no other, the building dictates the requirements, as to tensile strength, of its beams. And so, I wish to show, the culture identifies the events that explain and justify the culture. And, in consequence, we must ask ourselves, are not the literary records of events so constituted as to dictate the shape of the parts by appeal to the necessities of the whole? For it is my view that the system forms its events, not as a matter of mere consciousness, but as a *diktat* of culture. History therefore emerges as not the source for the explanation of culture, but rather as the best evidence for the shape, structure, and system that a culture comprises.

Let us take as our initial instance not Judaism but a different matter altogether, one that gives us perspective on our question, what, in Judaism, is an event, and how, from Judaism, do we learn about the hermeneutics of events? It is the clash of cultures that produced a long-remembered event indeed, the death of Captain Cook in Hawaii two hundred years ago. Marshall Sahlins argues[1] in behalf of the view, adumbrated in my remarks, that "history is culturally ordered, differently so in different societies, according to meaningful schemes of things."[2] Sahlin further cites Clifford Geertz's observation that "an event is a unique actualization of a general phenomenon, a contingent realization of the cultural pattern." Sahlin selects as his probative case the death of Captain Cook, because he is able, through his analysis of exactly what happened, to show the cultural indicators to which "events" testify – and which explain "events." To state matters briefly, "When the English anchored next year at Kealakekua, Hawaiian priests were able to objectify their interpretation of Cook as the Year-God Lonon, on his annual return to renew the fertility of the land." Then, when Cook came back to repair the broken main mast, he violated the rules and had to be, and was, killed. In his "Anthropology of History," Sahlin states the upshot with lapidary clarity: "Different cultural orders have their own modes of historical action, consciousness, and determination – their own historical practice."[3] That is not to argue in favor of historical, let alone intellectual, relativity. It is only to insist upon the study of what a culture, as represented by its documents, defines as its past: the events, their order and connection, the meanings to be derived from them. History therefore serves as a capital indicator of the hermeneutics, and hermeneutics defines the system and structure – theirs but ours, too – that all together form intellect.

When we come to the case of Judaism, we bring with us a substantial intellectual heritage, composed, as a matter of fact, of misinformation or no information. First, we wrongly take for granted that Judaism (whatever else it may be) is the religion of the Old Testament. Then we have as an established fact the utter misrepresentation that Judaism is a historical religion, in that it appeals for its worldview to not myth about gods in Heaven but the history of Israel upon earth – interpreted in relationship to the acts of God in Heaven to be sure. Whether history in this form materially differs from myth in the Greek form is not at issue here. I take it as a broadly held conviction, third, that Judaism is a religion that appeals to history, that is, to events, defined in the ordinary way, important happenings, for its source of testing and establishing truth.

---

[1] In his landmark work, *Islands of History* (Chicago, 1985: University of Chicago Press).
[2] p. vii.
[3] p. 34.

What, Exactly, Do We Mean by "An Event" in Judaism?

True, what the Old Testament writers deem events is not to be gainsaid: God descending to Sinai surely proves more dramatic than the failure of rain on a village, but to Amos, what does not happen defines an event as rich in revelation as, to the Yahwist, Elohist, and Priestly authors of the strands of the Pentateuch, what does happen defines an event. The fundamentally historical character of the Old Testament narratives, with their beginnings, middles, ends, their lessons and their demonstrations – that basic historical character is so broadly held as not to require comment. And so I shall refrain from comment, even though I doubt that anyone in this august assembly can concur, as I cannot concur, that there is a shred of historical consciousness, as distinct from mythic fantasy, in the Old Testament. But then, I need hardly rehearse Professor Paul Veyne's arguments on "the constitutive imagination," in his *Did the Greeks Believe in their Myths?* – a book waiting to be written for ancient Israel as well.

But Judaism, of course, is not only the religion of the Old Testament, and, as a case in the study of the cultural definition of events, only in its full canonical expression does Judaism serve to show us how culture identifies event through its own cognitive processes. Judaism is the religion of not the Old Testament but the Torah, and the canonical Torah encompasses the Old Testament only as it is reworked, as an object of rewriting and revision, in the vast canon of the two Talmuds and the Midrash compilations that took shape in late antiquity, the first seven centuries A.D., under the title, the Oral Torah. That labor of rewriting and recasting of one thing in light of something else that produced the Judaism of the Dual Torah forms a rich set of cases in cultural transformation, in the determination, by a system, of its own past, in the identification, within a system, of its own resources. For, after all, while a system speaks through its canon, and while theologians commonly read the canon to describe the system, in point of fact it is the canon that recapitulates the system, the system that speaks, in detail to be sure, through the canon.

When, therefore, we can affirm, with Sahlin, that "the different cultural orders studied by anthropology have their own historicities," the result of that affirmation is not a conclusion (the relativity of historical knowledge) but a question: How shall we frame history into a cultural indicator? In the case of the Judaism of the Dual Torah, the answer to that question proves quite accessible, for that Judaism makes ample use of the Old Testament in its account of itself. We should therefore anticipate that the canon of the Dual Torah will encompass narrative history, but it does not. We should expect to find therein accounts of events of not only times past but also the present explained by the past, but we do not. We should go in search of the description of one-time, unique happenings – events in the conventional sense – but, if we did, we should return disappointed. The result will be quite opposite. When we read matters properly, we shall find out how to read. For the archaeology of texts uncovers abstract structure in the identification and explication of the concrete event.[4]

This brings me directly to the problem at hand, what exactly does Judaism mean by events? To answer that question succinctly is simple. When we know how Judaism classifies events, we shall have the answer to the question of definition. So too, when we know how Judaism utilizes events, the heuristic value, the probative standing, of events, we once again shall have our answer. What I shall show is that, in the canonical literature of the Judaism of the Dual Torah, formed between the second and the seventh centuries and authoritative to this day, events find their place, within the science of learning of *Listenwissenschaft* that characterizes this literature, along with sorts of things that, for our part, we should not characterize as events at all. Events have no autonomous standing; events are not unique, each unto itself; events have no probative value on their own. Events form cases, along with a variety of other cases, making up lists of things that, in common, point to or prove one thing. Not only so, but events do not make up their own list at all, and this is what I found rather curious when I first noted that fact. Events will appear on the same list as persons, places, things. That means that events not only have no autonomous standing on their own, but also that events constitute no species even within a genus of a historical order. For persons, places, and things in our way of thinking do not belong on the same list as events; they are not of the same order. Within the logic of our own minds, we cannot classify the city, Paris, within the same genus as the event, the declaration of the rights of man, for instance, nor is Sinai of the same order of things as the Torah.

What then will you make of a list that encompasses within the same taxic composition events and things? One such list made up of events, persons, and places, is as follows: [1] Israel at the sea; [2] the ministering angels; [3] the tent of meeting; [4] the eternal house [= the Temple]; [5] Sinai. That mixtures an event (Israel redeemed at the sea), a category of sensate being (angels), a location (tent of meeting, Temple), and then Sinai, which can stand for a variety of things but in context stands for the Torah. In such a list an event may or may not stand for a value or a proposition, but it does not enjoy autonomous standing; the list is not defined by the eventfulness of events and their meaning, the compilation of matters of a single genus or even a single species (tent of meeting,

---

[4]cf. Sahlin, p. 72.

What, Exactly, Do We Mean by "An Event" in Judaism?   181

eternal house, are the same species here). The notion of event as autonomous, even unique, is quite absent in this taxonomy.

Another such list moves from events to other matters altogether, finding the whole subject to the same metaphor, hence homogenized. First come the events that took place at these places or with these persons: Egypt, the sea, Marah, Massah and Meribah, Horeb, the wilderness, the spies in the Land, Shittim, for Achan/Joshua and the conquest of the Land. Now that mixture of places and names clearly intends to focus on particular things that happened, and hence, were the list to which I refer to conclude at this point, we could define an event for Judaism as a happening that bore consequence, taught a lesson or exemplified a truth, in the present case, an event matters because it the mixture of rebellion and obedience. But there would then be no doubt that "event" formed a genus unto itself, and that a proper list could not encompass both events, defined conventionally as we should, and also other matters altogether.

But the literary culture at hand, this textual community proceeds, in the same literary context, to the following items: [1] the Ten Commandments; [2] the show fringes and phylacteries; [3] the *Shema* and the Prayer; [4] the tabernacle and the cloud of the Presence of God in the world to come. Why we invoke, as our candidates for the metaphor at hand, the Ten Commandments, show fringes and phylacteries, recitation of the *Shema* and the Prayer, the tabernacle and the cloud of the Presence of God, and the mezuzah, seems to me clear from the very catalogue. These reach their climax in the analogy between the home and the tabernacle, the embrace of God and the Presence of God. So the whole is meant to list those things that draw the Israelite near God and make the Israelite cleave to God. And to this massive catalogue, events are not only exemplary – which historians can concede without difficulty – but also subordinated.

They belong on the same list as actions, things, persons, places, because they form an order of being that is not to be differentiated between events (including things that stand for events) and other cultural artifacts altogether. A happening is no different from an object, in which case "event" serves no better, and no worse, than a hero, a gesture or action, recitation of a given formula, or a particular locale, to establish a truth. It is contingent, subordinate, instrumental. I can think of no more apt illustration of Geertz's interesting judgment: "an event is a unique actualization of a general phenomenon, a contingent realization of the cultural pattern." And why find that fact surprising, since all history comes to us in writing, and it is the culture that dictates how writing is to take place; that is why history can only paraphrase the affirmations of a system, and that is why events recapitulate in acute and concrete ways the system that classifies one thing that happens as event, but another thing is not only not an event but is not classified at all. In the present instance, an event is not at all eventful; it is merely a fact that forms part of the evidence for what is, and what is eventful is not an occasion at all, but a condition, an attitude, a perspective and a viewpoint. Then, it is clear, events are subordinated to the formation of attitudes, perspectives, viewpoints – the formative artifacts of not history in the conventional sense but culture in the framework of Sahlin's generalization, "history is culturally ordered, differently so in different societies, according to meaningful schemes of things."

To make more concrete the evidence on which I have drawn to join the public discussion, let me refer to one important compilation of lists, of the sixth century A.D., Song of Songs Rabbah, a reading of the Song of Songs as a metaphorization of God's relationship of intense love for Israel, and Israel's relationship of intense love for God. In that document we find sequences, or combinations, of references to Old Testament persons, events, actions, and the like. These bear the rhetorical emblem, "another matter," in long lists of composites of well-framed compositions.[5] Each entry on a given list will be represented as "another matter," meaning, another interpretation of reading of a given verse in the Song of Songs. As a matter of fact, however, that "other matter," one following the other, turns out to be the same matter in other terms. These constructions form lists out of diverse entries. When in Song of Songs Rabbah we have a sequence of items alleged to form taxon, that is, a set of things that share a common taxic indicator, of course what we have is a list. The list presents diverse matters that all together share, and therefore also set forth, a single fact or rule or phenomenon. That is why we can list them, in all their distinctive character and specificity, on a common catalogue of "other things" that pertain all together to one thing.

Since, on these lists, we find classified within a single taxon events, persons, places, objects and actions, it is important to understand how they coalese. The rhetoric is the key indicator, since it is objective and superficial. When we find the rhetorical formula, "another matter," that is, *davar aher*, what follows says the same thing in other words, or at least something complementary and necessary to make some larger point. That is why I insist the constructions form lists. William Scott Green states the matter, in his analysis of a single passage, in these words:

---

[5] I estimate that approximately 80 percent of the document in bulk is comprised of "another-matter" compositions. The list in this form defines the paramount rhetorical medium and logical structure of the document.

What, Exactly, Do We Mean by "An Event" in Judaism?

> Although the interpretations in this passage are formally distinguished from one another...by the disjunctive device *davar aher* ('another interpretation'), they operate within a limited conceptual sphere and a narrow thematic range....Thus rather than 'endless multiple meanings,' they in fact ascribe to the words 'doing wonders' multiple variations of a single meaning....By providing multiple warrant for that message, the form effectively restricts the interpretive options....[6]

When we have a sequence of *davar aher* passages forming a *davar aher* construction, the message is cumulative, and the whole as a matter of fact forms a sum greater than that of the parts; it will then be that accumulation that guides us to what is if implicit yet fundamental in the exact sense: at the foundation of matters; there is where we should find that system, order, proportion, cogency that all together we expect a theology to impart to discrete observations about holy matters.

In general, "another matter" signals "another way of saying the same thing"; or the formula bears the sense, "these two distinct things add up to one thing," with the further proviso that both are necessary to make one point that transcends each one. Not only so, but in Song of Songs Rabbah the fixed formula of the *davar aher* compilation points toward fixed formulas of theological thought: sets of coherent verbal symbols that work together. These "other things" encompass time, space, person and object, action and attitude, and join them all together, for instance, David, Solomon, Messiah at the end of time; this age, the age to come; the Exodus from Egypt, Sinai, the age to come all may appear together within a single list. Let me give a single example of the list that makes it possible to redefine "event" into a category of quite ahistorical valence.

Chapter Five. Song of Songs Rabbah to Song 1:5

I.1   A.   "I am very dark, but comely, [O daughters of Jerusalem, like the tents of Kedar, like the curtains of Solomon]" (Song 1:5):
       B.   "I am dark" in my deeds.
       C.   "But comely" in the deeds of my forebears.
I.2   A.   "I am very dark, but comely":
       B.   Said the Community of Israel, "'I am dark' in my view, 'but comely' before my Creator."
       C.   For it is written, "Are you not as the children of the Ethiopians to Me, O children of Israel, says the Lord" (Amos 9:7):
       D.   "As the children of the Ethiopians" – in your sight.
       E.   But "to Me, O children of Israel, says the Lord."
I.3   A.   Another interpretation of the verse, ""I am very dark": In Egypt.
       B.   "But comely": In Egypt.

---

[6]In Jacob Neusner with William Scott Green, *Writing with Scripture. The Authority and Uses of the Hebrew Bible in the Torah of Formative Judaism* (Minneapolis, 1989: Fortress Press), p. 19.

	C.	"I am very dark" in Egypt: "But they rebelled against me and would not hearken to me" (Ezek. 20:8).
	D.	"But comely" in Egypt: With the blood of the Passover-offering and circumcision, "And when I passed by you and saw you wallowing in your blood, I said to you, In your blood live" (Ezek. 16:6) – in the blood of the Passover.
	E.	"I said to you, In your blood live" (Ezek. 16:6) – in the blood of the circumcision.
I.4	A.	Another interpretation of the verse, "I am very dark": At the sea, "They were rebellious at the sea, even the Red Sea" (Ps. 106:7).
	B.	"But comely": At the sea, "This is my God and I will be comely for him" (Ex. 15:2) [following Simon's rendering of the verse].
I.5	A.	"I am very dark": At Marah, "And the people murmured against Moses, saying, 'What shall we drink'" (Ex. 15:24).
	B.	"But comely": At Marah, "And he cried to the Lord and the Lord showed him a tree, and he cast it into the waters and the waters were made sweet" (Ex. 15:25).
I.6	A.	"I am very dark": At Rephidim, "And the name of the place was called Massah and Meribah" (Ex. 17:7).
	B.	"But comely": At Rephidim, "And Moses built an altar and called it by the name 'the Lord is my banner'" (Ex. 17:15).
I.7	A.	"I am very dark": At Horeb, "And they made a calf at Horeb" (Ps. 106:19).
	B.	"But comely": At Horeb, "And they said, 'All that the Lord has spoken we will do and obey'" (Ex. 24:7).
I.8	A.	"I am very dark": In the wilderness, "How often did they rebel against him in the wilderness" (Ps. 78:40).
	B.	"But comely": In the wilderness at the setting up of the tabernacle, "And on the day that the tabernacle was set up" (Num. 9:15).
I.9	A.	"I am very dark": In the deed of the spies, "And they spread an evil report of the land" (Num. 13:32).
	B.	"But comely": In the deed of Joshua and Caleb, "Save for Caleb, the son of Jephunneh the Kenizzite" (Num. 32:12).
I.10	A.	"I am very dark": At Shittim, "And Israel abode at Shittim and the people began to commit harlotry with the daughters of Moab" (Num. 25:1).
	B.	"But comely": At Shittim, "Then arose Phinehas and wrought judgment" (Ps. 106:30).
I.11	A.	"I am very dark": Through Achan, "But the children of Israel committed a trespass concerning the devoted thing" (Josh. 7:1).
	B.	"But comely": Through Joshua, "And Joshua said to Achan, 'My son, give I pray you glory'" (Josh. 7:19).
I.12	A.	"I am very dark": Through the kings of Israel.
	B.	"But comely": Through the kings of Judah.
	C.	If with my dark ones that I had, it was such that "I am comely," all the more so with my prophets.
II.5	A.	[As to the verse, "I am very dark, but comely," R. Levi b. R. Haita gave three interpretations:
	B.	"'I am very dark': All the days of the week.
	C.	"'But comely': On the Sabbath.
	D.	"'I am very dark': All the days of the year.

> E. "'But comely': On the Day of Atonement.
> F. "'I am very dark': Among the Ten Tribes.
> G. "'But comely': In the tribe of Judah and Benjamin.
> H. "'I am very dark': In this world.
> I. "'But comely': In the world to come."

The contrast of dark and comely yields a variety of applications; in all of them the same situation that is the one also is the other, and the rest follows in a wonderfully well-crafted composition. What is the repertoire of items? Dark in deeds but comely in ancestry; dark in my view but comely before God; dark when rebellious, comely when obedient, a point made at Nos. 3, for Egypt, 4, for the sea, and 5 for Marah, 6, for Massah and Meribah, 7 for Horeb, 8 for the wilderness, 9 for the spies in the Land, 10 for Shittim, 11 for Achan/Joshua and the conquest of the Land, 12 for Israel and Judah. But look what follows: the week as against the Sabbath, the weekdays as against the Day of Atonement, the Ten Tribes as against Judah and Benjamin, this world as against the world to come. Whatever classification these next items demand for themselves, it surely will not be that of events. Indeed, if by event we mean something that happened once, as in "once upon a time," then Sabbath as against weekday, Day of Atonement as against ordinary day form a different category; the Ten Tribes as against Judah and Benjamin constitute social entities, not divisions of time; and this age and the age to come form utterly anti-historical taxa altogether.

Events not only do not form a taxon, they also do not present a vast corpus of candidates for inclusion into some other taxon. The lists in the document at hand form selections from a most limited repertoire of candidates. If we were to catalogue all of the exegetical repertoire encompassed by *davar aher* constructions in this document, we should not have a very long list of candidates for inclusion in any list. And among the candidates, events are few indeed. They encompass Israel at the sea and at Sinai, the destruction of the first Temple, the destruction of the second Temple, events as defined by the actions of some holy men such as Abraham, Isaac, and Jacob (treated not for what they did but for who they were), Daniel, Mishael, Hananiah and Azariah, and the like. It follows that the restricted repertoire of candidates for taxonomic study encompasses remarkably few events, remarkably few for a literary culture that is commonly described as quintessentially historical!

Then what taxic indicator dictates which happenings will be deemed events and which not? What are listed throughout are not data of nature or history but of theology: God's relationship with Israel, expressed in such facts as the three events, the first two in the past, the third in the future, namely, the three redemptions of Israel, the three patriarchs, and holy persons, actions, events, what have you. These are facts that are assembled and grouped; in Song of Songs Rabbah the result is not propositional at all, or, if propositional, then essentially the repetition of familiar propositions through unfamiliar data. What we have is a kind of recombinant theology, in which the framer ("the theologian") selects from a restricted repertoire a few items for combination, sometimes to make a point (for example, the contrast of obedient and disobedient Israel we saw just now), sometimes not. What is set on display justifies the display: putting this familiar fact together with that familiar fact in an unfamiliar combination constitutes what is new and important in the list; the consequent conclusion one is supposed to draw, the proposition or rule that emerges – these are rarely articulated and never important. True, the list in Song of Songs Rabbah may comprise a rule, or it may substantiate a proposition or validate a claim; but more often than not, the effect of making the list is to show how various items share a single taxic indicator, which is to say, the purpose of the list is to make the list. The making of connections among ordinarily not connected things is then one outcome of *Listenwissenschaft*. What I find engaging in *davar aher* constructions is the very variety of things that, on one list or another, can be joined together – a list for its own sake. What we have is a kind of subtle restatement, through an infinite range of possibilities, of the combinations and recombinations of a few essentially simple facts (data). It is as though a magician tossed a set of sticks this way and that, interpreting the diverse combinations of a fixed set of objects. The propositions that emerge are not the main point; the combinations are.

That seems to me an important fact, for it tells me that the culture at hand has defined for itself a repertoire of persons and events and conceptions (for example, Torah study), holy persons, holy deeds, holy institutions, presented candidates for inclusion in *davar aher* constructions, and the repertoire, while restricted and not terribly long, made possible a scarcely limited variety of lists of things with like taxic indicators. That is to say, since the same items occur over and over again, but there is no pattern to how they recur. By a pattern I mean that items of the repertoire may appear in numerous *davar aher* constructions or not; they may keep company with only a fixed number of other items, or they may not. Most things can appear in a *davar aher* composition with most other things.[7]

---

[7]To make this point concrete, here is a survey of sequences of components of such lists:

Joseph, righteous men, Moses, and Solomon;

patriarchs as against princes, offerings as against merit, and Israel as against the nations; those who love the king, proselytes, martyrs, penitents;

first, Israel at Sinai; then Israel's loss of God's presence on account of the golden calf; then God's favoring Israel by treating Israel not in accord with the requirements of justice but with mercy;

Dathan and Abiram, the spies, Jeroboam, Solomon's marriage to Pharaoh's daughter, Ahab, Jezebel, Zedekiah;

Israel is feminine, the enemy (Egypt) masculine, but God the father saves Israel the daughter;

Moses and Aaron, the Sanhedrin, the teachers of Scripture and Mishnah, the rabbis;

the disciples; the relationship among disciples, public recitation of teachings of the Torah in the right order; lections of the Torah;

the spoil at the sea = the Exodus, the Torah, the Tabernacle, the ark;

the patriarchs, Abraham, Isaac, Jacob, then Israel in Egypt, Israel's atonement and God's forgiveness;

the Temple where God and Israel are joined, the Temple is God's resting place, the Temple is the source of Israel's fecundity;

Israel in Egypt, at the sea, at Sinai, and subjugated by the gentile kingdoms, and how the redemption will come;

Rebecca, those who came forth from Egypt, Israel at Sinai, acts of loving kindness, the kingdoms who now rule Israel, the coming redemption;

fire above, fire below, meaning heavenly and altar fires; Torah in writing, Torah in memory; fire of Abraham, Moriam, bush, Elijah, Hananiah, Mishael, and Azariah;

the Ten Commandments, show fringes and phylacteries, recitation of the Shema and the Prayer, the tabernacle and the cloud of the Presence of God, and the mezuzah;

the timing of redemption, the moral condition of those to be redeemed, and the past religious misdeeds of those to be redeemed;

Israel at the sea, Sinai, the Ten Commandments; then the synagogues and schoolhouses; then the redeemer;

the Exodus, the conquest of the Land, the redemption and restoration of Israel to Zion after the destruction of the first Temple, and the final and ultimate salvation;

the Egyptians, Esau and his generals, and, finally, the four kingdoms;

Moses's redemption, the first, to the second redemption in the time of the Babylonians and Daniel;

the litter of Solomon: the priestly blessing, the priestly watches, the Sanhedrin, and the Israelites coming out of Egypt;

Israel at the sea and forgiveness for sins effected through their passing through the sea; Israel at Sinai; the war with Midian; the crossing of the Jordan and entry into the Land; the house of the sanctuary; the priestly watches; the offerings in the Temple; the Sanhedrin; the Day of Atonement;

God redeemed Israel without preparation; the nations of the world will be punished, after Israel is punished; the nations of the world will present Israel as gifts to the royal messiah, and here the base verse refers to Abraham, Isaac, Jacob, Sihon, Og, Canaanites;

the return to Zion in the time of Ezra, the Exodus from Egypt in the time of Moses;

the patriarchs and with Israel in Egypt, at the Sea, and then before Sinai;

Abraham, Jacob, Moses;

The upshot is simple. Listmaking is accomplished within a restricted repertoire of items that can serve on lists; the listmaking then presents interesting combinations of an essentially small number of candidates for the exercise. But then, when making lists, one can do pretty much anything with the items that are combined; the taxic indicators are unlimited, but the data studied, severely limited. And that fact returns us to our starting point, the observations on history as a cultural artifact that form the premise for the study of history within the archaeology of knowledge. In fact, in Judaism history serves the theological sciences and therefore cannot be said to constitute history in any ordinary sense at all; but that is a trivial and obvious observation. More to the point, history, in the form of events, contributes to a rather odd way of conducting theological science.

For, forming part of the *davar aher* construction, history constitutes one among a variety of what I call, for lack of more suitable language at this point, theological "things"[8] – names, places, events, actions deemed to bear theological weight and to affect attitude and action. The play is worked out by a reprise of available materials, composed in some fresh and interesting combination. When three or more such theological "things" – whether person, whether event, whether action, whether attitude – are combined, they form a theological structure, and, viewed all together, all of the theological "things" in a given document constitute the components of the entire theological structure that the document affords. The propositions portrayed visually, through metaphors of sight, or dramatically, through metaphors of action and relationship, or in attitude and emotion, through metaphors that convey or provoke feeling and sentiment, when translated into language prove familiar and commonplace. The work of the theologian in this context is not to say something new or even persuasive, for the former is unthinkable by definition, the latter unnecessary in context. It is rather to display

---

Isaac, Jacob, Esau, Jacob, Joseph, the brothers, Jonathan, David, Saul, man, wife, paramour;

Abraham in the fiery furnace and Shadrach Meshach and Abednego, the Exile in Babylonia, now with reference to the return to Zion.

[8]I find myself at a loss for a better word-choice and must at this stage resort to the hopelessly inelegant "'theological' things" to avoid having to repeat the formula that seems to me to fit the data, namely, "names, places, events, actions deemed to bear theological weight and to affect attitude and action." Still, better a simple Anglo-Saxon formulation than a fancy German or Greek or Latin one. And Hebrew, whether Mishnaic or modern, simply does not serve for analytical work except when thought conceived in some other language is translated back into that language, should anyone be interested.

theological "things" in a fresh and interesting way, to accomplish a fresh exegesis of the canon of theological "things."

The combinations and recombinations defined for us by our document form events into facts, sharing the paramount taxic indicators of a variety of other facts, comprising a theological structure within a larger theological structure: a reworking of canonical materials. An event is therefore reduced to a "thing," losing all taxic autonomy, requiring no distinct indicator of an intrinsic order. It is simply something else to utilize in composing facts into knowledge; the event does not explain, it does not define, indeed, it does not even exist within its own framework at all. Judaism by "an event" means, in a very exact sense, nothing in particular. It is a component in a culture that combines and recombines facts into structures of its own design, an aspect of what I should call a culture that comes to full expression in recombinant theology.

We have been prepared for such a result by Jonathan Z. Smith, who has made us aware of critical issue of the recombinancy of a fixed canon of "things" in his discussion of sacred persistence, that is, "the rethinking of each little detail in a text, the obsession with the significance and perfection of each little action." In the canonical literature of Judaism, these minima are worked and reworked, rethought and recast in some other way or order or combination – but always held to be the same thing throughout. In this context I find important Smith's statement:

> An almost limitless horizon of possibilities that are at hand...is arbitrarily reduced...to a set of basic elements....Then a most intense ingenuity is exercised to overcome the reduction...to introduce interest and variety. This ingenuity is usually accompanied by a complex set of rules.[9]

The possibilities out of which the authorship of our exemplary document has made its selections are limited not by the metaphorical potential of the Song of Songs (!) but by the contents of the Hebrew Scriptures as the textual community formed of the Judaic sages defined those contents within their Torah.

For every Abraham, Isaac, and Jacob that we find, there are Job, Enoch, Jeroboam, or Zephaniah, whom we do not find; for every sea/Sinai/entry into the Land that we do find, there are other sequences, for example, the loss of the ark to the Philistines and its recovery, or Barak and Deborah, that we do not find. Ezra figures, Haggai does not; the Assyrians play a minor role, Nebuchadnezzar is on nearly every page. Granted, Sinai must enjoy a privileged position throughout. But

---

[9]"Sacred Persistence: Towards a Redescription of Canon," in William Scott Green, ed., *Approaches to Ancient Judaism* 1 (1978): 11-28. Quotation: p. 15.

why prefer Shadrach, Meshach and Abednego, Hananiah, Mishael, and Azariah, over other trilogies of heroic figures? So the selection is an act of choice, a statement of culture in miniature. But once restricted through this statement of choice, the same selected theological "things" then undergo combination and recombination with other theological things, the counterpart to Smith's "interest and variety." If we know the complex set of rules in play here, we also would understand the system that makes this document not merely an expression of piety but a statement of a theological structure: orderly, well-composed and proportioned, internally coherent and cogent throughout.

The canonical, therefore anything but random, standing of events forms a brief chapter in the exegesis of a canon. That observation draws us back to Smith, who observes:

> The radical and arbitary reduction represented by the notion of canon and the ingenuity represented by the rule governed exegetical enterprise to apply the canon to every dimension of human life is that most characteristic, persistent, and obsessive religious activity....The task of application as well as the judgment of the relative adequacy of particular applications to a community's life situation remains the indigenous theologian's task; but the study of the process, particularly the study of comparative systematics and exegesis, ought to be a major preoccupation of the historian of religions.[10]

Smith speaks of religion as an "enterprise of exegetical totalization," and he further identifies with the word "canon" precisely what we have identified as the substrate and structure of the list. If I had to define an event in this canonical context, I should have to call it merely another theological thing: something to be manipulated, combined in one way or in another, along with other theological things.

Have we access to other examples of cultures that define for themselves canonical lists of counterparts to what I have called "theological things"? Indeed, defining matters as I have, I may compare the event to a fixed object in a diviner's basket of the Ndembu, as Smith describes that divinitory situation:

> Among the Ndembu there are two features of the divinitory situation that are crucial to our concern: the diviner's basket and his process of interrogating his client. The chief mode of divination consists of shaking a basket in which some twenty-four fixed objects are deposited (a cock's claw, a piece of hoof, a bit of grooved wood...withered fruit, etc.). These are shaken in order to winnow out 'truth from falsehood' in such a way that few of the objects end up on top of the heap. These are 'read' by the diviner both with respect to

---

[10]*Ibid.*, p. 18.

their individual meanings and their combinations with other objects and the configurations that result.[11]

In Song of Songs Rabbah, Abraham, Isaac, Jacob, or the sea and Sinai, or Hananiah, Mishael, and Azariah, are the counterpart to the cock's claw and the piece of hoof. The event, in Judaism, is the counterpart to a cock's claw in the Ndembu culture. Both will be fixed, but will combine and recombine in a large number of different ways. But then what of "the lessons of history," and how shall we identify the counterpart to historical explanation? I find the answer in the Ndembu counterpart, the mode of reading "the process of interrogating the client." Again Smith:

> The client's situation is likewise taken into account in arriving at an interpretation. Thus...there is a semantic, syntactic, and pragmatic dimension to the 'reading.' Each object is publicly known and has a fixed range of meanings....The total collection of twenty-four objects is held to be complete and capable of illuminating every situation....What enables the canon to be applied to every situation or question is not the numbr of objects....Rather it is that, prior to performing the divination, the diviner has rigorously questioned his client in order to determine his situation with precision....It is the genius of the interpreter to match a public set of meanings with a commonly known set of facts...in order to produce a quite particular plausibility structure which speaks directly to his client's condition, which mediates between that which is public knowledge and the client's private perception of his unique situation.[12]

That concludes our inquiry, since it draws us to the task of the exegesis of exegesis. Events then form a problem of exegesis, in which, from what a culture defines as a consequential happening, we find our way back to the system and structure that that culture means to form. The work before us will teach us, in the case of Judaism, how from the study of what are defined as events to describe the process of interrogation that has produced the result we see before us, this particular plausibility structure that has persuaded holy Israel, from then to now (as indeed all the Israels that revere the Song of Songs have been persuaded), to read the erotic as the best, the only way to express precisely who is God in relationship to Israel, and who is Israel in relationship to God. The theology of this Judaism – that is to say, our account of the worldview that comes to expression within this literary culture and textual community – will take shape within the exegesis of that exegesis.

---

[11]*Ibid.*, p. 25.
[12]*Ibid.*, p. 25.

Part Four

TORAH, ISRAEL, AND GOD

8

The Transformation of the Torah

Judaism as we know it at the end of late antiquity reached its now familiar definition when "the Torah" lost its capital letter and definite article and ultimately became "torah." What for nearly a millennium had been a particular scroll or book thus came to serve as a symbol of an entire system. When a rabbi spoke of torah, he no longer meant only a particular object, a scroll and its contents. Now he used the work to encompass a distinctive and well-defined worldview and way of life. Torah had come to stand for something one does. Knowledge of the Torah promised not merely information about what people were supposed to do, but ultimate redemption or salvation.

The Torah of Moses clearly occupied a critical place in all systems of Judaism from the closure of the Torah book, the Pentateuch, in the time of Ezra onward. But in late antiquity, for one group alone the book developed into an abstract and encompassing symbol, so that in the Judaism that took shape in the formative age, the first seven centuries A.D., everything was contained in that one thing. How so? When we speak of torah, in rabbinical literature of late antiquity, we no longer denote a particular book, on the one side, or the contents of such a book, on the other. Instead, we connote a broad range of clearly distinct categories of noun and verb, concrete fact and abstract relationship alike. "Torah" stands for a kind of human being. It connotes a social status and a sort of social group. It refers to a type of social relationship. It further denotes a legal status and differentiates among legal norms. As symbolic abstraction, the word encompasses things and persons, actions and status, points of social differentiation and legal and normative standing, as well as "revealed truth." In all, the main points of insistence of the whole of Israel's life and history come to full symbolic expression in that single word. If people wanted to explain how they would be saved, they would use the word Torah. If they wished to sort out their parlous relationships with gentiles, they would use the word Torah. Torah stood for salvation and accounted for Israel's this-worldly condition and the hope, for both individual and national alike, of life in the world to come. For the kind of Judaism under discussion, therefore, the word Torah stood for everything. The Torah symbolized the whole, at once and entire. When, therefore, we wish to describe the unfolding of the definitive doctrine of Judaism in its formative period, the first exercise consists in paying close attention to the meanings imputed to a single word.

Every detail of the religious system at hand exhibits essentially the same point of insistence, captured in the simple notion of the Torah as the generative symbol, the total, exhaustive expression of the system as a whole. That is why the definitive ritual of the Judaism under study consisted in studying the Torah as the generative symbol, the total, exhaustive expression of the system as a whole. That is why the definitive myth explained that one who studied Torah would become holy, like Moses "our rabbi," and like God, in whose image humanity was made and whose Torah provided the plan and the model for what God wanted of a humanity created in his image. As for Christians it was in Christ God made flesh, so the framers of the system of Judaism at hand found in the Torah that image of God to which Israel should aspire, and to which the sage in fact conformed.

The meaning of the several meanings of the Torah should require only brief explanation.

When the Torah refers to a particular thing, it is to a scroll containing divinely revealed words.

The Torah may further refer to revelation, not as an object but as a corpus of doctrine.

When one "does Torah" the disciple "studies" or "learns," and the master "teaches," Torah. Hence while the word Torah never appears as a verb, it does refer to an act.

The word also bears a quite separate sense, torah as category or classification or corpus of rules, for example, "the torah of driving a car" is a usage entirely acceptable to some documents. This generic usage of the word does occur.

The word Torah very commonly refers to a status, distinct from and above another status, as "teachings of Torah" as against "teachings of scribes." For the two Talmuds that distinction is absolutely critical to the entire hermeneutic enterprise. But it is important even in the Mishnah.

Obviously, no account of the meaning of the word Torah can ignore the distinction between the two Torahs, written and oral. It is important only in the secondary stages of the formation of the literature.

The Transformation of the Torah

Finally, the word Torah refers to a source of salvation, often fully worked out in stories about how the individual and the nation will be saved through Torah. In general, the sense of the word "salvation" is not complicated. It is simply salvation in the way in which Deuteronomy and the Deuteronomic historians understand it: kings who do what God wants win battles, those who do not, lose. So, too, here, people who study and do Torah are saved from sickness and death, and the way Israel can save itself from its condition of degradation also is through Torah.

Upon its closure, the Mishnah gained an exalted political status as the constitution of Jewish government of the Land of Israel. Accordingly, the clerks who knew and applied its law had to explain the standing of that law, meaning its relationship to the law of the Torah. But the Mishnah provided no account of itself. Unlike biblical law codes, the Mishnah begins with no myth of its own origin. It ends with no doxology. Discourse commences in the middle of things and ends abruptly. What follows from such laconic mumbling is that the exact status of the document required definition entirely outside the framework of the document itself. The framers of the Mishnah gave no hint of the nature of their book, so the Mishnah reached the political world of Israel without a trace of self-conscious explanation or any theory of validation.

The one thing that is clear, alas, is negative. The framers of the Mishnah nowhere claim, implicitly or explicitly, that what they have written forms part of the Torah, enjoys the status of God's revelation to Moses at Sinai, or even systematically carries forward secondary exposition and application of what Moses wrote down in the wilderness. Later on, I think two hundred years beyond the closure of the Mishnah, the need to explain the standing and origin of the Mishnah led some to posit two things. First, God's revelation of the Torah at Sinai encompassed the Mishnah as much as Scripture. Second, the Mishnah was handed on through oral formulation and oral transmission from Sinai to the framers of the document as we have it. These two convictions, fully exposed in the ninth-century letter of Sherira, in fact emerge from the references of both Talmuds to the Dual Torah. One part is in writing. The other was oral and now is in the Mishnah.

As for the Mishnah itself, however, it contains not a hint that anyone has heard any such tale. The earliest apologists for the Mishnah, represented in Abot and the Tosefta alike, know nothing of the fully realized myth of the Dual Torah of Sinai. It may be that the authors of those documents stood too close to the Mishnah to see the Mishnah's standing as a problem or to recognize the task of accounting for its origins. Certainly they never refer to the Mishnah as something out there, nor speak of the document as autonomous and complete. Only the two Talmuds reveal that conception – alongside their mythic explanation of where the document came from and why it should be obeyed. So the Yerushalmi marks the change. In any event, the absence of explicit expression of such a claim in behalf of the Mishnah requires little specification. It is just not there.

But the absence of an implicit claim demands explanation. When ancient Jews wanted to gain for their writings the status of revelation, of torah, or at least to link what they thought to what the Torah had said, they could do one of four things. They could sign the name of a holy man of old, for instance, Adam, Enoch, Ezra. They could imitate the Hebrew style of Scripture. They could claim that God had spoken to them. They could, at the very least, cite a verse of Scripture and impute to the cited passage their own opinion. These four methods – pseudepigraphy, stylistic imitation (hence, forgery), claim of direct revelation from God, and eisegesis – found no favor with the Mishnah's framers. to the contrary, they signed no name to their book. Their Hebrew was new in its syntax and morphology, completely unlike that of the Mosaic writings of the Pentateuch. They never claimed that God had anything to do with their opinions. They rarely cited a verse of Scripture as authority. It follows that, whatever the authors of the Mishnah said about their document, the implicit character of the book tells us that they did not claim God had dictated or even approved what they had to say. Why not? The framers simply ignored all the validating conventions of the world in which they lived. And, as I said, they failed to make explicit use of any others.

It follows that we do not know whether the Mishnah was supposed to be part of the Torah or to enjoy a clearly defined relationship to the existing Torah. We also do not know what else, if not the Torah, was meant to endow the Mishnah's laws with heavenly sanction. To state matters simply, we do not know what the framers of the Mishnah said they had made, nor do we know what the people who received and were supposed to obey the Mishnah thought they posessed.

A survey of the uses of the word Torah in the Mishnah, to be sure, provides us with an account of what the framers of the Mishnah, founders of what would emerge as rabbinic Judaism, understood by that term. But it will not tell us how they related their own ideas to the Torah, nor shall we find a trace of evidence of that fully articulated way of life – the use of the word Torah to categorize and classify persons, places, things, relationships, all manner of abstractions – that we find fully exposed in some later redacted writings.

True, the Mishnah places a high value upon studying the Torah and upon the status of the sage. A "mamzer disciple of a sage takes priority

The Transformation of the Torah

over a high priest am-haares," as at M. Hor. 3:8. But that judgment, distinctive though it is, cannot settle the question. All it shows is that the Mishnah pays due honor to the sage. But if the Mishnah does not claim to constitute part of the Torah, then what makes a sage a sage is not mastery of the Mishnah in particular. What we have in hand merely continues the established and familiar position of the wisdom writers of old. Wisdom is important. Knowledge of the Torah is definitive. But to maintain that position, one need hardly profess the fully articulated Torah myth of rabbinic Judaism. Proof of that fact, after all, is the character of the entire wisdom literature prior to the Mishnah itself.

So the issue is clearly drawn. It is not whether we find in the Mishnah exaggerated claims about the priority of the disciple of a sage. We do find such claims. The issue is whether we find in the Mishnah the assertion that whatever the sage has on the authority of his master goes back to Sinai. We seek a definitive view that what the sage says falls into the classification of Torah, just as what Scripture says constitutes Torah from God to Moses. That is what distinguishes wisdom from the Torah as it emerges in the context of rabbinic Judaism. To state the outcome in advance: we do not find the Torah in the Mishnah, and the Mishnah is not part of the Torah.

When the authors of the Mishnah surveyed the landscape of Israelite writings down to their own time, they saw only Sinai, that is, what we now know as Scripture. Based on the documents they cite or mention, we can say with certainty that they knew the pentateuchal law. We may take for granted that they accepted as divine revelation also the Prophets and the Writings, to which they occasionally make reference. That they regarded as a single composition, that is, as revelation, the Torah, Prophets, and Writings appears from their references to the Torah, as a specific "book," and to a Torah scroll. Accordingly, one important meaning associated with the word Torah was concrete in the extreme. The Torah was a particular book or sets of books, regarded as holy, revealed to Moses at Sinai. That fact presents no surprise, since the Torah scroll(s) had existed, it is generally assumed, for many centuries before the closure of the Mishnah in 200.

What is surprising is that everything from the formation of the canon of the Torah to their own day seems to have proved null in their eyes. Between the Mishnah and Mount Sinai lay a vast, empty plain. From the perspective of the Torah myth as they must have known it, from Moses and the prophets, to before Judah the Patriarch, lay a great wasteland. So the concrete and physical meaning attaching to the word Torah, that is the Torah, the Torah revealed by God to Moses at Mount Sinai (including the books of the Prophets and the Writings), bore a contrary implication. Beyond The Torah there was no torah. Besides the Pentateuch, Prophets, and Writings, not only did no physical scroll deserve veneration, but no corpus of writings demanded obedience. So the very limited sense in which the words the Torah were used passed a stern judgment upon everything else, all the other writings that we know circulated widely, in which other Jews alleged that God had spoken and said "these things."

The range of the excluded possibilities that other Jews explored demands no survey. It includes everything, not only the Gospels (by 200 A.D. long since in the hands of outsiders), but secret books, history books, psalms, wisdom writings, rejected works of prophecy – everything excluded from any biblical canon by whoever determined there should be a canon. If the library of the Essenes at Qumran tells us what might have been, then we must regard as remarkably impoverished the (imaginary) library that would have served the authors of the Mishnah: The Book of Books, but nothing else. We seldom see so stern, so austere a vision of what commands the status of holy revelation among Judaisms over time. The tastes of the Mishnah's authors express a kind of literary iconoclasm, but with a difference. The literary icons did survive in the churches of Christendom. But in their own society and sacred setting, the judgment of Mishnah's authors would prevail from its time to ours. Nothing in the Judaisms of the heritage from the Hebrew Scripture's time to the Mishnah's day would survive the implacable rejection of the framers of the Mishnah, unless under Christian auspices or buried in caves. So when we take up that first and simplest meaning associated with the word Torah, "The Torah," we confront a stunning judgment: this and nothing else, this alone, the thing alone of its kind and no other thing of similar kind.

We confront more than a closing off of old possibilities, ancient claims to the status of revelation. For, at the other end, out of the Torah as a particular thing, a collection of books, would emerge a new and remarkably varied set of meanings. Possibilities first generated by the fundamental meaning imputed to the word Torah would demand realization. How so? Once the choice for the denotative meaning of the Torah became canonical in the narrowest possible sense, the ranges of connotative meaning imputed to the Torah stretched forth to an endless horizon. So the one concrete meaning made possible many abstract ones, all related to that single starting point. Only at the end shall we clearly grasp, in a single tableau, the entire vista of possibilities. To begin with, it suffices to note that the Mishnah's theory of the Torah not only closed, but also opened, many paths.

Abot draws into the orbit of Torah talk the names of authorities of the Mishnah. But Abot does not claim that the Mishnah forms part of the Torah. Nor, obviously, does the tractate know the doctrine of the two Torahs. Only in the Talmuds do we begin to find clear and ample evidence of that doctrine. Abot, moreover, does not understand by the word Torah much more than the framers of the Mishnah do. Not only does the established classification scheme remain intact, but the sense essentially replicates already familiar usages, producing no innovation. On the contrary, I find a diminution in the range of meanings.

Yet Abot in the aggregate does differ from the Mishnah. The difference has to do with the topic at hand. The other sixty-two tractates of the Mishnah contain Torah sayings here and there. But they do not fall within the framework of Torah discourse. They speak about other matters entirely. The consideration of the status of Torah rarely pertains to that speech. Abot, by contrast, says a great deal about Torah study. The claim that Torah study produces direct encounter with God forms part of Abot's thesis about the Torah. That claim, by itself, will hardly have surprised Israelite writers of wisdom books over a span of many centuries, whether those assembled in the Essene commune at Qumran, on the one side, or those represented in the pages of Proverbs and in many of the Psalms, or even the Deuteronomistic circle, on the other.

A second glance at tractate Abot, however, produces a surprising fact. In Abot, Torah is instrumental. The figure of the sage, his ideals and conduct, forms the goal, focus and center. To state matters simply: Abot regards study of Torah as what a sage does. The substance of Torah is what a sage says. That is so whether or not the saying relates to scriptural revelation. The content of the sayings attributed to sages endows those sayings with self-validating status. The sages usually do not quote verses of Scripture and explain them, nor do they speak in God's name. Yet, it is clear, sages talk Torah. What follows? It is this: if a sage says something, what he says is Torah. More accurately, what he says falls into the classification of Torah. Accordingly, as I said, Abot treats Torah learning as symptomatic, an indicator of the status of the sage, hence, as I said, as merely instrumental.

The simplest proof of that proposition lies in the recurrent formal structure of the document, the one thing the framers of the document never omit and always emphasize: (1) the name of the authority behind a saying, from Simeon the Righteous on downward, and (2) the connective attributive "says." So what is important to the redactors is what they never have to tell us. Because a recognized sage makes a statement, what he says constitutes, in and of itself, a statement in the status of Torah.

To spell out what this means, let us look at the opening sentences. "Moses received Torah," and it reached "the Men of the Great Assembly." "The three things" those men said bear no resemblance to anything we find in written Scripture. They focus upon the life of sagacity – prudence, discipleship, a fence around the Torah. And, as we proceed, we find time and again that, while the word Torah stands for two things, divine revelation and the act of study of divine revelation, it produces a single effect, the transformation of unformed man into sage. One climax comes in Yohanan ben Zakkai's assertion that the purpose for which a man (an Israelite) was created was to study Torah, followed by his disciples' specifications of the most important things to be learned in the Torah. All of these pertain to the conduct of the wise man, the sage.

We have to locate the document's focus not on Torah but on the life of sagacity (including, to be sure, Torah study). But what defines and delimits Torah? It is the sage himself. So we may simply state the tractate's definition of Torah: Torah is what a sage learns. Accordingly, the Mishnah contains Torah. It may well be thought to fall into the classification of Torah. But the reason, we recognize, is that authorities whose sayings are found in the Mishnah possess Torah from Sinai. What they say, we cannot overemphasize, is Torah. How do we know it? It is a fact validated by the association of what they way with their own names.

So we miss the real issue when we ask Abot to explain for us the status of the Mishnah, or to provide a theory of a Dual Torah. The principal point of insistence – the generative question – before the framers of Abot does not address the status of the Mishnah. And the instrumental status of the Torah, as well as of the Mishnah, lies in the net effect of their composition: the claim that through study of the Torah sages enter God's presence. So study of Torah serves a further goal, that of forming sages. The theory of Abot pertains to the religious standing and consequence of the learning of the sages. To be sure, a secondary effect of that theory endows with the status of revealed truth things sages say. But then, as I have stressed, it is because they say them, not because they have heard them in an endless chain back to Sinai. The fundament of truth is passed on through sagacity, not through already formulated and carefully memorized truths. That is why the single most important word in Abot also is the most common, the word "says."

At issue in Abot is not the Torah, but the authority of the sage. It is that standing that transforms a saying into a Torah saying, or to state matters more appropriately, that places a saying into the classification of the Torah. Abot then stands as the first document of the doctrine that the sage embodies the Torah and is a holy man, like Moses "our rabbi," in the likeness and image of God. The beginning is to claim that a saying falls into the category of Torah if a sage says it as Torah. The end will be to view the sage himself as Torah incarnate.

The Mishnah is held in the Talmud of the Land of Israel to be equivalent to Scripture (Y. Hor. 3:5). But the Mishnah is not called Torah.

The Transformation of the Torah

Still, once the Mishnah entered the status of Scripture, it would take but a short step to a theory of the Mishnah as part of the revelation at Sinai – hence, Oral Torah. In the first Talmud we find the first glimmerings of an effort to theorize in general, not merely in detail, about how specific teachings of Mishnah relate to specific teachings of Scripture. The citing of scriptural prooftexts for Mishnah propositions, after all, would not have caused much surprise to the framers of the Mishnah; they themselves included such passages, though not often. But what conception of the Torah underlies such initiatives, and how do Yerushalmi sages propose to explain the phenomenon of the Mishnah as a whole? The following passage gives us one statement. It refers to the assertion at M. Hag. 1:8D that the laws on cultic cleanness presented in the Mishnah rest on deep and solid foundations in the Scripture.

Y. Hagigah 1:7

V. A. The laws of the Sabbath [M. 1:8B]: R. Jonah said R. Hama bar Uqba raised the question [in reference to M. Hag. 1:8D's view that there are many verses of Scripture on cleanness], "And lo, it is written only, 'Nevertheless a spring or a cistern holding water shall be clean; but whatever touches their carcass shall be unclean' (Lev. 11:36). And from this verse you derive many laws. [So how can M. 8:8D say what it does about many verses for laws of cultic cleanness?]"

B. R. Zeira in the name of R. Yohanan: "If a law comes to hand and you do not know its nature, do not discard it for another one, for lo, many laws were stated to Moses at Sinai, and all of them have been embedded in the Mishnah."

The truly striking assertion appears at B. The Mishnah now is claimed to contain statements made by God to Moses. Just how these statements found their way into the Mishnah, and which passages of the Mishnah contain them, we do not know. That is hardly important, given the fundamental assertion at hand. The passage proceeds to a further, and far more consequential, proposition. It asserts that part of the Torah was written down, and part was preserved in memory and transmitted orally. In context, moreover, that distinction must encompass the Mishnah, thus explaining its origin as part of the Torah. Here is a clear and unmistakable expression of the distinction between two forms in which a single Torah was revealed and handed on at Mount Sinai, part in writing, part orally.

While the passage below does not make use of the language, Torah in-writing and Torah by-memory, it does refer to "the written" and "the oral." I believe myself fully justified in supplying the word Torah in square brackets. The reader will note, however, that the word Torah likewise does not occur at K, L. Only when the passage reaches its climax, at M, does it break down into a number of categories – Scripture, Mishnah, Talmud, laws, lore. It there makes the additional point that everything comes from Moses at Sinai. So the fully articulated theory of two Torahs (not merely one Torah in two forms) does not reach final expression in this passage. But short of explicit allusion to Torah in-writing and Torah by-memory, which (so far as I am able to discern) we find mainly in the Talmud of Babylonia, the ultimate theory of Torah of formative Judaism is at hand in what follows.

Y. Hagigah 1:7

V. D. R. Zeirah in the name of R. Eleazar: "'Were I to write for him my laws by ten thousands, they would be regarded as a strange thing' (Hos. 8:12). Now is the greater part of the Torah written down? [Surely not. The oral part is much greater.] But more abundant are the matters which are derived by exegesis from the written [Torah] than those derived by exegesis from the oral [Torah]."

E. And is that so?

F. But more cherished are those matters which rest upon the written [Torah] than those which rest upon the oral [Torah]....

J. R. Haggai in the name of R. Samuel bar Nahman, "Some teachings were handed on orally, and some things were handed on in writing, and we do not know which of them is the more precious. But on the basis of that which is written, 'And the Lord said to Moses, "Write these words; in accordance with these words I have made a covenant with you and with Israel"' (Ex. 34:27), [we conclude] that the ones which are handed on orally are the more precious."

K. R. Yohanan and R. Yudan b. R. Simeon – One said, "If you have kept what is preserved orally and also kept what is in writing, I shall make a covenant with you, and if not, I shall not make a covenant with you."

L. The other said, "If you have kept what is preserved orally and you have kept what is preserved in writing, you shall receive a reward, and if not, you shall not receive a reward."

M. With reference to Deut. 9:10: "And on them was written according to all the words which the Lord spoke with you in the mount,"] said R. Joshua b. Levi, "He could have written, 'On them,' but wrote, 'And on them.' He could have written, 'All,' but wrote, 'According to all.' He could have written, 'Words,' but wrote 'The words.' [These then serve as three encompassing clauses, serving to include] Scripture, Mishnah, Talmud, laws, and lore. Even what an experienced student in the future is going to teach before his master already has been stated to Moses at Sinai."

N. What is the Scriptural basis for this view?

O. "There is no remembrance of former things, nor will there be any remembrance of later things yet to happen among those who come after" (Qoh. 1:11).

P. If someone says, "See, this is a new thing," his fellow will answer him, saying to him, "this has been around before us for a long time."

The Transformation of the Torah

Here we have absolutely explicit evidence that people believed part of the Torah had been preserved not in writing but orally. Linking that part to the Mishnah remains a matter of implication. But it surely comes fairly close to the surface, when we are told that the Mishnah contains Torah traditions revealed at Sinai. From that view it requires only a small step to the allegation that the Mishnah is part of the Torah, the oral part.

To define the category of the Torah as a source of salvation, as the Yerushalmi states matters, I point to a story that explicitly states the proposition that the Torah constitutes a source of salvation. In this story we shall see that because people observed the rules of the Torah, they expected to be saved. And if they did not observe, they accepted their punishment. So the Torah now stands for something more than revelation and life of study, and (it goes without saying) the sage now appears as a holy, not merely a learned, man. This is because his knowledge of the Torah has transformed him. Accordingly, we deal with a category of stories and sayings about the Torah entirely different from what has gone before.

Y. Taanit 3:8

II. A. As to Levi ben Sisi: Troops came to his town. He took a scroll of the Torah and went up to the roof and said, "Lord of the ages! If a single word of this scroll of the Torah has been nullified [in our town], let them come up against us, and if not, let them go their way."

B. Forthwith people went looking for the troops but did not find them [because they had gone their way].

C. A disciple of his did the same thing, and his hand withered, but the troops went their way.

D. A disciple of his disciple did the same thing. His hand did not wither, but they also did not go their way.

E. This illustrates the following apophthegm: You can't insult an idiot, and dead skin does not feel the scalpel.

What is interesting here is how taxa into which the word Torah previously fell have been absorbed and superseded in a new taxon. The Torah is an object: "He took a scroll...." It also constitutes God's revelation to Israel: "If a single word...." The outcome of the revelation is to form an ongoing way of life, embodied in the sage himself: "A disciple of his did the same thing...." The sage plays an intimate part in the supernatural event: "His hand withered...." Now can we categorize this story as a statement that the Torah constitutes a particular object, or a source of divine revelation, or a way of life? Yes and no. The Torah here stands not only for the things we already have catalogued. It represents one more thing which takes in all the others. Torah is a source of salvation. How so? The Torah stands for, or constitutes, the way in which the people Israel saves itself from marauders. This straightforward sense of salvation will not have surprised the author of Deuteronomy.

In the canonical documents up to the Yerushalmi, we look in vain for sayings or stories that fall into such a category. True, we may take for granted that everyone always believed that, in general, Israel would be saved by obedience to the Torah. That claim would not have surprised any Israelite writers from the first prophets down through the final redactors of the Pentateuch in the time of Ezra and onward through the next seven hundred years. But, in the rabbinical corpus from the Mishnah forward, the specific and concrete assertion that by taking up the scroll of the Torah and standing on the roof of one's house, confronting God in Heaven, a sage in particular could take action against the expected invasion – that kind of claim is not located, so far as I know, in any composition surveyed so far.

Still, we cannot claim that the belief that the Torah in the hands of the sage constituted a source of magical, supernatural, and hence salvific power, simply did not flourish prior, let us say, to ca. 400 A.D. We cannot show it, hence we do not know it. All we can say with assurance is that no stories containing such a viewpoint appear in any rabbinical document associated with the Mishnah. So what is critical here is not the generalized category – the genus – of conviction that the Torah serves as the source of Israel's salvation. It is the concrete assertion – the speciation of the genus – that in the hands of the sage and under conditions specified, the Torah may be utilized in pressing circumstances as Levi, his disciple, and the disciple of his disciple, used it. That is what is new.

To generalize: this stunningly new usage of Torah found in the Talmud of the Land of Israel emerges from a group of stories not readily classified in our established categories. All of these stories treat the word Torah (whether scroll, contents, or act of study) as source and guarantor of salvation. Accordingly, evoking the word Torah forms the centerpiece of a theory of Israel's history, on the one side, and an account of the teleology of the entire system, on the other. Torah indeed has ceased to constitute a specific thing or even a category or classification when stories about studying the Torah yield not a judgment as to status (that is, praise for the learned man) but promise for supernatural blessing now and salvation in time to come.

To the rabbis the principal salvific deed was to "study Torah," by which they meant memorizing Torah sayings by constant repetition, and, as the Talmud itself amply testifies (for some sages) profound analytic inquiry into the meaning of those sayings. The innovation now is that

The Transformation of the Torah

this act of "study of Torah" imparts supernatural power of a material character. For example, by repeating words of Torah, the sage could ward off the angel of death and accomplish other kinds of miracles as well. So Torah formulas served as incantations. Mastery of Torah transformed the man engaged in Torah learning into a supernatural figure, who could do things ordinary folk could not do. The category of "Torah" had already vastly expanded so that through transformation of the Torah from a concrete thing to a symbol, a Torah scroll could be compared to a man of Torah, namely, a rabbi. Now, once the principle had been established, that salvation would come from keeping God's will in general, as Israelite holy men had insisted for so many centuries, it was a small step for rabbis to identify their particular corpus of learning, namely, the Mishnah and associated sayings, with God's will expressed in Scripture, the universally acknowledged medium of revelation.

The key to the first Talmud's theory of the Torah lies in its conception of the sage, to which that theory is subordinate. Once the sage reaches his full apotheosis as Torah incarnate, then, but only then, the Torah becomes (also) a source of salvation in the present concrete formulation of the matter. That is why we traced the doctrine of the Torah in the salvific process by elaborate citation of stories about sages, living Torahs, exercising the supernatural power of the Torah, and serving, like the Torah itself, to reveal God's will. Since the sage embodied the Torah and gave the Torah, the Torah naturally came to stand for the principal source of Israel's salvation, not merely a scroll, on the one side, or a source of revelation, on the other.

The history of the symbolization of the Torah proceeds from its removal from the framework of material objects, even from the limitations of its own contents, to its transformation into something quite different and abstract, quite distinct from the document and its teachings. The Torah stands for this something more, specifically, when it comes to be identified with a living person, the sage, and endowed with those particular traits that the sage claimed for himself. While we cannot say that the process of symbolization leading to the pure abstraction at hand moved in easy stages, we may still point to the stations that had to be passed in sequence. The word Torah reached the apologists for the Mishnah in its long-established meanings: Torah scroll, contents of the Torah scroll. But even in the Mishnah itself, these meanings provoked a secondary development, status of Torah as distinct from other (lower) status, hence, Torah teaching in contra-distinction to scribal teaching. With that small and simple step, the Torah ceased to denote only a concrete and material thing – a scroll and its contents. It now connoted an abstract matter of status. And once made abstract, the symbol entered a secondary history beyond all limits imposed by the concrete object, including its specific teachings, the Torah scroll.

I believe that Abot stands at the beginning of this process. In the history of the word Torah as abstract symbol, a metaphor serving to sort out one abstract status from another regained concrete and material reality of a new order entirely. For the message of Abot, as we saw, was that the Torah served the sage. How so? The Torah indicated who was a sage and who was not. Accordingly, the apology of Abot for the Mishnah was that the Mishnah contained things sages had said. What sages said formed a chain of tradition extending back to Sinai. Hence it was equivalent to the Torah. The upshot is that words of sages enjoyed the status of the Torah. The small step beyond, I think, was to claim that what sages said was Torah, as much as what Scripture said was Torah. And, a further small step (and the steps need not have been taken separately or in the order here suggested) moved matters to the position that there were two forms in which the Torah reached Israel: one [Torah] in writing, the other [Torah] handed on orally, that is, in memory. The final step, fully revealed in the Talmud at hand, brought the conception of Torah to its logical conclusion: what the sage said was in the status of the Torah, was Torah, because the sage was Torah incarnate. So the abstract symbol now became concrete and material once more. We recognize the many, diverse ways in which the Talmud stated that conviction. Every passage in which knowledge of the Torah yields power over this world and the next, capacity to coerce to the sage's will the natural and supernatural worlds alike, rests upon the same viewpoint.

The first Talmud's theory of the Torah carries us through several stages in the processes of the symbolization of the word Torah. First transformed from something material and concrete into something abstract and beyond all metaphor, the word Torah finally emerged once more in a concrete aspect, now as the encompassing and universal mode of stating the whole doctrine, all at once, of Judaism in its formative age.

While both the national and the individual dimensions of salvation mark the measure of the word Torah in the Babylonian Talmud, the national proves the more interesting. For the notion of private salvation through "Torah" study and practice, of which we hear much, presents no surprise. When, by contrast, we find God saying, "If a man occupies himself with the study of Torah works of charity, and prays with the community, I account it to him as if he had redeemed me and my children from among the nations of the world" (B. Ber. 8a), we confront a concept beyond the imagination of the framers of Abot and the other compositions of that circle. Still more indicative of the importance for Israel as a whole, imputed to Torah learning, is the view that those who

The Transformation of the Torah

master the Torah do not require protection by this-worldly means. Rabbis need not contribute to the upkeep of the walls of a town, "because rabbis do not require protection" (B. B.B. 8a). Sayings such as these focus to be sure upon the individual who has mastered the Torah. But the supernatural power associated with the Torah here is thought to protect not the individual alone, but Israelites in general associated with the individual Torah master. So, given the social perspective of our sages, all Israel enjoys salvation through the Torah.

9

The Redefinition of "Israel": Judaism and Its Social Metaphors

A Religious System and Its Social Component

I mean to ask a small question about a large problem. I want to know what a word means when it appears in the authoritative writings of a particular Judaism. Specifically, I want to find out how people bring to concrete and vivid expression their thought about the social entity that in their minds they imagine that they, with their families and others of like opinion and life-pattern, constitute. When they speak of "Israel," to what sort of social group do they refer, and how do they think about that group? At stake in the answers is insight into the solution of a much larger problem, the way in which religious systems take shape, the relationship, in the formation of religious systems, between circumstance and context, contents and convictions.

By religious system I mean the composition of three things: a worldview, a way of life, and an address to a defined social entity, which, all together, encompass (at least in someone's mind) the social world of a given social entity. Within that framework a Judaism is [1] a worldview, which explains [2] a way of life, both of which are addressed to, and allegedly characterize, [3] an "Israel." I say "a Judaism" and "an Israel" because – as everyone now recognizes full well – history yields not one by many Judaisms, not one but many theories of who, and what, is (an) "Israel." Hence a "Judaism" is a Judaic system, and an "Israel" is the "Israel" (whether social group, whether caste, whether family, whether class or "population," and whether any of the many social entities admirably identified by sociology) defined by a "Judaism."

The particular "Judaism" of which I speak is the one that took shape in the first six centuries of the Common Era and is represented by a variety of holy books beginning with the Mishnah, a philosophical law code completed at ca. A.D. 200, and ending with the Talmud of Babylonia, a systematic commentary on passages of both the Mishnah and also Scripture, or the Hebrew Bible, completed at ca. A.D. 600. That Judaism differs from all other Judaisms because of its appeal, unique among Judaisms, to the symbol and myth of a Dual Torah, one in writing, the other oral, explained by the myth that at Sinai God revealed to Moses, called "our rabbi," revelation, or the Torah, in two media, one in writing, the other to be formulated and transmitted for oral transmission, that is, by memory, hence a written and an Oral Torah. The Mishnah and the works that flowed from it constitute, for late antiquity, that writing down of the originally Oral Torah.

What I shall now show is a proposition bearing interesting implications for the study of religion. An "Israel" will find its definition within the Judaic system which it serves. An "Israel" will prove wholly congruent to the shape and structure of that system and will be formed of materials selected by the systemic authorship out of a miscellaneous, received or invented repertoire of possibilities.[1] The opposite proposition is that the social entity, "Israel," will appeal to facts dictated by the social world "out there," so that the system will struggle to absorb and assimilate the givens of a politics and imagination not formed by the system itself. That opposite, but quite plausible proposition is false for the data we have examined. An "Israel" within a given system is the invention of the system builders, with those traits found relevant to the larger system – without appeal to facts or realities beyond the range of systemic control. Any notion that the character of the "Israel" will find definition in a received corpus of facts not subject to the system's own processes of selection is false. Any conception that the system builders – sages, in the present instance, over a period of centuries – compose their "Israel" through collection of information and generalization of what they find – is improbable. The system responds to its inner logic and makes things up from there. That is why neither the social data nor the repertoire of available "Israel"s makes a contribution on their own initiatives, respectively. The simple fact is that religious ideas – systems – constitute what in sociology are called independent variables. Ideas matter and make the world. Now to the case at hand.

The Two Stages in the Formation of the Judaism of the Dual Torah

The writings produced by sages, or rabbis, of late antiquity in the Land of Israel ("Palestine") and Babylonia, mainly the former location

---

[1] System builders, as we see, do not find themselves bound to remain with an inherited repertoire, though they may survey the possibilities made available by it.

fall into two groups, each with its own plan and program, the one produced in the second and third centuries, the second in the fourth and fifth. The first of these groups of writings begins with the Mishnah, a philosophical law book brought to closure at ca. A.D. 200, later on called the first statement of the Oral Torah. In its wake, the Mishnah drew tractate Abot, ca. A.D. 250, a statement of concluded a generation after the Mishnah on the standing of the authorities of the Mishnah; Tosefta, ca. A.D. 300, a compilation of supplements of various kinds to the statements in the Mishnah; and three systematic exegeses of books of Scripture or the Written Torah, Sifra, to Leviticus, Sifré to Numbers, and another Sifré, to Deuteronomy, of indeterminate date but possibly concluded by A.D. 300. These books overall form one stage in the unfolding of the Judaism of the Dual Torah, in which emphasis stressed issues of sanctification of the life of Israel, the people, in the aftermath of the destruction of the Temple of Jerusalem in A.D. 70, in which, it was commonly held, Israel's sanctification came to full realization in the bloody rites of sacrifice to God on high. I call this system a Judaism without Christianity, because the issues found urgent in the documents representative of this phase address questions not pertinent to the Christian *défi* of Israel at all.

The second set of the same writings begins with the Talmud of the Land of Israel, or Yerushalmi, generally supposed to have come to a conclusion at ca. A.D. 400, Genesis Rabbah, assigned to about the next half century, Leviticus Rabbah, ca. A.D. 450, Pesiqta deRab Kahana, ca. A.D. 450-500, and, finally, the Talmud of Babylonia or Bavli, assigned to the late sixth or early seventh century, ca. A.D. 600. The two Talmuds systematically interpret passages of the Mishnah, and the other documents, as is clear, do the same for books of the Written Torah. Some other treatments of biblical books important in synagogue liturgy, particularly the Five Scrolls, for example, Lamentations Rabbati, Esther Rabbah, and the like, are supposed also to have reached closure at this time. This second set of writings introduces, alongside the paramount issue of Israel's sanctification, the matter of Israel's salvation, with doctrines of history, on the one side, and the Messiah, on the other, given prominence in the larger systemic statement.

The first of the two stages in the formation of the Judaism of the Dual Torah exhibits no sign of interest in, or response to, the advent of Christianity. The second, from the Yerushalmi forward, lays points of stress and emphasis that, in retrospect, appear to respond to, and to counter, the challenge of Christianity. The point of difference, of course, is that from the beginning of the legalization of Christianity in the early fourth century, to the establishment of Christianity at the end of that same century, Jews in the Land of Israel found themselves facing a challenge that, prior to Constantine, they had found no compelling reason to consider. The specific crisis came when the Christians pointed to the success of the Church in the politics of the Roman state as evidence that Jesus Christ was king of the world, and that his claim to be Messiah and King of Israel had now found vindication. When the Emperor Julian, 361-3, apostasized and renewed state patronage of paganism, he permitted the Jews to begin to rebuild the Temple, part of his large plan of humiliating Christianity. His prompt death on an Iranian battlefield supplied further evidence for Heaven's choice of the Church and the truth of the Church's allegations concerning the standing and authority of Jesus as the Christ. The Judaic documents that reached closure in the century after these events attended to those questions of salvation, for example, doctrine of history and of the Messiah, authority of the sages' reading of Scripture as against the Christians' interpretation, and the like, that had earlier not enjoyed extensive consideration. In all, this second Judaism, which I characterize as a Judaism despite Christianity, met the challenge of the events of the fourth century. The Judaic system of the Dual Torah, expressed in its main outlines in the Yerushalmi and associated compilations of biblical exegeses concerning Genesis, Leviticus, and some other scriptural books, culminated in the Bavli, which emerged as the authoritative document of the Judaism of the Dual Torah from then to now.

"Israel" as Chosen Metaphor

The fundamental act of metaphorization, from which all else follows, is the *comparison* of persons – Jews – of the here and now to the "Israel" of which the Hebrew Scriptures – "the Torah" – speak, and the identification of those Jews with that "Israel." Treating the social group – two or more persons – as other than they actually are in the present, as more than a (mere) given, means that the group is something else than what it appears to be. That supererogatory act of imagination constitutes the metaphorical reading of the social group. Prior to all the specific metaphors comes that act of metaphorization. For no facticity or givenness explains why people should treat the group they form as extraordinary and undertake comparisons and contrasts between the given and a variety of projections of the group they propose to discuss. It was hardly self-evident that the social group formed more than an "us," that is to say, "our village," "our household," perhaps extending also to people like "us" in other villages or other households. These constituted the hardest of hard social facts. Any meaning imputed to the group beyond these statements of the "us" of the here and now by definition constituted an act of metaphorization.

The Redefinition of "Israel": Judaism and Its Social Metaphors

The most surprising metaphor is the one operative in the Mishnah and related writings[2] as they take up the social entity, the social group they have chosen to discuss. It is the simple allusion to "Israel" when speaking of the "us" – of Jewry today. When sages in the Mishnah spoke of "Israel," the word bore two identical meanings: the "Israel" of (all) the Jews now and here, but also the "Israel" of which Scripture – the Torah – spoke.[3] That word choice, which applies to both individual and social group, comes prior to all definitions of who and what (an) "Israel" is. And the word dictates for the system all of the metaphors, both in the first and in the second phases of the documents. "Israel" accomplishes therefore is the simple but astonishing comparison of the Jews of the here and now to that "Israel" of which Scripture speaks.

When sages engaged in a process of treating as concrete things what begin as imaginary entities, that process of reification drew them into what I think is a work of supererogatory imagination that we may justifiably call metaphor – specifically, the metaphorization of the social group.[4] For sages in the Mishnah did not merely describe a group; they portrayed it as they wished to. They did not assemble facts and define the social entity, the social group, as a matter of mere description of the given. They imputed to the social group, Jews, the standing of the systemic entity, "Israel." They furthermore assigned to that entity indicative and definitive traits that, to begin with, take form in the distant reaches of mind, for example, belief in the resurrection of the dead as a scriptural doctrine. For to characterize as a social group, for example, a people, even a holy people, persons who did not, after all, see and know one another, persons long dead or in faraway lands, to identify those persons in the here and now with that "Israel" of which Scripture speaks – these seem to me daring acts of metaphorization, the most remarkable ones that we shall witness in the formative processes of the Judaism of the Dual Torah. And the powerful argumentation assigned to the metaphorization of the social group consisted of treating as fact what was a statement of imagination, poetry: always calling

---

[2] And not of those writings alone. What marks any Judaism is that the social entity of the system will be called (an) "Israel."

[3] And that encompassed both the individual and the group, without linguistic differentiation of any kind. Thus in the Mishnah "Israel" may refer to an individual Jew (always male) or to "all Jews," that is, the collectivity of Jews. The individual woman is nearly always called *bat yisrael*, daughter of (an) Israel(ite). Judith R. Wegner, *Woman as Person and Chattel in the System of the Mishnah* (New York, 1988: Oxford University Press), discusses this matter further.

[4] For a broader reading of the issue of metphor and metaphorization, cf. Fitz John Porter Poole, "Metaphors and Maps: Towards Comparison in the Anthropology of Religion." *JAAR* 54 (1986): 411-460.

"Israel" the group, the individual, in the everyday world of mundane discourse of which the Mishnah is composed. Let me now frame and state emphatically the question before us: *What is it that made self-evident the identification of the persons or groups with a single group, what made obvious the connection between that single group and the "Israel" of received Scripture?*

To others within Jewry it was not at all self-evident that "all Jews" constituted one "Israel,"[5] and that that one "Israel" formed the direct and immediate continuation, in the here and now, with the "Israel" of holy writ and revelation. The Essene community at Qumran did not come to that conclusion, and the sense and meaning of "Israel" proposed by the authorships of the Mishnah and related writings did not strike Philo as the main point at all. Paul, for his part, reflected on "Israel" within categories not at all symmetrical with those of the Mishnah.

The identification of Jewry in the here and now with the "Israel" of Scripture therefore constituted an act of metaphor, comparison, contrast, identification and analogy, and I point to "Israel" as that Judaism's most daring social metaphor. The fact that through the ages it has seemed self-evident, a given of the Jews' everyday circumstance, shows us the success of the Judaism of the Dual Torah, as much as, seeing that metaphor as a choice among alternatives shows us the reason for that success. Seeing Jews and calling them "Israel" – an act of imaginative daring indeed – forms the metaphor that gives the system its energy, and from that metaphor all else derived its momentum. No wonder, then, that when we first took up the initial statement of the Judaism of the Dual Torah, we found fresh and unprecedented in context the doctrine of "Israel" as "all Israel." That doctrine, a statement of metaphor, now proves to be the key to the system as a whole.

Transitive "Israel"

In the Mishnah, "Israel" finds definition in antonymic relationships of two sorts, first, "Israel" as against "not-Israel," gentile, and second, "Israel" as against "priest," or "Levite."[6] Accordingly, "Israel serves as a taxonomic indicator, specifically part of a more encompassing system of hierarchization; "Israel" defined the frontiers, on the outer side of society, and the social boundaries within, on the other. To understand

---

[5]In modern Zionist parlance, from Theodor Herzl onward, ein *Volk, ein* Volk, "a *people, one* people," and in Reconstructionism, people gains a capital P and theological standing. The processes under discussion characterize all Judaisms at all times, so far as I can see.

[6]In my *"Israel": Judaism and its Social Metaphors* (in press), I provide the data to back up these statements.

The Redefinition of "Israel": Judaism and Its Social Metaphors

the meaning of "Israel" as the Mishnah and its associated documents of the second and third centuries sort matters out, we consider the sense of "gentile," for one of the two persistent meanings of "Israel" is "not-gentile," the other being "not-priest." Specifically, does the authorship of the Mishnah differentiate when speaking of gentiles? The answer is no, for the gentiles represent an undifferentiated mass. To the system of the Mishnah, whether or not a gentile is a Roman or an Aramaean or a Syrian or a Briton does not matter. And, it is also the fact, to the system of the Mishnah, that in the relationship at hand, "Israel" is not differentiated either. The upshot is that just as "gentile" is an abstract category, so is "Israel." "Kohen" is a category, and so is "Israel." For the purposes for which Israel/priest are defined, no further differentiation is undertaken. That is where matters end. But to the Judaic system represented by the Yerushalmi and its associated writings, "gentile" may be Roman or other-than-Roman, for instance, Babylonia, Media, or Greece. That act of further differentiation – we may call it "speciation" – makes a considerable difference in the appreciation of gentile.

"Israel" serves in a more immediate way as classifier and taxonomic category. In the Mishnah's authorship's "Israel," we confront an abstraction in a system of philosophy. The shift, later on, will carry us to an "Israel" that bears that socially vivid sense that the metaphor implicitly requires: a real social entity, with a story attached. Systemically, so, too, will the counterpart, Rome, gain that speciation that "the gentiles" lack.

The Mishnah's first and most systematic apologetic, tractate Abot, brought to closure a generation beyond the Mishnah, in ca. A.D. 250, presents us with the only truly general statement, in the form of aphorisms to be sure, of the Mishnah's system, its Judaism. From a gathering of two persons on upward, the framers of Abot explicitly identify what they mean by a social entity, a social group. But this entity the do not call an "Israel." They have another socially definitive category in mind, and they invoke their own indicators to say what they mean:

3:2B. R. Hananiah b. Teradion says, "[If] two sit together and between them do not pass teachings of the Torah, lo, this is a seat of the scornful, as it is said, 'Nor sits in the seat of the scornful' (Ps. 1:1).
"But two who are sitting, and words of the Torah do pass between them – the Presence is with them, as it is said, 'Then they that feared the Lord spoke with one another, and the Lord hearkened and heard, and a book of remembrance was written before him, for them that feared the Lord and gave thought to his name' (Mal 3:16)."
"I know that this applies to two. How do I know that even if a single person sits and works on the Torah, the Holy One, blessed be He, set aside

>
> a reward for him? As it is said, 'Let him sit alone and keep silent, because he has laid it upon him' (Lam. 3:28)."

3:3
> R. Simeon says, "Three who ate at a single table and did not talk about teachings of the Torah while at that table are as though they ate from dead sacrifices (Ps. 106:28), as it is said, 'For all tables are full of vomit and filthiness [if they are] without God' (Ps. 106:28).
>
> "But three who ate at a single table and did talk about teachings of the Torah while at that table are as if they ate at the table of the Omnipresent, blessed is He, as it is said, 'And he said to me, This is the table that is before the Lord' (Ezek. 41:22)."

3:6
> R. Halafta of Kefar Hananiah says, "Among ten who sit and work hard on the Torah the Presence comes to rest, as it is said, 'God stands in the congregation of God' (Ps. 82:1).
>
> "And how do we now that the same is so even of five? For it is said, 'And he has founded his group upon the earth' (Amos 9:6).
>
> "And how do we know that this is so even of three? Since it is said, 'And he judges among the judges' (Ps. 82:1).
>
> "And how do we know that this is so even of two? Because it is said, 'Then they that feared the Lord spoke with one another, and the Lord hearkened and heard' (Mal. 3:16).
>
> "And how do we know that this is so even of one? Since it is said, 'In every place where I record my name I will come to you and I will bless you' (Ex. 20:24)."

These sayings represent the bulk of what the framers of Abot have to tell us about the social entity of their system. A social entity, a social group in particular is not called an "Israel"! The social entity takes shape in one of two ways, either because people do exchange Torah teachings, or because they do not do so. The one type of entity is differentiated from the other by that sole indicator, which conforms to the larger system at hand. Here we have another social entity that is sui generis, though it is not called (an) Israel.

Along these same lines, the individual and "Israel" serve as examples of the same thing, namely, God's love, which is all the greater because the person and the social entity are informed of that love. "Israel" is systemically inert, not generating a proposition but contributing to the statement of one. The proposition has to do with God's love, illustrated, by the way, in the condition of Israel too. So we see how a systemically neutral "Israel" plays its part in making the points important to the system, and how the traits of "Israel" fail to generate distinctive propositions:

3:14A.
> *He would say, "Precious is the human being, who was created in the image [of God]. It was an act of still greater love that it was made known to him that he was created in the image [of God], as it is said, 'For in the image of God he made man' (Gen. 9:6)."*

3:14B.
> *Precious is Israel [that is, are Israelites], who are called children to the Omnipresent. It was an act of still greater love that it was made known to*

	them that they were called children to the Omnipresent, as it is said, "You are the children of the Lord your God" (Deut. 14:1).
3:14C.	Precious are Israelites, to whom was given the precious thing. It was an act of still greater love that it was made known to them that to them was given that precious thing with which the world was made, as it is said, "For I give you a good doctrine. Do not forsake my Torah" (Prov. 4:2).

Once more we observe an "Israel" that is sui generis, beginning with a simple fact. "Israel" here means "Israelite," not the social entity viewed as a collectivity, but those who belong to the entity – and therefore constitute that entity, even one by one. These are the children of the Lord, as Scripture says; "Israel[ites]" are shown to be beloved because the Torah was given to them and because that fact was made known to them. In making these statements, the central issue is the Torah, not Israel. What is celebrated is the gift of the Torah, here, the information therein. The upshot is simple. We cannot point to these sayings as evidence of an unfolding social metaphor, fully exposed, richly exploited. That would come much later, and, in the contrast, we shall see how flat and one-dimensional is the use of "Israel" in the present passage, aimed as it is not at "Israel" but at celebration of the Torah. What that tells us is a simple fact. Tractate Abot spins out the inner logic of Torah study; that is what forms of the sayings a cogent statement – and not the issue of "Israel." Then "Israel" serves as a minor detail, helping to make the points that the authorship of Abot wishes to make about Torah study. When we speak of categorical imperatives and categorically tangential entities, here is a case of what is at stake.

Proof of the inconsequentiality of the category, "Israel," in the context of tractate Abot derives from one simple fact. Among the scores of sayings of which the document is composed, all of those concerning a social entity in general, and Israel in particular, make an appearance only as part of a larger case concerning the centrality of the Torah in the salvific process of individual life. The social entity is peripheral to that salvific process, as it is to the teleology of the Mishnah as defined by tractate Abot.[7] The social entity, Israel, makes no contribution on its own, and, more consequentially, receives no sustained attention in its own right. That, sum and substance, constitutes the thought I can locate in tractate Abot, on issues of the social entity in general and on Israel in particular. That doctrine conforms to the prevailing emphasis, within tractate Abot, on Torah study, which is its principal theme. The point of the whole, of course, is that God revealed the Torah to Moses, who

---

[7] I have dealt with this matter in *Messiah in Context. Israel's History and Destiny in Formative Judaism* (Philadelphia, 1983: Fortress Press).

handed it on through a chain of tradition to the present. Within that context, social thought in general takes a decidedly subordinated role.

We have to wonder where is that "Israel" in the middle range, that is, a social group possessing traits of its own, defined intransitively, within its own terms and not always in a transitive relationship. Why do we not deal, in the writings of the Mishnah and its continuators, with an "Israel" possessed of a social tangibility, a facticity in the here and now? These traits which appear in the second stage of the unfolding of the Judaism of the Dual Torah prove to be noteworthy by their absence. The second phase of the literature represents "Israel" on its own terms and with its own traits, an "Israel" that is sui generis but also substantive and immediate, not solely an aspect of the supernatural. When we account for the shape and character of the social metaphors before us, we shall also set our path toward the next passage, with its metaphors that yield a quite palpable and real "Israel."

Intransitive Israel

Two metaphors, rarely present and scarcely explored in the writings of the first stage in the formation of the Judaism of the Dual Torah, in the second stage came to prominence, first, the view of "Israel" as a family, the children and heirs of the man, Israel; second, the conception of Israel as sui generis.[8] While "Israel" in the first phase of the formation of Judaism perpetually finds definition in relationship to its opposite, "Israel" in the second phase constituted an intransitive entity, defined in its own terms and not solely or mainly in relationship to other comparable entities. The enormous investment in the conception of "Israel" as sui generis makes that point blatantly. But "Israel" as family bears that same trait of autonomy and self-evident definition. In the first phase, just as "gentile" was an abstract category, so was "Israel." "*Kohen*" was a category, and so, too, "Israel." When we see "Israel" as classifier and taxonomic category, we confront an abstraction in a system of philosophy. The "Israel" we see in the second stratum of the literature of the Dual Torah by contrast bears a socially vivid sense. The contrast is clear. "Israel" when viewed in the this-worldly framework of most of the Mishnah's discussions emerges through a series of contrasts and comparisons, not as intrinsically important, systemically determinative

---

[8]To be sure, "Israel" as sui generis does make an appearance in M. San. 10:1ff., which identifies (an) "Israel" as one who affirms certain beliefs. But the incomparability of the social entity, "Israel," to any other social entity, which we find as the premise and proposition of documents of the fourth and fifth century, finds no counterpart in the earlier writings.

facts. We know in that literature what "Israel" or "an Israel" is mainly when we can specify the antonym.

"Israel" in the second phase of the canon of the Judaism of the Dual Torah therefore stands for a real social group, not merely an entity in theory. "Israel" forms a family, and an encompassing theory of society, built upon that conception of "Israel," permits us to describe the proportions and balances of the social entity at hand, showing how each component both is an "Israel" and contributes to the larger composite as well. "Israel" as sui generis carried in its wake a substantial doctrine of definition, a weighty collection of general laws of social history governing the particular traits and events of the social group. In comparing transitive to intransitive "Israel," we move from "Israel" as not-gentile and "Israel" as not-priest to powerful statements of what "Israel" is. Now to specify in concrete terms the reasons I adduce to explain the rather striking shift before us. I see two important changes to account for the metaphorical revolution at hand, one out at the borders, the other within, the Jews' group.

Between 200 and 300, the approximate and rough dates for the closure of the first statement of the Judaism of the Dual Torah, and 400 and 500, the counterpart dates for the second, two decisive changes in the Jews' political life took place. One was in the political context of the world beyond, the other, the political circumstance of the world within, "Israel." The political control of the world at large in the fourth and fifth centuries, first, lay in Christian, not pagan, hands. Second, the picture we have of the position of sages, the authorship of the writing at hand, in the fourth and fifth centuries points to a group of lawyer-philosophers who now exercised practical authority and carried out the everyday administration of the life of the communities in which they lived. Nothing in the Mishnah and related writings portrays the authorships of those documents in a comparable position. Indeed, the very theoretical character of the Mishnah's political conceptions suggests that the sage as administrator lay beyond the imagination of the authorship of the Mishnah, with shifts in the perspective of the authorship(s) of the Tosefta suggesting incipient change in how the political world may be imagined.

By claiming that "Israel" constituted "Israel after the flesh," the actual, living, present family of Abraham and Sarah, Isaac and Rebecca, Jacob and Leah and Rachel, sages met head-on the Christian claim that there was – or could ever be – some other "Israel," of a lineage not defined by the family connection at all, and that the existing Jews no longer constituted "Israel." By representing "Israel" as sui generis, sages moreover focused upon the systemic teleology, with its definition of salvation, in response to the Christian claim that salvation is not of Israel but of the Church, now enthroned in this world as in Heaven. The sage, model for Israel, in the model of Moses, our rabbi, on earth represented the Torah that had come from Heaven. Like Christ, in earth as in Heaven, like the Church, the body of Christ, ruler of earth (through the emperor) as of Heaven, the sage embodied what Israel was and was to be. So Israel as family in the model of the sage, like Moses our rabbi, corresponded in its social definition to the Church of Jesus Christ, the New Israel, the source of salvation of the savior of humanity. The metaphors given prominence in the late fourth and fifth century sages' writings formed a remarkable counterpoint to the social metaphors important in the mind of significant Christian theologians, as both parties reflected on the political revolution that had taken place.

In response to the challenge of Christianity, sages' thought about "Israel" centered on the issues of history and salvation, issues made not merely chronic but acute by the political triumph. That accounts for what I believe is an unprecedented reading of the outsider, contained in the two propositions of Rome, first, as Esau or Edom or Ishmael, that is, as part of the family, second, of Rome as the pig. Differentiating Rome from other gentiles represented a striking concession indeed. Rome is represented as only Christian Rome can have been represented: it looks kosher but it is unkosher. Pagan Rome cannot ever have looked kosher, but Christian Rome, with its appeal to ancient Israel, could and did and moreover claimed to. It bore some traits that validate, but lacked others that validate.

The other metaphor – that of the family – proved equally pointed. Sages framed their political ideas within the metaphor of genealogy, because to begin with they appealed to the fleshly connection, the family, as the rationale for Israel's social existence. A family beginning with Abraham, Isaac, and Jacob, Israel today could best sort out its relationships by drawing into the family other social entities with which it found it had to relate. So Rome became the brother. That affinity came to light only when Rome had turned Christian, and that point marked the need for the extension of the genealogical net. But the conversion to Christianity also justified sages' extending membership in the family to Rome, for Christian Rome shared with Israel the common patrimony of Scripture – and said so. The character of sages' thought on Israel therefore proved remarkably congruent to the conditions of public discourse that confronted them. But the substance of their doctrine – the rejection of metaphor in favor of the claim that Israel formed an entity that was sui generis – derived from within.

When we grasp how the authorship understood itself, we may compare that representation of matters to its thinking about the larger social group subject to revisioning in the systematic statement at hand. "Israel" writ large represented sages' conception of themselves. A small social group reflecting on a larger social group, sages projected outward their sense of their own group. Their social metaphors germinated, to begin with, out of the seed of that singular authorship's own social imagination of itself. This thesis then is to be tested against the authorship's representation of its own social entity. Since we have, in the Yerushalmi and its related writings, the results of a social group reflecting upon a social group, we turn to the representation of their own standing in Heaven and earth as imagined by the authorship of the Yerushalmi. All things, in that portrait, stood in hierarchical connection and relationship, with sages at the end of the chain begun at Sinai (a conception that will not have surprised the authorship of tractate Abot). The Yerushalmi's authorship portrays the rabbi as an effective authority over the everyday affairs and social life of the social group ("Israel").

The Metaphor of the Family, "Israel"

When sages wished to know what (an) "Israel" was, in the fourth century they reread the scriptural story of Scripture's "Israel"'s origins for the answer. To begin with, as Scripture told them the story, "Israel" was a man, Jacob, and his children are "the children of Jacob." That man's name was also "Israel," and, it followed, "the children of Israel" comprised the extended family of that man. By extension, "Israel" formed the family of Abraham and Sarah, Isaac and Rebecca, Jacob and Leah and Rachel. "Israel" therefore invoked the metaphor of genealogy to explain the bonds that linked persons unseen into a single social entity; the shared traits were imputed, not empirical. That social metaphor of "Israel" – a simple one, really, and easily grasped – bore consequences in two ways. First, children in general are admonished to follow the good example of their parents. The deeds of the patriarchs and matriarchs therefore taught lessons on how the children were to act. Of greater interest in an account of "Israel" as a social metaphor, "Israel" lived twice, once in the patriarchs and matriarchs, a second time in the life of the heirs as the descendants relived those earlier lives. The stories of the family were carefully reread to provide a picture of the meaning of the latterday events of the descendants of that same family. Accordingly, the lives of the patriarchs signaled the history of Israel.[9]

---

[9] I maintain that the original act of metaphorization is what made inevitable the identification of the social entity now with the family of Abraham, Isaac, and Jacob. But how that metaphor would serve, and the weight of meaning it would have to bear, are hardly dictated by the fact that the group now is "Israel" then. After all, the meanings imputed to the fact of "being Israel" by sages hardly correspond to those imputed to that same fact by Christian theologians of the same age. See my *Judaism and Christianity in the Age of Constantine. Issues in the Initial Confrontation* (Chicago, 1988: University of Chicago Press).

The polemical purpose of the claim that that abstraction, "Israel," was to be compared to the family of the mythic ancestor lies right at the surface. With another "Israel," the Christian Church, now claiming to constitute the true one, Jews found it possible to confront that claim and to turn it against the other side. "You claim to form 'Israel after the spirit.' Fine, and *we* are Israel after the flesh – and genealogy forms the link, that alone." (Converts did not present an anaomly, of course, since they were held to be children of Abraham and Sarah, who had "made souls," that is, converts, in Haran, a point repeated in the documents of the period.) That fleshly continuity formed of all of "us" a single family, rendering spurious the notion that "Israel" could be other than genealogically defined. But that polemic seems to me adventitious and not primary. At the same time the metaphor provided a quite separate component to sages' larger system.

A Social Metaphor and a Field Theory of Society:
"Israel" and the Social Contract

The metaphor of Israel as family supplied an encompassing theory of society, accounting for that sense of constituting a corporate social entity that clearly infused the documents of the Judaism of the Dual Torah from the very outset.[10] Such a theory explained not only who "Israel" as a whole was. It also set forth the responsibilities of Israel's social entity, its society; it defined the character of that entity; it explained who owes what to whom at why, and it accounted for the inner structure and interplay of relationship within the community, here and now, constituted by Jews in their villages and neighborhoods of towns. Accordingly, "Israel" as family bridged the gap between an account of the entirety of the social group, "Israel," and a picture of the components of that social group as they lived out their lives in their households and villages. An encompassing theory of society, covering all components from least to greatest, holding the whole together in correct order and proportion, derived from "Israel" viewed as extended family.[11]

---

[10]The conception of an encompassing "theory of society" originally came to me in the plenary lecture of Professors Betsy Fox-Genovese and Eugene Genovese at the American Academy of Religion meeting in Atlanta in 1986. That is what stimulated the reflections of this part of the paper.

[11]Whether or not such a theory of society as a whole and in its constituents can be identified in other Judaisms seems to me an interesting question. For a systemic statement on the social entity, the "Israel," may exhibit diverse qualities and serve a range of theoretical purposes. Such a statement need not address the issues worked out in an encompassing theory of society. My sense is that the Priestly Code accounted for the whole, all together and all at once. Whether other of the pentateuchal statements did, whether we may locate in the prophetic

The Redefinition of "Israel": Judaism and Its Social Metaphors

Can we say that the Mishnaic phase had presented an encompassing theory of society as a whole? In general terms, yes, But in specifics, no. Invoking the metaphor, "Israel," for a group subjected to metaphor and so identified with the biblical "Israel," the Mishnah accounted for the whole. And as to the parts, the here and the now of household and village, the Mishnah's "Israel" accomplished a suitable explanation. But the space in between the large and theoretical and the mundane was left vacant. The Mishnah's system had explained by "Israel" the identification of that large entity, the entirety of the social group, with biblical "Israel," and, in its extraordinary exegesis of the everyday as modality of the sacred, had also infused in the parts that sense that the whole was meant to make. But the parts remained just that: details of a larger whole that derived place and proportion only in that whole. That abstraction of "Israel" as not "not-Israel," holy and not gentile: holy people, left the middle range components of society unaccounted for.

The Mishnah could explain village and "all Israel," just as its system used the word "Israel" for individual and entire social entity. But the region and its counterparts, the "we" composed of regions, the corporate society of the Jews of a given country, language group, and the like, the real life world of communities that transcended particular locations – these social facts of the middle distance did not constitute subdivisions of the "Israel" that knew all and each, but nothing in between. The omitted entity, I see, was the family itself, which played no important role in the Mishnah's system, except as one of the taxonomic indicators. By contrast "Israel" as family imparted to the details an autonomy and a meaning of their own, *so that each complex component of the whole formed a microcosm of the whole: family to village to "Israel" as one large family.*

The village then comprised "Israel," as much as did the region, the neighborhood, the corporate society people could empirically identify, the theoretical social entity they could only imagine – all formed "all Israel," viewed under the aspect of Heaven, and, of still greater consequence, each household – that is, each building block of the village community – constituted in itself a model of, the model for, "Israel." The utter abstraction of the Mishnah had left "Israel" as individual or as "all Israel," thus without articulated linkage to the concrete middle range of the Jews' everyday social life. Dealing with exquisite detail and the intangible whole, the Mishnah's system had left that realm of the society of Jews in the workaday household and village outside the metaphorical

---

ideology a theory of society at large and in detail – these are questions I do not know how to answer. The comparison of Judaisms (as of other systems) will find in this consideration a taxonomic trait, I should imagine.

frame of "Israel," and "Israel" viewed in the image, after the likeness of family made up that omitted middle range.

That theory of "Israel" as a society made up of persons who because they constituted a family stood in a clear relationship of obligation and responsibility to one another corresponded to what people much later would call the social contract, a kind of compact that in palpable ways told families and households how in the aggregate they formed something larger and tangible. The web of interaction spun out of concrete interchange now was spun out of not the gossamer thread of abstraction and theory but the tough hemp of family ties. "Israel" formed a society because "Israel" was compared to an extended family. That, sum and substance, supplied to the Jews in their households (themselves a made-up category which, in the end, transformed the relationship of the nuclear family into an abstraction capable of holding together quite unrelated persons) an account of the tie from household to household, from village to village, encompassing ultimately "all Israel."

Now if we ask the authorship of the Mishnah to point to its encompassing theory of "Israel" as an ongoing society, where will they lead us? If they tell us that "Israel" forms a society because it is not "not-Israel," they evade the question altogether. For "not-Israel" formed an undifferentiated other. It did not constitute a society, but only a category. And for the same reason "Israel" as caste contained no elements that could be spun out into a theory of interpersonal relationships that would account for the ongoing life of households in community, villages, towns, and upward. The theory of society that infuses the Mishnaic system forms part of a larger abstract program: "Israel" constitutes a holy people, a people apart, a people different from all other peoples; "Israel" constitutes a caste. But how everyday "Israel" forms a community, how in the aggregate everyday relationships are composed and held together, and how to account for the corresponding middle range aggregates of "non-Israel" – these are not questions answered by the Mishnah's metaphors for "Israel."

Obviously, as I have underscored already, the Mishnah's system answers these questions in exquisite detail. We know how everyday relationships are to be ordered, whether involving a gored ox or a bereaved king. We may tease out of these threads and strands a fabric of community at large. But we find ourselves awed into silence by the requirement to state the connection between "Israel" at large and that social theory, that theory of society, that is expressed *in these details*. For no one, in the Mishnaic system, draws the connection, and the available metaphors do not suggest that there was one (though there assuredly is). The contrast, then, to the power of the metaphor of "Israel" as family hardly requires specification. If "we" form a family, then we know full

The Redefinition of "Israel": Judaism and Its Social Metaphors

well what links us, the common ancestry, the obligations imposed by common ancestry upon the cousins who make up the family today. The link between the commonplace interactions and relationships that make "us" into a community, on the one side, and that encompassing entity, "Israel," "all Israel," now is drawn. The large comprehends the little, the abstraction of "us" overall ("the circumcized," for instance) gains concrete reality in the "us" of the here and now of home and village, all together, all forming a "family." In that fundamental way, the metaphor of "Israel" as family therefore provided the field theory of "Israel" linking the most abstraction component, the entirety of the social group, to the most mundane, the specificity of the household. One theory, framed in that metaphor of such surpassing simplicity, now held the whole together. That is what I mean when I propose that the metaphor of family provided an encompassing theory of society, an account of the social contract encompassing all social entities, Jews' and gentiles' as well, that, so far as I can see, no other metaphor accomplished.

Israel as Family: The Patriarchs and Matriarchs and the Extended Family of Israel

"Israel" as family comes to expression in, among other writings of the fifth century, the document that makes the most sustained and systematic statement of the matter, Genesis Rabbah. In this theory we should not miss the extraordinary polemic utility, of which, in passing, we have already taken note. "Israel" as family also understood itself to form a nation or people. That nation people held a land, a rather peculiar, enchanted or holy, Land at that, one that, in its imputed traits, was as sui generis as (presently we shall see) in the metaphorical thought of the system at hand, Israel also was. Competing for the same territory, Israel's claim to what it called the Land of Israel – thus, *of Israel* in particular – now rested on right of inheritance such as a family enjoyed, and this was made explicit. The passage shows how high the stakes were in the claim to constitute the genealogical descendant of the ancestors.

Genesis Rabbah LXI

VII.1   A.   "But to the sons of his concubines, Abraham gave gifts, and while he was still living, he sent them away from his son Isaac, eastward to the east country" (Gen. 25:6):
        B.   In the time of Alexander of Macedonia the sons of Ishmael came to dispute with Israel about the birthright, and with them came two wicked families, the Canaanites and the Egyptians.
        C.   They said, "Who will go and engage in a disputation with them."
        D.   Gebiah b. Qosem [the enchanter] said, "I shall go and engage in a disputation with them."

E. They said to him, "Be careful not to let the Land of Israel fall into their possession."
F. He said to them, "I shall go and engage in a disputation with them. If I win over them, well and good. And if not, you may say, 'Who is this hunchback to represent us?'"
G. He went and engaged in a disputation with them. Said to them Alexander of Macedonia, "Who lays claim against whom?"
H. The Ishmaelites said, "We lay claim, and we bring our evidence from their own Torah: 'But he shall acknowledge the firstborn, the son of the hated' (Deut. 21;17). Now Ishmael was the firstborn. [We therefore claim the land as heirs of the firstborn of Abraham.]"
I. Said to him Gebiah b. Qosem, "My royal lord, does a man not do whatever he likes with his sons?"
J. He said to him, "Indeed so."
K. "And lo, it is written, 'Abraham gave all that he had to Isaac' (Gen. 25:2)."
L. [Alexander asked,] "Then where is the deed of gift to the other sons?"
M. He said to him, "'But to the sons of his concubines, Abraham gave gifts, [and while he was still living, he sent them away from his son Isaac, eastward to the east country]' (Gen. 25:6)."
N. [The Ishmaelites had no claim on the land.] They abandoned the field in shame.

The metaphor now shifts, with the notion of Israel today as the family of Abraham, as against the Ishmaelites, also of the same family, gives way. But the theme of family records persists. Canaan has no claim, for Canaan was also a family, comparable to Israel – but descended from a slave. The power of the metaphor of family is that it can explain not only the social entity formed by Jews, but the social entities confronted by them. All fell into the same genus, making up diverse species. The theory of society before us thus accounts for all societies, and, as we shall see when we deal with Rome, does so with extraordinary force.

O. The Canaanites said, "We lay claim, and we bring our evidence from their own Torah. Throughout their Torah it is written, 'the land of Canaan.' So let them give us back our land."
P. Said to him Gebiah b. Qosem, "My royal lord, does a man not do whatever he likes with his slave?"
Q. He said to him, "Indeed so."
R. He said to him, "And lo, it is written, 'A slave of slaves shall Canaan be to his brothers' (Gen. 9:25). So they are really our slaves."
S. [The Canaanites had no claim to the land and in fact should be serving Israel.] They abandoned the field in shame.

The same metaphor serves both "Israel" and "Canaan." Each formed the latterday heir of the earliest family, and both lived out the original paradigm. The mode of thought at hand imputes the same genus to both

The Redefinition of "Israel": Judaism and Its Social Metaphors

social entities, and then makes its possible to distinguish among the two species at hand. We shall see the same mode of thought – the family, but which wing of the family – when we consider the confrontation with Christianity and with Rome, in each case conceived in the same personal way. The metaphor applies to both and yields its own meanings for each. The final claim in the passage before us moves away from the metaphor of family. But the notion of a continuous, physical descent is implicit here as well. "Israel" has inherited the wealth of Egypt. Since the notion of inheritance forms a component of the metaphor of family (a conception critical, as we shall see in the next section, in the supernatural patrimony of the "children of Israel" in the merit of the ancestors), we survey the conclusion of the passage.

> T. The Egyptians said, "We lay claim, and we bring our evidence from their own Torah. Six hundred thousand of them left us, taking away our silver and gold utensils: 'They despoiled the Egyptians' (Ex. 12:36). Let them give them back to us."
>
> U. Gebiah b. Qosem said, "My royal lord, six hundred thousand men worked for them for two hundred and ten years, some as silversmiths and some as goldsmiths. Let them pay us our salary at the rate of a *denar* a day."
>
> V. The mathematicians went and added up what was owing, and they had not reached the sum covering a century before the Egyptians had to forfeit what they had claimed. They abandoned the field in shame.
>
> W. [Alexander] wanted to go up to Jerusalem. The Samaritans said to him, "Be careful. They will not permit you to enter their most holy sanctuary."
>
> X. When Gebiah b. Qosem found out about this, he went and made for himself two felt shoes, with two precious stones worth twenty-thousand pieces of silver set in them. When he got to the mountain of the house [of the Temple], he said to him, "My royal lord, take off your shoes and put on these two felt slippers, for the floor is slippery, and you should not slip and fall."
>
> Y. When they came to the most holy sanctuary, he said to him, "Up to this point, we have the right to enter. From this point onward, we do not have the right to enter."
>
> Z. He said to him, "When we get out of here, I'm going to even out your hump."
>
> AA. He said to him, "You will be called a great surgeon and get a big fee."

The Ishmaelites, Abraham's children, deprived as they were of their inheritance, fall into the same genus as does Israel. So, too, as I said, did Canaan. As to the Egyptians, that is a different matter. Now "Israel" is that same "Israel" of which Scripture spoke. The social metaphor shifts within the story, though, of course, the story is not affected.

Israel as Sui Generis: The Rules of Nature, the Rules of History, and Supernatural Governance of Israel in Leviticus Rabbah

The definition of "Israel" comes to us not only in what people expressly mean by the word, but also in the implicit terms yielded by how they discuss the social entity. In Leviticus Rabbah the conception of "Israel" as sui generis reaches expression in an implicit statement that Israel is subject to its own laws, which are distinct from the laws governing all other social entities. These laws may be discerned in the factual, scriptural record of "Israel"'s past, and that past, by definition, belonged to "Israel" alone. It followed, therefore, that by discerning the regularities in "Israel"'s history, implicitly understood as unique to "Israel," sages recorded the view that "Israel" like God was not subject to analogy or comparison. Accordingly, while not labeled a genus unto itself, Israel is treated in that way.

To understand how this view of "Israel" comes to expression, we have to trace the principal mode of thought characteristic of the authorship of Leviticus Rabbah.[12] It is an exercise in the proving of hypotheses by tests of concrete facts. The hypotheses derive from theology of Israel. The tests are worked out by reference to those given facts of social history that Scripture, for its part, contributes. As with the whole range of ancient exegetes of Scripture, typified in this context by Aphrahat and the rabbinic exegetes of Genesis Rabbah, cited in the preceding chapter, so the authorship at hand treated Scripture as a set of facts. These facts concerned history, not nature, but they served, much as did the facts of nature availed the Greek natural philosophers, to prove or disprove hypotheses. The hypotheses concerned the social rules to which Israel was subjected, and, as I said, the upshot was that Israel was subject to its own rules, revealed by the historical facts of Scripture.

If I had to point to the single most common way in which sages made the implicit statement that "Israel" is sui generis, I would point to their "as-if" mode of seeing "Israel"'s reality. Sages read "Israel"'s history not as it seems – that is, not as it would appear when treated in accord with the same norms as the histories of other social entities – but as a series of mysteries. The facts are not what appearances suggest. The deeper truth is not revealed in those events that happen, in common, to "Israel" and to (other) nations over the face of the earth. What is really happening to "Israel" is wholly other, different from what seems to be

---

[12]I must confess that of all rabbinic documents I have studied beginning to end and attempted to describe in a systematic and thorough way, Leviticus Rabbah turned out to be the single most subtle and attractive one. Since I found myself profoundly moved by all of the writings of late antiquity I have translated and analyzed, that is a considerable judgment.

The Redefinition of "Israel": Judaism and Its Social Metaphors

happening and what is happening to ordinary groups. The fundamental proposition pertinent to "Israel" in Leviticus Rabbah is that things are not what they seem. "Israel"'s reality does not correspond to the perceived facts of this world.

Now if we ask ourselves the source of this particular mode of thinking about "Israel," we find no difficulty in identifying the point of origin. The beginning of seeing "Israel" as if it were other than the here and now social group people saw lay in the original metaphorization of the social group. When people looked at themselves, their households and villages, their regions and language group, and thought to themselves, "What more are we? What else are we?" they began that process of abstraction that took the form of an intellectual labor of comparison, contrast, analogy, and, as is clear, consequent metaphorization. The group is compared to something else (or to nothing else) and hence is treated as not fully represented by the here and the now but as representative, itself, of something else beyond. And that very mode of seeing things, lying in the foundations of the Mishnah's authorship's thought, implicit in the identification of the survivors as the present avatar of Scripture's "Israel," yielded an ongoing process of metaphorization. The original use of the metaphor, "Israel," to serve as the explanation of who the surviving groups were made it natural, from that time forward, to see "Israel" under the aspect of the "as-if." How this mode of thought worked itself out in the documents at hand is clear. The exegetes at hand maintained that a given statement of Scripture, in the case of Leviticus, stood for and signified something other than that to which the verse openly referred. If – as was a given for these exegetes – water stands for Torah, the skin disease mentioned in Leviticus 13, in Hebrew called *saraat* and translated as leprosy, stands for, is caused by, evil speech, the reference to some thing to mean some other thing entirely, then the mode of thought at hand is simple.

And what is decisive for our inquiry is that that mode of thought pertained to "Israel" alone. Solely in the case of "Israel" did one thing symbolize another, speak not of itself but of some other thing entirely. When other social entities, for example, Babylonia, Persia, or Rome, stood for something else, it was in relationship to "Israel," and in the context of the metaphorization of Israel. When treated in a natural context, by contrast, we find no metaphors, for example, Alexander of Macedonia in the story considered earlier is a person, and no symbol stands for that person. When Greece appears in the sequence of empires leading finally to the rule of "Israel," then Greece may be symbolized by the hare. And there is another side of the matter too. Other things – the bear, the eagle – could stand for the empires, but – in that metaphorical context – then "Israel" stands only for itself. Whichever way we have it, therefore, implicit in that view and mode of thought is the notion of "Israel" as sui generis, lacking all counterpart or parallel entity for purposes of comparison and contrast. The importance of the mode of reading Scripture "as if" it meant something else than what it said, in the case of the exegesis of Leviticus Rabbah, should not be missed. What lies beneath or beyond the surface – there is the true reality, the world of truth and meaning.

"Israel" and the Social Rules of Judaisms

Systems by definition attend to a social entity; otherwise all we have is a book. And social groups – two or more persons sharing distinctive traits – commonly perceive what is not there to be seen, namely, something other, and more, than what they are. Concrete traits stand for an abstract social entity, present even when not perceived, indeed, imposing other traits besides those that are palpable. Accordingly, if our survey and analysis of how "Israel" serves as a metaphor for groups Jews form, and how the metaphors imputed to an "Israel" express shared concerns of such groups, is to serve, we have now to generalize. Success in such an exercise will yield lessons for the description, analysis, and interpretation of other systems and their social entities, other groups and their shared metaphors for themselves. But we require also an account of where and how Jews' groups, with their intense awareness of forming a social entity subject to stipulation and condition, may differ from others. Accordingly, I have now to propose hypotheses for general discourse deriving from the particular case at hand. And, to begin with, that requires comparison of the Judaism we have treated with other Judaisms.

The First Law: The Shape and Meaning Imputed to the Social Component, "Israel," Will Conform to the Larger Interests of the System and in Detail Express the System's Main Point. The Case of Paul and "Israel" after the Spirit.

We appeal, for proof that the law is not particular to the case, to the "Israel" defined by Paul. In his representation of his "Israel," Paul presents us with a metaphor for which, in the documents of the Judaism of the Dual Torah, I can find no counterpart in this context.[13] "Israel" compared to an olive tree, standing for "Israel" encompassing gentiles who believe but also Jews by birth who do not believe, "Israel" standing

---

[13] My picture of Paul's thought is meant to give the consensus of learning at this time. I mean to illustrate my theoretical model by reference to that consensus. I owe thanks to my colleague at Brown University, Stanley Stowers, for reading this section of the book. He has a quite different interpretation of Paul on "Israel," which is to be dealt with once it has been published.

for the elect and those saved by faith and therefore by grace – these complex and somewhat disjoined metaphors and definitions form a coherent and simple picture when we see them not in detail but as part of the larger whole of Paul's entire system. For the issue of "Israel" for Paul forms a detail of a system centered upon a case in favor of salvation through Christ and faith in him alone, even without keeping the rules of the Torah. So does the conesensus of the familiar and rich corpus of scholarship on Paul present matters, and I take the results as definitive.[14]

The generative problematic that tells Paul what he wishes to know about "Israel" derives from the larger concerns of the Christian system Paul proposes to work out. That problematic was framed in the need, in general, to explain the difference, as to salvific condition, between those who believed, and those who did not believe, in Christ.[15] But it focused, specifically, upon the matter of "Israel," and how those who believed in Christ but did not derive from "Israel" related to both those who believed and also derived from "Israel" and those who did not believe but derived from "Israel." Do the first-named have to keep the Torah? Are the non-believing Jews subject to justification? Since, had Paul been a "gentile" and not an "Israel," the issue cannot have proved critical in the working out of an individual system (but only in the address to the world at large), we may take for granted that Paul's own Jewish origin made the question at hand important, if not critical. What transformed the matter from a chronic into an acute question – the matter of salvation through keeping the Torah – encompassed, also, the matter of who is "Israel."

For his part, Paul appeals, for his taxic indicator of "Israel," to a consideration we have not found commonplace at all, namely, circumcision. It is certainly implicit in the Torah, but the Mishnah's laws, we recall, accommodate as "Israel" persons who (for good and sufficient reasons) are not circumcised, and treat as "not-Israel" persons who are circumcised but otherwise do not qualify. So for the Mishnah's system circumcision forms a premise, not a presence, a datum, but not a decisive taxic indicator. But Paul, by contrast, can have called "Israel" all those who are circumcized, and "not-Israel" all those who are not circumcized – pure and simple. That has been shown, just now, by Jonathan Z.

---

[14] I had the advantage of the comments on my treatments, in this and the following sections, of the Essenes of Qumran, Paul and Philo of Professors Bruce Chilton, Yale University, Robert Berchman, University of Virginia, Stanley Stowers, Brown University, and Burton Mack, Claremont Graduate School.
[15] Stowers sees these as coordinate but separate.

Smith.[16] He states, "The strongest and most persistent use of circumcision as a taxic indicator is found in Paul and the deutero-Pauline literature. Paul's self-description is framed in terms of the two most fundamental halakic definitions of the Jewish male: circumcision and birth from a Jewish mother....'Circumcised' is consistently used in the Pauline literature as a technical term for the Jew, 'uncircumcised,' for the gentile." It must follow, as I said, that for Paul, "Israel" is "the circumcized nation," and an "Israel" is a circumcized male. The reason for the meaning attached to "Israel" is spelled out by Smith:

> What is at issue...is the attempt to establish a new taxon: 'where there cannot be Greek and Jew, circumcised and uncircumcised, barbarian and Scythian' (Col. 3:11), 'for neither circumcision counts for anything but uncircumcision but a new creation' (Gal. 6:15).

It follows that for Paul, the matter of "Israel" and its definition forms part of a larger project of reclassifying Christians in terms not defined by the received categories, now (as we recall from Chapter One) a third race, a new race, a new man, in a new story. Smith proceeds to make the matter entirely explicit to Paul's larger system: "Paul's theological arguments with respect to circumcision have their own internal logic and situation: that in the case of Abraham, it was posterior to faith (Rom. 4:9-12); that spiritual things are superior to physical things (Col. 3:11-14); that the Christian is the 'true circumcision' as opposed to the Jew (Phil. 3:3)....But these appear secondary to the fundamental taxonomic premise, the Christian is a member of a new taxon."

In this same context Paul's Letter to the Romans presents a consistent picture. In Chapters Nine through Eleven he presents his reflections on what and who is (an) "Israel." Having specified that the family of Abraham will inherit the world not through the law but through the righteousness of faith (Rom. 4:13), Paul confronts "Israel" as family and redefines the matter in a way coherent with his larger program. Then the children of Abraham will be those who "believe in him that raised from the dead Jesus our Lord, who was put to death for our trespasses and raised for our justification" (Rom. 4:24-5). For us the critical issue is whether or not Paul sees these children of Abraham as "Israel." The answer is in his address to "my kinsmen by race. They are Israelites, and to them belong the sonship, the glory, the covenants, the giving of the law, the worship, and the promises; to them belong the patriarchs, and of their race, according to the flesh, is the Christ. God who is over all be

---

[16]In "Fences and Neighbors," in W. S. Green ed., *Approaches to Ancient Judaism* (Missoula, 1978: Scholars Press for Brown Judaic Studies) 2:1-25 = Jonathan Z. Smith, *Imagining Religion. From Babylon to Jonestown* (Chicago, 1982: University of Chicago Press), pp. 1-18.

The Redefinition of "Israel": Judaism and Its Social Metaphors

blessed for ever" (Rom. 9:3-4). "Israel" then is the holy people, the people of God. But Paul proceeds to invoke a fresh metaphor, "Israel" as olive tree, and so to reframe the doctrine of "Israel" in a radical way:

> Not all who are descended from Israel belong to Israel, and not all are children of Abraham because they are his descendants...it is not the children of the flesh who are the children of God, but the children of the promise are reckoned as descendants (Rom. 9:6-7).

Here we have an explicit definition of "Israel," now not after the flesh but after the promise. "Israel" then is no longer a family in the concrete sense in which, in earlier materials, we have seen the notion. "Israel after the flesh" who pursued righteousness which is based on law did not succeed in fulfilling that law because they did not pursue it through faith (Rom. 9:31), "and gentiles who did not pursue righteousness have attained it, that is, righteousness through faith" (Rom. 9:30). Now there is an "Israel" after the flesh but *also* "a remnant chosen by grace...the elect obtained it..." (Rom. 11:5-6), with the consequence that the fleshly "Israel" remains, but gentiles ("a wild olive shoot") have been grafted "to share the richness of the olive tree" (Rom. 11:17). Do these constitute "Israel"? Yes and no. They share in the promise. They are "Israel" in the earlier definition of the children of Abraham. There remains an "Israel" after the flesh, which has its place as well. And that place remains with God: "As regards election they are beloved for the sake of their forefathers. For the gifts and the call of God are irrevocable" (Rom. 11:28-29).

This very rapid and schematic account makes the point at hand and illustrates the law with which we began: the shape and meaning imputed to the social component, "Israel," here conform to the larger interests of the system constructed by Paul, both episodically, and, in Romans, quite systematically. "Israel" as a detail expresses, also, the system's main point. For Paul's Judaic system, encompassing believing (former) "gentiles" but also retaining a systemic status for non-believing Jews, "Israel" forms an important component within a larger structure. Not only so, but, more to the point, "Israel" finds definition on account of the logical requirements of that encompassing framework. Indeed, I cannot imagine making sense of the remarkably complex metaphor introduced by Paul – the metaphor of the olive tree – without understanding the problem of thought that confronted him, and that he solved through, among other details, his thinking on "Israel." The notion of entering "Israel" through belief but not behavior ("works") in one detail expresses the main point of Paul's system, which concerns not who is "Israel" but what faith in Christ means.[17]

The Second Law:
What an "Israel" is Depends on Who Wants to Know.
Philosophers Imagine a Philosophical "Israel,"
and Politicians Conceive a Political "Israel."
The Cases of Philo and of the Essenes of Qumran.

By philosopher in the present context I mean an intellectual who attempts to state as a coherent whole, within a single system of thought and (implicit) explanation, diverse categories and classifications of data. By politician I mean a person of public parts, one who undertakes to shape a social polity, a person of standing in a social group, for example, a community, who proposes to explain in some theoretical framework the meaning and character of the life of that group or nation or society or community. I should classify the framers of the Mishnah as philosophers, those of the Yerushalmi and related writings (by their own word) as politicians. The related but distinct systems made by each group exhibit traits of philosophy and politics, respectively, for reasons I have now spelled out. The generalization is before us. Does it apply to more than our own case? For purposes of showing that the same phenomenon derives from other cases and therefore constitutes a law, not a mere generalization out of a case, I appeal to an individual, a philosopher, and an authorship, the formative intellects of the community at Qumran. Philo, the Jewish philosopher of Alexandria, serves as our example of the former, and the authorship of the more important writings of the Essene community of Qumran, the latter.

For Philo, Israel forms a paradigmatic metaphor, bearing three meanings. The first is ontological, which signifies the places of "Israel" in God's creation. The second is epistemological. This signifies the knowledge of God that Israel possesses. The third is political, referring to the polity that "Israel" possesses and projects in light of its ontological place and epistemological access to God.[18] Not wishing to pretend to know things that, firsthand, in fact I do not know, I turn to a quick survey of the role assigned to "Israel" in Philo's system, as that role is portrayed in the systematic pictures provided by the two modern masters of the subject, Harry A. Wolfson and Erwin R. Goodenough.[19]

---

[17]Or, as Stowers sees it, what gentiles' being blessed through Abraham means.
[18]I owe this formulation to Robert Berchman, University of Virginia.
[19]Once more I depend upon generous colleagues to save me needless error based on mere ignorance. I owe special thanks for the reading of this section by Robert Berchman.

The Redefinition of "Israel": Judaism and Its Social Metaphors

Our point of interest is achieved when we perceive even from a distance the basic contours of Philo's vision of "Israel." What we shall see is that, for Philo, "Israel" formed a category within a larger theory of how humanity knows divinity, an aspect of ontology and epistemology. True, "Israel" emerges as, if not unique, then sui generis. But that is only in the framework of a system of classification, so "Israel" is not really sui generis in the way in which, in the second phase of the Judaism of the Dual Torah, "Israel" has no counterpart in kind, not merely in species. What makes an "Israel" into "Israel" for Philo is a set of essentially philosophical considerations, concerning adherence to or perception of God. In the philosophical system of Philo, "Israel" constitutes a philosophical category, not a social entity in an everyday sense.[20]

Seeing "Israel" as "the people which is dedicated to his service," Philo holds that "Israel" is the best of races and is capable of seeing God, and this capability of seeing God is based upon the habit of his service to God.[21] The upshot of capacity to receive a type of prophecy that comes directly from God, and one must be descended from "Israel" to receive that type of prophecy. An Egyptian, Hagar, cannot see the Supreme Cause.[22] The notion of inherited "merit" (in this context an inappropriate metaphor) bears more than a single burden; here "merit" or inherited capacity involves a more clear perception of God than is attained by those without the same inheritance – a far cry indeed from the "merit of the ancestors" as the fourth-century sages would interpret it.[23] Mere moral and intellectual qualifications, however, do not suffice. One has to enjoy divine grace, which Moses had, and which, on account of the merit of the patriarchs, the people have. Wolfson comments, "This view, that

---

[20]That is not to suggest that Philo does not see Jews as a living social entity, a community. The opposite is the case. But when he constructs his philosophical statement, the importance of "Israel" derives from its singular capacity to gain knowledge of God which other categories of the system cannot have. When writing about the Jews in a political context, Philo does not appeal to their singular knowledge of God, and when writing about the Jews as "Israel" in the philosophical context, he does not appeal to their forming a this-worldly community.

[21]Harry Austryn Wolfson, *Philo. Foundations of Religious Philosophy in Judaism, Christianity, and Islam* (Cambridge, 1948: Harvard University Press), II, p. 51-2.

[22]*Ibid.*, p. 51.

[23]Goodenough's critique of Wolfson for his insistence upon finding rabbinic parallels to Philo's ideas seems to me absolutely on target, beginning, middle, and end. That critique is now in print in Ernest S. Frerichs and Jacob Neusner, eds., *Goodenough on History of Religion and on Judaism* (Atlanta, 1986: Scholars Press for Brown Judaic Studies). Wolfson extended to Philo the interpretive system of George Foot Moore's *Judaism*, composing of the whole – rabbis, Philo – a single, unitary, and normative statement, a Judaism.

the revelation of the Law was a special gift to Israel, was by the time of Philo a common belief among the Jews, as is evidenced from Sirach."[24]

If Philo, serving as the counterpart to the authorship of the Mishnah, represents an intellectual's thinking about the entity, "Israel," we do well to identify a political reading, placing into perspective, for comparison and contrast, the deeply political definitions of "Israel" formed by the authorships of the Yerushalmi, Genesis Rabbah, and Leviticus Rabbah. For they appeal to political metaphors – metaphors of the group as *polis*. They see "Israel" as a political entity, matched against "Rome," or treated as sui generis, or compared to a family – anything but a mere category, by happenstance, a classification of persons, rather than of pears or sexual abnormalities, to be set into a hierarchical system. For that purpose we turn to the library that was selected by, and therefore presumably speaks for, the builders of an "Israel" that is the best documented, in its original site and condition, of any in antiquity: the Essene community of Qumran.[25] Just as, for Philo, I appealed to the foremost authorities for guidance, so, for the Essene community at Qumran, I do the same.[26] Geza Vermes, translator of the more important documents and authority on the community, draws our attention to what is critical.[27]

The Essenes of Qumran serve as a test case for two distinct laws, first, that what matters to begin with is dictated by the traits of the one to whom the subject is important, not by the objective and indicative characteristics of the subject itself; second, that the importance of a topic

---

[24]*Ibid.*, p. 52.

[25]I take as fact the current consensus the identification with Essenes of the community that valued the books found by the Dead Sea. I have no vested interest in the matter, which has slight bearing upon our inquiry.

[26]While the monographic literature on the Essene library and community of Qumran is truly formidable, the systemic description, analysis, and interpretation of that community has yet to begin. I cannot point to a single sustained and encompassing account of not the literature but the religious system, the Judaism, of the Essenes of Qumran, read inductively. Vermes's summary of knowledge, cited below, seems to me definitively to show (to the time of his writing) not only what has been accomplished, but also what awaits attention. I think the reason we do not have a picture of the Judaism of the Essenes of Qumran is that most scholars who have worked on the subject have come from the disciplines of not the history of religion but philology, text criticism, history, or theology, and a great many of them have found the library of Qumran of special interest in the theological study of the earliest Christian writings. That is an important topic, but it is, from the viewpoint of the history of religions, epiphenomenal (that is, rather beside the point).

[27]I rely on his *The Dead Sea Scrolls. Qumran in Perspective* (London, 1977: Collins), and, for the texts, his *The Dead Sea Scrolls in English* (Harmondsworth, 1975: Penguin Books, second edition).

The Redefinition of "Israel": Judaism and Its Social Metaphors

derives from the character of the system that takes up that topic. In both matters – we recall – I have to show that my generalizations pertain to more than a single case. We turn first to the systemic definition of "Israel": what kind of "Israel" and for what purpose, then to the importance, within a system, of an "Israel."

By "Israel" the authorships of the documents of the Essene library of Qumran mean "us" – and no one else. We start with that "us" and proceed from there to "Israel." In this way I show that – as with the authorship of the documents of the second phase of the Dual Torah – the movement of thought began with the particular and moved outward to the general. The group's principal documents comprised a Community Rule, which "legislates for a kind of monastic society," the Damascus Rule, "for an ordinary lay existence," and the War Rule and Messianic Rule, "...while associated with the other two, and no doubt reflecting to some extent a contemporary state of affairs, plan for a future age."[28] Among the four,[29] the first two will tell us their authorships' understanding of the relationship between "us" and "Israel," and that is what is critical to the picture of the type of "us" which (as we shall see) is "Israel" at hand.

Stated simply, what our authorships meant by "us" was simply "Israel," or "the true Israel." That is why the group[30] organized itself as a replication of "all Israel," as they read about "Israel" in those passages of Scripture that impressed them. They structured their group – in Vermes's language, "so that it corresponded faithfully to that of Israel itself, dividing it into priests and laity, the priests being described as the 'sons of Zadok' – Zadok was High Priest in David's time – and the laity grouped after the biblical model into twelve tribes."[31] This particular Israel then divided itself into units of thousands, hundreds, fifties, and

---

[28]Vermes, *Perspective*, p. 87. The Temple scroll, published after Vermes's account, is asymmetrical to our question, and can be set aside at the moment. But further study on our issue will certainly demand a rereading of that document for the purpose of its picture of "Israel." This first statement of the larger theses and hypothesis suffices with the first two items.

[29]I do not mean to neglect the numerous other important writings, but the ones at hand suffice for the limited purpose of this exercise.

[30]To call them a "sect" is inappropriate, since we do not know what type of group they were, and, from our perspective, the question is irrelevant. A group in its larger context constitutes a sect only if we have decided that that group is not what it conceives itself to be, which is, in this case, not the sect but the entirety of society ("church"). We need not make such an assessment in our context – and in fact, cannot.

[31]Vermes, *Perspective*, p. 88.

tens.³² The Community Rule further knows divisions within the larger group, specifically, "the men of holiness," "the men of perfect holiness," within a larger "Community." The corporate being of the community came to realization in common meals, prayers, and deliberations. Vermes says, "Perfectly obedient to each and every one of the laws of Moses and to all that was commanded by the prophets, they were to love one another and to share with one another their knowledge, powers, and possessions."³³ The description of the inner life of the group presents us with a division of a larger society. But – among many probative ones – one detail tells us that this group implicitly conceived of itself as "Israel."

It is that the group lived apart from the Temple of Jerusalem and had its liturgical life worked out in utter isolation from that central cult. They had their own calendar, which differed from the one people take for granted was observed in general, for their calendar was reckoned not by the moon but by the sun. This yielded different dates for the holy days and effectively marked the group as utterly out of touch with other Jews.³⁴ The solar calendar followed by the Essene community at Qumran meant that holy days for that group were working days for others and vice versa. The group furthermore had its own designation for various parts of the year. The year was divided into seven fifty-day periods, as Vermes says, each marked by an agricultural festival, for example, the Feast of New Wine, Oil, and so on.³⁵ On the Pentecost, treated as the Feast of the Renewal of the Covenant, the group would assembly in hierarchical order: "the priests first, ranked in order of status, after them the Levites, and lastly 'all the people one after another in their Thousands, Hundreds, Fifties, and Tens, that every Israelite may know his place in the community of God according to the everlasting design.'"³⁶ There can be no doubt from this passage – and a vast array of counterparts can be assembled – that the documents at hand address "Israel."

What an "Israel" is depends on who wants to know. Philo has given us a philosophical "Israel." The authorships of the documents preserved by the Essenes of Qumran define "Israel" not as a fictive entity possessing spiritual traits alone or mainly, but as a concrete social group, an entity in the here and now, that may be defined by traits of persons

---

³²Why using as the base ten rather than the scriptural and Mesopotamian base six I cannot say, but the analogy to the Iranian preference for base ten, for example, the *hazarapats*, should not be missed, for whatever it is worth.

³³Vermes, *Perspective*, p. 89.

³⁴Vermes, *Perspective*, p. 176.

³⁵*Ibid.*, p. 177.

³⁶*Ibid.*, p. 178.

The Redefinition of "Israel": Judaism and Its Social Metaphors

subject to the same sanctions and norms, sharing the same values and ideals. Builders of a community or a *polis*, and hence, politicians, the authorships of the Essenes of Qumran conceived and described in law a political "Israel." Their "Israel" and Philo's bear nothing in common. The one "Israel" – the Essenes' – constitutes a political entity and society. The "Israel" of the Essenes is the "Israel" of history and eschatology of Scripture, as much as the "Israel" of the authorship of the Yerushalmi, Genesis Rabbah, and Leviticus Rabbah refers back to the "Israel" of Genesis and Leviticus. The other "Israel" – Philo's – comprises people of shared intellectual traits in a larger picture of how God is known, as much as the "Israel" of the authorship of the Mishnah and related writings exhibits taxonomic traits and serves a function of classification. Both sets of politicians present us with political "Israel"s, that is, each with an "Israel" that exhibits the traits of a *polis*, a community ("people," "nation"). Both sets of philosophers offer a philosophical "Israel," with traits of a taxonomic character – one set for one system, another set for the other – that carry out a larger systemic purpose of explanation and philosophical classification. We have, therefore, not a generalization of a particular case, but a rule that can be tested in three cases.

The Third Law: The Systemic Importance of the Category, "Israel," Depends on the Generative Problematic – the Urgent Question – of the System Builders, and Not on Their Social Circumstance. The Place of "Israel" within the Self-Evidently True Response Offered by the System Will Prove Congruent to the Logic of the System – that Alone. The Cases of Paul, Philo, the Essenes of Qumran, and the Sages of the Dual Torah.

The proposed law is that the systemic question – the precipitating crisis that leads several generations of intellectuals to rethink the grounds of social being and to reconsider all fundamental questions in a new way – determines the importance of any category within the system. The negative version of the same law is obvious. The paramount character of a category in the social facts out there, in the streets and households (in the case of the social entity), has slight bearing upon the proportions and order of the system. Stated in the positive, the rule is that the systemic logic in here dictates all issues of proportion, balance, and order. We therefore ask ourselves how on objective grounds and by appealing to data, not mere impressions, we may assess the relative importance of a given systemic structural category when we compare one system to another.

Whether or not "Israel" takes an important place in a system is decided by the system and its logic, not the circumstance of the Jews in the here and now. *Systemopoeia* is a symbolic transaction worked out in imagination, not a sifting and sorting of facts. But how do we know whether or not any systemic component plays a more, or a less, important role? A judgment on the importance of a given entity or category in one system by comparison to the importance of that same entity or category in another need not rely upon subjective criteria. A reasonably objective measure of the matter lends hope to test the stated law. That criterion is whether or not the system remains cogent without consideration of its "Israel." Philo's does, the Mishnah's does, Paul's does not, the Essenes' does not, and the second stage in Judaism's does not.

The criterion of importance therefore does not derive from merely counting up references to "Israel." What we must do to assess the role and place of the social entity in a system by asking a simple question. *Were the entity or trait "Israel" to be removed from a given system, would that system radically change in character or would it merely lose a detail?* What is required is a mental experiment, but not a very difficult one. What we do is simply present a reprise of our systemic description. Let me state some bald facts.

First, without an "Israel," Paul would have had no system. The generative question of his system required him to focus attention on the definition of the social entity, "Israel." Paul originated among Jews but addressed both Jews and gentiles, seeking to form the lot into a single social entity "in Christ Jesus." The social dimension of his system formed the generative question with which he proposed to content.

Second, without an "Israel," Philo, by contrast, can have done very well indeed. For even our brief and schematic survey of the Philo described by Wolfson and Goodenough has shown us that, whatever mattered, "Israel" did not. It was a detail of a theory of knowledge of God, not the generative problematic even of the treatment of the knowledge of God, let alone of the system as a whole (which we scarcely approached, and had no reason to approach!). We may therefore say that "Israel" formed an important category for Paul and not for Philo. Accordingly, the judgment of the matter rests on more than mere word counts, on the one side, or exercises of impression and taste, on the other. It forms part of a larger interpretation of the system as a whole and what constitutes the system's generative problematic.[37]

---

[37] It is not only the problematic, but the topical program and category structure and organization of a system will provide probative testimony to issues of importance or peripherality. And these matters constitute statements of an entirely factual order. But considerations of space require postponing this matter.

If, moreover, we ask whether "Israel" is critical to the Essenes of Qumran, a simple fact answers our question. Were we to remove "Israel" in general and in detail from the topical program at hand, we should lose, if not the entirety of the library, then nearly the whole of some documents, and the larger part of many of them. The Essene library of Qumran constitutes a vast collection of writings about "Israel," its definition and conduct, history and destiny. We cannot make an equivalent statement of the entire corpus of Philo's writings, even though Philo obviously concerned himself with the life and welfare of the "Israel" of which, in Alexandria as well as world over, he saw himself a part. The reason for the systemic importance among the Essenes of Qumran of "Israel," furthermore, derives from the meanings imputed to that category. The library stands for a social group that conceives of itself as "Israel," and that wishes, in these documents, to spell out what that "Israel" is and must do. The system as a whole forms an exercise in the definition of "Israel" as against that "non-Israel" composed not of gentiles but of erring (former) Israelites. The saving remnant is all that is left: "Israel."

Our survey of four Judaisms yield a single rule. If we wish to know whether "Israel" will constitute an important component in a Judaism, we ask about the categorical imperative and describe, as a matter of mere fact, the consequent categorical composition of that system, stated as a corpus of authoritative documents. A system in which "Israel" – the social entity to which the system's builders imagine they address themselves – plays an important role will treat "Israel" as part of its definitive structure. The reason is that the system's categorical imperative will find important consequences in the definition of its "Israel." A system in which the system's builders work on other questions entirely than social ones, explore the logic of issues different from those addressing a social entity, also will not yield tractates on "Israel" and will not accord to the topic of "Israel" that categorical and systemic importance that we have identified in some Judaisms but not in others. Discourse on "Israel," in general (as in the second phase of the Judaism of the Dual Torah) or in acute detail concerning internal structure (as in the Essene writings of Qumran) comes about because of the fundamental question addressed by the system viewed whole.

The Hypothesis: The System Builders' Social (Including Political) Circumstance Defines the Generative Problematic which Imparts Self-Evidence to the Systemically Definitive Logic, Encompassing its Social Component. The Cases of Paul, the Essenes of Qumran, and the Sages of the Dual Torah.

The systemically generative circumstance finds its definition in the out there of the world in which the system builders – and their imagined audience – flourish. Extraordinary political crises, ongoing tensions of society, a religious crisis that challenges theological truth – these in time impose their definition upon thought, seizing the attention and focusing the concentration of the *systemopoieic* thinkers who propose to explain matters. Systems propose an orderly response to a disorderly situation, and that is their utility. Systems then come into existence at a point, and in a context, in which thoughtful people identify questions that cannot be avoided and must be solved. Such a circumstance, for the case at hand, emerges in the *polis*, that is, in the realm of politics and the context of persons in community, in the corporate society of shared discourse. The acute *systemopoieic* question then derives from out there, the system begins somewhere beyond the mind of the thoughtful intellects who build systems. Having ruled out the *systemopoieic* power of authors' or authorships' circumstance, therefore, I now invoke the *systemopoieic* power of the political setting of the social group of which the system builders form a part (in their own minds, the exemplification and realization).

Systemic logic enjoys self-evidence. But it is circumstance that dictates that absolute given, that sense of fittingness and irrefutable logic, that people find self-evident. By circumstance I do not mean the particular setting within which an authorship finds itself, for, as I just said, a collective authorship may produce an abstract or a concrete "Israel," so, too, an individual writer. How then does circumstance shape matters? System building forms a symbolic transaction, and, by definition, represents symbol change for the builders and their building. On the one hand, it is a social question that sets the terms and also the limits of the symbolic transaction, so symbol change responds to social change (at least for some). On the other hand, symbol change so endures as to impose a new shape upon a social world, as we can show was the case at Qumran for the Essenes and in the aftermath of Constantine for the Jews who then constituted "Israel." It follows that social change comes about through symbol change. How shall we account for the origin of a system? We can show correlation between a system and its circumstance, and, it must follow, between the internal logic of a system and the social givens in which the system flourishes. But correlation is not explanation. And the sources of explanation lie beyond the limits of cases, however many. The question facing system builders carries with it one set of givens, not some other, one urgent and ineluctable question, which, by definition, excludes others. The context of the system builders having framed the question before them, one set of issues, and not some other, issues of one type, rather than some other, predominate. Now to the cases at hand.

Matters in regard to Paul's and the Essenes' systems hardly require detailed specification. Paul's context told him that "Israel" constituted a categorical imperative, and it also told him what, about "Israel" he had to discover in his thought on the encounter with Christ. The Essenes of Qumran by choice isolated themselves and in that context determined upon the generative issue of describing an "Israel" that, all by itself in the wilderness, would survive and form the saving remnant.

Paul – all scholarship concurs – faced a social entity ("church" or "Christian community") made up of Jews but also gentiles, and (some) Jews expected people to obey the law, for example, to circumcise their sons. Given the natural course of lives, that was not a question to be long postponed, which imparts to it the acute, not merely chronic, character that it clearly displayed even in the earliest decade beyond Paul's vision.[38] And that fact in my judgment explains why, for Paul, circumcision formed a critical taxic indicator in a way in which, for Philo, for the Mishnah, and other Judaic systems, it did not.

The circumstance of the Essenes of Qumran is far better documented, since that community through its rereading of Scripture tells us that it originated in a break between its founder(s) and other officials. Consequently, my characterizing the Essenes of Qumran hardly moves beyond the evidence in hand. They responded to their own social circumstance, isolated and alone as it was, and formed a community unto itself, hence seeing their "Israel," the social entity of their system, as what there was left of Scripture's "Israel," that is, the remnant of Israel.[39]

---

[38] I am not equivalently clear on the crisis that provoked and defined Philo's program of stating in philosophical terms the Judaism he proposed to expound and defend. Scholarship generally concurs that he took as his task the labor of mediation, but whether or not we can characterize that program as a response to an urgent crisis I cannot say.

[39] That fact contrasts with the clear premise of the Mishnah's authorship that "Israel" meant "all the Jews," except, of course, for the exceptions. But in no detail do I find in any rabbinic document of late antiquity the conception that the "Israel" of whom the document speaks is the saving remnant, leaving out all non-believing or non-conforming Jews. Sages saw themselves as special within the context of a general society to be transformed in the image and after the likeness of sages. That is a totally opposite conception from the one that reads "us" as "all Israel," "all Israel" as "us," and omits everyone else. Paul's system, we note,

The sages of the Dual Torah made their documentary statements in reply to two critical questions, the one concerning sanctification, presented by the final failure of efforts to regain Jerusalem and restore the temple cult, the other concerning salvation, precipitated by the now unavoidable fact of Christianity's political triumph.[40]

Once each of the three Judaisms for which a precipitating (in my jargon, *systemopoieic*) crisis can be identified passes before us, we readily see how the consequent program flowed from the particular politically generative crisis.[41] The case of the sages in both phases in the unfolding of the Dual Torah is the obvious example of the interplay of context and contents. There we see with great clarify both the precipitating event and the logic of self-evidence out of which a system spun its categorical program. That program, correlated with the *systemopoieic* event, would then define all else. If sanctification is the issue imposed by events, then the Mishnah will ask a range of questions of detail, at each point providing an exegesis of the everyday in terms of the hermeneutics of the sacred: Israel as different and holy within the terms specified by Scripture. If salvation proves the paramount claim of a now successful rival within "Israel," then the authorship of Genesis Rabbah will ask the matriarchs and patriarchs to spell out the rules of salvation, so far as they provide not merely precedents but paradigms of salvation. The authorship of Leviticus Rabbah will seek in the picture of sanctification supplied by the book of Leviticus the rules and laws that govern the salvation of "Israel." The history of an "Israel" that is a political entity – family, sui generis, either, both, it hardly matters – will dictate for the authorship for which the Yerushalmi speaks a paramount category.

And yet an element of a priori choice proves blatant in the three systems upon which we have come to focus. And that matter of selectivity points toward symbol change as the prior, social change as the consequent, fact. That is to say, social change forms a necessary, but not sufficient, explanation. There is a simple fact that seems to me to validate that judgment. It is that many Jews confronted the social change to which the system builders responded in the way they did. But – by definition – only the system builders[42] reached the conclusions that they

---

entertained no such possibility, which was irrelevant to Philo's too. Clearly, one taxic classifier among Judaisms will be the character of the social entity of the system: inclusive or exclusive, in a variety of senses of those words.

[40]That is the argument of my *Judaism and Christianity in the Age of Constantine* (Chicago, 1987: University of Chicago Press).

[41]Once more, "political" stands for "pertaining to the *polis*, the corporate community."

[42]That is not to neglect those who responded to their judgment of the self-evident and the logical.

reached and composed the system that they created. There were other Jews who reached other conclusions (or none at all). Hence social crisis tells us the problem that engaged the system builders, but the character and structure of the crisis, viewed by itself, could not tell us the system that they would build.

Sages formed that group of Jews that identified the critical issue as that of sanctification, involving proper classification and ordering of all of the elements and components of Israel's reality. Not all Jews interpreted events within that framework, however, and it follows, circumstances by themselves did not govern. The symbol change worked for those for whom it worked, which, ultimately, changed the face of the Jews' society. But in the second and fourth centuries were Jews who found persuasive a different interpretation of events – whether the defeat of Bar Kokhba or the conversion of Constantine – and became Christian.[43]

Nor did all Christians concur with Paul that Jews and gentiles now formed a new social entity, another "Israel" than the familiar one; the same social circumstance that required Paul to design his system around "Israel" persuaded a later set of authorships to tell the story of Jesus's life and teachings, a story in which (as in the Mishnah's system) "Israel" formed a datum, a backdrop, but hardly the main focus of discourse or the precipitating consideration. It took a century for Paul's reading of matters to gain entry into the canon, and before Luther, Paul's system was absorbed and hardly paramount.

So, too, with the Essenes. Diverse groups in the age in which the Essenes of Qumran took shape and produced their library, hence the system expressed in their books, formed within the larger society of the Jews in the Land of Israel. And not all such smaller groups seized upon the option of regarding themselves as the whole of (surviving) "Israel." Many did not. One such group, the Pharisees, presents an important structural parallel, in its distinctive calculation of the holy calendar, in its provision of stages for entry into the group, in its interest in the rules of purity governing meals which realized, in a concrete communion, the social existence of the group, and in diverse other ways.[44] The Pharisees did not regard themselves as co-existent with "all Israel," even while they remained part of the everyday corporate community. They proposed to exemplify their rules in the streets and marketplaces and to

---

[43]We return to this matter presently.
[44]Indeed, the earliest debates on the identification of the sponsorship of the ancient library dug up at Qumran encompassed the position that the authors were Pharisees in particular. For an encompassing account of the matter, see Vermes, *Perspective*, pp. 116-136.

attain influence in the people at large. So merely forming what we now call a sect did not require a group to identify itself as "all Israel," as did the Essenes of Qumran.[45]

When we point to the correlation between problem and program, context and contents, we do not explain matters. We only beg the question. True, the system builders' social (including political) circumstance defines the generative problematic which imparts self-evidence to the systemically definitive logic, encompassing its social component. But that important point of correspondence cannot by itself account in the end for the particular foci and the generative problematic of a system. I claim that a single political problem, a crisis that we can identify and describe, persuaded one group of the self-evidence of a given set of cogent truths, which yielded, for an author or authorship, the materials of a systematic rereading of all things in light of some one thing – thus, the documents that form the canon of that system.[46] But that same circumstance did not impose upon another group in the same time, place, and situation, the same sense of the self-evidence of that system's matters identified as important and read in one way and not in some other. Paul had opposition within precisely the sort of groups that he identified as the center of interest: mixed groups of Jews and gentiles. Different groups responded in diverse ways to the same crisis, which is proved by the fact that diverse systems, reaching documentary expression in canons of varying contents, did emerge from the same circumstances and did appeal to precisely the same foundation document, the Hebrew Scriptures. Issues of the first century and the destruction of the temple, issues of the fourth and the conversion of the government of Rome to Christianity – these generated more than a single canon, as the history of the West testifies.

Since I have focused upon the Judaism of the Dual Torah, let me spell out the insufficiency of appeal to the precipitating circumstance in explaining the character of that system. Sages' Mishnah and Yerushalmi and related writings, at both of the two phases in their unfolding, solved the problem on which they focused for sages. But others did not necessarily concur on either the urgent question or the self-evident answer. To take one example, some Jews in the second century did conclude that "Judaism" was over. Justin's Trypho may typify these Jews, and, it may well be, among those who adopted the Gnostic way of seeing things and rejected both the Creator God and the Torah were Jews

---

[45]The utility of my proposed taxic indicator for systemic comparison is here illustrated.

[46]I underline the matter of canon because of what follows in the concluding section.

disgusted by the perfidy of destruction and disappointment.[47] To take another example, Avi-Yonah plausibly maintains that in the fourth and fifth centuries, Christians became the absolute majority of the population of the Land of Israel, and Jews formed a minority.[48] The political triumph of Christianity may have persuaded numbers of Jews that their ancestors had erred in rejecting Jesus as Christ the King of the world, as he now appeared to be. That that issue proved paramount I believe is a fact, and that in consequence, Jews did adopt Christianity and therefore rejected sages' explanation of matters seems to me a reasonable view of matters.[49]

Society and System

We cannot, in the end, explain the origin of Judaic systems. Stated in general terms, the issue is whether symbol change generates (for some) social change, or social change precipitates symbol change. In the setting of this argument, it is whether society sets the issue, which the system then works out, or whether the inner logic of the system dictates the proportions and order and logic, which, as a matter of fact, serves very well where and when it serves. But that impasse in finding the reason why need not impede our reaching one solid conclusion concerning systems and the symbolic transactions realized in them. *It is the priority of the social entity in systemic formation.*

Systems begin in the social entity, whether of two persons or two hundred or ten thousand – there, and not in their canonical writings, which come only afterward, or even in their politics. The social group, however formed, frames the system, the system then defines its canon within, and addresses the larger setting, the *polis* without. For our part, to be sure, we describe systems from their end products, the writings which are our sole entry. But we have then to work our way back from canon to system. We cannot be so deceived as to imagine either that the canon is the system, or that the canon creates the system. The canonical writings speak, in particular, to those who can hear, that is, to the

---

[47]In my *Judaism: The Evidence of the Mishnah* (Chicago, 1981: University of Chicago Press), pp. 37-43 I go over this matter. I know of no concrete evidence that Jews formed an important part in the Gnostic groups.

[48]See M. Avi Yonah, *The Jews of Palestine: A Political History from the Bar Kokhba War to the Arab Conquest* (New York, 1976: Oxford University Press, pp. 220ff., and my *Judaism in Society. The Evidence of the Yerushalmi. Toward the Natural History of a Religion* (Chicago, 1983: University of Chicago Press), pp. 9-23.

[49]But an account of sages' opposition as reflected in the polemics mounted by them must encompass, also, the Gnostic position that is the opposite of the recurrent points of emphasis of Genesis Rabbah's authorship's reading of creation. See my "Israel and Creation," *Journal for the Study of Judaism*.

members of the community, who, on account of that perspicacity of hearing, constitute the social entity or systemic community. The community then comprises that social group the system of which is recapitulated by the selected canon. The group's exegesis of the canon in terms of the everyday imparts to the system the power to sustain the community in a reciprocal and self-nourishing process. The community through its exegesis then imposes continuity and unity on whatever is in its canon.

While, therefore, we cannot account for the origin of a system, we can explain its power to persist. That power to persist derives from interchange and movement, like electricity from magnetism via a dynamo, specifically as a symbolic transaction. It is one in which social change comes to expression in symbol change. That symbolic transaction, specifically, takes place in its exegesis of the systemic canon, which, in literary terms, constitutes the social entity's statement of itself.[50] So, once more, the texts recapitulate the system. The system does not recapitulate the texts. The system comes before the texts and defines the canon. The exegesis of the canon then forms that ongoing social action that sustains the whole. A system does not recapitulate its texts, it selects and orders them, imputes to them as a whole cogency, one to the next, that their original authorships have not expressed in and through the parts. A system expresses through the composition formed of the documents its deepest logic, *and it also frames that just fit that, we have observed, joins system to circumstance.* The whole works its way out through exegesis, and the history of any religious system – that is to say, the history of religion writ small – is the exegesis of its exegesis. And the first rule of the exegesis of systems is the simplest, and the one with which I conclude: *the system does not recapitulate the canon. The canon recapitulates the system.*

The system forms a statement of a social entity, specifying its worldview and way of life in such a way that, to the participants in the system, the whole makes sound sense, beyond argument. So in the beginning are not words of inner and intrinsic affinity, but (as Philo would want us to say) the Word: the transitive logic, the system, all together, all at once, complete, whole, finished. Then the word awaits only that labor of exposition and articulation that the faithful, for centuries to come, will lavish at the altar of the faith. That is why, as Jonathan Z. Smith has said, the history of religion is the exegesis of exegesis.

---

[50] And that is why, of course, we have focused analysis upon the canonical evidences of the Judaism of the Dual Torah. The social facts outside, uncovered by archaeology, for one example, are systemically inert and uninteresting.

A religious system therefore presents a fact not of history but of immediacy, of the eternal, social present. The issue of why a system originates and survives, if it does, or fails, if it does, by itself proves impertinent to the analysis of a system. A system is like a language. A language forms an example of language if it produces communication through rules of syntax and verbal arrangement. That paradigm serves full well however many people speak the language, or however long the language serves. Two people (two hundred, ten thousand) who understand each other form a language community, even – or especially – if no one understands them. So, too, by definition religions address the living, constitute societies, frame and compose cultures. For however long, at whatever moment in historic time, a religious system always grows up in the perpetual present, an artifact of its day, whether today or a long-ago time. The only appropriate tense for a religious system is the present. A religious system always *is*, whatever it was, whatever it will be. Why so? Because its traits address a condition of humanity in society, a circumstance of an hour – however brief or protracted the hour and the circumstance.

When we ask that a religious composition speak to a society with a message of the *is* and the *ought* and with a meaning for the everyday, we focus on the power of that system to hold the whole together: the society the system addresses, the individuals who compose the society, the ordinary lives they lead, in ascending order of consequence. And that system then forms a whole and well composed structure. Yes, the structure stands somewhere, and, indeed, the place where it stands will secure for the system either an extended or an ephemeral span of life. But the system, for however long it lasts, serves. And that focus on the eternal present justifies my interest in analyzing why a system works (the urgent agenda of issues it successfully solves for those for whom it solves those problems) when it does, and why it ceases to work (loses self-evidence, is bereft of its Israel, for example) when it no longer works.[51] The phrase, the *history* of a *system*, presents us with an oxymoron. Systems endure in that eternal present that they create. They evoke precedent, they do not have a history. A system relates to context, but, as I have stressed, exists in an enduring moment (which, to be sure, changes all the time). We capture the system in a moment, the worm consumes it an hour later. That is the way of mortality, whether for us one by one, in all mortality, or for the works of humanity in society.

---

[51] I have performed this analysis in my *Death and Birth of Judaism. The Impact of Christianity, Secularism, and the Holocaust on Jewish Faith* (New York, 1987: Basic Books). These remarks paraphrase the meditation on systemic analysis that forms the appendix of that book.

10

God: Principle, Presence, Person, and Personality in the Formation of Judaism

The Mishnah's God of the Philosophers. God as Premise and as Presence

Philosophy is the queen of sciences, since all other disciplines of learning emerged from it. But it is also the most abstract and difficult to follow, and once we grasp how the Torah was set forth in philosophical modes of thought, everything else will prove rather easy by comparison. But the Mishnah, which states its share of the oral part of the Torah in a philosophical way, is the foundation document of the Oral Torah, and we naturally expect that it will state what we know about God in an intellectually rigorous and demanding way. And we are not going to be disappointed.

In the Mishnah – as in all other writings of Judaism – God is present not merely in details, when actually mentioned, but at the foundations. To characterize the encounter with God, whether intellectual or concrete and everyday, we must therefore pay attention not alone to passages that speak of God in some explicit way, but, even more so, to the fundamental givens on which all particular doctrines or stories of a document depend. What that fact means in the case of the Mishnah is simple. That great philosophical law code demonstrates over and over again that all things are one, complex things yield uniform and similar components, and, rightly understood, there is a hierarchy of being, to be discovered through the proper classification of all things. What this means is that, for the philosophers who wrote the Mishnah, the most important thing they wished to demonstrate about God is that God is one. And this they proposed to prove by showing, in a vast array of everyday circumstances, [1] the fundamental order and unity of all things, all being and [2] the unity of all things in an ascending order to God. So all things point through their unity and order to one thing, and all being derives from One God.

In the Mishnah, many things are placed into sequence and order – "hierarchized" – and the order of all things is shown to have a purpose, so that the order, or hierarchization, is purposive, or "teleological." The Mishnah time and again demonstrates these two contrary propositions: [1] many things join together by their nature into one thing, and [2] one thing yields many things. These propositions of course complement each other, because, in forming matched opposites, the two set forth an ontological judgment. It is that all things are not only orderly, but, in their deepest traits of being, so are ordered that many things fall into one classification, and one thing may hold together many things of a single classification. For this philosophy then rationality consists in the hierarchy of the order of things, a rationality tested and proved, time and again, by the possibility always of effecting the hierarchical classification of all things. The proposition that is the Mishnah's then is a theory of the right ordering of each thing in its classification (or taxon), all the categories (or taxa) in correct sequence, from least to greatest. And showing that all things can be ordered, and that all orders can be set into relationship with one another, we transform the ontological message into its components of proposition, argument, and demonstration.

The Mishnah's authorship's sustained effort therefore is to demonstrate how many classes of things – actions, relationships, circumstances, persons, places – really form one class. This work of classification then explores the potentialities of chaos – but that exploration is a journey en route to explicit order. It is classification transformed from the *how* of intellection to the *why* and the *what for* and, above all, the *what does it all mean* of philosophical conviction. And the goal is to show, through the very qualities of the natural and social world, that all things point to the plan and purpose of the one God, who so ordered creation as to reveal the divine plan for a well-ordered world: everything in its proper place, each with its rightful name, all things in the order in which, in six days, they were made.

Recognition that one thing may fall into several categories and many things into a single one comes to expression, for the authorship of the Mishnah in a simple way. The authorship shows over and over again that diversity in species or diversification in actions follows orderly lines, thus confirming the claim that there is that single point from which many lines come forth. Carried out in proper order [1] the many form one

God: Principle, Presence, Person, and Personality

thing, [2] one thing yields many, the demonstration then leaves no doubt as to the truth of the matter.

The upshot may be stated very simply. The species point to the genus, the classes to one class, all classes of things, or taxa, properly hierarchized then rise to the top of the structure and the system forming one taxon. So all things ascend to and reach one thing. All that remains is for the philosopher to define that one thing: God. But that is a step that the philosophers of the Mishnah did not take, at least, not in an articulated way. I assume that the reason was that they did not think they had to make such an obvious point. But I think there is a further, and different reason altogether. It is because, as a matter of fact, they were philosophers who were not theologians at all. The document they produced pursues issues of natural history, never working out a proposition of a theological character – not in a single line! And to philosophers while God serves as premise and principle, the system does not derive its generative problematic from that fact. It is not that on which the system builders propose to work.

By showing that all things can be ordered, and that all orders can be set into relationship with one another, we transform method into message. The message of hierarchical classification is that many things really form a single thing, the many species a single genus, the many genera an encompassing and well-crafted, cogent whole. Every time we speciate, we affirm that position; each successful labor of forming relationships among species, for example, making them into a genus, or identifying the hierarchy of the species, proves it again. Not only so, but when we can show that many things are really one, or that one thing yields many (the reverse and confirmation of the former), we say in a fresh way a single immutable truth, the one of this philosophy concerning the unity of all being in an orderly composition of all things within a single taxon.

To show how this works, I turn to a very brief sample of the Mishnah's authorship's sustained effort to demonstrate how many classes of things – actions, relationships, circumstances, persons, places – really form one class. This supererogatory work of classification then works its way through the potentialities of chaos to explicit order. It is classification transformed from the how of intellection to the why and the what for and, above all, the what does it all mean. Recognition that one thing may fall into several categories and many things into a single one comes to expression, for the authorship of the Mishnah, in diverse ways. One of the interesting ones is the analysis of the several taxa into which a single action may fall, with an account of the multiple consequences, for example, as to sanctions that are called into play, for a single action. The right taxonomy of persons, actions, and things will show the unity of all being by finding many things in one thing, and that forms the first of the two components of what I take to be the philosophy's teleology.

The two matched and complementary propositions – many things are one, one thing encompasses many – complement each other, because, in forming matched opposites, the two provide a single, complete and final judgment of the whole of being, social, natural, supernatural alike. Showing that all things can be ordered, and that all orders can be set into relationship with one another, we of course transform method into message. The message of hierarchical classification is that many things really form a single thing, the many species a single genus, the many genera an encompassing and well-crafted, cogent whole. Every time we speciate, we affirm that position. Each successful labor of forming relationships among species, for example, making them into a genus, or identifying the hierarchy of the species, proves it again. Not only so, but when we can show that many things are really one, or that one thing yields many (the reverse and confirmation of the former), we say in a fresh way a single immutable truth, the one of this philosophy concerning the unity of all being in an orderly composition of all things within a single taxon. Exegesis always is repetitive – and a sound exegesis of the systemic exegesis must then be equally so, everywhere explaining the same thing in the same way.

The sustained effort to demonstrate how many classes of things – actions, relationships, circumstances, persons, places – are demonstrated really to form one class bears implications for theology, but it is not a theological effort. The point is important nonteheless. Just as God, in creation, ordered all things, each in its class under its name, so in the Mishnah classification works its way through the potentialities of chaos to explicit order. As in the miracle of God's creation of the world in six days, here, too, is classification transformed from the *how* of intellection to the *why* and the *what for* and, above all, the *what-does-it-all-mean*.

The issue concerns nature, not supernature, and sorts out and sifts the everyday data of the here and the now. It will prove its points, therefore, by appeal to the palpable facts of creation, which everyone knows and can test. So recognition that one thing may fall into several categories and many things into a single one comes to expression, for the authorship of the Mishnah, in secular ways. One of the interesting ones is the analysis of the several taxa into which a single action may fall, with an account of the multiple consequences, for example, as to sanctions that are called into play, for a single action. The right taxonomy of persons, actions, and things will show the unity of all being by finding many things in one thing, and that forms the first of the two components of what I take to be the philosophy's teleology.

Mishnah-tractate Keritot 3:9

A. There is one who ploughs a single furrow and is liable on eight counts of violating a negative commandment:
B. [Specifically, it is] he who (1) ploughs with an ox and an ass (Deut. 22:10), which are (2,3) both Holy Things, in the case of (4) [ploughing] mixed seeds in a vineyard (Deut. 22:9), (5) in the Seventh Year (Lev. 25:4), (6) on a festival (Lev. 23:7) and who was both a (7) priest (Lev. 21:1) and (8) a Nazirite (Num. 6:6) [ploughing] in a graveyard.
C. Hanania b. Hakhinai says, "Also: He is [ploughing while] wearing a garment of diverse kinds" (Lev. 19:19, Deut. 22:11).
D. They said to him, "This is not within the same class."
E. He said to them, "Also the Nazir [B8] is not within the same class [as the other transgressions]."

Here is a case in which more than a single set of flogging is called for. B's felon is liable to 312 stripes, on the listed counts. The ox is sanctified to the altar, the ass to the Temple upkeep (B2,3). Hanania's contribution is rejected since it has nothing to do with ploughing, and sages' position is equally flawed. The main point, for our inquiry, is simple. The one action draws in its wake multiple consequences. Classifying a single thing as a mixture of many things then forms a part of the larger intellectual address to the nature of mixtures. But it yields a result that, in the analysis of an action, far transcends the metaphysical problem of mixtures, because it moves us toward the ontological solution of the unity of being.

So much for actions. How about substances? Can we say that diverse things, each in its own classification, form a single thing? Indeed so. Here is one example, among a great many candidates, taken from Mishnah-tractate Hallah. The tractate takes as its theme the dough-offering to which the framers assume Num. 15:17-21 refers: "of the first of your coarse meal you shall present a cake as an offering." The tractate deals with the definition of dough liable to the dough-offering, defining the bread, the process of separating dough-offering, and the liability of mixtures.

Mishnah-tractate Hallah 1:1

A. [Loaves of bread made from] five types [of grain] are subject to dough-offering:
B. (1) wheat, (2) barley, (3) spelt, (4) oats, and (5) rye;
C. lo, [loaves of bread made from] these [species] are subject to dough-offering,
D. and combine with each other [for the purpose of reckoning whether or not a batch of dough comprises the minimum volume subject to dough-offering (M. Hal. 1:4, 2:6, M. Ed. 1:2)].

E. And products of these species are forbidden for common use until Passover under the category of new produce [produce harvested before the waving of the first sheaf (Lev. 23:14)].
F. And grasses of these species may not be reaped until the reaping of the first sheaf.
G. And if they took root prior to the waving of the first sheaf, the waving of the first sheaf releases them for common use;
H. but if they did not take root prior to the waving of the omer, they are forbidden for common use until the next omer.

1:3

A. Grain in the following categories is liable to dough-offering when made into dough but exempt from tithes:
B. Gleanings, forgotten sheaves, produce in the corner of a field, that which has been abandoned, first tithe from which heave-offering of the tithe has been removed, second tithe, and that which is dedicated to the Temple which has been redeemed, the left over portion of grain which was harvested for the offering of the first sheaf, and grain which has not reached a third of its anticipated growth.
C. R. Eliezer says, "Grain which has not reached one-third of its growth is exempt from dough-offering when made into dough."

M. Hal. 1:1 addresses the issuing of whether or not five species of grain join together to produce dough of sufficient volume to incur liability to the dough-offering. Since they share in common the trait that they are capable of being leavened (*himus*), they do. So the genus encompasses all of the species, with the result that the classification process is neatly illustrated. "Joining together" or connection then forms a statement that these many things are one thing. M. 1:2 makes the same point about the five species. The interstitial cases at M. Hal. 1:3 are subject to ownership other than that of the farmer. But that fact does not change their status as to dough-offering. We take no account of the status with regard to ownership, past or present use as another type of offering, or the stage of growth of the grain whence the dough derives. This then forms the other side of the taxonomic labor: indicators that do not register distinguish. The upshot is as I said: many things are one thing; one rule applies to a variety of classes of grains.

The real interest in demonstrating the unity of being lies not in things but in abstractions, and, among abstractions, as we have already seen in other connections, types of actions take the centerstage. As before, I present in evidence not episodic compositions, but the better part of a complete composite, a tractate, which, I maintain, is formulated to address the issue of method that I deem critical. For that purpose I point to Mishnah-tractate Keritot, because its governing purpose is to work out how many things are really one thing. This is accomplished by showing that the end or consequence of diverse actions to be always one and the

God: Principle, Presence, Person, and Personality

same. The issue of the tractate is the definition of occasions on which one is obligated to bring a sin-offering and a suspensive guilt-offering. The tractate lists those sins that are classified together by the differentiating criterion of intention. If one deliberately commits those sins, he is punished through extirpation. If it is done inadvertently, he brings a sin-offering. In case of doubt as to whether or not a sin has been committed (hence: inadvertently), he brings a suspensive guilt-offering. Lev. 5:17-19 specifies that if one sins but does not know it, he brings a sin-offering or a guilt-offering. Then if he does, a different penalty is invoked, with the suspensive guilt-offering at stake as well. While we have a sustained exposition of implications of facts that Scripture has provided, the tractate also covers problems of classification of many things as one thing, in the form of a single sin-offering for multiple sins, and that problem fills the bulk of the tractate.

Mishnah-tractate Keritot 1:1
A. Thirty-six transgressions subject to extirpation are in the Torah....

1:2
A. For those [transgressions] are people liable, for deliberately doing them, to the punishment of extirpation,
B. and for accidentally doing them, to the bringing of a sin-offering,
C. and for not being certain of whether or not one has done them, to a suspensive guilt-offering [Lev. 5:17] –
D. "except for the one who imparts uncleanness to the sanctuary and its Holy Things,
E. "because he is subject to bringing a sliding scale-offering (Lev. 5:6-7, 11)," the words of R. Meir.
F. And sages say, "Also: [Except for] the one who blasphemes, as it is said, 'You shall have one law for him that does anything unwittingly' (Num. 15:29) – excluding the blasphemer, who does no concrete deed."

1:7
A. The woman who is subject to a doubt concerning [the appearance of] five fluxes,
B. or the one who is subject to a doubt concerning five miscarriages
C. brings a single offering.
D. And she [then is deemed clean so that she] eats animal sacrifices.
E. And the remainder [of the offerings, A, B] are not an obligation for her.
F. [If she is subject to] five confirmed miscarriages,
G. or five confirmed fluxes,
H. she brings a single offering.
I. And she eats animal sacrifices.
J. But the rest [of the offerings, the other four] remain as an obligation for her [to bring at some later time] –

K. M'SH S: A pair of birds in Jerusalem went up in price to a golden denar.
L. Said Rabban Simeon b. Gamaliel, "By this sanctuary! I shall not rest tonight until they shall be at [silver] denars."
M. He entered the court and taught [the following law]:
N. "The woman who is subject to five confirmed miscarriages [or] five confirmed fluxes brings a single offering.
O. "And she eats animal sacrifices.
P. "And the rest [of the offerings] do not remain as an obligation for her."
Q. And pairs of birds stood on that very day at a quarter-denar each [one one-hundredth of the former price].

3:2

A. [If] he ate [forbidden] fat and [again ate] fat in a single spell of inadvertence, he is liable only for a single sin-offering,
B. [If] he ate forbidden fat and blood and remnant and refuse [of an offering] in a single spell of inadvertence, he is liable for each and every one of them.
C. This rule is more strict in the case of many kinds [of forbidden food] than of one kind.
D. And more strict is the rule in [the case of] one kind than in many kinds:
E. For if he ate a half-olive's bulk and went and ate a half-olive's bulk of a single kind, he is liable.
F. [But if he ate two half-olive's bulks] of two [different] kinds, he is exempt.

3:4

A. There is he who carries out a single act of eating and is liable on its account for four sin-offerings and one guilt-offering:
B. An unclean [lay] person who ate (1) forbidden fat, and it was (2) remnant (3) of Holy Things, and (4) it was on the Day of Atonement.
C. R. Meir says, "If it was the Sabbath and he took it out [from one domain to another] in his mouth, he is liable [for another sin-offering]."
D. They said to him, "That is not of the same sort [of transgression of which we have spoken heretofore since it is not caused by eating (A)]."

M. Ker. 1:7 introduces the case of classifying several incidents within a single taxon, so that one incident encompasses a variety of cases and therefore one penalty or sanction covers a variety of instances. That same conception is much more amply set forth in Chapter Two. There we have lists of five who bring a single offering for many transgressions, five who bring a sliding scale-offering for many incidents, and the like, so M. 2:3-6. Then M. 3:1-3 we deal with diverse situations in which a man is accused of having eaten forbidden fat and therefore of owing a sin-offering. At M. 3:1 the issue is one of disjoined testimony. Do we treat as one the evidence of two witnesses. The debate concerns whether two cases form a single category. Sages hold that the case are hardly the same, because there are differentiating traits. M. 3:2-3 show us how we differentiate or unify several acts. We have several acts of transgression in a single spell of inadvertence; we classify them all as one action for purposes of the penalty. That at stake is the problem of classification and how we invoke diverse taxic indicators is shown vividly at M. 3:2 in particular. Along these same lines are the issues of M. Ker. 3:3, 4-6: "There is he who carries out a single act of eating and is liable on its account for four sin-offerings and one guilt-offering; there is he who carries out a single act of sexual intercourse and becomes liable on its account for six sin-offerings," with the first shown at M. 3:4.

Showing that many things are really of one kind because they produce a single consequence – the same offering – proves inadequate. The reason is that that mode of argument by appeal to outcome or consequence ignores the traits of things, which the Mishnah's system, so it seems, deems paramount. So the approach provides a demonstration that bears three negative traits. It is formal, not substantive. It is static, not dynamic, and so fails to deal with movement and change, which is where diversity takes place. And it addresses consequence, not essence; and that teleological proof leaves open the question of whether or not being as it is, not only as they are meant to be, really forms a unity. For proving (or, at least, illustrating) that proposition, which demands a far more important place in the philosophical program meaning to state the unity of ontology, we have to find a different sort of proof altogether. It is one that appeals – not surprisingly! – to processes of classification of things *as they are*, not as to their consequences but as to their essence or very being. And this draws us – as is our way – to ask whether there is a complete tractate that is devoted to showing the unity of *phenomenona*. And indeed there is, and an odd one at that. The survey of one of the strangest tractates in the Mishnah will show us how the intrinsic and inherent traits of things on their own prove the besought proposition.

The issue of how many things are one thing is spelled out in detail in Mishnah-tractate Negaim. This is not an easy tractate; it is a kind of geometry, very abstract conceptions being expressed in quite concrete notions. Mishnah-tractate Negaim takes up the issues of Leviticus Chapters Thirteen and Fourteen, the uncleanness and purification of those affected by *saraat*, often mistranslated "leprosy." The principle of the unity of phenomena is not made articulate, but it does serve throughout the document in all cases. This is done through classification and then the joining of taxa. And that fact shows us the teleology of the methods we have now identified as critical to the philosophical enterprise of Judaism, stating the proposition that is implicit in them.

Mishnah-tractate Negaim 1:1

A. The appearances of plagues are two, which are four:
B. (1) A bright spot is as bright white as snow. (2) And secondary to it is [a shade as white] as the lime of the Temple.
C. (3) "And the swelling is [as white] as the skin of an egg. (4) And secondary to it is [a shade as white] as white wool," the words of R. Meir.
D. And sages say, "(1) The swelling is [as white] as white wool. (2) Secondary to it is [a shade as white] as the skin of an egg."

1:2

A. "The [reddish] mixture which is in the snow-white is like wine mixed in snow.
B. "The [reddish] mixture in the lime is like the blood which is mixed in milk," the words of R. Ishmael.
C. R. Aqiba says, "The reddishness which is in this and in this is like wine mixed in water.
D. "But that which is in the snow-white is strong, and that which is in lime is duller than it."

1:3

A. These four appearances join together with one another – (1) to clear [of uncleanness], and (2) to certify [the sign to be unclean], and (3) to shut up [quarantine for a week]:
B. (3) To shut up: That which stands [unchanged] at the end of the first week.
C. (1) To declare clear: That which stands unchanged at the end of the second week.
D. (2) And to certify: That in which quick flesh or white hair appears,
E. (a) in the first instance, (b) at the end of the first week, (c) at the end of the second week, (d) after the clearance.
F. (2) To certify: That in which a spreading appears,
G. (a) at the end of the first week, (b) at the end of the second week, (c) after the clearance.
H. (2) To certify: That which turns entirely white (d) after the clearance.
I. To declare clear: That which turns entirely white after the certification or after the shutting up.
J. These are the appearances [colors of plagues, upon which all plagues depend].

M. Negaim 1:1-6 presents a systematic classification of colors and shades that, appearing upon the skin, signify that uncleanness is present, and, further, addresses the issue of how these shades join together to form the affected space requisite for imparting uncleanness. The four colors or shades of white signify the presence of the skin disease in particular; they join together and form a common mixture. There are, further, three stages of inspection, and when they take place, color and other matters are inspected to find out whether diseased skin signifies uncleanness. The joining together means that if a bit of skin is of one shade and an adjacent bit is of another, the two are regarded as a single bright spot. A vast amount of information is held together, and the principal issues of classification and mixture are imposed upon it. Unity among diverse data is gained through appeal to standard taxa, for example, Israel as against the nations, the classifications within Israel of the several castes.

This is accomplished in Chapter Three. M. 3:1 classifies those subject to being affected by the skin uncleanness and those suitable for examining it. In the former are all persons except gentiles and resident aliens, in the latter, all informed persons, with the priest in charge of stating the outcome. Another medium for unification of data, of course, is to show the simplicity of classifying extremely diverse phenomena. Formal traits – recurrent patterns – bear the substantive message, which is set forth with exceptional clarity.

Mishnah-tractate Negaim 3:3

A. The skin of the flesh is made unclean within two weeks and by three tokens: With white hair, and with quick flesh, and with spreading.
B. With white hair and with quick flesh –
C. in the beginning, or by the end of the first week, or by the end of the second week, after the [declaration of] clearance.
D. And by spreading –
E. at the end of the first week, and at the end of the second week, after the clearance.
F. And it is made unclean within two weeks –
G. which are thirteen days.

3:4

A. The boil and the burning are made unclean in one week and with two tokens: With white hair and spreading.
B. With white hair –
C. in the beginning, at the end of the first week, after the clearance.
D. And with spreading –
E. at the end of a week, after the clearance.
F. And they are made unclean within one week –
G. which are seven days.

M. Negaim 3:3-8 take up – in the model of the sample given here, which is repeated with great consistency throughout – the scriptural laws and organize them in a set of classifications of the following taxic indicators: specification of the form of the ailment; the period of time over which it is inspected; the signs of contamination that may occur. These items are then set forth with respect to the skin of the flesh, M. 3:3, the boil and burning, M. 3:4, bald spot on the forehead and on the back of the head, clothing, and houses. Once more a sizable body of diverse information is reorganized into well-formed classifications.

The other half of the matter – the differentiation within a unity, once demonstrated, follows in Mishnah-tractate Negaim Chapter Four. Here again we see the logical order in which a tractate investigates its topic. We first show unities, then differentiate within them. That underlines the polemic of the philosophy as a whole: everything is really one thing, even though one thing yields many things. One proposition without the other is simply incomplete. In the case at hand, once the taxic indicators have classified the various kinds of skin disease, the next step is to compare one species of the skin ailment to another, and this is accomplished at M. 4:1-3.

Mishnah-tractate Negaim 4:1

A. There are [strict rules applying] to white hair which do not [apply] to spreading, and there are [rules applying] to spreading which do not [apply] to white hair.
B. For white hair (1) renders unclean in the first [inspection], and (2) renders unclean in any appearance [shade] of whiteness, and (3) no token of cleanness applies to it.
C. There are [strict rules applying] to spreading, for the spreading (1) renders unclean in any size whatever, and (2) renders unclean in all plagues, (3) [though] outside the plague [itself], which is not the case for white hair [which must be encompassed by the bright spot] –

4:2

A. There are [strict rules applying] to the quick flesh which do not apply to spreading, and there are [rules applying] to spreading which do not [apply] to quick flesh.
B. For the quick flesh (1) renders unclean in the first [inspection], and (2) renders unclean in any appearance [color], and (3) no token of cleanness applies to it.
C. There are [rules applying] to spreading, for the spreading (1) renders unclean in any size whatever, and (2) renders unclean in all plagues, (3) [though] outside the plague, which is not the case with quick flesh.

The relationship between an indicator and the skin concerning which the indicator testifies is compared from item to item. We begin with the skin of the flesh, that is, the point at which we started, with M. 3:3, affected by three indicators, white hair, quick flesh, and spreading. Then the impact of the indicator over a sequence of inspections is worked out, and then strict rules applying to one indicator but not another are specified. How a more perfect mode of taxonomy and hierarchical classification can have been devised I simply do not know. The whole of Chapter Four (4:4-4:11) is captured at M. Negaim 4:5.

Mishnah-tractate Negaim 4:5

A. A bright spot the size of a split bean –
B. and a streak extends from it –
C. if there is in it [the streak] the breadth of two hairs,
D. it [the streak] subjects it [the bright spot] to [the restrictions in respect of] white hair and spreading, but not to [that in respect of] the quick flesh.
E. Two bright spots –
F. and a streak goes forth from one to the other –
G. if there is in it a breadth of two hairs,
H. it joins them together. And if not, it does not join them together.

The issue is whether a streak extending from a bright spot affects the bright spot. For example, if in the streak we have two white hairs, or if the spreading affects the streak but not the primary symptom, what is the rule? The answer is that if we have the stated breadth, sufficient for the growth of two hairs, the streak subjects the primary symptom to the restrictions which occur in the streak (which is then connected and through which a complete mixture is formed), and if not, it does not. The same point is made twice. Connection, classification – these yield a single point, that everything is subject to one coherent rule, and many things serve in their unity to demonstrate the essential unity of all things. That demonstration derives from the possibility of ordering many things in a single way.

However many times we construct problems for solution, theorems for demonstration, we return to that same point. How about humble things, simple matters – things that ordinary people can understand, in a way in which the remote abstractions of Mishnah-tractate Negaim cannot be visualized? Let us turn to the corpse and the diverse fluids and substances that the corpse yields. Here we see in the application of reason and the practical uses of logic the one and the many, the many and the one. The laws about tents at Num. 19:11-22 hold that if a corpse is located in a tent, whatever else is found underneath that same tent, even not touching the corpse, is contaminated by uncleanness produced by the corpse, which lasts for seven days and requires a purification rite.

Mishnah-tractate Ohalot 2:1

A. These contaminate in the Tent: (1) The corpse, and (2) an olive's bulk [of flesh] from the corpse, and (3) an olive's bulk of corpse dregs, and (4) a ladleful of corpse mould; (5) the backbone, and the skull, and (6) a limb from the corpse, and (7) a limb from the living person on which is an appropriate amount of flesh;
B. (8) a quarter-qab of bones from the larger part of the frame [of the skeleton] or (9) from the larger number; and (10) the larger part of the frame or (11) the larger number of the corpse, even though there is not among them a quarter-qab, are unclean.

C. How much is the "larger number"? One hundred twenty-five.

2:2

A. (12) A quarter-log of blood and (13) a quarter-log of mingled blood from a single corpse [render unclean in a Tent].
B. R. Aqiba says, "From two corpses."
C. The blood of a minor, all of which has exuded –
D. R. Aqiba says, "Any amount."
E. And sages say, "A quarter-log."
F. An olive's bulk of a worm whether living or dead –
G. R. Eliezer declares unclean like its flesh.
H. And sages declare clean.
I. The ash of burned people –
J. R. Eliezer says, "Its measure is a quarter-qab."
K. And sages declare clean.
L. A ladleful and a bit more of grave dirt is unclean.
M. R. Simeon declares clean.
N. A ladleful of corpse mould which one kneaded with water is not a connector for uncleanness.

On the surface the issue of M. Oh. 2:1-2 is the familiar one of mixtures and connection. But underneath the proposition is that many things are really one thing, producing a single consequence not in everyday action – a given mode of execution, for instance – but in the very nature of being, here, classification. The issue is whether two species of the genus, that which contaminates by reason of corpse uncleanness, join together to form the requisite volume for conveying uncleanness; whether two corpses may contribute to the formation of the requisite volume, and the like. Must the requisite blood derive from a single corpse, or may blood from two corpses combine, since they fall into a single taxon? There is no clearer way of raising the question of the relationship of species of the same genus than is precipitated by the odd categories at hand.

Can what was many things become one thing? Indeed so. The problem of M. 2:7 then is a special one: a bone the size of a barley corn which was divided into two parts; a quarter-qab of crushed bones, in any one of which there is not a bone the size of a barley corn – that is to say, connection and mixtures once more. More to the point, many things may be joined together by a common function or by being subject to a common function.

Mishnah-tractate Ohalot 3:6-7 provides an ideal demonstration of how in action being is made – shown to be – one. Let me explain what is going to happen here. M. Ohalot 3:6-7 work out the problem of how many things are one thing. At stake is how the tent functions to spread about uncleanness that is underneath it. On the surface the issue is the definition of the tent. But the operative question is how one tent relates

God: *Principle, Presence, Person, and Personality* 267

to another beyond itself, beside itself, or within itself. Scripture's rule is that a tent spreads corpse uncleanness. But a tent may also interpose and prevent the spread of corpse uncleanness. And then the issue is affording protection against corpse uncleanness or interposition; and that, in the end, is a question of whether we classify the tent as an autonomous and protected area or as an area that is joined with and part of a larger area. That is the basis for my judgment that at stake is the relationship of demarcated spaces, hence, spatial mixtures.

Mishnah-tractate Ohalot 3:6

A. An olive's bulk of a corpse – its opening is a handbreadth. And the corpse – its opening is four handbreadths.
B. To afford protection for the [other] openings against uncleanness.
C. But to give passage for the uncleanness [to go to an adjacent space], an opening of a handbreadth [suffices].
D. More than a handbreadth is like a corpse.
E. R. Yose says, "The backbone and the skull are like the corpse."

3:7

A. A cubic handbreadth introduces the uncleanness and interposes before the uncleanness.
B. How?
C. A drain which is arched under the house –
D. it is a handbreadth wide, and its outlet is a handbreadth wide –
E. uncleanness is in it –
F. the house is clean.
G. Uncleanness is in the house –
H. what is in it is clean,
I. for the way of the uncleanness is to exude, and it is not its way to seep in.
J. It is a handbreadth wide, and its outlet is not a handbreadth wide –
K. the uncleanness is in it –
L. the house is unclean.
M. Uncleanness is in the house.
N. What is in it is clean,
O. for it is the way of the uncleanness to exude, and it is not its way to seep.
P. It is not a handbreadth wide, and its outlet is not a handbreadth wide –
Q. uncleanness is in it –
R. the house is unclean.
S. Uncleanness is in the house –
T. what is in it is unclean.
U. All the same is the hole dug by water or insects, or which saltpetre has eaten through –
V. and so a row of stones, and so a pile of beams.
W. R. Judah says, "Any tent which is not made by man is no tent."
X. But he agrees concerning the clefts and overhanging rocks.

The general rule then assigns (as with Miqvaot) an area that permits the joining of two other ways distinct units of space: "'An olive's bulk of a corpse – its opening is a handbreadth. And the corpse – its opening is four handbreadths. To afford protection for the [other] openings against uncleanness. But to give passage for the uncleanness [to go to an adjacent space], an opening of a handbreadth [suffices]." That is, the specified areas of space serve to open two distinct spaces into one another or to close off two areas of space from one another.

So much for the impalpable and invisible realm of classification and status. There we can conjure, but cannot touch or feel or see, the lines of structure and division. Order is imputed and imagined. What about the visible world of space? Here we can frame a question that permits a highly tangible representation of the complexity of unity and diversity, the demonstration that one thing encompasses many things, so many things form one thing. The question is asked in this way: When is a field a field, and when is it two or ten fields? That taxonomic problem of how many are one, or how one is deemed many, is addressed at Mishnah-tractate Peah, which concerns itself with giving to the poor produce abandoned at the corner of a field. Then we have to know what constitutes a field, hence the question of when one thing is many things, or when many things are one thing, framed in terms of spatial relations:

Mishnah-tractate Peah 2:1

A. And these [landmarks] establish [the boundaries of a field] for [purposes of designating] peah:
B. (1) a river, (2) pond, (3) private road, (4) public road, (5) public path, (6) private path that is in use in the hot season and in the rainy season, (7) uncultivated land, (8) newly broken land, (9) and [an area sown with] a different [type of] seed.
C. "And [as regards] one who harvests young grain [for use as fodder – the area he harvests] establishes [the boundaries of a field]," the words of R. Meir.
D. But sages say, "[The area he harvests] does not establish [the boundaries of a field], unless he has also ploughed [the stubble] under."

2:5

A. One who sows his field with [only] one type [of seed], even if he harvests [the produce] in two lots
B. designates one [portion of produce as] peah [from the entire crop].
C. If he sowed [his field] with two types [of seeds], even if he harvests [the produce] in only one lot,
D. he designates two [separate portions of produce as] peah, [one from each type of produce].
E. He who sows his field with two types of wheat –
F. [if] he harvests [the wheat] in one lot, [he] designates one [portion of produce as] peah.

God: Principle, Presence, Person, and Personality 269

G. [But if he harvests the wheat in] two lots, [he] designates two [portions of produce as] peah.

3:5

A. [Two] brothers who divided [ownership of a field which previously they had jointly owned]
B. give two [separate portions of produce] as peah [each designates peah on behalf of the produce of his half of the field].
C. [If] they return to joint ownership [of the field]
D. [together] they designate one [portion of produce] as peah [on behalf of the entire field].
E. Two [men] who [jointly] purchased a tree [together] designate one [portion of produce] as peah [on behalf of the entire tree] –
F. But if one purchased the northern [half of the tree], and the other purchased the southern [half of the tree],
G. the former designates peah by himself, and the latter designates peah by himself.

The principle of division rests upon the farmer's attitude and actions toward a field. If the farmer harvests an area as a single entity, that action indicates his attitue or intentionality in regard to that area and serves to mark it as a field. For each patch of grain the householder reaps separately a peah share must be designated; the action indicates the intentionality to treat the area as a single field. But natural barriers intervene; rivers or hills also may mark off a fields boundaries, whatever the farmer's action and therefore a priori intentionality or attitude. So in classifying an area of ground as a field, there is an interplay between the givens of the physical traits and the attitude, confirmed by action, of the farmer.

If then many things become one thing, how about the one thing that yields the many? If we can show that a single classification may be *subdivided*, then the unity of the many in the one is demonstrated from a fresh angle. If so, the systemic contention concerning the fundamental and essential unity of all being finds reinforcement. That the question is faced may be shown, as usual in so coherent a piece of writing as the Mishnah, at a variety of passages. To take only a single instance, M. Makkot 3:5, 7-9 raise a question familiar to us from Mishnah-tractate Horayot: when are many actions classified as a single action, or a single action as many. But, more to the point, let us turn immediately to a very concrete reflection on the nature of actions and differentiating among them.

Mishnah-tractate Nazir 6:4

A. A Nazir who was drinking wine all day long is liable only on one count.

B. [If] they said to him, "Don't drink it!" "Don't drink it!" and he continues drinking, he is liable on each and every count [of drinking].
C. [If] he was cutting his hair all day long, he is liable only on a single count.
D. [If] they said to him, "Don't cut it!" "Don't cut it!" and he continued to cut his hair, he is liable for each and every count [of cutting].
E. [If] he was contracting corpse uncleanness all day long, he is liable on only one count.
F. If they said to him, "Don't contract corpse uncleanness!" "Don't contract corpse uncleanness!" and he continued to contract corpse uncleanness, he is liable for each and every count.

6:5

A. Three things are prohibited to a Nazir: [Corpse] uncleanness, cutting the hair, and anything which goes forth from the grapevine.
B. A more strict rule applies to corpse uncleanness and haircutting than applies to that which comes forth from the grapevine.
C. For corpse uncleanness and haircutting cause the loss of the days already observed, but [violating the prohibition against] that which goes forth from the vine does not cause the loss of the days already observed.
D. A more strict rule applies to that which goes forth from the vine than applies to corpse uncleanness and haircutting.
E. For that which goes forth from the vine allows for no exception, but corpse uncleanness and haircutting allow for exceptions,
F. in the case of [cutting the hair for] a religious duty and in the case of finding a neglected corpse [with no one else to provide for burial, in which case, the Nazir is absolutely required to bury the corpse].
G. A more strict rule applies to corpse uncleanness than to haircutting.
H. For corpse uncleanness causes the loss of all the days previously observed and imposes the liability for an offering.
I. But haircutting causes the loss of only thirty days and does not impose liability for an offering.

At M. Naz. 6:4 we take up the issue of disjoined actions, for each of which one is liable, when these actions are of a single species. What distinguishes one action from another, when all are of the same species, is that one is made aware each time he does the prohibited action that he is forbidden to do so. Then each action is individual. But if not, then all of the actions form a single sustained action, for which one is liable on only one count. This interesting conception then imposes upon the differentiation of actions the consideration of intentionality: the man now knows that the particular action he is about to undertake is prohibited. Hence it seems to me a case in which we invoke intentionality in the work of the classification of actions (=counts of culpability). What is at stake in the issue? It is the application of hierarchical classification, which as we know forms the goal of the philosophy's method of classification. So we see the unity of philosophical medium and

God: Principle, Presence, Person, and Personality

philosophical message. For M. Naz. 6:5 takes the facts of Scripture and forms of them a composition of hierarchical classification, in which the taxic indicators are laid out in accord with a single program.

I have repeatedly claimed that the recognition that one thing becomes many does not challenge the philosophy of the unity of all being, but confirms the main point. Why do I insist on that proposition? The reason is simple. If we can show that differentiation flows from within what is differentiated – that is, from the intrinsic or inherent traits of things – then we confirm that at the heart of things is a fundamental ontological being, single, cogent, simple, that is capable of diversification, yielding complexity and diversity. The upshot is to be stated with emphasis. *That diversity in species or diversification in actions follows orderly lines confirms the claim that there is that single point from which many lines come forth.* Carried out in proper order – [1] the many form one thing, and [2] one thing yields many – the demonstration then leaves no doubt as to the truth of the matter. Ideally, therefore, we shall argue from the simple to the complex, showing that the one yields the many, one thing, many things, two, four.

Mishnah-tractate Shabbat 1:1

A. [Acts of] transporting objects from one domain to another, [which violate] the Sabbath, (1) are two, which [indeed] are four [for one who is] inside, (2) and two which are four [for one who is] outside.
B. How so?
C. [If on the Sabbath] the beggar stands outside and the householder inside,
D. [and] the beggar stuck his hand inside and put [a beggar's bowl] into the hand of the householder,
E. or if he took [something] from inside it and brought it out,
F. the beggar is liable, the householder is exempt.
G. [If] the householder stuck his hand outside and put [something] into the hand of the beggar,
H. or if he took [something] from it and brought it inside,
I. the householder is liable, and the beggar is exempt.
J. [If] the beggar stuck his hand inside, and the householder took [something] from it,
K. or if [the householder] put something in it and he [the beggar] removed,
L. both of them are exempt.
M. [If] the householder put his hand outside and the beggar took [something] from it,
N. or if [the beggar] put something into it and [the householder] brought it back inside,
O. both of them are exempt.

M. Shab. 1:1 classifies diverse circumstances of transporting objects from private to public domain. The purpose is to assess the rules that classify as culpable or exempt from culpability diverse arrangements. The operative point is that a prohibited action is culpable only if one and the same person commits the whole of the violation of the law. If two or more people share in the single action, neither of them is subject to punishment. At stake therefore is the conception that one thing may be many things, and if that is the case, then culpability is not incurred by any one actor.

The consequence of showing that one thing is many things is set forth with great clarity in the consideration not of the actor but of the action. One class of actions is formed by those that violate the sanctity of the Sabbath. Do these form many subdivisions, and, if so, what difference does it make? Here is a famous passage that shows how a single class of actions yields multiple and complex speciation, while remaining one:

Mishnah-tractate Shabbat 7:1

A. A general rule did they state concerning the Sabbath:
B. Whoever forgets the basic principle of the Sabbath and performed many acts of labor on many different Sabbath days is liable only for a single sin-offering.
C. He who knows the principle of the Sabbath and performed many acts of labor on many different Sabbaths is liable for the violation of each and every Sabbath.
D. He who knows that it is the Sabbath and performed many acts of labor on many different Sabbaths is liable for the violation of each and every generative category of labor.
E. He who performs many acts of labor of a single type is liable only for a single sin-offering.

7:2

A. The generative categories of acts of labor [prohibited on the Sabbath] are forty less one:
B. (1) He who sews, (2) ploughs, (3) reaps, (4) binds sheaves, (5) threshes, (6) winnows, (7) selects [fit from unfit produce or crops], (8) grinds, (9) sifts, (10) kneads, (11) bakes;
C. (12) he who shears wool, (13) washes it, (14) beats it, (15) dyes it;
D. (16) spins, (17) weaves,
E. (18) makes two loops, (19) weaves two threads, (20) separates two threads;
F. (21) ties, (22) unties,
G. (23) sews two stitches, (24) tears in order to sew two stitches;
H. (25) he who traps a deer, (26) slaughters it, (27) flays it, (28) salts it, (29) cures its hide, (30) scrapes it, and (31) cuts it up;
I. (32) he who writes two letters, (33) erases two letters in order to write two letters;
J. (34) he who builds, (35) tears down;
K. (36) he who puts out a fire, (37) kindles a fire;

God: Principle, Presence, Person, and Personality

L. (38) he who hits with a hammer; (39) he who transports an object from one domain to another –

M. lo, these are the forty generative acts of labor less one.

Now we see how the fact that one thing yields many things confirms the philosophy of the unity of all being. For the many things all really are one thing, here, the intrusion into sacred time of actions that do not belong there. M. Shab. 7:1-2 presents a parallel to the discussion, in Mishnah-tractate Sanhedrin, of how many things can be shown to be one thing and to fall under a single rule, and how one thing may be shown to be many things and to invoke multiple consequences. It is that interest at M. 7:1 which accounts for the inclusion of M. 7:2, and the exposition of M. 7:2 occupies much of the tractate that follows. Accordingly, just as at Mishnah-tractate Sanhedrin the specification of the many and diverse sins or felonies that are penalized in a given way shows us how many things are one thing and then draws in its wake the specification of those many things, so here we find a similar exercise. It is one of classification, working in two ways, then: the power of a unifying taxon, the force of a differentiating and divisive one. The list of the acts of labor then gives us the categories of work, and performing any one of these constitutes a single action in violatiuon of the Sabbath.

How, exactly, do these things work themselves out? If one does not know that the Sabbath is incumbent upon him, then whatever he does falls into a single taxon. If he knows that the Sabbath exists and violates several Sabbath days in succession, what he does falls into another taxon. If one knows that the Sabbath exists in principle and violates it in diverse ways, for example, through different types of prohibited acts of labor, then many things become still more differentiated. The consideration throughout, then, is how to assess whether something is a single or multiple action as to the reckoning of the consequence.

I have repeatedly pointed to the philosophical unity of mode of argument, medium of expression, and fundamental proposition. In this connection let us turn back to our consideration of the rules of speciation. These form the methodological counterpart to the proposition that one thing yields many things. Here is the consequence, in the context of the exposition of the one and the many, of the rule of sub- and super-speciation:

Mishnah-tractate Shabbat 10:6

A. He who pares his fingernails with one another, or with his teeth,

B. so, too, [if he pulled out the hair of] his (1) head, (2) moustache, or (3) beard –

C. and so she who (1) dresses her hair, (2) puts on eye shadow, or (3) rouges her face –

D. R. Eliezer declares liable [for doing so on the Sabbath].

E. And sages prohibit [doing so] because of [the principle of] Sabbath rest.
F. He who picks [something] from a pot which has a hole [in the bottom] is liable.
G. [If he picks something from a pot] which has no hole [in the bottom], he is exempt.
H. And R. Simeon exempts him on this account and on that account.

The interest in the classification of acts of labor draws attention, at M. 10:6, to the lesson of superspeciation. We make a distinction between a derivative of the generative categories of prohibited acts, commission of which invokes a penalty, and an act which is not to be done by reason of the general principle of "Sabbath rest," but which is not culpable under the list of thirty-nine specifically prohibited acts of labor. From superspeciation – acts that cannot be speciated but that fall into the genus of prohibited deeds – we move, in Chapters Twelve through Sixteen, to the subspecies of the thirty-nine categories of prohibited acts of labor. Here we ask about the extent to which one must perform a prohibited act of labor in order to be subject to liability; Chapter Twelve addresses building, ploughing, writing; in Chapter Thirteen, we proceed to weaving and hunting (one who completes an action is liable, one who does not is exempt; one who does not intend by his action to violate the Sabbath is not liable and one who does intend to violate the Sabbath is liable; if two people together do a single act of prohibited labor, neither is liable); Chapter Fifteen moves on to knot tying; Chapter Sixteen, to saving things from the fire even though that involves moving objects across the boundary between private and public domain.

The Sabbath exposition appears so apt and perfect for the present proposition that readers may wonder whether the authorship of the Mishnah could accomplish that same wonder of concision of complex thought more than a single time. Joining rhetoric, logic, and specific (no longer general, methodological) proposition transforms thought into not merely expository prose but poetry. Have I given a proof consisting of one case? Quite to the contrary, the document contains a plethora of exercises of the same kind. My final demonstration of the power of speciation in demonstrating the opposite, namely, the generic unity of species and the hierarchy that orders them, derives from the treatment of oaths, to which we now turn. The basic topical program of Mishnah-tractate Shabuot responds systematically to the potpourri of subjects covered by Leviticus Chapters Five and Six within the (to the priestly author) unifying rubric of those who bring a guilt-offering. Lev. 5:1-6 concerns oaths, an oath of testimony, and one who touches something unclean in connection with the Temple cult, and finally, one who utters a rash oath.

Mishnah-tractate Shabuot 1:1

A. Oaths are of two sorts, which yield four subdivisions.
B. Awareness of [having sinned through] uncleanness is of two sorts, which yield four subdivisions.
C. Transportation [of objects from one domain to the other] on the Sabbath is of two sorts, which yield four subdivisions.
D. The symptoms of negas are of two sorts, which yield four subdivisions.

1:2

A. In any case in which there is awareness of uncleanness at the outset and awareness [of uncleanness] at the end but unawareness in the meantime – lo, this one is subject to bringing an offering of variable value.
B. [If] there is awareness [of uncleanness] at the outset but no apprehension [of uncleanness] at the end, a goat which [yields blood to be sprinkled] within [in the Holy of Holies], and the Day of Atonement suspend [the punishment],
C. until it will be made known to the person, so that he may bring an offering of variable value.

2:1

A. Awareness of uncleanness is of two sorts, which yield four subdivisions [M. 1:1B].
B. (1) [If] one was made unclean and knew about it, then the uncleanness left his mind, but he knew [that the food he had eaten was] Holy Things,
C. (2) the fact that the food he had eaten was Holy Things left his mind, but he knew about [his having contracted] uncleanness,
D. (3) both this and that left his mind, but he ate Holy Things without knowing it and after he ate them, he realized it –
E. lo, this one is liable to bring an offering of variable value.
F. (1) [If] he was made unclean and knew about it, and the uncleanness left his mind, but he remembered that he was in the sanctuary;
G. (2) the fact that he was in the sanctuary left his mind, but he remembered that he was unclean,
H. (3) both this and that left his mind, and he entered the sanctuary without realizing it, and then when he had left the sanctuary, he realized it – lo, this one is liable to bring an offering of variable value.

M. Shabuot 1:1-7, 2:1-5 accomplish the speciation of oaths, on the one side, and uncleanness in regard to the cult, on the other. That work of speciation then joins two utterly disparate subjects, oaths and uncleanness, so showing a unity of structure that forms a metaphysical argument for the systemic proposition on the unity of being. We do so in a way that is now to be predicted. It is by showing that many things are one thing, now, as I said, oaths, uncleanness. When the priestly author joined the same subjects, it was because a single offering was involved for diverse and distinct sins or crimes. When the Mishnaic author does, it is because a single inner structure sustains these same diverse and distinct sins or crimes. Comparing the priestly with the Mishnah's strategy of exposition underlines the remarkable shift accomplished by our philosophers. Their power of formulation – rhetoric, logic together – of course, works to demonstrate through the medium the message that these enormously diverse subjects in fact can be classified within a simple taxonomic principle. It is that there are two species to a genus, and two subspecies to each species, and these are readily determined by appeal to fixed taxic indicators. An abstract statement of the rule of classification (and, it must follow, also hierarchization) will have yielded less useful intellectual experience than the remarkably well balanced concrete exemplification of the rule, and that is precisely what we have in Mishnah-tractate Shabuot Chapters One and Two.

And that process of speciation and subspeciation is where the uniformity of oaths is established, with the consequence, given our starting point, that many things are really one thing, for, as we see at the outset, they come from one thing.

Mishnah-Tractate Shabuot 3:1

A. Oaths are of two sorts, which yield four subdivisions [M. 1:1A].
B. (1) "I swear I shall eat," and (2) "...I shall not eat,"
C. (3) "...that I ate," and (4) "...that I didn't eat."
D. "[If one said], 'I swear I won't eat,' and he ate anything [in any volume] whatsoever, he is liable," the words of R. Aqiba.
E. They said to R. Aqiba, "Where have we found that someone who eats anything in any negligible volume is liable, that this one should be deemed liable?"
F. Said to them R. Aqiba, "And where have we found that one who merely speaks has to bring an offering?"
G. "I swear that I won't eat," and he ate and drank – he is liable on only one count.
H. "I swear that I won't eat and drink," and he ate and drank – he is liable on two counts.

3:2

A. "I swear I won't eat" –
B. and he ate a piece of bread made of wheat, a piece of bread made of barley, and a piece of bread made of spelt, he is liable on one count only.
C. "I swear that I won't eat a piece of bread made of wheat, a piece of bread made of barley, and a piece of bread made of spelt," and he ate –
D. he is liable on each and every count.

3:8

A. What is a vain oath?
B. [If] one has taken an oath to differ from what is well known to people.
C. If he said (1) concerning a pillar of stone that it is made of gold,
D. (2) concerning a man that he is a woman,
E. (3) concerning a woman that she is a man –
F. [if] one has taken an oath concerning something which is impossible –
G. (1) "...If I did not see a camel flying in the air...,"
H. (2) "...If I did not see a snake as thick as the beam of an olive press...,"
I. (3) [If] he said to witnesses, "Come and bear witness of me,"
J. [and they said to him,] "We swear that we shall not bear witness for you" –
K. [if] he took an oath to nullify a commandment –
L. (1) not to build a sukkah, (2) not to take lulab and (3) not to put on phylacteries –
M. this is a vain oath,
N. on account of the deliberate making of which one is liable for flogging, and on account of the inadvertent making of which one is exempt [from all punishment] –

3:9

A. "I swear that I shall eat this loaf of bread," "I swear that I shall not eat it" –
B. the first statement is a rash oath, and the second is a vain oath.
C. [If] he ate it, he has violated a vain oath.
D. [If] he did not eat it, he has violated a rash oath.

3:11

A. [The law governing] a vain oath applies (1) to men and women, (2) to those who are not related and to those who are related, (3) to those who are suitable [to bear witness] and to those who are not suitable [to bear witness],
B. (4) before a court and not before a court.
C. (5) [But it must be stated] by a man out of his own mouth.
D. And they are liable for deliberately taking such an oath to flogging, and for inadvertently taking such an oath, one is exempt [from all punishment].
E. All the same are this oath and that oath:
F. he who was subjected to an oath by others is liable.
G. How so?
H. [If] one said, "I did not eat today, and I did not put on phylacteries today,"
I. [and his friend said,] "I impose an oath on you [that that is so],"
J. and he said, "Amen,"
K. he is liable.

The speciation and subspeciation of oaths occupies the rest of the tractate. Not only so, but we now find out what is at stake in the matter. It has to do with the number of counts for which one is liable, which is to say, the division of a given action or statement into its components and the identification of each completed action or statement, which is to say, the number of counts of liability. All of this is entirely familiar. It is the point at which we started. But here, that point emerges in the analysis of the language one has used in the oath at hand. Since one has taken one oath, there is one point of liability. But since he has in the oath specified two or more actions, he is liable for violating the oath as to each of those actions. Thus at Mishnah-tractate Shabuot 3:1ff., we have the speciation of oaths into four types, then the demonstration of the subspeciation of a given type by appeal to the language that is used. M. 3:1-6 go over oaths in general. M. 3:2 shows how one thing yields many things. M. 3:7-11 deals with the vain oath, differentiating that from the rash oath. These show us the model that is followed, with variations required by the subject matter, for the rest.

Once we reflect on the simple fact that nearly the whole of Mishnah-tractate Negaim and the entirety of Mishnah-tractate Shabuot perform precisely the same tasks in exactly the same way, we realize how fully and broadly our authorship has accomplished its philosophical goal. It has shown that any topic allows for the same demonstration of the same proposition in a single way, and that means everything really does fall into one simple pattern. The very diversity of the topical program of the Mishnah then forms on its own an argument in behalf of the philosophy's single proposition. For if one wants to show that many things are really one, and that one thing yields many things, the best way to do it is to show that you can say the same thing about many things – the more, the better.

To conclude: the species point to the genus, all classes to one class, all taxa properly hierarchized then rise to the top of the structure and the system forming one taxon. So all things ascend to, reach one thing. All that remains is for the theologian to define that one thing: God. But that is a step that the philosophers of the Mishnah did not take. Perhaps it was because they did not think they had to. But I think there is a different reason altogether. It is because, as a matter of fact, they were philosophers. And to philosophers, as I said at the outset, God serves as premise and principle (and whether or not it is one God or many gods, a unique being or a being that finds a place in a class of similar beings hardly is germane!), and philosophy serves not to demonstrate principles or to explore premises, but to analyze the unknown, to answer important questions.

In such an enterprise the premise, God, turns out to be merely instrumental, and the given principle, so to be merely interesting. But for philosophers, intellectuals, God can live not in the details, but in the unknowns, in the as-yet unsolved problem and the unresolved dilemma. So, I think, in the Mishnah, God lives, so to speak, in the excluded middle, is revealed in the interstitial case, is made known through the phenomena that form a single phenomenon, is perceived in the one that is many, is encountered in the many that are one. For that is the dimension of being – that, so I claim, immanental and sacramental dimension of being – that defines for this philosophy its statement of ultimate concern, its recurrent point of tension, its generative problematic. That then is the urgent question, the ineluctable and self-evidently truthful answer: God in the form, God in the order, God in the structure, God in the heights, God at the head of the great chain of well-ordered being, in its proper hierarchy. True, God is premise, scarcely mentioned. But it is because God's name does not have to be mentioned when the whole of the order of being says that name, and only that name, and always that name, the Name unspoken because it is always in the echo, the silent, thin voice, the numinous in all phenomena of relationship: the interstitial God of the Mishnah.

The Talmud of the Land of Israel's God in Person

Had Judaism emerged from the Mishnah, philosophers over the ages would have found themselves with an easy task in setting forth in a systematic and abstract way the doctrine of God and our relationship with God: the first principle, much like the unmoved mover of Greek philosophy, the premise, the presence, above all, the one who made the rules and keeps them in place. And in the context of tractate Abot, knowing God through the Torah is something that philosophers find a familiar task. But most people encounter the world in not mind alone but also heart and soul, in not the processes of thought primarily but mostly in things that happen, cannot have found the portrait of a presence and a principle entirely pertinent. And that philosophical God will have puzzled the faithful over time, who found in the Written Torah the commandment to "love the Lord your God with all your heart, with all your soul, and with all your might," a commandment not readily carried out in behalf of the unmoved mover, the principle and premise of being. Such a God as the philosophers set forth is to be affirmed and acknowledged, but by knowledge few are changed, and all one's love is not all that easily lavished on an abstract presence. When we come to the Talmud of the Land of Israel we meet God in both familiar, but also fresh representation.

In the writings of sages of the Land of Israel that reached closure at the end of the fourth and the beginning of the fifth century, the Talmud of the Land of Israel, a massive commentary to thirty-nine tractates of the sixty-three tractates of the Mishnah, brought to a conclusion at the end of the fourth century and beginning of the fifth, ca. 400 A.D., recast and enriched the received Oral Torah. This reconsideration and re-presentation of matters responded to a critical challenge. In the early part of the fourth century, the Roman emperor, Constantine, made Christianity a licit religion, and, by the end of that same century, Christianity, representing itself as the completion and fulfillment of ancient Israel's revelation and prophecies, had become the state religion of the Roman empire.

The symbolic system of Christianity, with Christ triumphant, with the cross as the now-regnant symbol, with the canon of Christianity now defined and recognized as authoritative, called forth from the sages of the Land of Israel a symbolic system strikingly responsive to the crisis. Our sages of blessed memory laid renewed stress upon three matters: [1] the coming of the Messiah set as the teleology of the system of Judaism as they defined that system, [2] the symbol of the Torah expanded to encompass the whole of human existence as the system laid forth the limns of that existence, [3] the canon of Sinai broadened to take account of the entirety of the sages' teachings, as much as of the Written Torah everyone acknowledged as authoritative. In that same context, the representation of God in man, God incarnate, in Jesus Christ, as the Christians saw him, found a powerful reply in the re-presentation of God as person, individual and active. God is no longer only, or mainly, the premise of all being, nor is God only or mainly the one who makes the rules and enforces them. God is now presented in the additional form of the one who makes decisions in the here and now of every day life, responding to the individual and his or her actions. Not only so, but the actions of an individual are treated one by one, in the specific context of the person, and not all together, in the general context of the social world overall. And, as we saw in the Mishnah, that is not the primary activity of God at all.

That God gave the Torah of course forms a premise of all discourse, but God's person or personality in giving the Torah is not set forth. So too, it is taken for granted that God, as ruler of all, assigned traits to this one or to that, for example, "The Holy One, blessed be He, gave to Israel three good qualities: modesty, kindness, and caring" (Y. San. 6:7.II.Z). Along these same lines, God, or Heaven, is responsible for sending rain, as in the following colloquy between a holy man, who can bring rain, and our sages:

God: Principle, Presence, Person, and Personality

He came down to them and asked, "Why have the rabbis troubled themselves to come here today?"

They said to him, "We want you to pray for rain."

He said to them, "Now do you really need my prayers? Heaven has already done its miracle."

Y. Ta. 1:4

Obviously, the premise is that God has done the miracle of making rain without the wonder-worker's intervention. But the passage does not invoke the presence or person of God in particular; it makes exactly the opposite point, that there is nothing distinctive about the event. Countless passages of such a character restate the simple fact that God forms the premise of all discourse in the Yerushalmi, as in the other writings of the canon of the Judaism of the Dual Torah.

But, overall, that fact does not yield a rich statement of God as premise. For instance, God's act of revealing the Torah is not augmented or amplified. Rather, we find the passive, for example, "All those forty days that Moses served on the mountain, he studied the Torah but forgot it. In the end it was given to him as a gift" (Y. Hor. 3:4.I.E). God of course not only gave the Torah but also enforced its laws. That premise of all discourse hardly has to be proven. Just punishment for sin, just reward for merit – these are ordinary facts of life under God's rule. God rules over land and sea, but we have no stories about God's doing so, in person, in any one case (cf., for example, Y. A.Z. 4:1.III.Hff.): "An earthly king rules only on dry land but not on the sea, but the Holy One...is not so. He is ruler by sea and ruler by land" (Y. A.Z. 4:1.III.L).

In the following passage, God serves as the origin of all great teachings, but as we have seen, that fact bears no consequences for the description of God as a person or personality:

E. "Given by one shepherd" –
F. Said the Holy One, blessed be He, "If you hear a teaching from an Israelite minor, and it gave pleasure to you, let it not be in your sight as if one has heard it from a minor, but as if one has heard it from an adult,
G. "and let it not be as if one has heard it from an adult, but as if one has heard it from a sage,
H. "and let it not be as if one has heard it from a sage, but as if one has heard it from a prophet,
I. "and let it not be as if one has heard it from a prophet, but as if one has heard it from the shepherd,
J. "and there is as a shepherd only Moses, in line with the following passage: 'Then he remembered the days of old, of Moses his servant. Where is he who brought out of the sea the shepherds of his flock? Where is he who put in the midst of them his holy Spirit?' (Isa. 63:11).

K. "It is not as if one has heard it from the shepherd but as if one has heard it from the Almighty."
L. "Given by one Shepherd" – and there is only One who is the Holy One, blessed be He, in line with that which you read in Scripture: "Hear, O Israel: the Lord our God is one Lord" (Deut. 6:4).

Y. San. 10:1.IX

In studying the Torah, sages and disciples clearly met the living God and recorded a direct encounter with and experience of God through the revealed word of God. But in a statement such as this, alluding to, but not clearly describing, what it means to hear the word of the Almighty, God at the end of the line simply forms the premise of revelation. There is no further effort at characterization. The exposition of the work of Creation (Y. Hag. 2:1.IIff.) refers to God's deeds, mainly by citing verses of Scripture, for example, "Then he made the snow: 'He casts forth his ice like morsels' (Ps. 147:17)," and so on. So, too, God has wants and desires, for example, what God wants is for Israel to repent, and which time God will save Israel (Y. Ta. 1:1X.U), but there is no effort to characterize God.

God is understood to establish a presence in the world. This is accomplished both through intermediaries such as a retinue or angels and also through the hypostatization of divine attributes, for example, the Holy Spirit, the Presence of Shekhinah, and the like. The Holy Spirit makes its appearance, for example, "They were delighted that their opinion proved to be the same as that of the Holy Spirit" (Y. Hor. 3:5.III.PP, Y. A.Z. 3:1.II.AA, etc.). God is understood to enjoy a retinue, a court (Y. San. 1:1IV.Q); God's seal is truth. These and similar statements restate the notion that God forms a living presence in the world. Heaven reaches decisions and conveys them to humankind through the working of chance, for example, a lottery:

> "To whoever turned up in his hand a slip marked 'Elder,'" he said, 'They have indeed chosen you in Heaven.' To whoever turned up in his hand a blank slip, he would say, 'What can I do for you? It is from Heaven.'"

Y. San. 1:4.V.FF-GG

The notion that the lottery conveys God's will, therefore represents God's presence in the decision making process, will not have surprised the authorship of the book of Esther. It is one way in which God's presence is given concrete form. Another, also supplied by Scripture, posited that God in the very Presence intervened in Israel's history, for example, at the Sea of Reeds:

> When the All-Merciful came forth to redeem Israel from Egypt, he did not send a messenger or an angel, but the Holy One, blessed be He, himself came forth, as it is said, "For I will pass through the Land of

God: Principle, Presence, Person, and Personality 283

> Egypt that night" (Ex. 12:12) – and not only so, but it was he and his entire retinue.
>
> Y. San. 2:1.III.O

The familiar idea that God's presence went into Exile with Israel recurrs (Y. Ta. 1:1.X.Eff.]. But I do not know of a single passage in the entire Yerushalmi in which it is claimed that God's personal presence at a historical event in the time of sages changed the course of events. The notion that God's presence remained in Exile leaves God without personality or even ample description.

Where God does take up a presence, it is not uncommonly a literary device, with no important narrative implications. For example, God is assumed to speak through any given verse of Scripture. Therefore the first person will be introduced in connection with citing such a verse, as at Y. San. 5:1.IV.E, "[God answers,] '"It was an act of love which I did...[citing a verse,] for I said, 'The world will be built upon merciful love'"' (Ps. 89:2)." Here since the cited verse has an "I," God is given a presence in the colloquy. But it is a mere formality. So, too, we may say that God has made such and such a statement, which serves not to characterize God but only to supply an attribution for an opinion:

> It is written, "These are the words of the letter which Jeremiah...sent from Jerusalem to the rest of the elders of the exiles" (Jer. 29:1).
>
> Said the Holy One, blessed be He, "The elders of the exile are valuable to me. Yet more beloved to me is the smallest circle which is located in the Land of Israel than a great sanhedrin located outside of the Land."
>
> Y. Ned. 6:9.III.CCCCf.

All we have here is a paraphrase and restatement of the cited verse.

Where actions are attributed to God, we have of course to recognize God's presence in context, for example, "The Holy One, blessed be He, kept to himself [and did not announce] the reward that is coming to those who carry out their religious duties, so that they should do them in true faith [without expecting a reward]" (Y. Qid. 1:7.IX.B). But such a statement hardly constitutes evidence that God is present and active in a given circumstance. It rather forms into a personal statement the principle that one should do religious duties for the right motive, not expecting a reward – a view we found commonplace in tractate Abot. So, too, statements of God's action carry slight characterization, for example, "Even if 999 aspects of the argument of an angel incline against someone, but a single aspect of the case of that angel argues in favor, the Holy One...still inclines the scales in favor of the accused" (Y. Qid. 1:9.II.S). It remains to observe that when we find in the Yerushalmi a sizable narrative of intensely important events, such as the destruction of

Betar in the time of Bar Kokhba (Y. Ta. 4:5.Xff.), God scarcely appears except, again, as premise and source of all that happens. There is no characterization, nor even the claim that God intervened in some direct and immediate way, though I do not believe we can imagine anyone thought otherwise. That simple affirmation reaches expression, for instance, in the observation, in connection with the destruction of the Temple, "It appears that the Holy One, blessed be He, wants to exact from our hand vengeance for his blood" (Y. Ta. 4:5.XIV.Q). That sort of intrusion hardly suggests a vivid presence of God as part of the narrative scheme, let alone a characterization of God as person.

Sages in the Yerushalmi may have made up conversations between biblical heroes and God, but when it came to their own day, such conversations took the form of prayers. As to the former:

> At that very moment, David said to the Holy One, blessed be He, "Master of the Universe, shall your presence descend upon the earth? May your presence rise up from among them!..." [David is urging God to remain over the earth and not among gossipmongers on earth.]
> Y. Pe. 1:1.XXV.C
> (trans. by Roger Brooks)

In this case, a conversation between God and David is made up; I cannot point in the Yerushalmi to equivalent conversations involving sages.

But of course God does occur as a "you" throughout the Yerushalmi, most commonly, of course, in a liturgical setting. As in the earlier documents of the oral part of the Torah, so in the Yerushalmi, we have a broad range of prayers to God as "you," illustrated by the following:

> R. Ba bar Zabeda in the name of Rab: "[The congregation says this prayer in an undertone:] 'We give thanks to you, for we must praise your name. "My lips will shout for joy when I sing praises to you, my soul also which you have rescued" (Ps. 71:23). Blessed are you, Lord, God of praises.'"
> Y. Ber. 1:4.VIII.D
> (trans. by Tzvee Zahavy)

Since the formula of the blessing invokes "you," we find nothing surprising in the liturgical person imagined by the framers of various prayers. God's ad hoc intervention, as an active and participating personality, in specific situations is treated as more or less a formality, in that the rules are given and will come into play without ordinarily requiring God to join in a given transaction:

> When one enters the study hall, what does he say? "May it be your will, Lord my God, God of my fathers, that I shall not be angry with my colleagues and they not be angry with me; that we not declare what is clean to be unclean and vice versa; that we not declare what is permitted

God: Principle, Presence, Person, and Personality

to be forbidden and vice versa; lest I find myself put to shame in this world and in the world to come."

Y. Ber. 4:2.I.Aff.
(trans. by Tzvee Zahavy)

Here we see yet another fine instance in which God is a "you," but in which that "you" does not intervene in a particular case or engage in a concrete and ad hoc transaction. "May it be your will...," a standard liturgical formula, never is followed by a tale showing how, on a specific occasion, God showed that that was, indeed, the divine will (or the opposite). God was encountered as a very real presence, actively listening to prayers, as in the following:

> See how high the Holy One, blessed be He, is above his world. Yet a person can enter a synagogue, stand behind a pillar, and pray in an undertone, and the Holy One, blessed be He, hears his prayers, as it says, "Hannah was speaking in her heart; only her lips moved, and her voice was not heard" (1 Sam. 1:13). Yet the Holy One, blessed be He, heard her prayer.

Y. Ber. 9:1.VII.E

When, however, we distinguish God as person, "you," from God as a well-portrayed active personality, liturgical formulas give a fine instance of the one side of the distinction. In the Yerushalmi's sizable corpus of such prayers, individual and community alike, we never find testimony to a material change in God's decision in a case based on setting aside known rules in favor of an episodic act of intervention, and, it follows, thought on God as person remains continuous with what has gone before. Sages, like everyone else in Israel, believed that God hears and answers prayer. But that belief did not require them to preserve stories about specific instances in which the rules of hearing and answering prayer attested to a particular trait of personality or character to be imputed to God. A specific episode or incident never served to highlight the characterization of divinity in one way, rather than in some other, in a manner parallel to Scripture's authorships' use of stories to portray God as a sharply etched personality.

For yet another example of God as person in a liturgical passage, Y. Ta. 2:1I.G-H (among many instances) uses the imperative: "[They sound the horns] as if to say, 'Consider us as if we cry like a beast before you.'" But in the personification of God, referred to in context as "Lord of the world," we find very few sustained conversations, in which God takes an active role in discourse. An example of the essentially passive character of god as "you" is in the following:

> R. Simeon b. Yohai taught, "The book of Deuteronomy went up and spread itself out before the Holy One, blessed be He, saying before him, 'Lord of the world! You have written in your Torah that any covenant,

part of which is null is wholly nullified. Now lo, Solomon wishes to uproot a Y of mine.' Said to him the Holy One, blessed be He, 'Solomon and a thousand like him will be null, but not one word of yours will be nullified.'"

Y. San. 2:6.II.AA-DD

Here as commonly is the case, the depiction of God follows the logic of the story. God has no particular traits imputed by the narrative, rather serving as a conversation partner for the book of Deuteronomy. Still, God is portrayed as a person, not merely a presence.

One aspect of personhood is capacity to carry out deeds, and, it goes without saying, in the document at hand God is represented as doing things, past, present, and future, for example:

> R. Berekhiah in the name of R. Abba bar Kahan: "In the future, the Holy One, blessed be He, is going to set the place of the righteous closer to his throne than the place of the ministering angels. The ministering angels will ask them and say to them, 'What has God wrought?' (Num. 23:23). That is, what did the Holy One, blessed be He, teach you?"
>
> Said R. Levi bar Hayyuta, "Did he not do so in this world?..."
>
> Y. Shab. 6:9.II.HH-II

God's doing this or that forms part of a larger portrait of God as a person capable of carrying out purposive deeds. When, presently, we meet God as a fully etched personality, God will be shown to do the deeds human beings do in the way that human beings do them. At this point, by contrast, even a very long catalogue of the great deeds of God cannot yield much of a picture of God as a "you," a person people may know and love.

Not only so, but the representation in the Yerushalmi of God as a person does not fully work out the potential of a given subject that invites it. For example, God is angry – so Scripture says – on account of idolatry. Yet in the Yerushalmi's exposition of the pertinent chapters of Abodah Zarah, for example, Chapters Three ff., I find not a single story of God's anger embodied in a picture of God as a person, let alone as a personality. The matter is left as a prevailing attitude or principle. When God does appear, it is as an essentially passive participant, for example, the conversation partner who asks, "Why?" or who confirms what the protagonist proposes, as in the following:

> I. But the Holy One, blessed be He, said to Elijah, "This Hiel is a great man. Go and see him [because his sons have died]."
> J. He said to him, "I am not going to see him."
> K. He said to him, "Why?"
> L. He said to him, "For if I go and they say things which will outrage you, I shall not be able to bear it."

God: Principle, Presence, Person, and Personality 287

> M. He said to him, "Then if they say things which outrage me, whatever you decree against them I shall carry out."
>
> Y. San. 10:2.III

Here God is person and not abstract principle or premise, but not a vividly etched personality. The conversation consists of an exchange of conventional theological positions, not a transaction between two distinctive personalities, each entering into a one-time exchange with the other. Another example of the same phenomenon is as follows:

> O. It is written, "Then the word of the Lord came to Isaiah: 'Go and say to Hezekiah, "Thus says the Lord, the God of David your father: I have heard your prayer, I have seen your tears; behold I will add fifteen years to your life"'" (Isa. 38:4-5).
> P. [Isaiah] said to him, "Thus I've already told him, and how thus do I say to him?
> Q. "He is a man occupied with great affairs, and he will not believe me."
> R. [God] said to him, "He is a very humble man, and he will believe you. And not only so, but as yet the rumor has not yet gone forth in the city."
> S. "And before Isaiah had gone out of the middle court, [the word of the Lord came to him]" (2 Kgs. 20:4).
>
> Y. San. 10:2.VI

Here once again God is a mere conversation partner, a straight-man once more, pointing to facts already established in context and not doing more than moving the narrative along by word or deed. When God serves as the protagonist of a story and leads the conversation, and when God's part in the conversation is particular to that context and not simply the proclamation of well-known theological principles, then we shall meet God as a fully spelled out and individual personality: divinity in the form of humanity. But it is not in the present compilation, so far as I have been able to discover. Yet another case is in the same context:

> Q. Now all the ministering angels went and closed the windows, so that the prayer of Manasseh should not reach upward to the Holy One, blessed be He.
> R. The ministering angels were saying before the Holy One, blessed be He, "Lord of the world, a man who worshipped idols and put up an image in the Temple – are you going to accept him back as a penitent?"
> S. He said to them, "If I do not accept him back as a penitent, lo, I shall lock the door before all penitents."
> T. What did the Holy One, blessed be He, do? He made an opening [through the heavens] under his throne of glory and listened to his supplication.
> U. That is in line with the following verse of Scripture: "He prayed to him, and God received his entreaty ('TR) and heard his supplication

and brought him again [to Jerusalem into his kingdom]. [Then Manasseh knew that the Lord was God]" (2 Chr. 33:13).

Y. San. 10:2.VII

Here we have a more concrete characterization of a deed done by God, which shows God's character as merciful. Yet another passage that shows the same tendency is as follows:

> Said R. Phineas, "'Good and upright is the Lord. Therefore he instructs sinners in the way' (Ps. 25:8). Why is he good? Because he is upright. And why upright? Because he is good. 'Therefore he instructs sinners in the way' by teaching them the way to repentance."
>
> They asked Wisdom, "As to a sinner, what is his punishment?"
>
> She said to them, "Evil pursues the evil" (Prov. 13:21).
>
> They asked prophecy, "As to a sinner, what is his punishment?"
>
> She said to them, "The soul that sins shall die" (Ezek. 18:20).
>
> They asked the Holy One, blessed be He, "As to a sinner, what is his punishment?"
>
> He said to them, "Let the sinner repent, and his sin will be forgiven for him,' as it is said, 'Therefore he instructs sinners in the way' (Ps. 25:8). He shows sinners the way to repentance."
>
> Y. Mak. 2:6.IV

This is a further excellent example of how God as person represents a mere hypostatization, without concrete and particular traits. When God is represented as a "you," it turns out (thus far) to form a mere formality of rhetoric.

Imputing thoughts or public statements to God therefore does not much change the picture, as in the following:

> Said R. Levi, "What is the meaning of slow to 'anger'?
>
> "The matter may be compared to a king who had two tough legions. He said, 'If they live here with me in the capital, of the city-folk anger me, they will immediately put them down with brute force. I shall send them a long way away, so that if the city folk anger me, while I am yet summoning the legions, the people will appease me and I shall accept their plea.'
>
> "Likewise, the Holy One, blessed be He, said, 'Anger and wrath are angels of destruction. Lo, I shall send them a long way away, and if Israel angers me, while I am summoning and bringing them to me, Israel will repent and I shall accept their repentance.'"
>
> Y. Ta. 2:1.XI.I-K

God may further serve as an active voice, but only in the paraphrase of an available verse of Scripture, as in the following:

> Said R. Judah b. Pazzi, "[God said,] 'That [dew] which I gave as a bequest which may be nullified to Abraham, I give [to his descendants

God: Principle, Presence, Person, and Personality

> as a gift which can never be nullified], "May God give you of the dew of heaven" (Gen. 27:28.'"
>
> Y. Ber. 5:2.I.D

Here we have assigned to God simply an amplification of the cited verse of Scripture. Yet another case in which God speaks without emerging as a well-etched personality is the following:

> Said R. Samuel bar Nahman, "Said the Holy One, blessed be He, to David, 'David, I shall count out for your a full complement of days. I shall not give you less than the full number. Will Solomon, your son, not build the Temple in order to offer sacrifices in it? But more pious to me are the just and righteous deeds which you do than the offerings which will be made in the Temple'"
>
> Y. Sheq. 2:6.VI.D

Numerous examples will not vastly change the picture. God is represented as a person, but not as much of a personality. God's rulings, rather than God's attitudes or emotions or deeds in a concrete narrative, are simply restated in dialogue form. That establishes God as a person, but does not then provide a rich characterization at all.

While God makes a statement in the first person, in fact it is nothing more than a restatement of the point of the parable and does not, therefore, constitute a characterization of God in some particular framework. The reason I think so is that if the storyteller had spoken in the third person, that is, instead of "I," using simply "the Holy One," in no way would the course of the story have shifted. The point of the story lies in imputing to the divinity the trait of patience, not in describing a patient personality in some particular framework. Not only so, but even when parables are drawn, they commonly illustrate principles or traits, rather than serving to characterize a highly individual personality. For example, in the following parable, God is shown to be more loyal as a patron than a human counterpart. But this turns out merely to illustrate a point Scripture has made and hardly serves to etch in words a vivid personality:

> R. Yudan in the name of R. Isaac gave four discourses: "A person had a human patron. One day they came and told the patron, 'A member of your household has been arrested.'
>
> "He said to them, 'Let me take his place.'
>
> "They said to him, 'Lo, he is already going out to trial.'
>
> "He said to them, 'Let me take his place.'
>
> "They said to him, 'Lo, he is going to be hanged.'
>
> "Now where is he, and where his patron?

> "But the Holy One, blessed be He, [will save his subjects just as he] saved Moses from the sword of Pharaoh. This is in accord with what is written, 'He delivered me from the sword of Pharaoh' (Ex. 18:4)."
>
> Y. Ber. 9:1.VIII.B-C
> (trans. by Tzvee Zahavy)

The passage goes through a sequence of examples deriving from Scripture of the same fact, namely, God's personal salvation of the saints. God is further portrayed as loyal and humble, identifying with Israel even in their poverty, ignorance, and humiliation (Y. Ber. 9:1.XI, for one important example). But at no point in the exposition do we find either an immediate case, deriving from sages' own time, or, more to the point, a clear characterization of God in specific and vivid terms. God acts, as Scripture has made clear, and evidence of God's will and person all derive from Scripture. For instance, while everyone believed God answers prayers, where evidence of that fact is adduced, it is from Scripture's cases:

> Said R. Judah b. Pazzi, "Even if a woman in labor is already seated in the delivery chair, God can change the sex of the foetus, in accord with the verse, 'Behold like clay in the hand of the potter, so you are in my hand, O house of Israel' (Jer. 18:6)."
>
> Rabbi in the name of the house of Yannai: "Originally Dinah was a male. After Rachel prayed, she was changed into a female. So it says, 'Afterwards she bore a daughter and called her Dinah' (Gen. 30:21). It was after Rachel prayed that Dinah was changed into a female."
>
> Y. Ber. 9:3.VI.B-C
> (trans. by Tzvee Zahavy)

The evidence is then expounded wholly within the framework of principles established by biblical facts, without a further effort to transform these facts into the portrait of a living personality. God emerges as a person, vital and alive in the life of Israel, but in no way incarnate in everyday encounters, stories of a personality people might know and engage in conversation.

Now that we have surveyed familiar territory, let us stand back and examine matters from a different perspective altogether. When we asked about the Mishnah's presentation of God, we began with not specific statements but a general question concerning the character of the document as a whole: What do the authors of the Mishnah propose to say over and over again? And the answer to that question, that many things resolve into one thing, and that from one thing emanate many things, showed us what the Mishnah says about God everywhere and throughout, mostly when it is not speaking about God at all. So can we now ask the same question: What is principal in the Judaic world of the Talmud of the Land of Israel, and can that fundamental and pervasive conception guide us to a deeper insight into the Yerushalmi's representation of God?

The answer to that question is contained in a single word, *zekhut*, which refers to our capacity for uncoerced action, and the result of God's response to that uncoerced action of ours. That category, which on the face of it refers to moral conduct, in fact formed the foundation for the Yerushalmi's conception of political economy for the social order of Israel. It defined economics and politics – an economics and a politics that made powerlessness into power, disinheritance into wealth. The structure of Israel's political economy therefore rested upon divine respone to acts of will consisting of submission, on one's own, to the will of Heaven; these acts, as we shall see, endowed Israel with a lien and entitlement upon Heaven. What we cannot by will impose, we can by will evoke. What we cannot accomplish through coercion, we can achieve through submission. God will do for us what we cannot do for ourselves, when we do for God what God cannot make us do. In a wholly concrete and tangible sense, love God with all the heart, the soul, the might, we have. God then stands above the rules of the created world, because God will respond not to what we do in conformity to the rules alone, but also to what we do beyond the requirement of the rules. God is above the rules, and we can gain a response from God when, on some one, unique occasion, we, too, do more than obey – but love, spontaneously and all at once, with the whole of our being. That is the conception of God that *zekhut*, as a conception of power in Heaven and power in humanity, contains. In the relationship between God and humanity expressed in the conception of *zekhut*, we finally reach the understanding of what the Torah means when it tells us that we are in God's image and after God's likeness: we are then, "in our image," the very mirror image of God. What can that possibly mean? And what can that tell us about God?

From Rule to Exception: God Makes Choices

The systemic statement made by the usages of *zekhut* speaks of relationship, function, the interplay of humanity and God. One's store of *zekhut* derives from a relationship, that is, from one's forebears. That is one dimension of the relationships in which one stands. *Zekhut* also forms a measure of one's own relationship with Heaven, as the power of one person, but not another, to pray and so bring rain attests. What sort of relationship does *zekhut*, as the opposite of sin, then posit? It is not one of coercion, for Heaven cannot force us to do those types of deeds that yield *zekhut*, and that, story after story suggests, is the definition of a deed that generates *zekhut:* doing what we ought to do but do not have to do. But then, we cannot coerce Heaven to do what we want done either, for example, by carrying out the commandments. These are obligatory, but do not obligate Heaven.[1]

Whence then our lien on Heaven? It is through deeds of a supererogatory character – to which Heaven responds by deeds of a supererogatory character: supernatural favor to this one, who through deeds of ingratiation of the other or self-abnegation or restraint exhibits the attitude that in Heaven precipitates a counterpart attitude, hence generating *zekhut*. The simple fact that rabbis cannot pray and bring rain, but a simple ass driver can, tells the whole story. The relationship measured by *zekhut* – Heaven's response by an act of uncoerced favor to a person's uncoerced gift, for example, act of gentility, restraint, or self-abnegation – contains an element of unpredictability for which appeal to the *zekhut* inherited from ancestors accounts. So while I cannot coerce heaven, I can through *zekhut* gain acts of favor from Heaven, and that is by doing what Heaven cannot require of me.

This is what it means to love God with all one's heart, soul and mind, but it also tells us what they understand God to be. For Heaven then responds to my attitude in carrying out my duties – and more than my duties. That act of pure disinterest – giving the woman my means of livelihood – is the one that gains for me Heaven's deepest interest. And what that tells us about God is that our God is a God of love, and love is always specific, and love is never bound by rules. That is what makes love love. *Zekhut* is the power of the powerless, the riches of the disinherited, the Valuation and valorization of the will of those who have no right to will. What has this to do with God? These – weak and disinherited, the streetpeople of the ages – are the very opposite of God, they form the mirror image of God, and they realize what it means to be "in our image, after our likeness."

---

[1]The exposition of *zekhut* in *Transformation* is not repeated here, but the conclusion is, since that forms the important component in the unfolding of the personality of God in the sequential documents.

Index

Aaron, 77, 81, 83, 89, 136, 170, 187
Abba bar Kahana, 77, 79, 125
Abbahu, 22, 74, 146
Abiathar, 77
Abihu, 83
Abijah, 156
Abimelech, 89
Abin, 78-79, 85, 137
Abiram, 187
Abodah Zarah, 4, 286
abomination, 84
Abot, 25, 164-165, 197, 200-202, 208, 213, 217-219, 223, 279, 283
Abraham, 24, 78-80, 84-85, 89, 122-129, 133-134, 142-143, 170, 185, 187, 189, 191, 221-224, 227-229, 234-236, 289
Abram, 78-79, 85, 129
Achan, 181, 184-185
act of labor, 272-274
Adam, 84-85, 198
Adda bar Ahbah, 20
Aha, 138, 148
Ahab, 187
Ahasuerus, 141, 156

Aibu, 156
Alexander of Macedonia, 123-124, 227-228, 231
Alexandria, 236, 243
All-Merciful, 282
altar, 63, 75, 141, 184, 187, 250, 257
Amen, 277
Ammi, 157
Amos, 139, 179, 183, 218
analogy, 92, 109, 111, 176, 181, 216, 230-231, 240
angel, 5, 72, 84-85, 88-89, 127, 140, 150, 180, 207, 282-283, 286-287, 289
angel of death, 207
animal sacrifice, 259-260
anoint, 64-65, 136, 140, 162, 171
Aphrahat, 230
apocalyptic, 96, 104, 165, 169
appendix, 116, 251
Aqiba, 18, 262, 266, 276
Arab, 76, 249
Aramaeans, 89, 217
Aramaic, 73
Aristotle, 4-10, 17
ark, 84, 187, 189

Asa, 156
Assyrian, 189
atonement, 112-113, 185, 187, 260, 275
authorship, 5-6, 8-9, 189, 212, 217, 219, 221-223, 226, 230-231, 236, 238-239, 241, 244-246, 248-249, 254-256, 274, 278, 282
autonomy, 42, 167, 189, 220, 225
Avi Yonah, M., 249
Azariah, 128, 143, 185, 187, 190-191
Baalhanan, 156
Baba Mesia, 35, 61
Babylonia, 20, 71, 88, 121, 126, 128, 130, 139, 153, 166, 169, 187, 204, 212-213, 217, 231
Babylonian, 64, 112, 187
Babylonian Talmud, 208
Balaam, 87-90
Bar Hutah, 143
Bar Kokhba, 163, 167-170, 247, 283
Bar Kokhba War, 249
Barak, 189
Barnes, Jonathan, 5
Bavli, 213-214
Bela, 155-156
Ben Neser, 153
Benaiah, 126, 136
Benjamin, 135, 138-141, 185
Beor, 155-156
bereavement, 226
Berekhiah, 78, 128, 132, 140, 144-145, 286

Bible, 43-44, 71, 80, 91, 95-96, 98, 102, 105, 113-114, 116, 121, 126, 143, 151, 165, 169, 183, 197, 200, 212-214, 225, 239, 284, 290
blood, 126, 184, 260, 262, 266, 275, 284
Brooks, Roger, 284
burnt-offering, 126
Caesar Hadrian, 167
Cain, 113
Caleb, 77, 184
Canaan, 124, 129, 132, 228-229
Canaanites, 123-124, 187, 227-228
canon, 4, 11, 18, 30, 51, 57, 69, 91, 94, 96, 106-108, 122, 164, 170, 173, 175, 179-180, 189-191, 199-200, 206, 221, 247-250, 280-281
carrion, 130
catalogue, 42-43, 47-48, 50-51, 54, 113, 118, 177, 181-182, 185, 205, 286
category formation, 3, 14, 16, 18, 68
children of Israel, 71, 89, 129, 138, 152, 183-184, 223, 229
Chilton, Bruce, 232
Chr., 76-78, 129, 288
Christ, 69, 142, 170, 196, 214, 222, 233-234, 236, 242, 245, 249, 280
Christianity, 25, 69, 98, 102, 122, 129, 133, 142, 147, 196, 200, 213-214, 221-224, 229, 233-234, 237-238, 245-249, 251, 280

Index

Chronicles, 75, 174

Church, 214, 221-222, 224, 239, 245

circumcision, 184, 233-234, 245

cleanness, 40, 203, 264

cogency, 4-5, 10, 33, 48, 71, 78, 105, 107-110, 115, 183, 190, 219, 242, 248, 250, 255-256, 271

commandment, 83, 86, 132, 146, 166-167, 170, 181, 187, 257, 277, 279, 292

comparison, 5, 9-11, 14, 16, 20, 34, 36, 45, 60, 67-68, 97, 154, 174, 214-216, 224, 230-232, 238, 242, 248, 253

compilation, 3, 17, 30, 45, 48, 57, 107-108, 121, 179-180, 182-183, 213-214, 287

composite, 39, 45, 78, 84, 109-110, 121, 166, 221, 258

congruence, 14, 33

consecration, 114

Constantine, 27, 126, 142, 159, 214, 223, 244, 246-247, 280

continuity, 224, 250

contrast, 3, 5, 7, 9-10, 14-15, 19-20, 31, 34, 37, 40-41, 44-46, 52, 58, 64-65, 67-68, 85, 90, 93, 97, 108-109, 111, 113, 147, 155, 174, 177, 185-186, 201, 208, 214, 216, 219-220, 225-226, 231-233, 238, 242, 245, 286

corpse, 265-268, 270

corpse uncleanness, 266-267, 270

counterpart category, 10, 12-19, 25-26

Creation, 45, 56, 66, 93, 104, 112, 118, 122-123, 164, 175, 234, 236, 249, 254, 256, 282

cult, 9, 55, 63, 65, 97, 114, 127, 162, 167, 240, 246, 274-275

Dan., 83, 138-140, 153

Daniel, 112, 138-139, 153-154, 185, 187

Dathan, 187

davar-aher, 182-183, 185-186, 188

David, 18, 79-80, 94, 96, 117, 148, 152, 155-156, 161, 183, 187, 239, 284, 287, 289

Day of Atonement, 185, 187, 260, 275

Dead Sea scrolls, 238

death, 22-23, 87, 128, 130, 137, 141-142, 178, 197, 214, 234, 251, 287

Deborah, 189

debt, 22

Deut., 73, 75, 79, 86-88, 124, 140, 147, 153, 169, 204, 219, 228, 257, 282

Deuteronomic historians, 197

Deuteronomist, 201

Deuteronomy, 3, 18, 71, 134, 197, 206, 213, 286

Divine Name, 83

Divine Presence, 137

divorce, 127

doctrine, 94, 98-99, 110, 196, 200-202, 207-208, 213-216, 219, 221-222, 235, 253, 279

dough-offering, 166, 257-258

Dual Torah, 179-180, 197, 202, 212-216, 220-221, 224, 232, 237, 239, 241, 243-244, 246, 248, 250, 281

eclecticism, 5

economics, 4, 6-8, 10-14, 17, 19, 24-26, 291

Edom, 98, 126, 130, 138, 140, 142, 146, 148-150, 152, 155-157, 222

Edomites, 151

Efes, 150

Egypt, 72, 74, 89, 112, 129, 134, 136-137, 181, 183-185, 187, 229, 282

Egyptian, 123-124, 187, 227, 229

eisegesis, 198

Eleazar, 81, 85, 125, 128, 168, 204

Eleazar b. R. Menahem, 88

Eleazar bar Abina, 138

Eliezer, 258, 266, 273

Elijah, 157, 187, 287

Emperor Julian, 214

English, 176, 178, 238

Enoch, 189, 198

Ephraim, 130

Erubin, 166

Esau, 98, 125, 130-131, 133-134, 140, 142-156, 187, 222

eschatology, 80, 125, 139, 155, 162, 164, 167, 169, 171, 241

Essene, 103, 200-201, 216, 232, 236, 238-245, 247-248

Est., 130, 133, 135, 141

Esther, 141, 282

Esther Rabbah, 213

eternity, 68, 169

ethics, 100, 102, 119

ethos, 164

Europe, 177

Ex., 73, 76-77, 80-83, 89, 124, 129, 132, 136, 154, 184, 204, 218, 229, 282, 290

execution, 166, 266

exegesis, 12, 15, 29, 32, 34, 39-45, 47, 49, 51-52, 54-56, 70-71, 75, 81, 83, 86-87, 90-92, 95-96, 100, 102-103, 105-106, 110-111, 113, 121, 125, 127, 129, 131, 135, 147, 155, 170, 185, 189-191, 204, 213-214, 225, 230-232, 246, 250, 256

exile, 66, 122, 127, 187, 283

Exodus, 83, 112, 183, 187

extirpation, 259

Ezek., 138, 155, 170, 184, 218, 288

Ezra, 187, 189, 195, 198, 206

festival, 166, 240, 257

fire, 76, 187, 272, 274

firstling, 140

flog, 257, 277

foetus, 290

forbidden, 64-67, 258, 260, 270, 285

forgiveness, 113, 187

form-analysis, 33

fornication, 140

Fox-Genovese, Elizabeth, 224

Freedman, H., 129, 137, 143-145, 149, 151-152, 154-156

freewill-offering, 82

Frerichs, Ernest S., 237

Index

Garden of Eden, 84
Gebiah b. Qosem, 123-124, 227-229
Geertz, Clifford, 178, 181
Gen., 78, 84-85, 88-89, 123-131, 133-137, 139-141, 143-156, 170, 218, 227-228, 289-290
generation of the flood, 112-113
Genesis, 70, 121-123, 125, 129, 134-135, 142, 214, 241
Genesis Rabbah, 3, 70-71, 75, 91, 100, 103, 119, 121, 129, 141-142, 213, 227, 230, 238, 241, 246, 249
gentile, 44, 87-88, 96, 170, 187, 196, 216-217, 220-222, 225, 227, 232-236, 242-243, 245, 247-248, 263
German, 188
gloss, 3, 39, 41, 52-54, 133, 137, 146
gnosticism, 15, 248-249
God, 7-8, 16, 19, 25, 72-74, 76-89, 93, 96-98, 100, 102, 104, 112-114, 116, 118-119, 122, 125-126, 130, 132, 134, 136, 139-140, 143, 145, 148-149, 152, 154, 165-171, 178-179, 181-182, 184-185, 187, 191, 193, 196-203, 205-208, 212-213, 218-219, 230, 234-237, 240-242, 248, 253-256, 278-292
Gog and Magog, 136
Gomorrah, 112-113
Goodenough, Erwin R., 236-237, 242
Goshen, 129

Gospels, 136, 162, 200
grace, 20, 233, 235, 237
Greco-Roman, 4, 6-7, 9, 116
Greece, 4-5, 99, 117, 119, 126, 130, 139-140, 153, 178-179, 188, 217, 230-231, 234, 279
Green, William Scott, 182-183, 189, 234
guilt, 148
guilt-offering, 259-261, 274
Hadad, 156
Hadar, 156
Haggai, 73, 144, 146, 189, 204
Hagigah, 203-204
Halafta of Kefar Hananiah, 218
Hallah, 257
Hama, 75
Hama bar R. Hanina, 88, 127
Hama bar Uqba, 203
Haman, 112-113, 130, 135, 141, 156
Hana, 132
Hanan, 128
Hanan bar Berekiah, 132
Hananiah, 128, 185, 187, 190-191, 218, 257
Hananiah b. Teradion, 217
Hanina, 128, 133, 139
Hanina of Sepphoris, 157
Hannah, 285
harmonization, 39, 41, 84
Hasmonean, 140
heave-offering, 258

Heaven, 8-9, 19, 22-24, 76, 84-85, 127-128, 132, 149, 163-164, 167-168, 178, 206, 214, 221-223, 225, 280-282, 289, 291-292

Hebrew, 73, 128, 156, 183, 188, 198, 200, 212, 231

Hebrew Scriptures, 4, 69, 121, 189, 214, 248

Hebrews, 137

hekhalot, 108

Helbo, 145

hermeneutic, 52, 176-178, 196, 246

Herzl, 216

Hezekiah, 112, 287

hierarchy, 4-6, 16, 20, 24, 216, 223, 238, 240, 253-256, 264, 270-271, 274, 276, 279

high priest, 8-9, 19, 63-65, 128, 199, 239

Hillel, 80

Hinena bar Isaac, 126

historiography, 169

history of Judaism, 18, 39, 62, 167

history of religion, 237-238, 250

Hiyya, 87, 166

Hiyya bar Abba, 146

Holocaust, 251

Holy Land, 26, 55, 64, 98, 166, 227

Holy of Holies, 275

Holy One, 72, 74-77, 79-83, 85, 88-89, 126, 131, 133, 136, 139, 146, 148-149, 151-152, 169, 217, 280-290

Holy Place, 49, 98

Holy Things, 40, 55, 257, 259-260, 275

Horayot, 64, 269

Horeb, 181, 184-185

Hos., 74-75, 89, 204

Hoshaiah, 75, 89, 155

Hullin, 169

Huna, 144-145

husband, 22-24, 55

Husham, 156

hypothesis, 11, 110, 230, 232, 239, 244

Idi, 132

idolatry, 144, 286

incarnation of God, 280

intentionality, 269-270

interpretation, 3, 11, 14, 38, 62, 68, 92, 111, 137, 149-150, 169, 174, 176, 178, 182-184, 191, 214, 232, 238, 242, 247

Iram, 156-157

Isa., 75, 85, 88, 90, 125, 132, 138, 143, 146, 148-150, 156, 170, 281, 287

Isaac, 24, 73, 87, 123-131, 133, 142-144, 146-147, 155, 185, 187, 189, 191, 221-223, 227-228, 290

Isaiah, 103, 287

Ishbosheth, 156

Ishmael, 18, 123-124, 142-143, 222, 227-228, 262

Ishmaelites, 124-125, 228-229

Islam, 237

Index

Israel, 3-4, 6, 8-10, 12-13, 15-16, 19, 24-26, 29, 31, 34, 38-39, 42-56, 58, 61-65, 67-68, 69, 71, 73, 75-77, 79, 84-89, 94-104, 109, 112-119, 121-127, 129-143, 145-148, 152, 154-157, 161-171, 175, 178-180, 182-187, 191, 193, 195-197, 202, 204-209, 211-249, 251, 263, 279-280, 282-283, 285, 289-291

Israelites, 50, 63-65, 73-74, 86, 89-90, 103, 114-115, 118, 126, 129, 146, 155-156, 161, 165, 170, 181, 187, 199, 201-202, 206-207, 209, 218-219, 234, 240, 243, 281

Issachar, 88

Jacob, 24, 78, 87, 122, 125, 129, 131, 133-134, 138-142, 144-155, 185, 187, 189, 191, 221-223

Jehoiakin, 156

Jehoram, 156

Jehoshaphat, 156

Jer., 136, 139-140, 144, 146, 151, 283, 290

Jeremiah, 283

Jericho, 141

Jeroboam, 187, 189

Jerusalem, 9, 64-65, 71, 122, 124, 146, 148-149, 163, 183, 213, 229, 240, 246, 260, 283, 288

Jesus, 69, 162, 214, 222, 234, 242, 247, 249, 280

Jew, 9, 25, 55, 76, 91, 93-94, 98, 112, 114, 122, 129, 141, 145, 165-166, 170, 175, 197-198, 200, 213-216, 221, 224-228, 232-238, 240-242, 244-249, 251

Job, 88, 92, 137, 189

Jobab, 156

Jonah, 148, 203

Jonathan, 6, 187

Joseph, 133-138, 140, 186

Josh., 184

Joshua, 80, 126, 128, 132, 149, 181, 184-185

Joshua b. Levi, 75, 77, 86, 128, 136, 149, 156, 204

Joshua b. Qorhah, 77

Josiah, 117

Judah, 89, 130, 135, 138-139, 150, 185, 267

Judah bar Ilai, 77, 89, 147

Judah bar Simon, 77, 126, 149

Judah the Patriarch, 150, 154-155, 164, 199

Judaism, 3-7, 10-11, 13, 15-16, 18, 20, 24-26, 27, 39-40, 43, 45-47, 55, 62-65, 68, 69-71, 90-91, 93-94, 98-99, 103-104, 110, 121-122, 159, 161-162, 166-167, 171, 173, 177-181, 183, 188-189, 191, 195-196, 198-200, 204, 208, 211-217, 219-221, 223-224, 232, 234-235, 237-238, 242-243, 245-246, 248-251, 253, 261, 279-281, 291

Judg., 72, 140

judges, 156, 218

Julian, 98

Justin, 248

Keritot, 257-259

Kgs., 75-76, 126, 156, 170, 287

Kings, 77-78, 114, 152-153, 155-156, 170, 184, 197

knife, 154-155
Laban, 89, 134, 148, 150-151
Lam., 218
Lamentations Rabbati, 213
Land of Israel, 3, 9-10, 12, 15, 25, 29, 31, 34, 38-39, 42-56, 58, 61-62, 71, 100, 103, 118-119, 121-123, 127, 138, 164-167, 169, 171, 197, 202, 206, 212-213, 227-228, 247, 249, 279-280, 283, 291
Latin, 188
law, 4, 8-9, 21-22, 29, 35-36, 40-43, 45, 47-49, 51, 53-56, 59-60, 63, 67-68, 96-97, 99-101, 104, 113, 116-117, 119, 123, 125-126, 130, 134, 144, 162-164, 166, 169, 197-199, 203-204, 211, 213, 221, 230, 232-236, 238, 240-242, 245-246, 253, 259-260, 263, 265, 272, 277, 281
Leah, 221, 223
Lev., 73-75, 77-90, 132, 146, 153, 203, 257-259, 274
Levi, 76-78, 80, 126, 132, 136, 139-140, 144, 149, 153, 157, 206, 288
Levi bar Haita, 184
Levi ben Sisi, 205
Levite, 64-65, 77, 216, 240
Leviticus, 7, 71, 78, 91-92, 95, 97-100, 103, 113-114, 116, 118, 213-214, 231, 241, 246, 261, 274
Leviticus Rabbah, 3, 18, 69-71, 90-104, 105-115, 117-119, 213, 230-232, 238, 241, 246

liability, 86, 257-258, 270, 274, 278
Lieberman, Saul, 62, 90
listmaking, 102, 105, 113, 117, 119, 188
Listenwissenschaft, 5, 174, 180, 186
literature, 45, 91, 108, 169, 180, 189, 195-196, 199, 220-221, 234, 238
Litrinus, 157
logic, 12, 54, 66, 71, 90-91, 93, 95, 99, 101, 105-111, 114-118, 161, 174, 180, 212, 219, 234, 241, 243-244, 246, 248-250, 265, 274, 276, 286
Lord, 71-73, 77, 79, 81-85, 88-90, 124, 126-127, 131-132, 136, 138-139, 143, 145-146, 148, 150-152, 168-169, 183-184, 204-205, 217-219, 228-229, 234, 279, 282, 284-288
lulab, 277
Luther, Martin, 247
M. Ed., 257
M. Hag., 203
M. Hal., 257-258
M. Hor., 65, 199
M. Ker., 260-261
M. Mak., 269
M. Naz., 270-271
M. Ned., 127
M. Neg., 262-264
M. Oh., 266
M. San., 220
M. Shab., 271, 273

Index

M. Shabu., 275
M. Tem., 126
Magdiel, 156-157
Mal., 145, 217-218
mamzer, 64-65, 198
Manasseh, 287-288
Manoah, 72
Marah, 181, 184-185
Margulies, M., 71, 75, 77, 87, 90
marriage, 127, 147, 187
Massah, 181, 184-185
matriarchs, 98, 129, 223, 227, 246
Matthew, 103
Meir, 259-260, 262, 268
Mekhilta Attributed to R. Ishmael, 18
Meribah, 181, 184-185
Messiah, 64-65, 98, 136, 142, 146, 151, 155, 157, 161-164, 167, 169-171, 183, 187, 213-214, 219, 280
metaphor, 30, 40, 57, 176, 181, 208, 214-217, 219, 222-229, 231-232, 235-237
method, 4-6, 12, 14, 46, 100, 122-123, 165, 167, 255-256, 258, 270
mezuzah, 181, 187
Mic., 78, 131
Middle East, 7
Midian, 187
Midrash, 3, 44, 71, 96, 161
Midrash compilation, 3, 179
Midrash Wayyikra Rabbah, 71

Miqvaot, 268
Miriam, 136
Mishael, 128, 185, 187, 190-191
Mishnah, 3-10, 12-13, 15-19, 21, 24, 29-61, 63-68, 69-71, 90-91, 94-95, 100, 103-104, 105-108, 113, 117-119, 121, 126-127, 161-165, 167, 169-171, 187-188, 196-208, 211-213, 215-217, 219-221, 225-226, 231, 233, 236, 238, 241-242, 245-249, 253-259, 261-269, 271-276, 278-280, 290-291
mixed seeds, 257
Moab, 184
Moed Qatan, 4
Moore, George Foot, 237
Mordecai, 112, 135, 138-139, 141
Moses, 42, 54, 56, 69, 71-85, 88-90, 94, 96, 98, 104, 134, 136, 139-140, 147, 170, 184, 186-187, 195-197, 199, 201-204, 212, 219, 222, 237, 240, 281, 290
Mount Sinai, 54, 73-74, 79, 89, 199, 203
Mulgan, R. G., 9
murder, 77, 168
Nadab, 83
Nahum, 150
Nathan, 79, 83, 129
Nazir, 4, 257, 269-270
Nazirites, 257
Ndembu, 190-191
Near East, 7

Nebuchadnezzar, 112-113, 117, 156, 170, 189
Negaim, 261-265, 278
negative commandment, 257
Neh., 79, 138
Nehemiah, 144
Neusner, Jacob, 183, 237
New Testament, 100
New Year, 126
Niddah, 35, 40, 61
Noah, 84-85, 123
Num., 72, 79, 87-89, 131-132, 141, 184, 257, 259, 265, 286
Numbers, 71
oath, 127, 274, 277-278
Obad., 155
Ohalot, 265-267
Old Testament, 4, 69, 103, 142, 178-179, 182
Omnipresent, 218-219
ontology, 237, 261
Oral Torah, 69, 179, 203-204, 212-213, 253, 280
paganism, 98, 122, 170, 214, 221-222
Palestine, 9, 25, 212, 249
Palestinian, 30, 34, 57, 68
parables, 86, 92, 99-101, 104, 111, 119, 289
Passover, 136, 184, 258
Passover-offering, 184
patriarchs, 44, 64-65, 98, 112, 123, 126-127, 129, 151, 156, 185-187, 223, 227, 234, 237, 246

Paul, 179, 216, 232-236, 241-242, 244-245, 247-248
Peah, 268-269
Pentateuch, 7, 9-10, 103, 179, 195, 198-199, 206, 224
Pentecost, 240
pericope, 29-30, 34-36, 38-41, 43, 57, 60-61, 82, 107
Persia, 231
Pesiqta deRab Kahana, 3, 213
Pharaoh, 75-77, 81, 113, 135-137, 170, 187, 290
Pharisees, 247
Philistines, 189
Philo, 70, 216, 232, 236-238, 240-243, 245, 250
philology, 131, 238
philosophy, 3-20, 24, 26, 42, 68, 70, 100-104, 105, 117, 119-120, 125, 132, 134, 162-165, 171, 211, 213, 217, 220-221, 230, 236-237, 240-241, 245, 253-256, 261, 264, 270-271, 273, 276, 278-279
Phineas, 72, 78, 89, 126, 140-141, 147-148, 151, 288
phylactery, 181, 187, 277
Plato, 6-7, 9
Platonism (neo-Platonism), 4-6
Plotinus, 5-6
Polanyi, Karl, 6
politics, 4, 6-15, 17-19, 21, 24-26, 65, 93, 99-100, 102, 112, 119, 122, 142, 151, 171, 197, 212, 214, 221-222, 236-238, 241, 244, 246, 248-249, 291

Index

prayer, 21-24, 77, 83, 88, 161, 181, 187, 240, 281, 284-285, 287, 290

Presence of God, 76, 139, 145, 181, 187, 284

priest, 7-9, 19, 49, 55, 63-65, 77, 114, 128, 161-162, 178, 199, 216-217, 221, 239-240, 257, 263

priestly code, 7, 224

prohibition, 99, 270, 272-274

prooftext, 39, 41-42, 53-54, 69, 90, 102-103, 116, 131, 171, 175, 203

Prophet, 64, 72, 76, 88, 281

proposition, 4-6, 15-16, 24, 36, 38-39, 41, 46, 51-54, 58, 60, 71, 82, 86, 90-91, 94-97, 99, 102, 104, 105-109, 113-116, 118-119, 123, 129, 143, 167, 175-176, 180, 186, 188, 201, 203, 205, 212, 218, 220, 222, 231, 254-256, 261, 264, 266, 271, 273-275, 278

proselyte, 64-65, 74-75, 77, 186

Prov., 80-82, 88, 149, 152, 155, 219, 288

Proverbs, 92, 201

Ps., 18, 21, 72-76, 78-80, 83, 130-132, 134, 136, 143-144, 147-148, 151-152, 154-155, 168, 170, 184, 217-218, 282-284, 288

Psalms, 92, 148, 200-201

pseudepigrapha, 198

public domain, 271, 274

purification, 261, 265

Qid., 283

Qoh., 92, 131, 204

Qumran, 103, 200-201, 216, 232, 236, 238-241, 243-245, 247-248

Raamah, 145

Rab, 20

Rabbah, 3, 18, 69-71, 75, 90-104, 105-115, 117-119, 121, 129, 141-142, 213, 227, 230-232, 238, 241, 246, 249

Rabbi, 21, 40, 42, 44, 47-48, 52-56, 64, 69, 104, 150, 161, 195-196, 202, 207, 212, 222-223, 290

rabbinic, 43, 47-48, 50-51, 63-65, 69-70, 91, 94, 96, 100-101, 106-108, 117-118, 121, 161, 164, 167, 170-171, 195, 198-199, 206, 230, 237, 245

rabbis, 22-23, 39, 42, 44-45, 47, 49, 51, 63-64, 68, 70, 72, 75, 79, 88-89, 91, 96, 106, 117, 121, 128, 138, 154, 187, 206-207, 209, 212, 237, 281, 292

Rachel, 134, 140, 151, 221, 223, 290

redaction, 31, 33-39, 53, 58-63, 70, 74, 86, 90, 110, 121, 137, 141

Reformation, Protestant, 174-175

Rehoboam, 156

religion, 3, 6, 11-16, 20, 24-25, 69, 73, 97-98, 103-104, 161, 169, 173, 175, 178-179, 187, 190, 196, 202, 211-212, 215, 224, 234, 237-238, 244, 249-251, 270, 280, 283

repentance, 113, 288-289

resurrection, 69, 215

Reuben, 135, 138, 148

revelation, 20, 54, 81, 89, 104, 112, 125, 133, 165, 179, 196-203, 205, 207, 212, 216, 238, 280, 282

rhetoric, 12, 37-38, 54, 58, 66-67, 70-71, 87, 90-91, 102-103, 105-106, 108-109, 115, 117, 120, 182, 274, 276, 288

Roman Empire, 122, 142, 280

Rome, 4, 6-7, 9, 35, 97-98, 113, 116, 118, 125, 130, 133-134, 140-143, 145-157, 166, 214, 217, 222, 228-229, 231, 238, 248, 280

Sabbath, 184-185, 203, 260, 271-275

Sabbatical Year, 73-74

Sabteca, 145

sacrifice, 66, 81, 126-127, 213, 218, 259-260, 289

Sadoq, 77

sage, 5, 9, 15, 19-21, 24, 26, 42, 44-45, 52, 54-56, 63-68, 83, 95, 99-101, 119, 121-123, 125, 129, 133-134, 136, 141-143, 151, 153, 157, 161, 163, 167-170, 189, 196, 198-199, 201-203, 205-209, 212, 214-215, 221-224, 230, 237, 241, 244-249, 257, 259, 261-262, 266, 268, 274, 280-285, 290

Sahlin, 178-180, 182

salvation, 15, 97-100, 103-104, 109, 114-115, 117, 119, 122, 136, 142, 161-163, 167, 169, 187, 195-197, 205-209, 213-214, 219, 221-222, 233, 246, 290

Sam., 79, 140-141, 285

Samaritan, 124, 168, 229

Samlah of Masrekah, 155-156

Samuel bar Nahman, 83, 136, 140, 151, 204, 289

sanctification, 6, 9, 19-20, 63, 65, 97-98, 100, 114, 126, 138, 162, 165, 167, 169, 198, 213, 241, 246-247, 255-257, 260, 272

sanctuary, 124-125, 131-132, 138, 146, 187, 229, 259-260, 275

Sanhedrin, 8, 35, 41, 61, 187, 273, 283

Sarah, 143, 221, 223-224

Satan, 151

Saul, 140-141, 152, 156, 187

scribe, 18, 77, 196

Scripture, 3-4, 8, 15, 35, 39, 41-45, 47-51, 53-54, 69-73, 75-76, 78-82, 84, 86-104, 105, 112-113, 115-119, 121-123, 125-126, 129-130, 135, 137, 143, 151, 153, 155, 161, 164-165, 170-171, 175, 183, 187, 189, 197-204, 207-208, 212-216, 219, 222-223, 229-232, 239-241, 245-246, 248, 259, 263, 267, 271, 282-283, 285-286, 288-290

sea, 81, 134, 153, 180-181, 184-185, 187, 191, 281-282

Seir, 130, 148, 150

Sennacherib, 112-113

sexual relations, 135

Shabbat, 271-273

Shabuot, 274-276, 278

Shaul of Rehobot, 155-156

Shem, 128, 146

Shema, 83, 181, 187

Shemaiah, 77
Shittim, 181, 184-185
show fringe, 181, 187
Shushan, 133
Sifra, 3, 18, 70, 87, 91, 100, 103, 119
Sifra to Leviticus, 213
Sifré to Deuteronomy, 3, 18, 213
Sifré to Numbers, 3, 18, 213
Sifrés, 70
Simeon, 218, 266, 274
Simeon b. Azzai, 80
Simeon b. Gamaliel, 260
Simeon b. Laqish, 127, 144, 152, 154-155
Simeon b. Yohai, 75, 286
Simeon the Righteous, 201
Simon, 72, 75-78, 87, 126, 138, 147, 149, 184
sin, 8, 22-23, 96-97, 112-113, 137-138, 259-261, 281, 288, 292
sin-offering, 127, 259-261, 272
Sinai, 81, 85-86, 112, 179-180, 183, 185, 187, 189, 191, 197, 199, 202-205, 208, 212, 223, 280
sinner, 114, 288
Sisera, 113
skin ailment, 264
slave, 64-65, 93, 112, 122, 124, 143, 163, 228
Smith, Jonathan Z., 189-191, 233-234, 250
social entity, 4, 6, 8-9, 11, 13, 17, 19, 24, 101, 117, 134, 185, 211-212, 215, 217-225, 227-232, 237, 241-243, 245, 247, 249-250
sociology, 211-212
Sodom, 112-113
Sodomites, 113
Solomon, 131, 145, 156, 183, 186-187, 286, 289
Song of Songs Rabbah, 182-183, 186, 191
Song of Songs, 182, 189, 191
storyteller, 177, 289
successor system, 10-12, 14-15, 17-19
Sukkah, 35, 41, 61, 277
syllogism, 16, 71, 91, 97, 102, 105-110, 112, 115-116, 118-119, 121, 129, 145
synagogue, 20, 144-145, 187, 213, 285
Syria, 166
T. Hor., 64-65
Tabernacle, 82-83, 86, 181, 184, 187
Tabyomi, 75
Talmud, 15, 29-31, 34, 36-46, 48-68, 70, 75, 161, 167, 170-171, 179, 196, 198, 200, 203-204, 206-208, 213
Talmud of Babylonia, 121, 169, 204, 212-213
Talmud of the Land of Israel, 3, 10, 12, 15, 25, 29, 31, 34, 38-39, 42-56, 58, 61-62, 71, 100, 103, 118-119, 165-167, 169, 171, 202, 206, 213, 279-280, 291
Tanhum bar Hanilai, 79

Tanhuma, 77, 81
Tannaite, 18, 127, 144
Tarfon, 17-18
taxa, 5, 43, 45, 47, 49-50, 53, 173, 182, 185, 205, 234, 254-256, 260-261, 263, 266, 273, 278
taxonomy, 12, 29-30, 34, 45-47, 50-51, 57, 62, 93, 109, 111, 113, 162-164, 181, 185, 216-217, 220, 224-225, 234, 241, 255-256, 258, 264, 268, 276
teleology, 162, 164-167, 169, 171, 177, 206, 219, 221, 254, 256, 261, 280
Temple, 7, 9, 40, 49, 55, 63-67, 93, 112, 114, 122, 124, 127-128, 131, 141, 146, 162-163, 165-166, 180, 185, 187, 213-214, 229, 239-240, 246, 248, 257-258, 262, 274, 284, 287, 289
Ten Commandments, 132, 181, 187
Ten Tribes, 138, 185
Tent of Meeting, 71, 81, 85-87, 90, 180
text criticism, 39, 238
textual community, 181, 189, 191
theology, 15-16, 26, 41, 44, 48, 129, 161, 175, 177, 179, 183, 185-186, 188-191, 216, 222-223, 230, 234, 238, 244, 255-256, 278, 287
tithe, 146, 258
tithe, second, 258
Tobiah, 77

topic, 4, 12-13, 16, 31-32, 35, 37, 43, 45-46, 48-50, 59-60, 66, 70-71, 86, 89-91, 97, 99, 105-109, 112, 114-115, 118, 201, 238-239, 242-243, 264, 274, 278
Torah, 14-22, 25, 54, 69, 76-77, 85-87, 90, 92, 96, 98, 104, 111-112, 114, 122, 124-125, 133-134, 142-143, 154, 161, 164-165, 169-170, 179-180, 183, 187, 189, 193, 195-209, 212-222, 224, 228-229, 231-233, 237, 239, 241, 243-244, 246, 248, 250, 253, 259, 279-282, 284, 286, 291
Torah study, 15, 19-21, 24, 128, 186, 201-202, 208, 219
Tosefta, 30, 34-35, 39, 53-54, 57-58, 70, 94, 100, 103, 119, 197, 213, 221
traditions, 161, 205
transgression, 76, 126-127, 257, 259-261
translation, 12, 14, 29, 34-35, 71
Trypho, 248
uncircumcised, 234
uncleanness, 40, 55, 63, 84, 88, 203, 259-268, 270, 274-275, 285
unit of thought, 33, 38, 61, 71, 109
Valuation, 19, 25, 292
Vermes, Geza, 238-240, 247
violation, 85-86, 178, 257, 270-274, 277-278
voice, 73, 79, 86-87, 90, 99, 127-128, 146-147, 279, 285, 289
vow, 127
West, 142, 248

Index

whole-offering, 127
wife, 23-24, 72, 76-77, 89, 147, 187
witness, 16, 128, 169, 215, 261, 277
Wolfson, Harry Austryn, 236-237, 242
woman, 22-24, 55, 74, 128, 130, 143-144, 146-147, 154, 215, 259-260, 277, 290, 292
worldview, 4, 11, 13-14, 16, 18-19, 24, 40, 46, 48-51, 90, 122, 171, 178, 191, 195, 211, 250
wrath, 79, 166, 289
Written Torah, 204, 213, 279-280
Y. Hagigah, 203-204
Y. Taanit, 20-21, 167, 169, 205, 281-285, 289
Yannai, 21, 125, 290
Yerushalmi, 3, 12, 15, 31, 34-35, 38-40, 44, 58, 61-64, 166, 169, 198, 203, 205-206, 213-214, 217, 223, 236, 238, 241, 246, 248-249, 281, 283-286, 291
Yohanan, 72, 127, 139, 144, 147, 153-154, 166-167, 203-204
Yohanan ben Zakkai, 202
Yosé, 135, 267
Yudan, 126, 128, 134, 140, 290
Yudan bar Shillum, 143
Zadok, 77, 239
Zahavy, Tzvee, 284-285, 290
Zebahim, 4
Zech., 74, 126, 128, 130, 148, 168
Zedekiah, 187
zekhut, 20-25, 291-292
Zephaniah, 189
Zion, 75, 112, 130-131, 146, 155, 187
Zionism, 175

South Florida Studies in the History of Judaism

240001	Lectures on Judaism in the Academy and in the Humanities	Neusner
240002	Lectures on Judaism in the History of Religion	Neusner
240003	Self-Fulfilling Prophecy: Exile and Return in the History of Judaism	Neusner
240004	The Canonical History of Ideas: The Place of the So-called Tannaite Midrashim, Mekhilta Attributed to R. Ishmael, Sifra, Sifré to Numbers, and Sifré to Deuteronomy	Neusner
240005	Ancient Judaism: Debates and Disputes	Neusner
240006	The Hasmoneans and Their Supporters: From Mattathias to the Death of John Hyrcanus I	Sievers
240007	Approaches to Ancient Judaism: New Series Volume One	Neusner
240008	Judaism in the Matrix of Christianity	Neusner
240009	Tradition as Selectivity: Scripture, Mishnah, Tosefta, and Midrash in the Talmud of Babylonia	Neusner
240010	The Tosefta: Translated from the Hebrew: Sixth Division Tohorot	Neusner
240011	In the Margins of the Midrash: Sifre Ha'azinu Texts, Commentaries and Reflections	Basser
240012	Language as Taxonomy: The Rules for Using Hebrew and Aramaic in the Babylonia Talmud	Neusner
240013	The Rules of Composition of the Talmud of Babylonia: The Cogency of the Bavli's Composite	Neusner
240014	Understanding the Rabbinic Mind: Essays on the Hermeneutic of Max Kadushin	Ochs
240015	Essays in Jewish Historiography	Rapoport-Albert
240016	The Golden Calf and the Origins of the Jewish Controversy	Bori/Ward
240017	Approaches to Ancient Judaism: New Series Volume Two	Neusner
240018	The Bavli That Might Have Been: The Tosefta's Theory of Mishnah Commentary Compared With the Bavli's	Neusner
240019	The Formation of Judaism: In Retrospect and Prospect	Neusner
240020	Judaism in Society: The Evidence of the Yerushalmi,Toward the Natural History of a Religion	Neusner
240021	The Enchantments of Judaism: Rites of Transformation from Birth Through Death	Neusner
240022	The Rules of Composition of the Talmud of Babylonia	Neusner
240023	The City of God in Judaism and Other Comparative and Methodological Studies	Neusner
240024	The Bavli's One Voice: Types and Forms of Analytical Discourse and their Fixed Order of Appearance	Neusner
240025	The Dura-Europos Synagogue: A Re-evaluation (1932-1992)	Gutmann
240026	Precedent and Judicial Discretion: The Case of Joseph ibn Lev	Morell
240028	Israel: Its Life and Culture Volume I	Pedersen
240029	Israel: Its Life and Culture Volume II	Pedersen
240030	The Bavli's One Statement: The Metapropositional Program of Babylonian Talmud Tractate Zebahim Chapters One and Five	Neusner
240031	The Oral Torah: The Sacred Books of Judaism: An Introduction: Second Printing	Neusner

240032	The Twentieth Century Construction of "Judaism:" Essays on the Religion of Torah in the History of Religion	Neusner
240033	How the Talmud Shaped Rabbinic Discourse	Neusner
240034	The Discourse of the Bavli: Language, Literature, and Symbolism: Five Recent Findings	Neusner
240035	The Law Behind the Laws: The Bavli's Essential Discourse	Neusner
240036	Sources and Traditions: Types of Compositions in the Talmud of Babylonia	Neusner
240037	How to Study the Bavli: The Languages, Literatures, and Lessons of the Talmud of Babylonia	Neusner
240038	The Bavli's Primary Discourse: Mishnah Commentary: Its Rhetorical Paradigms and their Theological Implications	Neusner
240039	Midrash Aleph Beth	Sawyer
240040	Jewish Thought in the 20th Century: An Introduction	Schweid
	in the Talmud of Babylonia Tractate Moed Qatan	Neusner
240041	Diaspora Jews and Judaism: Essays in Honor of, and in Dialogue with, A. Thomas Kraabel	Overman/MacLennan
240042	The Bavli: An Introduction	Neusner
240043	The Bavli's Massive Miscellanies: The Problem of Agglutinative Discourse in the Talmud of Babylonia	Neusner
240044	The Foundations of the Theology of Judaism: An Anthology Part II: Torah	Neusner
240045	Form-Analytical Comparison in Rabbinic Judaism: Structure and Form in *The Fathers* and *The Fathers According to Rabbi Nathan*	Neusner
240046	Essays on Hebrew	Weinberg
240047	The Tosefta: An Introduction	Neusner
240048	The Foundations of the Theology of Judaism: An Anthology Part III: Israel	Neusner
240049	The Study of Ancient Judaism, Volume I: Mishnah, Midrash, Siddur	Neusner
240050	The Study of Ancient Judaism, Volume II: The Palestinian and Babylonian Talmuds	Neusner
240051	Take Judaism, for Example: Studies toward the Comparison of Religions	Neusner
240052	From Eden to Golgotha: Essays in Biblical Theology	Moberly
240053	The Principal Parts of the Bavli's Discourse: A Preliminary Taxonomy: Mishnah Commentary, Sources, Traditions and Agglutinative Miscellanies	Neusner
240054	Barabbas and Esther and Other Studies in the Judaic Illumination of Earliest Christianity	Aus
240055	Targum Studies: Volume One: Textual and Contextual Studies in the Pentateuchal Targums	Flesher
240057	The Motherhood of God and Other Studies	Gruber
240058	The Analytic Movement in Rabbinic Jurisprudence	Solomon
240059	Recovering the Role of Women: Power and Authority in Rabbinic Jewish Society	Haas
240060	The Relation between Herodotus History and Primary History	Freedman/Mandell
240061	The First Seven Days: A Philosophical Commentary on the Creation of Genesis	Samuelson
240062	The Bavli's Intellectual Character: The Generative Problematic: In Bavli Baba Qamma Chapter One And Bavli Shabbat	

240063	The Incarnation of God: The Character of Divinity in Formative Judaism: Second Printing	Neusner
240064	Moses Kimhi: Commentary on the Book of Job	Basser/Walfish
240065	Judaism and Civil Religion	Breslauer
240066	Death and Birth of Judaism: Second Printing	Neusner
240067	Decoding the Talmud's Exegetical Program	Neusner
240068	Sources of the Transformation of Judaism	Neusner